William Bradford's Books

William Bradford's Books

Of Plimmoth Plantation
and the Printed Word

DOUGLAS ANDERSON

The Johns Hopkins University Press   *Baltimore and London*

© 2003 The Johns Hopkins University Press
All rights reserved. Published 2003
Printed in the United States of America
on acid-free paper
2   4   6   8   9   7   5   3   1

The Johns Hopkins University Press
2715 North Charles Street
Baltimore, Maryland 21218-4363
www.press.jhu.edu

Library of Congress Cataloging-in-Publication Data

Anderson, Douglas, 1950–
William Bradford's books : Of Plimmoth Plantation
and the printed word / Douglas Anderson.
p.   cm.
Includes bibliographical references and index.
ISBN 0-8018-7074-7 (hardcover : alk. paper)
1. Bradford, William, 1588–1657. History of Plymouth
Plantation. 2. Massachusetts—History—New Plymouth, 1620–1691. 3. Pilgrims (New Plymouth
Colony) 4. Bradford, William, 1588–1657—Criticism
and interpretation. 5. Bradford, William, 1588–1657.
6. Pilgrims (New Plymouth Colony)—Biography.
I. Title.
F68 .B80733 2002
974.4′8202—dc21   2002001843

A catalog record for this book is available from
the British Library.

CONTENTS

R EADERS FAMILIAR with *Of Plimmoth Plantation,* in Samuel Eliot Morison's modernized text or in the anthology selections drawn from it, may be surprised to encounter Bradford's original spelling and punctuation in the following pages. As these chapters repeatedly emphasize, *Of Plimmoth Plantation* is the product of a particular literary world and rewards most generously those who approach its language with the practices and expectations of that world firmly in mind. Preserving William Bradford's English, as nearly as modern typography makes it practical to do so, is one way of persistently reminding the reader that a modernized text is always in danger of becoming an expurgated one. I have expanded Bradford's scribal contractions, silently deleted superfluous commas, and doubled consonants where called for by his diacritical marks, in the spelling of "Plimmoth," for instance. Otherwise, with the exception of a handful of cases where I replaced a semicolon with a period, in order to break up a particularly unwieldy sentence, all quotations reproduce the text of Bradford's manuscript.

Every scholar of early American literature and history is indebted to Morison's 1952 edition of William Bradford's book. Without Morison's effort and advocacy, *Of Plimmoth Plantation* might well have remained an obscure and inaccessible title, known only to a handful of specialists and even then seldom read in its entirety. Instead it has become a mainstay in college and university classrooms, where it is frequently the only seventeenth-century work of American letters presented to modern students in something approaching its complete form. To achieve this degree of currency with modern readers, however, Morison made significant concessions to modern practices of reading. My hope, in these pages, is not to supplant Morison's edition, or diminish the importance of his work, but to recover some critical features of the relationship between literary form and reading practice that are inherent in William Bradford's original design for his book.

I am grateful to the Special Collections department of the Millsaps College Library and to the University of Rochester Library for making their copies of the 1896 facsimile of Bradford's manuscript available to me through interlibrary loan, sometimes for quite extended periods, as I checked transcriptions. Virginia Fehrer and the Interlibrary Loan staff at the University of Georgia made it seem as if this scarce volume, along with many others, were housed in our own stacks. Mary Bicknell and her assistants, Karen Abramson and Christine Gebhard, at the George Fingold Library in the State House at Boston allowed me the luxury of a morning with Bradford's original manuscript—a much more beautiful volume than photographs are able to convey. The Photographic Services departments at the Folger Shakespeare Library and at the Houghton Library of Harvard University helped with securing specific illustrations from the work of John Foxe and Joseph Moxon. The Hargrett Rare Book Library and the Photographic Services staff at the University of Georgia were similarly helpful with assembling images from the work of Peter Martyr and from the Bradford facsimile. Peter Drummey and Carrie Foley, at the Massachusetts Historical Society, gathered together for me all the pages that the society owns in William Bradford's hand, including the text of his 1652 third "Dialogue," a particularly evocative example of Bradford's meticulous scribal discipline. Jeremy Bangs, of the American Pilgrim Museum at Leiden, shared with me his considerable knowledge of seventeenth-century material culture and New England town history. Karin Goldstein at the Pilgrim Hall Museum in Plymouth was equally generous with her knowledge of the Winslow family and of the Edward Winslow portrait exhibited there, along with a number of books and objects in the Museum collections that have survived from the era of the plantation's settlement. Robert J. Brugger and Melody Herr ably shepherded the manuscript through its review at the Johns Hopkins University Press. Lois R. Crum edited the text with exacting care.

I am especially indebted to the John Simon Guggenheim Memorial Foundation for awarding me a fellowship that supported a year of leave from teaching in order to write this book. The Franklin College of Arts and Sciences at the University of Georgia supplemented the resources of the Guggenheim Foundation, making it possible for me to concentrate on the writing without financial hardship or professional distractions. Wyatt Anderson, Dean of the College, and Hugh Ruppersburg, Associate Dean, along with Anne Williams, Head of the English Department, smoothed this process at every stage. David Shields, Philip Morgan, Frank Shuffleton, and Barbara Oberg all expressed their confidence, at an important phase of the research, that this book was indeed worth writing and that I was in a good position to write it. Michael McGiffert provided an acute and helpful reading of the entire typescript, further evidence of the fruitful and supportive conversation that has taken place between literary critics and historians in American colonial studies for over seventy years. I hope that these colleagues are not disappointed with the results.

I first learned to read William Bradford under the guidance of David Levin. His personal and professional example, along with that of his intellectual generation—many of whom trained in the Harvard undergraduate and graduate programs in history and literature during the years immediately following the Second World War—created the field of study in which people of my scholarly generation have been able to spend our careers. That immeasurable debt, too, I gratefully acknowledge.

William Bradford's Books

Introduction

The Operations of Print

God hath opened the presse to preache.

JOHN FOXE

*O*F PLIMMOTH PLANTATION, the "scribled writings" that William Bradford
reports that he began to set down in 1630 and "peeced up at times of leasure"
for the next twenty years, remained in manuscript for so long and survived so many
remarkable vicissitudes that the book's appearance in print for the first time, in the
Collections of the Massachusetts Historical Society for 1856, seems only a little less
miraculous than the survival of the tiny community whose story Bradford set out
to tell. Nathaniel Morton, William Hubbard, Cotton Mather, Thomas Prince, and
Thomas Hutchinson all knew the manuscript and made use of it, for more than a
century after Bradford's death, in compiling their own accounts of colonial history—a piecemeal fate for a book that had been so lovingly "peeced" together by its
author.[1]

The first of these historical legatees, Nathaniel Morton, cribbed directly from
Bradford's pages in *New England's Memoriall* (1669), published sixty years after the
harried congregation of dissenters from Scrooby, of which Bradford was a member,
had fled England and settled in Leiden, the first stage of a protracted emigration
that ended in 1620 at Cape Cod Bay. Unlike the Nottinghamshire or Yorkshire villages from which they came, Leiden was a city of 45,000 people, home of a famous
Dutch university, and a center of the English Protestant press in exile. There, having trained himself as a fustian weaver and begun his adaptation to an urban world,
twenty-year-old William Bradford continued the process of self-education that
occupied him throughout his life. He announced its last phase, a study of Hebrew,
in the front leaves of his Plymouth manuscript: "Though I am growne aged, yet I
have had a longing desire, to see with my owne eyes, somthing of that most ancient
language, and holy tongue, in which the Law, and oracles of God were write; and
in which God, and angels, spake to the holy patriarks, of old time; and what names
were given to things, from the creation . . . my aime and desire is, to see how the

words, and phrases lye in the holy texte; and to dicerne somewhat of the same for my owne contente."[2]

Within a few years of the appearance of Morton's *Memoriall,* William Hubbard was again consulting Bradford's pages for a "History of New England," which itself remained unpublished until 1815. Twenty years after Hubbard, Cotton Mather incorporated information from Bradford's text into *Magnalia Christi Americana,* written in the closing decade of the seventeenth century—a time of such incessant frontier warfare with the native peoples that Mather had termed it, in the title of an earlier book, *Decennium Luctuosum* (Decade of Sorrow). Thomas Prince drew on Bradford's account for his New England annals early in the eighteenth century and acquired Bradford's manuscript for his New England Library in 1728. Thomas Hutchinson discovered it there nearly forty years later, in time to help him prepare his two-volume *History of the Province of Massachusetts Bay* (1764–67), written during the opening stages of the contest over colonial taxation that ultimately drove Hutchinson into exile during the American Revolution.

After the evacuation of Boston by British troops early in the Revolutionary War, the manuscript disappeared. Alexander Young, a Unitarian clergyman, literary anthologist, and son of a well-known Boston printer, discovered the opening nine chapters of Bradford's book transcribed into the Plymouth Church Records—quite inaccurately, as it turned out—by Nathaniel Morton. Young published these chapters, together with other early sources of Plymouth history, in his *Chronicles of the Pilgrim Fathers* (1841). A little more than a decade later, an obscure bibliographical citation to some of the holdings in the library of the bishop of London, where Bradford's book had mysteriously come to rest, resulted in the discovery and transcription of the entire manuscript for the edition of 1856, still marred by inaccuracies but complete at last and in print more than two hundred years after Bradford had ceased working on the text and almost exactly two hundred years after Bradford's death in May 1657.

It was, perhaps, an inauspicious year for the lost work to resurface. The story of dispersal and dissolution that formed part of Bradford's theme in the history of Plymouth seemed to be reenacting itself on a much greater scale in 1856, with the impending dissolution of the federal Union. The year after Bradford's history finally appeared, Herman Melville produced his complex portrayal of the struggle between cynical self-interest and metaphysical idealism, *The Confidence-Man* (1857). Melville drew his title from nineteenth-century social experience on the eve of the Civil War, but it aptly describes a human phenomenon with which Bradford might readily have identified Thomas Weston, John Lyford, or Isaac Allerton—materialistic manipulators of confidence in seventeenth-century Plymouth who would have been perfectly suited to the smoking rooms and galleries of Melville's Mississippi river boat, the evocatively named *Fidele*.[3]

Bradford himself might have viewed the publication of his history on the threshold of America's secession crisis as a providential coincidence. In some measure his book had always been intimately associated with larger issues of war and peace and with the imperfectly resolved antagonisms to which both of those social conditions give expression. The intransigent policies of James I toward dissenting congregations in England—a kind of civil war within the religious "state"—had first driven John Robinson's church from Nottinghamshire to Amsterdam and then to Leiden, where the first twelve years of the church's residence had coincided exactly with the period of an extended truce between the United Provinces of the Netherlands and the Spanish, with whom the Dutch had been at war for over forty years.[4]

In Leiden, during the second decade of the seventeenth century, William Bradford and his English companions almost certainly heard tales of the famous siege that the city had withstood in 1574, surmounting starvation and plague within the city walls and military assault from without for five months before Dutch relief forces broke through an elaborate network of dikes in early October of that year, flooded the Spanish siege lines, and drove the invaders away.[5] The university at Leiden was established by William of Orange the following year in commemoration of the victory, a parable of endurance that quickly came to occupy a central place in patriotic narratives of Dutch history and identity. The citizens of Leiden held annual feasts of thanksgiving on the anniversary of their liberation, with a ritual menu of bread and herring, to commemorate the city's deliverance.[6] The social and spiritual efficacy of such a festal meal must have made a vivid impression on the English emigrants in their midst.

Later, from their New England outpost, Bradford and his neighbors witnessed the panorama of the Thirty Years War in Europe, the outbreak of civil war in England, and the deterioration of relations with the surrounding Indian tribes that eventually produced the massacres of the Pequot War in 1637, an example of English military ruthlessness that was not lost on the son of Massasoit, Plymouth's Wampanoag ally, whose own campaign against English encroachment, King Philip's War, broke out almost twenty years after Bradford's death. Word of Parliament's victories over King Charles in 1646 prompted Bradford to celebrate this evidence of the Lord's most recent judgmental intervention in English history on the reverse side of the opening pages of his Plymouth manuscript:

Why, art thou a stranger in Israll, that thou shouldest not know what is done? Are not those Jebusites overcome that have vexed the people of Israll so long . . . The tiranous bishops, are ejected, their courts disolved, their cannons forceless, their servise casheired, their ceremonies uselese, and despised; their plots for popery prevented, and all their superstitions discarded & returned to Roome from whence they came, and the monuments of Idolatrie rooted out of the land. And the proud and profane suporters, and cruell defenders of these (as bloody papists & wicked athists, and their malignante consorts) marvelously over throwne. And are not these great things? Who can deney it? (11)

Perhaps Thomas Hutchinson reflected on this long entanglement of American colonial idealism with imperial violence when he left Massachusetts in the hands of its revolutionary government and sailed to England two years ahead of General Howe's retiring British troops; it was a journey that Bradford's book also made sometime before the spring of 1776.

By 1897—when Bradford's original manuscript was finally returned to Boston and *Of Plimmoth Plantation* was republished in an edition that included photofacsimiles of Bradford's closely written pages—the profound insecurities of seventeenth- and eighteenth-century life were as alien to a United States about to prosecute its own brief war with Spain as Bradford's ornate script and archaic grammar were. In the introduction to his 1952 edition of the history, Samuel Eliot Morison almost wistfully reprints the menu of a lavish banquet hosted by the American Antiquarian Society to mark the presentation of Bradford's manuscript to the Commonwealth of Massachusetts.[7] There is no suggestion in Morison's account that the guests at the 1897 feast had any awareness of the deep ambivalence toward prosperity and success, in seventeenth-century Calvinist culture, that Simon Schama perceptively characterizes as the "embarrassment of riches."[8] On the threshold of the twentieth century, and in the year of John Philip Sousa's "Stars and Stripes Forever," the festivity is all riches and very little embarrassment—representing a human susceptibility that, once again, would not have been unfamiliar to the cosmopolitan observer, reader, and writer who produced the extraordinary narrative to which the banquet guests at the Parker House in 1897 paid homage.

Morison prepared his modernized edition of Bradford's book amid the ideological passions of the cold war and fresh memories of World War II—conditions that were likewise influential in shaping Bradford Smith's presentation of seventeenth-century experience in his 1951 biography of William Bradford. The prisons of the Tudor and Stuart monarchies, Smith asserted in grotesque hyperbole, "were not much better than Hitler's gas chambers."[9] Plymouth itself was initially a "communist" village that came quickly (and reassuringly) to dramatize the unworkable nature of communism. Like Smith, Morison thought he detected in William Bradford's pages suggestive parallels to the dilemmas of the mid–twentieth century. Seventeenth-century Plymouth appeared to be engaged in its own form of cold war, reflecting the anxieties and perplexities of a free people hemmed in by aggressive imperial neighbors. It wrestled with the contradictory demands of military security and an irenic faith, with the diplomatic quandaries of a "United Nations in miniature" that Morison believed he saw evidenced in the struggles of the United Colonies of New England to confront the challenge of seventeenth-century Narragansett aggression.[10]

Bradford, of course, could never have foreseen the role his narrative was going to play in the work of future historians, its influence upon subsequent observers of American life over the next three centuries, or the curious pertinence of his story to the shifting cultural circumstances of its readers in 1856, 1897, or 1952. But it is unlikely that he would have been entirely surprised by the wonderful durability of his book. Books were critical to the emerging Protestant communities of northern Europe in Bradford's lifetime, precisely because they were so adaptable, so mobile, and so durable. In his *Actes and Monuments,* John Foxe closely associated the progressive collapse of papal authority, since the burnings of John Huss and Jerome of Prague in 1415 and 1416, with the spread of printing, the steady decline in the price of books, the increase in literacy, and the expanding knowledge of foreign languages made possible by the diffusion of printed texts. Print was, at the same time, a moral rebuke to the persecutions of the Counter Reformation. "In this very tyme so dangerous and desperate," Foxe wrote, "where mans power could do no more, there the blessed wisedome and omnipotent power of the Lord began to worke for his Churche; not with sworde and tergate to subdue his exalted adversarie, but with printyng, writyng, and readyng: to convince darknesse by lyght, errour by truth, ignoraunce by learnyng. So that by this meanes of printyng, the secret operation of God hath heaped upon that proude kyngdome [of the Bishop of Rome] a double confusion."[11]

In Leiden the members of John Robinson's small church were direct participants in God's "secret operation" of printing, inciting the proud kingdom of England and the diplomatic agents of James I to lodge angry protests against the enclaves of the exile press in Holland. After a number of efforts to support himself and his family in their new Dutch home, primarily as a private tutor and an English teacher, William Brewster had become a printer. Bradford himself may have mortgaged part of his new house to a Leiden goldsmith for four hundred guilders in order to provide some portion of the capital for what historians have come to call the "Pilgrim Press," the imprint of Thomas Brewer and William Brewster in Choir Alley, Leiden.[12] Brewer and Brewster did not produce many books— twenty-one titles at most, some of which are dubious attributions—nor were they in business for very long.[13] The English ambassador to The Hague in 1619, Dudley Carleton, complained that they had been engaged in publishing "prohibited books and pamphlets" for the preceding three years only. After 1619 the distinctive typeface of the Pilgrim Press disappeared, but over its brief life span it succeeded in distributing a number of titles that incensed the English government, in particular David Calderwood's *Perth Assembly,* an account of the subversion of the Scottish Church by clerical agents of King James, who converted the Presbyterian Assembly of 1618 into a tool for the suppression of dissent and the imposition of episcopal government upon Scottish Protestants.[14]

The Dutch eventually agreed to turn over these troublesome Leiden printers to the English authorities, but Brewer was affiliated with the university and could be sheltered by its special legal immunities. William Brewster went into hiding somewhere in England, until he could get safely on board the *Mayflower,* under an assumed name, and escape to Plymouth Plantation.[15] The operations of printing were necessarily furtive in Bradford's day, not only because of God's apparent intention to mediate his direct agency in the work of religious reformation but also because earthly printers directly undermined the earthly authority of kings and bishops. Although the Marian persecutions that formed such a dramatic portion of John Foxe's account of Protestant martyrdom had come to an end with Elizabeth's accession to the throne, the treatment of unlicensed printing as sedition, particularly when it addressed deep-seated religious or political controversy, continued into the reigns of the Stuarts.[16]

Long periods of imprisonment without trial, flogging, branding, public mutilation, or execution often awaited a printer or an author who had offended a prince. Even the illustrious Elizabeth, to whom John Foxe had addressed the first English edition of the *Actes and Monuments* in 1563, could be a fiercely repressive monarch. Foxe called her, in his dedicatory letter to the second edition of his book, "our peaceable Salome," a seemingly honorific reference so charged with cautionary ambivalence that it is difficult to imagine that Foxe did not intend to warn his young queen about the responsibilities and the perils of her position. The biblical Elizabeth was the mother of John the Baptist, whose own martyrdom was precipitated by the sensuous dance of Herodias's daughter, whom Josephus identifies as Salome.[17] There were good reasons, then, why William Brewster might want to conceal himself during the months before the *Mayflower* and the *Speedwell* sailed, why he went on board under an assumed name, and why William Bradford placed so little emphasis, in the pages of his book, on Brewster's formative, public role in the early years of the plantation itself. Bradford initially wrote, of course, during the reign of Charles I and in the midst of the legal and political uncertainties of the English Civil War. Charles' father, employing diplomatic pressure alone, had been able to drive Brewster out of Holland. It was by no means impossible that his successors might choose to drive him out of New England as well.

Some of the customary slang of the seventeenth-century printing trade probably derives from this close association of religious controversy with the evolving technology of print. Joseph Moxon, in his *Mechanick Exercises: Or, the Doctrine of handy-works. Applied to the Art of Printing* (1683–84) explains that the printing house "is by the Custom of Time out of mind, called a *Chappel*" in recognition of the many books of divinity that flowed from Reformation presses.[18] The names for the physical parts of the press itself suggest half-playful, half-grim associations with the fate of an author or a printer unlucky enough to offend ecclesiastical authority. Although the press was a machine, Moxon noted, it was also a kind of body "consisting of many Members" (48). The upright wooden frame that housed all of its moving parts was termed the press's "cheeks." Its primary horizontal support was its "head." The bed in which the type forms rested was called the "coffin," the marble printing stone was supported by a framework of "ribs," and the part of the mechanism that slid the inked forms and dampened paper under the platen was called the "gallows" (fig. 1). Because the printer's boys "commonly black and Dawb themselves" with ink, Moxon notes in his printer's dictionary, "the Workmen do jocosely call them *Devils*."[19] The shavings and debris that littered the floor of a letter-founder's house were its "ashes," and they were said to be "fat" or "lean" depending on how much reusable metal could be retrieved from them.

William Brewster's brief involvement with this subversive and liberating technology, along with his secret presence on the *Mayflower*, makes all the more interesting another secreted item of cargo on board—not a person but a tool that played a crucial role in helping the vessel survive the late-autumn storms of the North Atlantic. During heavy weather at some point in midpassage, the concussion of the sea cracked one of the *Mayflower*'s main beams, a thick horizontal wooden support essential to the ship's ability to resist the persistent leaking that had forced the *Speedwell* to return to England earlier in the voyage. This crisis would appear to be exclusively the concern of the ship's captain and crew, not its passengers, but Bradford indicates that the passengers not only were consulted on the condition of the ship—a subject in which they would naturally take a deep personal interest—but they were, as well, the chief means of its preservation. They had with them, Bradford writes, a "great iron scrue . . . brought out of Holland" that they were able to

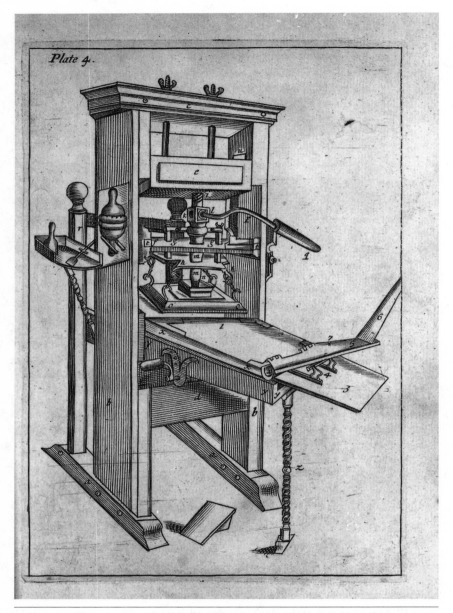

Fig. 1. From Joseph Moxon, *Mechanick Exercises: Or, the Doctrine of handy-works. Applied to the Art of Printing. The Second Volume* (London, 1683). This is Moxon's illustration of the "New-fashion'd *Presses* . . . used generally throughout all the *Low-Countries*." By permission of the Houghton Library, Harvard University.

employ as a jack to push the cracked beam back into position, where it could be reinforced with additional vertical posts until the ship's carpenter was satisfied that the vessel was secure (92).

Over the century and a half since the reemergence and the publication of Bradford's book, this curious piece of apparatus has attracted remarkably little attention from the book's editors and readers. Worthington Chauncey Ford's richly annotated 1912 edition of the history supplies a contemporary account of the contents of a typical ship carpenter's toolbox, but it passes over Bradford's enigmatic iron screw without comment. Morison's more recent edition is similarly disinterested. James and Patricia Deetz, with their historical archaeologist's eye for material evidence, recognize that the screw could be part of a printing press but dismiss the possibility as speculative, which of course it is.[20] Joseph Moxon's late-seventeenth-century discussion of the art of printing, however, helps shed light on this apparently unremarkable incident during the *Mayflower*'s voyage and the suggestive piece of hardware that was making its journey to the New World along with the Leiden emigrants.

The design of a hand press such as the one that William Brewster had partly owned and operated distributed the energy of the pressman evenly across the surface of the platen by means of a large "spindle" (as Moxon called it), threaded at one end and seated in a "nut" in the head of the press. When the pressman pulled at his bar, the "worms" (or threads) of the spindle turned in the nut, and as the "shank" and "toe" of the spindle descended, it pushed the platen down, evenly pressing the dampened sheet of paper to the inked letter forms beneath (fig. 2). Originally these large screws had been made of wood, as in the screw-driven presses used for the manufacture of linen or paper, and might have been threaded for their entire length rather than only at the end that was seated in the nut. But by Moxon's time, this crucial part of the printing press was made of iron. The one he described in his book was sixteen and one-half inches long and over two inches in diameter at its heaviest, threaded end. A single full revolution of the threads would produce a vertical movement of over two inches in the spindle itself, though Moxon added that a single pull from a pressman generally required only a one-quarter revolution to print the page beneath. Two inches of vertical movement would be ample to allow such a spindle and nut combination to function as a jack in an emergency such as the *Mayflower* encountered.[21]

Contemporary illustrations of presses dating from earlier in the seventeenth century suggest that the threaded screws that Moxon describes in 1683 might vary considerably in size. Certainly the large, standing presses used by printers to compress the finished leaves of a book before sending them to a bindery were driven by

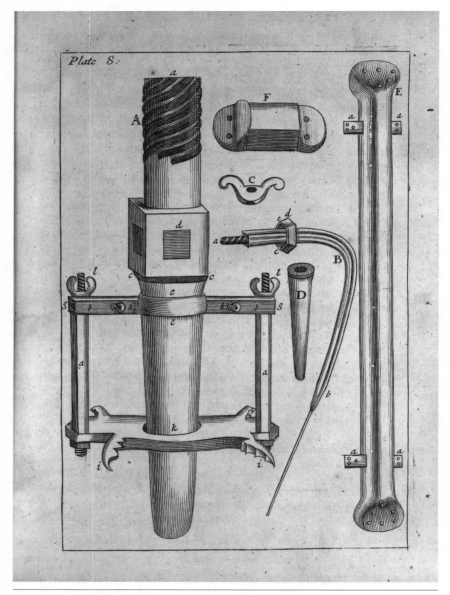

Fig. 2. From Joseph Moxon, *Mechanick Exercises* (London, 1683). "From the Top to the *Toe* of the *Spindle* [*A*] . . . is sixteen Inches and a half, the length of the Cilinder the *Worms* are cut upon is three Inches and a quarter, and the diameter of that Cilinder two Inches and a quarter." By permission of the Houghton Library, Harvard University.

much larger screws than the spindle on the printing press itself. Of all the mechanical "members" of a contemporary press, the most difficult pieces to reproduce or replace would have been the precisely threaded spindle and the nut that enabled it to move smoothly downward in response to the pressure of the bar. It seems a reasonable possibility, then, that along with William Brewster, the *Mayflower* was transporting to New England some portion of the Leiden printing press, perhaps exclusively the expensive metal parts that could only be secured in a European city, with a view to constructing the wooden frame at some future time when the circumstances of colonial life might have eased sufficiently to allow the secret operation of printing to resume.

We can never be certain, of course, that Bradford's great iron screw came from Brewster's Choir Alley press. Many of the Leiden emigrants worked in various weaving trades during their twelve years in Holland; at least some of those specialized trades probably involved the use of presses to shape or finish the fabric. The colonists would need to make clothes in their new home, using some of the skills they had acquired during their long Dutch apprenticeship. In New England, too, they planned to support their new plantation, initially at least, by commercial fishing and fur trading. The proceeds of their fishery they expected to salt, dry, and pack in barrels for shipment to the English market. A screw press of some kind could be used to pack the barrels as tightly as possible to keep moisture from penetrating the contents. A similar process of packing under pressure would have been applied to furs before consigning them to the damp hold of a seventeenth-century ship.[22] All of these purposes might require the transporting of a great iron screw on the *Mayflower*. Even if the settlers of Plymouth did envision the eventual revival of Brewster's press in the New World, their living circumstances in America during William Bradford's lifetime never eased enough that they could undertake such an expensive and risky enterprise.

About the nature of Plymouth's relationship to print itself, there is much less doubt. Bradford makes clear in the opening pages of his manuscript that he inhabits a sophisticated textual world—one in which books, as well as looms, fabric presses, hoes, and saws, were necessary tools in the support of individual and communal life. If in their earliest years together at Scrooby these particular English dissenters were a provincial people, as Bradford occasionally wishes his readers to believe, they were transformed by their residence on the Continent, assuming full status as citizens of the political and religious community with which John Foxe identifies his English martyrs. *Of Plimmoth Plantation*, at least in the eyes of its author, is not the record of a marginal outpost but of an experimental microcosm—a central rather than a peripheral action in the larger drama of the English Reformation.

THIS DEGREE of literary and historical self-consciousness is apparent even from the physical appearance of Bradford's pages, with their carefully maintained margins, centered and bordered chapter headings, and meticulous script. The first letter that Bradford inscribed in his title is an ornamental capital, with two vertical lines bisecting the character O in imitation of the sixteenth- and seventeenth-century black-letter typefaces that English printers frequently employed for works in the vernacular tongue (fig. 3). The manuscript's final page of text encloses formal headings for the two undocumented years, 1647 and 1648, between two pairs of parallel lines that run the width of the sheet, implying a deliberate act of closure rather than fatigue or interruption and linking Bradford's final page with the 1646 interjection on the English Civil War that he wrote and dated on the back of the sheets that contain the book's first chapter. The curvilinear ellipsis with which Bradford links the closing headings for 1647 and 1648 resembles a contemporary printer's decorative flourish (fig. 4). He has, it would seem, made every effort to serve as both the compositor and the author of his book.

Such efforts take still more elaborate form in the title page that Bradford designed in 1652 for the second of his two surviving manuscript dialogues on church government.[23] His recently acquired familiarity with Hebrew led him to incorporate three biblical epigraphs in Hebrew characters, between horizontal borders above his title, along with the same ornamental ellipsis, below the title, that had closed his history of Plymouth two years earlier (fig. 5). The formal preparation of an "author's book"—an autograph rather than a scribal copy of a presumably uncorrupted text—was an established feature of the medieval culture of scribal publication that continued to flourish in England throughout the seventeenth century, despite the development of printing. It is quite possible that Bradford's manuscript dialogues were prepared specifically for scribal circulation. *Of Plimmoth Plantation*, however, meets none of the essential criteria suggested by Harold Love as a means of determining whether a given manuscript, however meticulously written, was in fact "published."[24] The carefully prepared pages of Bradford's history clearly anticipate translation into type, reflecting as well their author's determination to guide that transformation as closely as possible.

These suggestive physical features underscore the relationship of Bradford's writing to the broader world of print. The introductory paragraphs in *Of Plimmoth Plantation* cite the fifth-century ecclesiastical historian Socrates Scholasticus, as well as Eusebius and John Foxe, in an effort to sketch the context in which Bradford wishes his narrative to be placed. He quotes from William Perkins' *Faithfull and plaine exposition upon the 2 chapter of Zephaniah* and from Emmanuel van Meteren's 1608 history of the Netherlands. He suggests that a reader interested in tracing the theological and political controversies within English Protestantism might profit from reading a 1575 account, traditionally ascribed to William Whittingham, of the struggle over the *Book of Common Prayer* that had broken out among the Marian exiles in Frankfort.[25] These opening pages invoke a bibliography, as well as a mythic understanding of the age-long conflict between Satan and the Saints, in order to position Bradford's work on a literary continuum extending over a thousand years. It is, moreover, a bibliography that explicitly recognizes a double-edged dimension to the book.

Writing is clearly a source of instruction, in Bradford's view, and print is an extraordinarily rich storehouse of collective memory, but books can be a means of coercion as well as instruments of enlightenment. The Frankfort "troubles" that William Whittingham describes involve the efforts of factions within the community of English exiles, in the mid–sixteenth century, to impose methods of worship on one another by enforcing conformity to a book. Neither the mediation of John Calvin nor the "commone persecution" of Mary Tudor's bishops could reconcile these hostile camps.[26] Whittingham's story, Bradford believes, "deserves better to be knowne and considred" at least in part because it makes evident the long history of ideological antagonism that drove the *Mayflower* emigrants to New England. It was a conflict nearly as old as English Protestantism itself, and like the wider Reformation of which they were a part, these troubles were founded upon and sustained by books.

Along with a select library of history and theology, Bradford clearly has at hand, as he writes, the complete correspondence that passed between the agents of the Leiden congregation and their English financial backers, the letters that the leadership at Plymouth received and sent by the various ships that visited New England, and copies of the two small books that Bradford and Edward Winslow had published in London, in 1622 and 1624, to inform the English public of the current state of the plantation. Although John Robinson was not himself present in New England to guide the activities of the colonists, his books shortly were. At some point during the early years of Plymouth's existence, both Bradford and William Brewster secured translations of the *Common Places* of Peter Martyr and Jean Bodin's *Six Bookes of a Commonweale* to enrich their theological, political, and historical collections.[27]

Brewster's library was well furnished by any seventeenth-century standard. It

Of Plimoth Plantation

And first of ỹ occasion, and Indusments ther vnto; the which
that I may truly vnfould, I must begine at ỹ very roote, & rise
of ỹ same. the which I shall endeuor to manefest in a playne
Stile; with singuler regard vnto ỹ simple trueth in all things,
at least as near as my slender Judgmente can attaine
the same.

1. Chapter

It is well knowne vnto ỹ godly, and judicious, how euer since ỹ
first breaking out of ỹ lighte of ỹ gospell, in our Honourable nation
of England (which was ỹ first of nations, whom ỹ Lord adorned ther with, after ỹ grosse darknes of popery which had couer-
ed, & ouerspred ỹ Christian worled) what warrs, & oppositions euer
since satan hath raised, maintained, and continued against the
sainctes, from time, to time, in one sorte, or other. Some times by
bloody death & cruell torments, other whiles Imprisonments, banish-
ments, & other hard vsages. As being loath his kingdom should goe
downe, the trueth preuaile; and ỹ Churches of god reuerte to their
anciente puritie; and recouer, their primatiue order, libertie, &
bewtie. But when he could not preuaile by these means, against
the maine truethes of ỹ gospell, but that they began to take rooting
in many places; being watered with ỹ blooud of ỹ martires,
and blesed from heauen with a gracious encrease. He then begane to take him to his anciente strategemes, vsed of old against
the first Christians. That when by ỹ bloody, & barbarous persecutions of ỹ Heathen Emperours, he could not stoppe, & subuerte
the course of ỹ gospell; but that it speedily ouerspred, with
a wounderfull celeritie, the then best known parts of ỹ world.
He then beganne to sow errours, heresies, and wounderfull
disentions amongst ỹ proffessours them selues (working vpon their
pride, & ambition, with other corrupte passions, Incidente to
all mortall men; yea to ỹ saints them selues in some measure)
By which wofull effects followed; as not only bitter contentions, &
hartburnings, schismes, with other horrible confusions. But
satan tooke occasion & aduantage therby to foyst in a number
of vile ceremoneys, with many vnprofitable Cannons, & decrees
which haue since been as snares, to many poore, & peaceable
souls, euen to this day. So as in ỹ anciente times, the persecuti-

contained an extensive array of Latin biblical commentaries by the most celebrated Reformation theologians and dozens of volumes of sermons, moral treatises, and anti-Catholic polemics. He had brought with him into exile many of the titles that he had printed at Leiden, including Calderwood's *Perth Assembly* and Thomas Cartwright's ambitious *Confutation* of the English Jesuit version of the New Testament. Secular histories, political tracts like Ralegh's *Prerogative of Parliaments,* and scholarly works like *The Twoo Bookes of Francis Bacon. Of the proficience and advancement of Learning, divine and humane* rounded out the collection—all of which was carefully inventoried at Brewster's death by his fellow bibliophile William Bradford. Bradford's own, much smaller library was not so well documented by his heirs, but it contained, along with many of the same theological titles that Brewster owned, Jeremy Taylor's 1647 argument for religious toleration, *A Discourse of The Liberty of Prophesying;* Pierre de la Primaudaye's sixteenth-century moral dialogues, *The French Academy;* and a volume cryptically set down as "the Guicciardin," in all likelihood an English translation of Francesco Guicciardini's *History of Italy.* So well supplied were Bradford and Brewster with books that in 1622, from

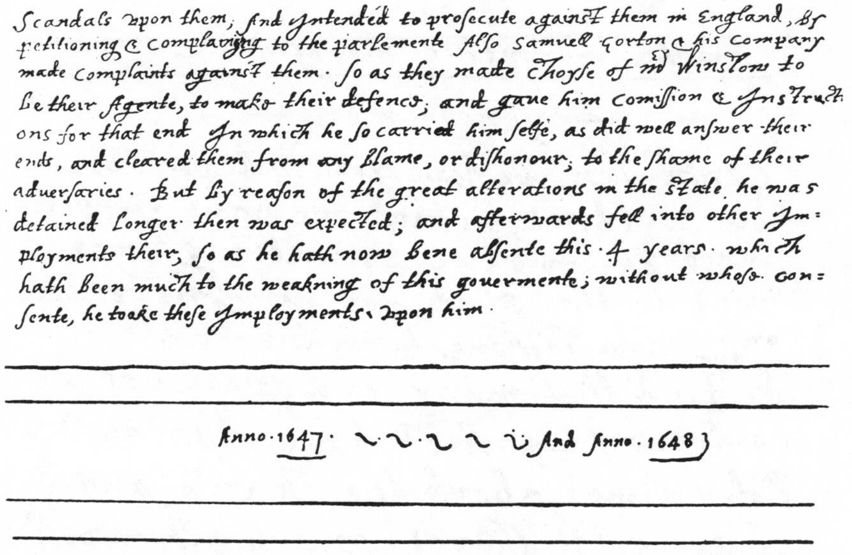
Scandals upon them; And intended to prosecute against them in England, by
petitioning & complaing to the parlemente. Also Samuell Gorton & his company
made complaints against them. so as they made Choyse of mr Winslow to
be their Agente, to make their defence; and gave him comission & Instructions for that end. In which he so carried him selfe, as did well answer their
ends, and cleared them from any blame, or dishonour; to the shame of their
adversaries. But by reason of the great alterations in the State, he was
detained longer then was expected; and afterwards fell into other Imployments their, so as he hath now bene absente this 4 years. which
hath been much to the weakning of this governmente; without whose con-
sente, he tooke these Imployments upon him.

Anno.1647. And Anno.1648

Fig. 3. (*left*) The first page of the history. Pages 1v and 2v are similarly ruled for margins but left blank. Bradford ceases ruling margins altogether on 14r. All images of the manuscript are from the 1896 facsimile, *History of the Plimoth Plantation* (London: Ward and Downey, 1896).

Fig. 4. (*above*) The last page of continuous narrative in *Of Plimmoth Plantation.*

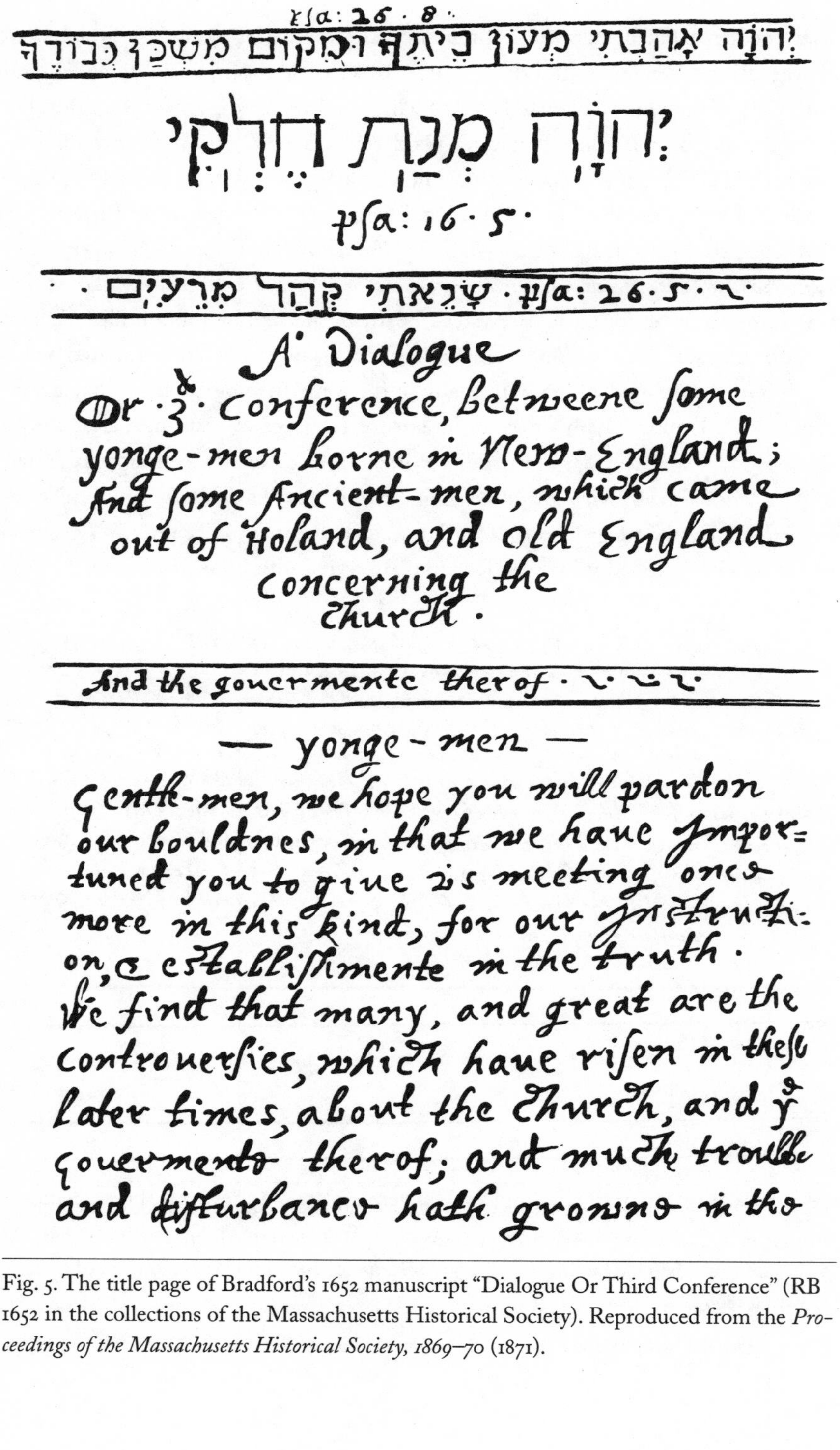

psa: 26. 8.

יְהוָה אָהַבְתִּי מְעוֹן בֵּיתֶךָ וּמְקוֹם מִשְׁכַּן כְּבוֹדֶךָ

יְהוָה מְנָת חֶלְקִי?

psa: 16. 5.

שָׂנֵאתִי קְהַל מְרֵעִים · psa: 26. 5. ·

A' Dialogue

Or ·3· Conference, betweene some
yonge-men borne in New-England;
And some Ancient-men, which came
out of Holand, and old England
concerning the
Church.

And the gouermente therof ·

— yonge-men —

Gentle-men, we hope you will pardon
our bouldnes, in that we haue ymportuned you to giue us meeting once
more in this kind, for our Instructi-on, & establishmente in the truth.
We find that many, and great are the
controuersies, which haue risen in these
later times, about the Church, and ye
gouerments therof; and much trouble
and disturbance hath growne in the

Fig. 5. The title page of Bradford's 1652 manuscript "Dialogue Or Third Conference" (RB 1652 in the collections of the Massachusetts Historical Society). Reproduced from the *Proceedings of the Massachusetts Historical Society, 1869–70* (1871).

their remote New England outpost, they were able to lend copies of Henry Ainsworth's commentaries on the five books of Moses and some of the works of John Robinson to John Pory, the secretary of Virginia, who was briefly visiting Plymouth on a return voyage to England and in need of good reading material.

Collectively, the books that Bradford and Brewster consulted in Plymouth form an apt representation of what Walter Ong has termed the most "riotously polemic" period in the history of print—the two centuries following Gutenberg, during which the deep antagonisms of the Reformation fuse with traditions of learning, in the late medieval and Renaissance world, that were founded upon disputation. Thomas Cartwright's *Confutation of the Rhemists Translation* (1618) captures this adversarial spirit not only in its title but also in its format, printing verses of the New Testament interspersed with the glosses provided by the college of English Jesuits at Reims, punctuated by Cartwright's frequently vituperative replies to his Jesuit opponents. From a modern point of view, it appears evident that the spectacle, not the outcome, of confutation is the book's subject.[28]

Among the other titles that Brewster had printed at Leiden, in addition to Cartwright's performance, were representative admonitions, pleas, apologies, answers, defenses, and two parts of a polemical discourse by Thomas Dighton on "refusing conformity to kneeling" during the Eucharist.[29] This nearly insatiable appetite for printed dispute influences the passages of accusation and reply that Bradford incorporates, often as dramatic dialogues, into portions of his history, but these are very much a vestigial presence in Bradford's text. *Of Plimmoth Plantation*, as its title alone might suggest, reflects the gradual process by which print slowly began to neutralize the antagonistic intellectual habits associated with what Ong playfully calls the "tribal lore" of male initiation into the academic culture of Learned Latin.[30]

The theological and ideological contests represented in Brewster's and Bradford's libraries are only one of the elements out of which Bradford came to "peece" together his book. Indeed, the process of composition and assembly itself quickly came to replace, in Bradford's mind, the oppositional passions captured in the polemical design of Thomas Cartwright's *Confutation*. *Of Plimmoth Plantation* is a study in the formation and maintenance of a "whole" out of disparate and sometimes stubbornly unaccommodating parts. The lessons of Bradford's residence in Leiden may be evident here, for the critical challenge confronting the Dutch, too, throughout the late sixteenth and early seventeenth centuries, was the problem of union. The United Provinces were composed from an unstable fabric of distinct civic and provincial loyalties, bound together in a loose confederation by the leadership of William the Silent, Prince of Orange, and by a common hostility toward Spain. The "strongly developed sense of nationality" that ultimately emerged among the Dutch states, Simon Schama observes, "was the result, not the cause, of the revolt against Spain."[31]

Near the end of the twelve-year truce in the bitter war between the Netherlands and Spain—as Bradford and his handful of English companions were preparing to leave Leiden for America—the Dutch weathered an internal political crisis that had pitted the policies and interests of Holland, the richest and largest of the seven United Provinces, against the *Stadtholder*, Maurice of Nassau; the commercial interests of Amsterdam; and the Dutch Church. In the course of this contest, Arminian theology was uprooted from the Dutch civic and educational establishment; Hugo Grotius, the most distinguished intellectual in the republic, was imprisoned; and the venerable Advocate of Holland, Johan van Oldenbarnevelt, William of Orange's close colleague during the opening decades of the Dutch revolt, was executed. The conflict was particularly intense in Leiden, where Arminius had been a professor at the university and where many of the city officials (though not the population as a whole) supported the so-called Remonstrants in their contest with the Calvinist authorities of the Reformed Church. Street battles broke out in 1617 and 1618 around the Leiden town hall, where the Arminians had constructed a defensive barricade topped with iron spikes, which their Calvinist opponents called, derisively, "Oldenbarnevelt's teeth."[32]

These events vividly illustrated the costs of irreconcilable conflict between "particular" parties who were equally determined to establish their claims to represent the "general" will. The terms themselves played important roles in Dutch political life; the Generality (*Generaliteits*) is the term that the Dutch used to designate the broad collective interests of the whole of the United Provinces, as opposed to the entrenched "particularism" of individual cities or provinces. Bradford's use of the "particular" and the "general" throughout *Of Plimmoth Plantation*, to characterize divisions of interest within the settlement, is more than an eccentricity of seventeenth-century usage. It echoes the configuration of the Dutch Remonstrant crisis of 1618 and 1619, which he witnessed. In yet another sense, too, the words are a constant reminder of the struggle between "particular" congregations and the doctrinal impositions of a "general" church that lay behind the English Reformation as a whole. The activity of "peecing" together, then, touches on a range of metaphorical significance that embraces much of Bradford's broader cultural and historical experience. Making a book could, in surprising ways, resemble as well as document the struggles entailed in making and preserving a compact religious and political community.

The resemblance, however, could be both reassuring and ominous. What is imperfectly pieced together may unexpectedly come undone. Separation and schism form an anxious, ever-present background to most of Bradford's narrative and directly occupy his attention in the first of the dialogues or "conferences" that he composed late in his life, which depict the generation of Plymouth's founders explaining their experiences to a group of younger listeners. Through the voice of his "ancient" men, Bradford insists that the original emigration of John Robinson's congregation from England to the Netherlands was not an act of separation at all but expressed their objection to the attempts of the English crown to enforce the concept of a "National Church."[33] In Bradford's view, it was the episcopal establishment and the Crown that, in seeking to impose a particular form of English national worship on the heterogeneous religious life of its people, had separated itself from the much broader theological experience of the Reformation as a whole. True religion could not be made coextensive with national boundaries or national language.

While the state had—Robinson and his supporters agreed—an undeniable interest in preserving piety and moral self-discipline among its citizens, that interest did not justify granting prescriptive authority to the Anglican liturgy. The reformed church, in its ideal form, was transnational and multilingual, with roots in Switzerland, in Germany, in France, and in the Dutch Republic, as well as in England and Scotland. Peter Martyr, or Pietro Martire Vermigli, author of the *Common Places* that Bradford owned, was an Italian monk whose Protestant views eventually forced him to leave Italy to teach Reformation theology at Strasbourg and at Oxford before ending his career at Zurich. Repeated experiences of emigration and exile had exposed English religious intellectuals to the extraordinary diversity of the trans-European Reformation, both before and after the period of the Marian persecution. "All English protestants," Patrick Collinson affirms, "were internationalists," but by force of necessity some were much more so than others.[34]

Charles V had begun the relentless process of attempting to root out the Protestant "infection" from the Holy Roman Empire with a series of edicts, beginning in 1522 and culminating in 1550 with an imperial declaration, directed largely at the Netherlands, that became known as the Edict of Blood. English textile centers near Norwich quickly began to profit from the knowledge and skill of Dutch fabric workers who fled Charles' (and later Philip of Spain's) increasingly comprehensive and ruthless inquisition.[35] William Whittingham, John Foxe, and John Knox acquired some of their familiarity with Calvinist church government in 1554 from French Protestant exiles in Frankfort, who made their English coreligionists welcome there and shared a church building with them until the conflict over the English Service Book split the English community in two, forcing Knox to flee to Zurich and Foxe to Basle, where he worked to support himself in the print shop of Johannes Oporinus.

John Robinson and William Brewster had been drawn to the Netherlands as a potential refuge for their Nottinghamshire congregation both because it was close and because a number of English congregations in exile were already established there before 1609.[36] The Dutch exile churches in the vicinity of Norwich had played a role in shaping the radical Separatism of Robert Browne in the closing decades of the sixteenth century. Browne eventually fled England to form an exile community of his own in Middelburg, where in 1582 he published the tracts that led to the association of his name with the schismatic "Brownists" from whom Robinson and Bradford were at pains to distinguish their own congregation. John Robinson too had his first clerical post in Norwich, a situation that may have familiarized him with Dutch religious practices and perhaps to a limited extent with their language. The reluctance of King James' agents to permit the small party of Scrooby emigrants to leave England in 1608, despite the king's professed willingness to harry nonconformists into just such a course, was due in some measure to the awareness on the part of English authorities that the Netherlands was rapidly becoming a staging ground for radical thought and radical exile communities.[37]

The emigration from Leiden to New England in 1620 was a singularly bold move for a Protestant congregation to undertake under any circumstances, but emigration itself was an established Reformation practice, a necessary tactic in the strategies of adjustment and survival that the ideological contests of the period compelled people to adopt. To insist upon foreclosing the processes of cultural exchange that this experience had fostered and sealing off the borders of a "National Church" seemed stifling to Robinson and his fellow worshipers. In some sense they viewed the English Church as the truly provincial institution, attempting to separate itself from the international currents of religious thought represented by the movement of people and of books across intellectual and political frontiers.

William Bradford's devotion to the study of Hebrew, late in his life, is a reflection of this appetite for intellectual movement. His interest in what he termed "the most ancient language" has none of the marks of self-subordination or naive deference that one associates with the primitivist determination to recover a lost age of ecclesiastical purity. "My aime and desire," Bradford writes, "is to see how the words, and phrases lye in the holy texte," to learn "what names were given to things, from the creation." In many respects, this curiosity suggests that of a comparative linguist, investigating the difficulties of translation and transmission across cultural boundaries that span vast stretches of time and space. Among some of Bradford's contemporaries, Hebrew was thought to be a pictorial or iconic script more ancient than Egyptian hieroglyphics, with a rich mystical potential that Old Testament scholars could hardly afford to ignore. Pradford's attraction to this area of inquiry is the expression of a cosmopolitan mind, not a provincial or a primitivist one.[38]

At the same time, writing and reading in themselves were troublingly insular, even static activities. Books might be "scurrilous," like that of Thomas Morton, as well as deserving, like the narrative of the Frankfort troubles, but only an alert and discerning reader would be equipped to detect the difference—relying, as readers inevitably must, on the page alone rather than on the full experiential world that the living author strove to recreate in print. Correspondents might compose their letters in good faith or in bad, and a recipient across the sea would be sorely taxed to distinguish between the two. The difficulty with writing and with print springs from the same property to which Bradford finds himself attracted in his study of Hebrew: the words and phrases lie fixed in the text, available to the student despite vast barriers of time and space between writer and reader but unresponsive to the kinds of spirited exchange or interrogation embodied in direct verbal contact.[39]

William Bradford was an intensely literate man living in a religious community that prized the evident sincerity and authority of spontaneous oral expression: the sermon or the prayer delivered from the heart rather than from a written text or a printed tool of liturgical uniformity. And yet sermons themselves, as Bradford and his fellow dissenters understood them, were invariably structured as detailed, dramatic enactments of how to read—an application to Scripture of the philological and textual consciousness of humanist scholarship. In this sense, too, Bradford was living at a point of conjunction between intellectual as well as geographic worlds. *Of Plimmoth Plantation* moves deliberately away from the old polemic culture of confutation and defense, but at the same time it remains deeply rooted in and nourished by the oral elements of an intimate spiritual and physical community.

This paradox finds wonderfully compressed expression in the epigraph from the *Actes and Monuments* with which this introduction begins: "God hath opened the presse to preache," John Foxe declared. His statement is an intriguing blend of agency and action. Books are opened, presses print, and preachers preach, but for Foxe these disparate activities are amalgamated—pieced together—in the exhilarating literary context of late-sixteenth-century Protestant thought. The succeeding chapters set out to demonstrate the extent to which William Bradford's book is a subtle and beautiful product of this richly amalgamated world.

❧

THE LIBERATING POSSIBILITIES OF PRINT, to which Foxe paid tribute, inevitably entailed an increased appreciation among contemporary thinkers for the complex phenomenology of reading. The widespread circulation of vernacular Bibles in the sixteenth and seventeenth centuries almost immediately aroused anxiety and excitement concerning how that potent anthology would be read by the heterogeneous population who could now afford to buy it. Nearly every dimension of the act of reading that Wolfgang Iser describes, in the context of eighteenth-, nineteenth-, and twentieth-century prose fiction, was familiar (under different descriptive terms) to sixteenth-and seventeenth-century thinkers: the "wandering viewpoint" of the interpretive consciousness; the continual interplay between expectation and memory, as the reader repeatedly restructures a cumulative textual experience; the proliferating network of figurative connections that develops through the cyclic reading journey—a journey, as Iser notes, that does not merely flow forward but also circulates freely throughout narrative time.[40] William Bradford's contemporaries would insist, too, that the reading journey does not merely "flow" among the pages of the book in hand but incorporates the memory of other books as well, invited or uninvited guests in the interpretive enterprise.

This appreciation for the complexity of reading encourages an equally complex sense of literary design in a writer like Bradford, who is deliberately constructing what Peter Gay has termed, perhaps with unintentional eloquence, a miniature in an enormous frame.[41] The first three chapters presented here undertake to explore this fruitful relationship between thematic scope and historical particulars, offering a wandering viewpoint of their own, which ranges backward and forward through the bulk of Bradford's book. The chapter titles, accordingly, are evocative rather than denotative labels. "Words and Wind," for instance, the title of the first chapter, refers in part to the structural importance of storms in the opening portions of Bradford's narrative but also to the rhetorical traditions of *copia*, which play a more explicit and formative role in the third chapter, "Artificial Persons." That chapter, in turn, revisits important elements of Bradford's story that precede the voyage of the *Mayflower* but that offer some of the most moving examples of Bradford's ability to sustain his narrative as an epistolary history. Letters are among the most significant artificial persons of Bradford's book, capturing as they do the intractable human friction that repeatedly threatened this fragile venture, as well as the extraordinary verbal resources that repeatedly met each challenge.

The second chapter, "Such Neighbors and Brethren As We Are," takes its title from a letter that John Winthrop wrote to Bradford in 1637, urging Plymouth's compliance with the military intentions of Massachusetts Bay in its rapidly escalating conflict with the Pequot people. In many senses this letter is not a neighborly document, but it offers a suggestive title for a consideration of Bradford's exploration of textual and geographic "neighbors" in the first years of Plymouth's existence, nearly a decade before Winthrop's much more extensive and more affluent colonizing enterprise made its appearance in New England. Plymouth's relations with Massachusetts Bay are more exclusively the focus of the fifth chapter, "Controller of Stories." That title derives not from Bradford's pages but from one of John Foxe's most elaborate defenses of the narrative credibility of his ecclesiastical history, a book that Bradford knew well and cited in the compressed account of the Reformation with which *Of Plimmoth Plantation* begins.[42] The second and fifth chapters, in turn, point to a recurrent theme throughout Bradford's book: the struggle to assert a measure of control over collective religious and political life without giving scope to the appetite for dominance that was so conspicuous in the recent historical experience of England or the European Continent.

Unlike Foxe, Bradford is not compiling a portrait of heroic resistance to Catholic persecution. His model is much closer to the "politic" historiography of Francesco Guicciardini, whose *History of Italy* Bradford (like many radical Protestants) mined for its scathing portrait of papal corruption, even as he ignored its equally scathing account of Martin Luther. Unsavory details culled from Guicciardini's book appear in a portion of Bradford's 1652 "Dialogue" on New England church government that addresses particularly egregious abuses of the Catholic Church. In *Of Plimmoth Plantation*, however, he invokes an oblique comparison between the collapse of the Italian alliances after the death of Lorenzo de' Medici in 1492 and the evolution of the collective polity of New England after the death of William Brewster. The connection to Guicciardini's narrative is sufficiently loose for common thematic elements to emerge, amid the clear differences that distinguish Bradford's own diminutive canvas from Guicciardini's greater one.

The fourth chapter prepares for this final phase of Bradford's story, in part by offering a close examination of justice and of "judgments," as they impinge on Plymouth's experience. A key element in the formation of Bradford's ethical imagination, as this chapter presents it, is John Robinson's *Observations Divine and Morall* (1625), the collection of essays that captures most vividly Robinson's exemplary presence within the Leiden community from which Plymouth's leaders came. William Brewster represented an authoritative emotional and psychological link to that community for the first twenty-five years of the colony's existence, but Brewster's personal example drew heavily upon Robinson's vivid literary legacy for support. To Bradford's mind, Robinson's example of principled resistance to all manifestations of human arrogance remained profoundly influential, both on the course of the colony's affairs and on his own literary practice, long after Robinson's early death.

This interwoven, rather than sequential, account of Bradford's artistic achievement is meant to provide a formal antidote to the elegiac treatment usually accorded *Of Plimmoth Plantation* in American literary history. These chapters do not flow in one direction only, following the gradient of declension so frequently invoked by contemporary scholarship on seventeenth-century New England. Even the implicit comparison that Bradford appears to invite to Guicciardini's grim record of cultural collapse ultimately stresses the vast circumstantial differences between the United Colonies of New England and their Italian precursors, differences that emerge most vividly as New England's more successful experience with confederated communities unfolds.

Bradford's book closes—as this one does—with an examination of human increase in Plymouth: a tabular presentation of the individual lives that are largely subsumed by their collective story in the preceding pages of the history itself. Separated by two blank manuscript leaves from the main body of the history, these tables portray the dense network of individual narratives that spring from the *Mayflower*'s original list of passengers—a profusion rather than a diminishment of human energies, suggesting limitless possibility rather than the emptiness that modern commentators have frequently asserted to be the meaning implied by Bradford's evocative blank leaves. The ruthless exactions of disease so conspicuous in 1620 and 1621 are interlaced with the triumphant census of 1650—absorbed by, rather than eclipsing, Plymouth's living record. In the biblical paradigms to which Bradford and his contemporaries most frequently appealed as models of historical design, a census is always associated with momentous beginnings.

CHAPTER ONE

Words and Wind

A MEASURE OF FAME is sometimes the fruit of persecution, particularly when grave injustices are borne in public, in "eminent places," and in a manner that leaves "a deep impression" on the minds of witnesses. William Bradford learned these lessons in publicity as a young man, both from his reading of John Foxe and from the experiences that he and a handful of his neighbors endured when they sold their homes in the north of England and tried to emigrate to Holland, hoping to conduct their religious lives without interference from civil or ecclesiastical police. This decision, and the hostile reaction that it provoked, had an impact out of all proportion to the actual number of prospective emigrants—deterring some supporters, Bradford remembers in the first chapter of his history, but animating many others, who were drawn "to looke into the same," to investigate the details of this extraordinary local story (21). *Of Plimmoth Plantation,* like the ships that figure so prominently in its pages, is heavily freighted with documents and details, but it is propelled by narrative energy—by a story that slowly disentangles itself from the larger tapestry of political and religious events in early-seventeenth-century Europe.

At a particularly dramatic moment in his book, Bradford instructs his readers and heirs to recite a commemorative speech beginning, "Our faithers were Englishmen," praising their ancestors' piety and courage in what may well be a deliberately ambivalent echo of the Lord's Prayer (96). But these ancestors were also twice uprooted and homeless, adrift in turbulent seas where much larger questions of political and cultural survival were at stake than simply the preservation of a coterie of devout nonconformists from Scrooby. This essential disproportion is seldom far from Bradford's mind as he reads and rereads the pages that he wrote during two of the most troubled decades in English history. Why were we not crushed by the forces at play around us—drowned, starved, wasted by disease, slaughtered by some vindictive Spanish, English, or Indian enemy? The question is unanswerable. But the circumstances that give rise to it can be formulated and reformulated as a survivor's tale. Indeed, the survivor's tale is the paradigmatic source of all stories. "Death is the sanction of everything that the storyteller can tell," Walter Benjamin once observed, in a seminal account of the origins of narrative: "He has borrowed his authority from death."[1] *Of Plimmoth Plantation* begins and ends as just such an inexplicable narrative of survival.

἖

EVEN IN ITS MOST ANXIOUS MOMENTS, the voyage of the *Mayflower* never brought its passengers and crew to a point of physical and spiritual crisis equal to the one that had confronted a handful of John Robinson's congregation on their journey across the North Sea to the Netherlands in 1608. This small party of men were the first members of Robinson's church to board the Dutch vessel that had arrived off the English coast, between Grimsby and Hull, to transport them. A "greate company" of armed men suddenly appeared on shore, frightening the Dutch captain, who immediately made sail, carrying the ship and its anguished passengers, now separated from their families, into "a fearfull storme at sea." For seven days they "neither saw son, moone, nor stars," William Bradford writes in his account of these events, "the mariners them selves often despairing of life," and at one point "with shrikes and cries" completely surrendering to their fate:

> But when mans hope, and helpe wholy failed, the Lords power and mercie appeared in their recoverie; for the ship rose againe, and gave the mariners courage againe to manage her. And if modestie woud suffer me, I might declare with what fervente prayres they cried unto the Lord in this great distres, (espetialy some of them,) even without any great distraction, when the water rane into their mouthes and ears; and the mariners cried out, we sinke, we sinke; they cried (if not with mirakelous, yet with a great hight or degree of devine faith), yet Lord thou canst save, yet Lord thou canst save; with shuch other expressions as I will forbeare. Upon which the ship did not only recover, but shortly after the violence of the storme begane to abate; and the Lord filed their afflicted minds with shuch comforts as every one cannot understand. And in the end brought them to their desired Haven, wher the people came flockeing admiring their deliverance, the storme having ben so longe, and sore in which much hurt had been don, as the masters freinds related unto him in their congrattulations. (19–20)

Some faint resemblance to the opening scene of William Shakespeare's *The Tempest* may account for the hold that this passage has exercised over many of William

Bradford's most perceptive readers. "What, must our mouths be cold?" Shakespeare's heroic boatswain asks, as his terrified crew cry out, "All lost! To prayers, to prayers!" (I, i, 48–49). The water that fills the mouths and muffles the ears of Bradford's small band of religious exiles seems to reflect the same mysterious hostility to speech that Shakespeare's boatswain grimly acknowledges in the face of the ocean's fury.

It is the outcome of Bradford's storm, however, rather than its intensity or menace, that has struck his readers as especially significant. Surely this is a definitive, Pauline moment for the Christian historiographer—a version of the storm at sea in Acts 27 (the work of "that tempestuous wind Euroclydon," as Melville's Ishmael recalls) when "neither sunne nor starres in manie dayes appeared," and only the sublime faith of the Apostle prevented the soldiers and the crew of his prison ship from abandoning hope.[2] *Of Plimmoth Plantation* illustrates repeatedly "the force of God's sustaining hand," in Alan Howard's words, reversing "the downward curve of failing strength," a providential pattern that is exemplified in this dramatic opening passage. Jesper Rosenmeier suggests that the whole episode is prophetic of Plymouth's ultimate triumph over the storms of history. Although Anthony Kemp does not discuss this specific incident in Bradford's book, he considers the emigration to Holland to be one stage in "an odyssey of removal after removal," as John Robinson's company strives hopelessly to recover "the ahistorical and atemporal form of the primitive church." It is, in Kemp's view, a process of spiritual and communal attrition that ends in "moral cataclysm" and private despair.[3]

Despair is surely not the tone that Bradford establishes at this early point in his story, but it is important to pay close attention to certain puzzling features of this famous passage that are not directly related to the providential theme of Protestant history. We cannot learn very much about how to survive the terrors of a storm at sea from Bradford's words. The Lord's power and mercy are not always on call, even for the faithful suppliant. But we can begin to acquire some of the necessary equipment for reading *Of Plimmoth Plantation*.

For all of its inherent drama, Bradford's description of this miraculous deliverance goes out of its way to remind us that we are not, in fact, experiencing these events, any more than a playgoer experiences Prospero's magical tempest. We are reading about them, at a considerable remove in time and space from the chaotic moment of the occurrence itself. The author, too, shares this sense of removal. His account is shaped by a degree of reflective "modestie" that calls attention to his status as narrator rather than participant. This retrospective freedom permits him to distinguish between the degrees of fervor with which "some" of the passengers cried out to the Lord, while others perhaps were less vocal or less urgent with their prayers. Is one kind of appeal more efficacious or more sincere than another? Is Bradford's modesty in reporting this moment of crisis a result of his admiration for the genuinely "devine faith" that the men displayed or of his awareness that their desperate interest in survival somehow fell short of being miraculous? Some of their expressions he records verbatim, while others he excludes from the account—in part, it would seem, to keep the reader's focus on the pen that is constructing this scene rather than on the principals who are living it.

The overt allusion to Paul's voyage in Acts underscores the textual complexity of this moment in Bradford's history. Not only is the author at liberty to probe beneath the surface and hint at the tangle of incompatible motives that afflicted the minds of these men, but he is also able to link their experience to contrasting scenes outside the immediate narrative that encourage the reader's own predisposition to make comparisons and draw distinctions that intensify the import of events. A vicarious, and ultimately misleading, indulgence in the experiences of others is the not the aim of this language; its purpose is to situate us outside the turmoil of life and permit us to observe its contending elements, to the best of the historian's ability, in an atmosphere that is free of bias or passion.

Not even the most gifted writer could make the reader fully appreciate what it must have been like to have survived this terrible experience. The rewards of the participants, as Bradford puts it, are "shuch comforts as every one cannot understand," nor will he undertake to explain them. Did a burst of confidence or religious certitude follow from this spectacular preservation? Did the Lord's apparent intervention imply an endorsement of the motives that had led Bradford's companions to risk the terrible vicissitudes of the North Sea? The history gives no indication that it did. Indeed, the inaccessible comforts that the survivors experience are extraneous to the purposes of the narrative—a syntactical parallel to "shuch other expressions" of religious fervor as Bradford elected to omit from the account of the storm.

Ecstatic faith, like ecstatic relief, is a narrative solvent, a simplifier, and Bradford does not understand either his craft or his subject in simple terms. Certainly it was the Lord's power and mercy that "appeared" in the ship's "recoverie"—words that seem to cloud rather than clarify the question of divine agency—but it was the ship itself that "rose againe, and gave the mariners courage againe to manage her." The Lord "in the end brought them to their desired Haven," but the shipmaster's friends, for all their admiration at his inexplicable deliverance, offer their congratulations to him rather than their gratitude to God. There is no indication that Bradford intends this mixed account of heavenly and earthly means to be read as an ironic disparagement of human effort or an attack on human blindness. However sincere his own convictions of providential oversight in worldly affairs, he does not insist upon those convictions in treating the elements of his story. It is clear how the religious sensibility of the passengers might interpret the events of their remarkable voyage; it is equally clear that other observers might formulate other interpretations.

Rather than impose a particular vision, Bradford chooses to invite another juxtaposition of scene with scene, similar to his original allusion to Acts but this time contrasting two moments in his own story: the fearful storm on the North Sea in 1608 with the series of crosswinds and "feirce stormes" that buffet the *Mayflower* in the North Atlantic twelve years later, leading the mariners "to feare the suffisiencie of the shipe" (91). This second crisis never reaches the extremity of the first. The crew is anxious but far from panic as the passengers enter "into serious consulltation with the master and other officers of the ship, to consider in time of the danger." Rather than risk "inevitable perill" they were willing, if need be, to return to England:

> And truly ther was great distraction and differance of oppinion amongst the mariners them selves; faine would they doe what could be done for their wages sake (being now near halfe the seas over) and on the other hand they were loath to hazard their lives too desperatly. But in examening of all oppinions, the master and others affirmed they knew the ship to be stronge and firme under water, and for the buckling of the maine beame, ther was a great iron scrue the passengers brought out of Holland, which would raise the beame into his place the which being done, the carpenter and master affirmed that with a post put under it, set firme in the lower deck, and otherways bounde, he would make it sufficiente. And as for the decks and uper workes they would calke them as well as they could, and though with the workeing of the ship they would not longe keepe stanch, yet ther would otherwise be no great danger, if they did not overpress her with sails; So they commited them selves to the will of God, and resolved to proseede. (92)

Not God's resistless power to save but the unknowable disposition of his will sustains the passengers on the *Mayflower.* They are no longer a band of harried fugitives driven from their farms and villages in the English countryside but a purposeful expedition, equipped with a degree of experience and gravity that earn the shipmaster's respect, as well as with a useful tool that can assist the ship's carpenter in making necessary repairs. They are resolute amid these challenges, more than they are afflicted or consoled. A sentence or two later, as Bradford recounts the story of John Howland being washed off the ship during "a mighty storme," a sturdy topsail halyard along with "a boat hooke and other means" play more conspicuous roles in Howland's eventual rescue than the divine pleasure to which Bradford's language pays a formulaic deference. "He would make it sufficiente," the ship's carpenter declares, as he outlines his plan for bracing and caulking the *May-flower's* strained timbers. Bradford's description of these events tends to the same end: establishing a tenuous human sufficiency in the face of elemental power. Faith is one instrument among many to be employed in accommodating the vastly disproportionate forces that shape Bradford's world.

The meaning of these contrasts is almost certainly not the one that most readily occurs to a modern reader: twelve years of urban life in Holland have turned these rural pietists into secular citizens of the world. On the contrary, religious faith plays as vital a role in the lives of the emigrants of 1620 as it did in the lives of the fugitives of 1608. Bradford concludes his account of the *Mayflower's* voyage by depicting another fervent cry to the Lord, prompted not by the terrors of the sea but by a complete retrospective grasp of the outcome of his history, focusing on the psychological tensions of landfall but embracing all that had preceded that event and all that had followed it, through the first decade of Plymouth's existence.

On the occasion of this second prayer, as if to confirm its structural and thematic relationship to the first, Bradford openly alludes to the aftermath of Paul's shipwreck, the outcome of the fearful storm of Acts 27, when the natives of Malta showed the Apostles and their companions "no smale kindness in refreshing them" and the survivors learned that they were not hopelessly distant from their destination (95). In contrast, the predicament of the *Mayflower* emigrants, arriving in early winter on a barren coast thousands of miles from home, is almost unrelievedly bleak:

> Besids what could they see, but a hidious and desolate wildernes, full of wild beasts, and willd men, and what multituds ther might be of them they knew not; nether could they (as it were) goe up to the tope of Pisga, to vew from this willdernes a more goodly cuntrie to feed their hops; for which way soever they turnd their eys (save upward to the heavens) they could have litle solace or content, in respecte of any outward objects, for summer being done, all things stand upon them with a wetherbeaten face; and the whole countrie (full of woods and thickets) represented a wild and savage heiw; If they looked behind them, ther was the mighty ocean which they had passed, and was now as a maine barr and goulfe, to separate them from all the civill parts of the world . . . Let it be also considred what weake hopes of supply, and succoure, they left behinde them that might bear up their minds in this sade condition and trialls they were under; and they could not but be very smale; It is true indeed the affections and love of their brethren at Leyden was cordiall and entire towards them,

but they had litle power to help them, or them selves; and how the case stoode
betwene them and the marchants, at their coming away hath already been declared.
What could now sustaine them, but the spirite of God and his grace? (96)

These sentences too are among the most famous in Bradford's book, and they complete the fabric of allusion that he has constructed over the first nine chapters of
the history: linking voyage with voyage, storm with storm, and prayer with prayer.[4]
The buckling of the *Mayflower's* "maine beame" in midocean was a trivial threat
compared to the "maine barr and goulfe" of space and time that now divides these
would-be planters from the far more familiar perils of England or Holland. Human sufficiency alone would appear to have reached its limits, but even at this critical juncture Bradford resists an uncontingent appeal to providential favor.

The passage closes with a question, not an assertion, pointing to resources of
character and conviction rather than the vindication of those human attributes by
miraculous intercession or design. It is for "the children of these fathers," Bradford
writes, to cite Deuteronomy, to remember the adversity that nearly overwhelmed
their parents on the stark New England coastline in 1620, to praise the Lord for his
goodness and his mercy. The historian may "stay and make a pause," as Bradford
puts it, much as he has figuratively recreated storms at sea, in order to provide room
for reflection (94). He may invite his reader to picture the startling and unfamiliar
circumstances that the emigrants faced—to note what in their anxiety they "could"
see, not what was there to be seen; what the landscape "represented," rather than
what it actually contained. He may solicit the reader's imaginative sympathy and
may even draft an appropriate prayer of thanksgiving or remembrance, reassuring
his audience (the author's figurative children) that they are only right to say it.

But the historian, as John Foxe once suggested, is a controller of stories, not a
prescriber of meanings. Although strong personal memories and deep feelings must
have attached themselves to these circumstances as Bradford described them—
recollections of old friends who had died during the first winter in New England,
or of his young wife, who drowned in the shallow harbor at the tip of Cape Cod
while Bradford was away searching for a place to establish their settlement—he has
an extraordinarily disciplined grasp of his narrative obligations and opportunities.
He is writing a history, not recalling his past—structuring a public, written account
with all the ingenuity at his disposal, so as to infuse it with a degree of vitality and
authority that will prove independent of merely personal or emotional appeal. Sustaining this commitment to his book—prompting the care with which he composed and preserved Plymouth's story—is a lifelong acquaintance with reading and
with print that encouraged Bradford to attach significance to the smallest details

of his manuscript, as well as to the most crucial scenes of his narrative. He weighs the implications of individual words in order to distinguish between the portrayals that he will offer of subjective as well as objective conditions. He develops parallels with biblical or with secular history that underscore the give and take between a broad interpretive framework and the stubbornly unassimilable nature of historical particulars. He invites his reader to identify narrative frames, such as these troubled voyages early in the history, that emphasize the twin elements of repetition and difference that structure temporal experience. All of these features of the historian's craft signal a lifetime of thoughtful preparation, as well as a network of complex ambitions, behind the pages of Bradford's book. To reconstruct a complete picture of these authorial ambitions, we will need to begin at the beginning.

৯

IT IS SURPRISINGLY EASY for William Bradford's modern reader to overlook certain traditional elements of the seventeenth-century book that Bradford clearly thought he was writing in 1630. *Of Plimmoth Plantation* is a late-Renaissance manuscript, but it has become so closely associated with its modern publication history that one almost unconsciously treats it as a modern book, particularly since the most widely circulated editions, in the twentieth century, have been so carefully modernized. Even the lovely 1896 photo-facsimile of Bradford's pages has the effect of superimposing one kind of technological context upon another.[5] *Of Plimmoth Plantation* was meant to be printed, not photographed, and set alongside other printed books of its own day, with many of which Bradford had considerable familiarity and with which he may have hoped his own work would be compared.

All the editions that have appeared since Charles Deane's 1856 transcription, with their varying approaches to the challenges that Bradford's manuscript presents, have secured its place in literary history at the expense of neglecting its relationship to the contemporary world of print. How, for instance, do Bradford's remarkably finished pages appear to accommodate or to exclude the customary front matter of a seventeenth-century book describing the progress of English settlement in the New World? *Of Plimmoth Plantation* has no elaborate title page, no prefatory letter seeking the favor of a prominent nobleman, no preliminary address to the reader explaining the author's sense of purpose or offering hints concerning his intended audience, no dedicatory or commendatory verse.

Some of these features, of course, are part of the apparatus of a printed book that, in Bradford's day, would have originated with a publisher rather than an author. At the same time, Bradford was perfectly familiar with contemporary typographic conventions. When he wanted to reproduce some of the effects of a traditional title page for the work that he called *A Dialogue or 3rd Conference betweene some yonge-men borne in New-England; And some Ancient-men, which came out of Holand, and Old England concerning the Church And the goverment therof,* he was perfectly willing, within the constraints of his manuscript, to suggest a design that successfully manages this cumbersome bibliographic label. Short titles do not make much impact on English letters until the mid–eighteenth century, especially when a book's subject matter might be promoted as novel or exotic. The title page was effectively a kind of advertising poster, an enticement for what William Wood called, on the title page of *New England's Prospect* (1634), the "mind-travelling Reader."[6]

Thomas Prince was an editor and historian ahead of his time when, in 1736, he mercifully abbreviated the full title of the first printed account of Plymouth Plantation to *Mourt's Relation.* When this modest book originally appeared, in 1622, it was called *A Relation or Journall of the beginning and proceedings of the English Plantation setled at Plimoth in New England, by certaine English Adventurers both Merchants and others. With their difficult passage, their safe arivall, their joyfull building of, and comfortable planting themselves in the now well defended Towne of New Plimoth.*[7] These words blend seamlessly into a table of contents that itemizes four journeys of discovery that the settlers had made among the nearby Indian "kingdoms" and closes with a promise to answer *all such objections as are any way made against the lawfullnesse of English plantations in those parts.* The entire elaborate preamble ends with an ornamental woodcut, followed by the customary termination of a contemporary title page: the city and year of publication, the publisher's name, and the location of his bookshop.

Some portion of *Mourt's Relation* was the work of William Bradford, but he was not in London when its title page was composed. Robert Cushman, a member of the Leiden congregation who had lost heart during the preliminary discouragements of the original voyage and never emigrated to New England, visited Plymouth in 1621 and took most of the manuscript back to London with him. The 1622 title probably reflects, in some measure, Cushman's engagingly prolix nature, as well as the heterogeneous contents of the book, but it is by no means inconsistent with the explanatory ambitions captured in the fulsome title of John Smith's famous account, published six years earlier: *A Description of New England: or The Observations, and discoveries, of Captain John Smith (Admirall of that Country) in the North of America, in the year of our Lord 1614: with the successe of six ships, that went the next yeare 1615; and the accidents befell him among the French men of warre: With the proofe of the present benefit this Countrey affords: whither this present yeare, 1616, eight voluntary Ships are gone to make further tryall.*[8]

Edward Winslow's *Good Newes from New-England* (1624) purported to be *A true Relation of things very remarkable at the Plantation of Plimoth in New-England. Shewing the wondrous Providence and goodnes of* GOD, *in their preservation and continuance; being delivered from many apparent deaths and dangers.*[9] The customs of the Indians and the commodities of the country are also subsumed, on the title page, under Winslow's good news. Francis Higginson, in *New England's Plantation* (1630), wrote the earliest account of the English settlements at Massachusetts Bay under the most succinct title of the period: *A Short and true Description of the Commodities and Discommodities of that Countrey.*[10] Thomas Morton's notorious *New English Canaan* (1637) offered an *Abstract of New England, composed in three bookes,* with the first *setting forth the originall of the natives, their manners and customes, together with their tractable nature and love towards the English.* In the second Morton addresses *the naturall indowments of the country,* and only after these preliminary descriptive tasks have been announced does the title page disclose, in Morton's third book, the subject that has rescued his work from obscurity: the religious and political behavior of the English settlers.[11] By 1645, when he began writing the second part of the history, William Bradford was almost certainly aware of the striking simplicity of the title that he had chosen for his book. *Of Plimmoth Plantation* immediately declared itself to be different from the customary relations, journals, descriptions, and surveys that had preceded it into the London bookshops.

This conspicuous contrast with the expansive, frequently sensationalized titles of the time is both illuminating and misleading. Bradford is no less interested than his contemporaries in establishing a claim upon the reader's attention, but he is clearly distinguishing his work from what J. Paul Hunter calls the moment-centered consciousness of seventeenth-century travel narratives: the broad preoccupation that they often display with the immediate, the novel, and the strange—features in which Hunter locates some of the early imaginative roots of eighteenth-century English fiction.[12] The up-to-the-minute implications of Smith's *Description of New England,* with its attention to "present" benefits and to the events of "this present yeare," perfectly illustrate the narrative temperament that Hunter describes. It is not very much of a leap from such a plot-saturated title page as that of John Smith or Edward Winslow to those of Daniel Defoe. *Of Plimmoth Plantation* apparently resists, rather than invites, these entanglements with plot, and except for its allusion to the novel enterprise of planting a colony in the New World, Bradford's title seems, if anything, faintly archaic—an English echo of the Latinate syntax in Livy's *Ab urbe condita* or Augustine's *De civitate Dei.*

The tiny English settlement at New Plymouth is, to be sure, a ludicrously insignificant subject in comparison with Livy's or Augustine's grand themes—a disparity that would have been apparent to the largely bilingual, educated audience of the early seventeenth century—but Bradford is intent on announcing, at the outset of the narrative, his interest in the mysterious potential of small beginnings. He makes this theme explicit on many occasions throughout the book, when he emphasizes dramatic growth or improvement in the colony's economic circumstances. But the comparative implications of Bradford's title point to more than just a trajectory of material success. No European or English historian in Bradford's lifetime ever considered taking as a subject the destiny of a handful of families in a remote village, seemingly isolated from the political and religious currents of metropolitan life. The reigns of princes, the affairs of great cities or nations, deserved the attention of historians, but not (as Leonard Dean has observed) the "inelegant trivialities of everyday life."[13]

The kind of close historical scrutiny of human motives or human means advocated by Francis Bacon or practiced by the Italian humanists applied largely to the agency of great figures on the stage of events. Otherwise histories would have little instructive or didactic impact on the course of the contemporary world. To this end, Bacon ranked narrative history over chronicles largely because chronicles tended to overlook "the smaller passages and Motions of men and Matters," precisely the subjects that narratives sought to expose. The most perfect histories, Bacon declared in a book that William Brewster owned, took careful note of God's propensity to "hang the greatest waight upon the smallest Wyars," but even the smallest wires that Bacon had in mind were subordinated to sweeping historical actions, like the history of England "from the Uniting of the Roses to the Uniting of the Kingdoms," which Bacon proposed as an illustration of what he meant by a concise historical subject and as a gesture to flatter his royal master.[14]

When a seventeenth-century writer undertook to examine regional or local circumstances in a historical context, he usually characterized his work as some sort of verbal topography, much as William Wood does in the title of *New England's Prospect*. John Smith's book is in some measure a historical and biographical narrative, but he calls it a "description" of New England, not a "history" of his voyages. Thomas Morton has specific historical ambitions for *New English Canaan,* but he still regards the book as an "abstract" of New England, a regional resource map as well as an indictment of the civil and religious activities of recent emigrant communities. This customary generic terminology likewise influences contemporary metropolitan figures like John Stow, when he calls his account of the growth and

development of London a "survey," or William Camden, when he titles his historical review of England's counties and shires "a Chorographicall Description" of the
three kingdoms of the British Isles.[15]

Even John Winthrop, who presided over a colonizing enterprise many times
larger, more wealthy, and more ambitious than that of the Plymouth settlers,
showed considerable ambivalence about the title that he applied to his journals. On
the cover of the last of his manuscript notebooks, Winthrop called his work the
"Annalls of N: England," though on the first page of the text itself he describes the
volume as a continuation of New England's "Historye." Noah Webster adopted the
term "journal" for his 1790 edition of the first two manuscript notebooks. In 1825
James Savage settled on *The History of New England* for the title of the first complete edition of Winthrop's work.[16]

As these vacillations make evident, the traditional expectations associated with
the term *history* caused considerable difficulty for writers at work in a fluid generic
medium. Much of the bibliographic uncertainty had been resolved by the time
James Savage confidently labeled John Winthrop's journal.[17] William Bradford's
contemporaries, however, would quickly have recognized a dramatic complexity in
his evocative title that the text underscores, a few pages into the narrative, when it
anticipates the story of sacrifice that "this ensewing historie will declare" (13). A
surprising measure of thematic confidence lies behind Bradford's determination to
declare in a history the tribulations of his immediate neighbors and companions.
Moreover, *Of Plimmoth Plantation* draws upon the kind of antecedent narrative
closely associated with much greater worldly enterprises. In the short preface that
precedes his opening chapter, Bradford declares that he must first loop backward
to consider occasions and inducements to the central story that slowly take root in
individual minds. A historical and psychological chain of causation—a tracing of
the relation between great weights and small wires—is the first subject to which
Bradford must devote his "plaine stile" and "slender judgment." Like the suggestive
brevity of his title, this preface has an intriguing relation to the conventional expectations and disclaimers of Bradford's day.

Sixteenth- and seventeenth-century historians and travelers routinely dispar-
aged their literary abilities in the process of soliciting the reader's favor at the outset of their books. This convention tended to prevail regardless of the stature of the
author or the importance of the work in question. The successive editions of John
Foxe's *Actes and Monuments of these latter and perillous dayes, touching matters of the
Church* (1563) are among the most formidable publishing enterprises attempted in
English during the era of the hand-operated press.[18] Foxe's comprehensive account
of the persecutions inflicted upon and perpetrated by the Catholic Church through

fifteen centuries of Christian history eventually fills two richly illustrated, double-column folios of more than a thousand pages each, with a correspondingly elaborate front matter in which Foxe confesses, in both Latin and English, to his personal deficiencies.

The English version of this bilingual disclaimer in the edition of the *Actes and Monuments* that Bradford cites addresses the issue of "what utilitie is to be taken by readyng of these Hystoryes." In it Foxe admits to feeling "both bashfull and fearfull" that he will prove unequal to "the perfection of so great a story." The world is already so "pestered" with histories, Foxe believes, and contemporary readers have grown so sophisticated that his audience will judge him to be too "weake a thing" for such a "weyghty enterprise." It is Foxe's reader, of course, who is likely to experience a sense of weakness and inadequacy in the face of Foxe's monumental accomplishment, but the formal expectation that an author introduce his work with a confession of his incompetence was sufficiently well established by the mid-sixteenth century that even the most authoritative work is compelled to honor it, regardless of how formulaic the confession itself may sound.[19]

Walter Ralegh's preface to *The History of the World* (1614) opens with a similar confession, cast in expansive terms that manage to convey Ralegh's sense of dramatic pleasure as he elaborates on the traditional apologetic role:

> How unfit, and how unworthy a choice I have made of my self, to undertake a worke of this mixture; mine owne reason, though exceeding weake, hath sufficiently resolved me. For had it been begotten then with my first dawne of day, when the light of common knowledge began to open it selfe to my yonger yeares: and before any wound received, either from Fortune or Time: I might yet well have doubted, that the darknesse of Age and Death would have covered over both It and Mee, long before the performance . . . I confesse that it had better sorted with my dissability, the better part of whose times are runne out in other travailes; to have set together (as I could) the unioynted and scattered frame of our English affaires, than of the universall: in whome had there been no other defect, (who am all defect) then the time of the day, it were enough . . . But those inmost, and soulepeircing wounds, which are ever aking while uncured: with the desire to satisfie those few friends, which I have tried by the fire of adversitie; the former enforcing, the later perswading; have caused mee to make my thoughts legible, and my selfe the Subiect of every opinion wise or weake.[20]

James I almost certainly scoffed at Ralegh's pointed claim that he could "set together" the disjointed affairs of England from his Tower prison cell, even if the boast only pertained to literary powers. Ralegh's celebrated irreverence for princes, however, did not prevent the king's daughter from securing a copy of the *History*, shortly after her marriage to the elector Palatine, and taking it with her to Prague for her brief reign as queen of Bohemia.[21]

Seventeenth-century presses and bookshops teemed with universal secular and ecclesiastical histories—accounts of the major religious or political empires of the earth, from Creation to whenever the energies of the author flagged or the resources of the printer ran out.[22] Ralegh's handsome folio—the first of three projected parts, only one of which was completed—begins with Genesis and closes with the Roman conquest of Macedonia in 168 B.C. Some of the universal histories published on the Continent dwarf even the efforts of John Foxe. The vast commonplace collection of the "historian rhapsodist," Theodor Zwinger, *Theatrum vitae humanae* (1565), grew through its first five editions to more than twice the length of the *Actes and Monuments*.[23] The *Magdeburg Centuries* (1559–74), a "violently partisan" history of the abuses of the Catholic Church through the year 1400, fills thirteen folio volumes, prepared by a consortium of authors known to their Catholic opponents as "the Centuriators."[24] William Bradford was familiar with this encyclopedic indictment, at least indirectly, through citations in a book by John Cotton.[25] The comprehensive ambitions of such works invariably evoke conventional expressions of authorial humility. Ralegh's elaborate preamble discloses with unusual candor the element of vanity that propels the writer or the compiler forward, however vivid a sense he may possess of his defects.

John Smith introduces *A Description of New England* with seven congratulatory poems from his friends and three prose dedications of his own—a display of energetic promotional excess that is delightfully consistent with Smith's personal traits. Two of the dedications contain confessions of authorial weakness that are clearly tailored to their recipients. To the "Lords, Knights, and Gentlemen" of the Council for New England, Smith expresses his awareness that even "the writings of the most wise" are often "traduced" by "Times opinionists." "What shall such an ignorant as I expect?" he asks. Nevertheless, Smith has confidence that the council's patronage will protect his "rude discourse" from maltreatment, "Not doubting but your goodnesse will pardon my rudenesse, and ponder errours in the balance of good will."[26]

In his dedication to the "Adventurers" or investors who stand to profit from Smith's knowledge, he takes a different approach, confessing the "imbecillitie" of his work but blaming its defects at least partly on the haste with which he has been forced to reply in print to his "taxers" and critics. The result is a characteristically pugnacious assertion from a man whose scorn for verbal accomplishments is evident:

> If the little Ant, and the sillie Bee seek by their diligence the good of their Com-
> monwealth; much more ought Man. If they punish the drones and sting them [that]
> steales their labour, then blame not Man. Little hony hath that hive, where there are
> more Drones then Bees; and miserable is that Land, where more are idle then well
> imployed. If the indeavours of those vermin be acceptable, I hope mine may be
> excuseable; Though I confesse it were more proper for mee, To be doing what I say,
> then writing what I knowe.[27]

The expedient nature of these contrasting dedications exposes rather than mutes
Smith's problematic personality, though in contrast to Ralegh's melancholy polish,
such clumsiness almost seems a virtue. Smith's excesses are those of a comparatively forthright man mimicking the rhetorical formalities of contemporary publication.

Like Smith, Robert Cushman lived most of his life with no expectation that he
would ever contribute to a published book. He was a prosperous wool comber,
originally from Canterbury, who had joined John Robinson's church at Leiden after
the congregation of English exiles in Amsterdam to which he had first belonged
was split by personal and theological quarrels.[28] Cushman had become a trusted
member of the Leiden community by the time they decided to emigrate to America; and along with John Carver, he went to England to negotiate the arrangements
for the voyage with government officials and with potential investors, whose support was necessary to defer the expenses of such an ambitious undertaking. This
task proved to be so exasperating and exhausting that at one point Cushman asked
if another member of the community might take his place "and let me come again
to my Coombes" (68). With Carver's steady encouragement, Cushman remained,
but the stress of managing the preparations played a considerable role in the collapse of health and confidence that kept Cushman in England when the *Mayflower*
finally sailed west. Part of his later contribution to *Mourt's Relation,* however, was
a defense of "the Lawfulness of Removing out of England into the Parts of America." Cushman was sufficiently well versed in the conventions of authorship to begin
his discussion with a disclaimer that is similar to the acknowledgment that Bradford later attaches to the beginning of his history.

Those who have been "ear-witnesses" to the exceptions made against emigration, Cushman observes, would do well to answer those exceptions. Although some
of the skeptics are motivated by selfishness or fear, others are surely moved by "tenderness of conscience" to doubt the nature of the call to such a drastic step:

> For whose cause especially I have beene drawne, out of my good affection to them, to
> publish some reasons that might give them content and satisfaction, and also stay and

stop the wilfull and wittie caviller; and herein I trust I shall not be blamed of any godly wise, though thorow my slender judgment I should misse the marke, and not strike the naile on the head, considering it is the first attempt that hath beene made (that I know of) to defend those enterprises. Reason would, therefore, that if any man of deeper reach and better judgment see further or otherwise, that he rather instruct me than deride me.[29]

In comparison with the truculence of John Smith, the courtly melancholy of Ralegh, or the pious formulas of Foxe, Cushman's words seem both simple and sincere, even given the convention within which he is working and the jumble that he makes of his cliches. They convey the impression of a common man writing in great earnest on an uncommon theme; if the effect is due merely to a performance, it is an extraordinarily restrained and subtle one.

Bradford's preparatory disclaimer to *Of Plimmoth Plantation* shares some of the properties of Cushman's appeal, but at the same time Bradford sets aside a key element of the tradition that Cushman, Smith, Ralegh, and Foxe all display. Foxe professes to be wary of the judgments of a readership grown sophisticated on the steady diet of books that had been made available during the first century of print. The fires of political adversity, Ralegh insists, have left him with few friends to sustain him in the hostile court of public opinion. Smith's sensitivity to his "taxers" is readily apparent, and even Cushman writes in conscious opposition to the "wilfull and wittie caviller" who prefers to mock rather than to instruct. All four writers— despite their extraordinary diversity of background and the obvious differences in the scope of their literary ambitions—structure their professions of inadequacy in the face of an oppositional readership. All four have imbibed elements of the adversarial frame of discourse that characterized the rhetorical arts of the sixteenth and seventeenth centuries.

Bradford's preface to *Of Plimmoth Plantation,* in contrast, has shed this influence altogether, moving purposefully from the title to the beginning of the first chapter with no clear syntactical pause, as if the subject alone, and not the reception of his work, is all that concerns him: "And first of the occasion, and indusments ther unto; the which that I may truly unfould, I must begine at the very roote, and rise of the same. The which I shall endevor to manefest in a plaine stile; with singuler regard unto the simple trueth in all things, at least as near as my slender Judgmente can attaine the same" (3). In Bradford's manuscript page, these words, along with his title, are set carefully in place between crisp vertical and horizontal lines that the author has situated in such a way as to suggest a locked form of types, perhaps imitating the printed design of Peter Martyr's *Common Places* (1583), a book that Bradford owned at his death. The double columns of text in Anthonie Marten's translation of Peter Martyr's work are carefully enclosed by overlapping horizontal and vertical lines, with neatly bracketed titles, precisely as Bradford prepared the opening pages to *Of Plimmoth Plantation* (figs. 6 and 7).

Insofar as a writer can expect to control the presentation of his unpublished work to posterity, Bradford has sought to exercise that control, detaching his account from the atmosphere of contemporary controversy that is so influential in the authorial postures of Cushman or Smith. Even the conventional reference to his "slender" judgment emerges naturally from Bradford's horticultural metaphor of narrative "roots," extending the alliterative series of modifiers that he applies to the "singuler regard" with which he has pursued the "simple trueth." Elsewhere in the opening pages of his book, Bradford addresses the disruptions of the contemporary world quite explicitly, even passionately, and with a disdain for ecclesiastical princes that compares favorably with the indictment of monarchy in the pages of Ralegh's preface to *The History of the World*. But these initial lines signal a different temperament altogether from that of the religious or political controversialist.

Moreover, by stripping his prefatory matter of the customary defensive (or offensive) apparatus, Bradford begins to address a number of the strictures on historical credibility established by Jean Bodin in his influential handbook for students on the "easy comprehension" of history, *Methodus ad facilem historiarum cognitionem* (1566). Bodin was widely admired as a political theorist by sixteenth- and seventeenth-century English thinkers who, like William Bradford and William Brewster, owned copies of Bodin's extensive treatise, *Six Bookes of a Commonweale*, in Richard Knolles' English translation (1606). An important chapter from the *Methodus* likewise appeared in English as the preface to Thomas Heywood's edition of the histories of Sallust (1609). It is impossible to establish whether Bradford knew the *Methodus* directly, but it seems likely that his interest in Bodin's political thought—and his ownership of the work that Bodin praised most highly in the *Methodus*, Guicciardini's *History of Italy*—would entail at least a general acquaintance with Bodin's tests for historical bias.[30]

Excessively censorious or eulogistic language in historians constituted the most prominent of these tests. Emphatic praise or blame, Bodin suggests, is the mark of an orator pleading a cause, not of a dispassionate student of human affairs. Be wary, too, of signs that the historian wishes to entertain his reader—an intention clearly implied by the elaborate nature of many contemporary title pages or by the histrionic excesses of Thomas Morton's narrative. Like Francis Bacon forty years later, Bodin disliked the intrusion of long passages of interpretive commentary into the texture of historical narration, a kind of authorial mediation that Bacon derisively

other thinys · yet if may not omite ȳ fruits that came her
by, for by these so publick troubls; in so many eminente
places, their caus became famouse, & ocasioned many
to looke into ȳ same; and their godly cariage, & Christian
behauiour was shuch, as left a deep ympression in the
minds of many · And though some few shrunk, at these
first conflicts, & sharp beginings (as it was no maruell)
yet many more came on, with fresh courage, & greatly
animated others · And in ȳ end notwithstanding all
these stormes of opposition; they all gat over at Length,
some at one time, & some at another; and some in one
place, & some in another · And mete togeather againe
according to their desires, with no small rejoycing ·

The · 3. Chap

Of their setling in Holand, &
their maner of liuing, and ·
entertainmente ther

Being now come into ȳ low countries, they saw many goodly
& fortified cities, strongly walled, and garded with troupes
of armed men · Also they heard a strange, & vncouth language, and beheld ȳ diferente maners, & custumes of ȳ people
with their strange fashons, and atires; all so farre differing
from ȳ of their plaine countrie villages (wherin they were
bred, & had so longe liued) as it seemed they were come into a new world · But these ware not ȳ things, they much
looked on, or long tooke vp their thoughts; for they had other work
in hand, & another kind of warr to wage, & maintaine · for
though they saw faire, & beutifull cities, flowing with a-
bundance of all sorts of welth, & riches · yet it was not
longe before they saw the grime, & grisly face of powertie
cie coming vpon them like an armed man; with whom
they must Bukle, & ẏncounter; and from whom they could
not flye; But they were armed with faith, & patience against
him, and all his encounters; and though they were sometimes foyled, yet by gods asistance they preuailed, and
got ȳ victorie ·
Now when mr robinson, mr brewster, & other principall
members were come over (for they were of ȳ last, & stayed to helpe ȳ weakest over before them) shuch things were

---

Fig. 6. A chapter division and heading from the first "book" of Bradford's manuscript.

termed "Ruminated History."[31] Rhetorical display of any sort was a disquieting sign in a genre that sought to keep the personal loyalties and judgments of its author in the background. On the whole it is best, Bodin thought, "to commit writings on present matters to posterity," so that the circumstances of posthumous publication can help put to rest all questions of prejudice or vanity on the part of the writer.[32] The preface to *Of Plimmoth Plantation* is clearly framed with these cautions in mind. Bradford's title and his introductory words are ready for the printer, but he has committed the printing to the future.

These initial signs of tactical disengagement from his story point to Bradford's acute sense of his historical liabilities. The ideal chronicler of Plymouth's experience, from the perspective of Bodin's *Methodus*, would be a writer who enjoyed Bradford's access to personal testimony and to detailed literary records of the colony's life, without sharing the vulnerability to bias associated with a direct and intimate involvement in the events that one sets out to describe. Indeed, in the opening pages of his book, Bradford vividly dramatizes the struggle that lay beneath the dispassionate surface of his plain style, producing an example of energetically ruminated history that is suggestively linked to the disinterested goal of his narrative: the pursuit of simple truth as he unfolds the tale of Plymouth Plantation.

This apparent disruption occurs on the fourth page of the manuscript, as Bradford cites a passage from William Perkins' *Faithfull and plaine exposition upon the 2 chapter of Zephaniah,* a classic text of prophetic rebuke to a corrupted people: "Gather your selves, even gather you, o nation not worthy to be loved, Before the decre come forthe, and ye be as chaffe that passeth in a day . . . Seke ye the Lord, all the meke of the earth, which have wrought his judgement: seke righteousness, seke lowliness, if so be that ye may be hid in the day of the Lord's wrath." Like Bradford's plain history, Perkins' plain commentary on these verses represents an attempt to impose a degree of rhetorical and emotional discipline upon the inherently explosive materials of the English Reformation. Zephaniah's passionate attack on the complacency and decadence of Israel ably represents those explosive materials, which Perkins undertakes to contain within the metaphor suggested by Sturbridge Fair in 1593, the place where he delivered the sermon that formed the basis of his printed book. "Everyone brings hither something to be solde," Perkins concludes his incitement to religious self-scrutiny and personal reform: "This is the marchandise that I bring and set to sale unto you," a heavenly rather than an earthly "commoditie," not costly but free.[33]

At precisely this moment in *Of Plimmoth Plantation,* as he cites Perkins' "exhortation to repentance," Bradford's narrative self-discipline appears briefly to desert

Monica the mother of Augustine.

especiallie of those things, which they thinke to be meet, and which they cannot discusse of themselues. Monica the mother of Augustine being desirous that hir sonne should marrie, for the auoiding of fornication, desired God, that euen in sleepe he would reueale vnto hir some thing as touching that matter: and she testified that shee obtained of God some taste, whereby the discerned the thing, which in sleepe she sawe of hirselfe, from those things, which were shewed by inspiration from God: which thing Augustine witteth in his sixt booke of Confessions, the 13 chapter. And we knowe assuredlie, that Daniel praied for the vnderstanding of Nabuchadnezars dreame, and this is without controuersie to be holden, that it is the part of godlie men to praie to GOD, that euen in our sleepe we may be preserued pure, and chaste, both in bodie and spirit. For those night visions, by the which either the mind is troubled, or the bodie defiled, are certeine punishments of sinne: especiallie of that which hath béene drawne from our first creation. For so it should not haue béene in paradise, if Adam had abidden in that truth, wherein he was made: as Augustine wrote in his sixt booke, and eight chapter against Iulian. Looke In Gen. chapter 20, verse 3.

Augustine.

Dan. 2, 18.

The sixt Chapter.

Of the holie scriptures; out of the Preface vpon the first epistle to the Corinthians.

A diuision.

N Ow wée must speake somthing of the holie scriptures, whereby wée are both encouraged to studie them, and somewhat also are holpen in the following of that studie: and this shall be done, if I touch first in few words the worthines and profit of them; secondlie, if we shew by what certeine marks & tokens we may be able to iudge, and saie what is the sense or meaning of them: and lastlie, if we shall open the waie and means how to challenge them vnto our selues. This diuision I mind to folowe, as being most conuenient for the vnderstanding of those things, which shall be spoken. And first of al, bicause we are to speake of the worthines and profit of the holie scriptures, I will giue this plaine and homelie definition of them. For it is a hard matter for anie man, perfectlie and exactlie to define those things which are of God. Wherefore let vs define the holie scriptures, to be a certeine declaration of the wisdome of God, inspired by the holie Ghost into godlie men, and then set downe in monuments & wri-

Of the dignitie and vtilitie of the holie scriptures.

A definition of the holie scriptures.

The holie scripture inspired by the spirit of God.

tings. That it is inspired by the inward motion of the holie Ghost, for the saluation and restoring of vs, Peter testifieth in the first chapter of his latter epistle, when he saith, that Prophesie came not in old time by the will of men, but holie men of GOD spake as they were moued by the holie Ghost. And verie great honour hath come thereunto, bicause as well Christ, as the apostles, and sound councels haue vsed the testimonie of it, for the confirmation of those things which were decréed: yea, we may not thinke that anie traditions be necessarie to saluation, which are not surelie and stronglie grounded thereupon.

1.Pet.1, 21.

The sure proofes of diuine things are takt out of the scriptures onlie.

And we must alwaies beare in mind, how wée are sent awaie by Christ, the best teacher of the church, to search out the scripture, when he saith in the fift of Iohns gospell: Search ye the scriptures. Moreouer, euerie facultie and learning borroweth his worthines from the matter, about which it is occupied. For, according as that doth excell, so is anie science accounted of more or lesse estimation. Wherefore, séeing this science of ours intreateth of nothing else but of Christ, it is so much the more to be accounted the head of all other, as Christ is the most excellent aboue all other things. And as I suppose no man doubteth, but that the new testament speaketh chieflie of Christ. But bicause some man perhaps doubteth, whether the old testament do so likewise, let him heare euen Paule writing to the Romans the 10. chapter; Christ is the end of the lawe. And in the fift of Iohn, when the Lord had said (that which euen now I recited) Search the scriptures; he added incontinent, For they beare witnes of me. And in the same chapter it is said of Moses; He hath written of me. And manie other places may be brought, to confirme this selfe-same thing; but let vs content our selues with these for this time.

Christ sent vs to the reading of the scriptures. Iohn.5,39.

The sum of all that is done in the scripture is Christ.

Rom. 10.

Iohn.5,39.

Iohn.5,46.

2 The holie scriptures also are highlie commended, through those excellent properties wherewith God hath adorned them. For they are so glorious, that they séeme vnto vs, which walke as it were in darknes, to be like a candle lighted of God: whereof Peter hath admonished vs in the first chapter of the second epistle, And we haue a sure speech of prophesie, whereunto if you giue heed, as vnto a light shining in a darke place, ye do well, till the daie appeare, and the daie star arise in your harts. In which words thou shalt note this also, that they be verie sure. For godlie men are so assured of the truth of them, that for them they feare not to suffer anie cruell death: which thing hath seldome or neuer happened among naturall philosophers, or mathematicians, that they confirmed the opinions of their knowledge with their blood, and with the losse of their liues. And vnto faithfull and godlie harts, there is in the scriptures no want of cléerenes, which they

The notable properties of the holie scripture.

They shine as a candle in the darknes.

2.Pet.1,19.

The holie scriptures be sure and certeine.

To the godlie they be cléere and perspicuous.

F. ij.   Gréeks

him. In the continuous historical account that forms the body of his work, he turns directly from Perkins' portrait of religious antagonism among English Protestants at the close of the sixteenth century to address what he terms his own "intendmente": the story of how the small congregation at Scrooby gradually came together, had "their ignorance and sins discovered unto them," and began to "reform their lives and make conscience of their ways" under the leadership of Richard Clyfton and John Robinson. He follows, in effect, a small party of satisfied patrons from William Perkins' figurative booth at Sturbridge through a spiritual and physical pilgrimage that will deposit them at the tip of Cape Cod in the winter of 1620.

Sixteen years after recording these events, however, he responds to this same passage in his book with an elaborate digression on the blank verso sheet of his manuscript that faces the citation from Perkins' sermon—a "Late Observation," as Bradford calls it, on the triumphs of the English Civil War, exulting in the downfall of the episcopal hierarchy and its civil apparatus of religious coercion that had driven John Robinson and his "litle handfull" of companions to Holland nearly thirty years earlier:

> May not the people of God now say (and these pore people among the rest), The Lord hath brought forth our righteousnes; come, let us declare in Sion the work of the Lord our God . . . Doe you not now see the fruits of your labours, O all yee servants of the Lord that have suffered for his truth, and have been faithfull witnesses of the same, and yee litle handfull amongst the rest, the least amongst the thousands of Israll? You have not only had a seede time, but many of you have seene the joyefull harvest; should you not then rejoyse, yea, and againe rejoyce, and say Hallelu-iah, salvation, and glorie, and honour, and power, be to the Lord our God; for true and righteous are his judgments. (10–11)

The tumultuous emotions of 1646 directly confront the gravity and restraint of 1630 in the pages of Bradford's history, with an exhilarating indifference to modern standards of textual continuity or consistency. The "Late Observation" poses, among other things, intractable editorial difficulties. It is evidently not a revision or a correction to the passages that it faces. But is it a gloss, a note, or an interpolation? Should it appear at the foot of the printed page, somewhere on the page itself, or in an appendix? What is the relation of this conspicuous and passionate intrusion

FACING PAGE

Fig. 7. From *The Common Places of Peter Martyr* (London, 1583). Bradford owned this work and seems to have applied elements of its page design to *Of Plimmoth Plantation*. Courtesy of the Hargrett Rare Book and Manuscript Library, University of Georgia Libraries.

to the story of sequential domestic disruptions that ultimately produce Plymouth Plantation?

Bradford is clearly treating his book in a manner that reflects a textual tradition quite different from our own—one in which the customary boundaries between author and audience appear to invite rather than preclude infringement, soliciting an elaborate interaction between "reader" and "writer" or promoting the coexistence of both roles in a single individual. It is, moreover, a tradition that is closely associated with the same prominent figure in English religious history whose commentary on Zephaniah prompts the first of many such synchronic asides to Bradford's primary "intendmente." William Perkins has both a religious and a rhetorical influence on *Of Plimmoth Plantation*. Over the course of his clerical career, he addressed himself not only to the continuing pertinence of the biblical prophets in the lives of his contemporaries but also to what he termed the art of prophesying, a phrase he adopted for the title of a guide to reading and writing that sheds considerable light on William Bradford's sense of literary design.

ૐ

"INTERPRETATION is the *opening* of the words and sentences of the scripture," William Perkins declares to the aspiring ministers who consulted his clerical instruction manual. The smallest linguistic elements of this momentous book are "books" in themselves—volumes that need to be "opened." *The Arte of Prophecying* (1607) begins, rather surprisingly, at a very rudimentary level, naming and classifying the books of the Bible, before analyzing the process of sermon preparation, from the initial choice of a topical verse through advice on appropriate bodily gestures and vocal modulation during delivery. In addition to being a celebrated preacher in his own right, Perkins was among the most widely read adapters of Augustinian biblical analysis to the needs of Reformation clergy, many of whom were not deeply learned men. Although it was originally published in Latin, in 1592, Perkins' book does not assume an extensive educational background, or even well-established habits of systematic study, in his audience. Moreover, the title page of the 1607 translation solicits the attention not only of ministers but of "men of all degrees" seeking instruction as readers of Scripture. The proliferation of vernacular Bibles, in affordable editions, had solved one problem in the struggle against the religious monopoly of the Catholic Church, but it had simultaneously created another: how could the inherently private process of individual reading be guided, shaped, or controlled?[34]

The Arte of Prophecying took as its epigraph some verses from Nehemiah that stressed the role of preaching as a public exercise in the explication of a complex text: "And they read in the book of the law of God distinctly, and gave the sense, and caused them to understand the reading." Accordingly, Perkins and his radical colleagues viewed the preacher not so much as the primary liturgical officer of the church but as an exemplary and ingenious reader, able to expose what Perkins termed "the true patterne" of biblical language, to alert his audience to critical elements of context and to the subtleties of narrative sequence, to engage in what Perkins vividly (if opaquely) described as the "right cutting" of words, the "untwisting" of a text "as a weaver's web" into "sundrie doctrines," and the careful cross-comparison and collation of passages "whereby places are set like parallels, one beside another, that the meaning of them may more evidentlie appeare."[35]

These analytical tactics derived ultimately from Augustine's *De Doctrina Christiana* and were enshrined in sixteenth-century humanist pedagogy. Tudor grammar schools taught their pupils to divide the works they read into discrete philological or rhetorical units for concentrated study, storing particularly memorable passages from the best classical authors in commonplace books for eventual retrieval and reassembly in the student's own compositions. Eugene Kintgen has explained that the reading practices of Protestant preachers—as reflected in the sermons they published—were strikingly similar in approach, amounting to a "severely analytical" textual exercise in which biblical passages were "divided and subdivided, by grammatical, rhetorical, logical, or theological analysis into smaller and smaller segments," focusing finally on "individual words, with all their possibilities for polysemy or ambiguity."[36]

Where the humanist reader compiled a collection of similar passages from different classical authors, organized by *topos* or topic, the religiously schooled reader employed verses from different parts of the Bible as interpretive glosses on one another—a process physically embedded in the design of the Geneva Bible, with its numbered verses and the working concordance included in its elaborate marginalia. Both interpretive strategies were intertextual in nature, but their ends were quite different. The humanist reader primarily sought to expand the rhetorical resources of his commonplace book, in preparation for some public career in which eloquence—the flow of abundant and varied language known as *copia*—would play a significant role in worldly success. The religiously schooled reader sought to confirm the internal consistency of biblical narrative, to explore its elaborate referential web, and to reform his life.

Such reading practices were by no means exclusively associated with dissenting clergymen. In 1622 John Donne preached a sermon on Acts 1:8 before the members of the Virginia Company, in which he professed to find the whole significance of the verse that he had selected in its first word, the conjunction "but," to which this particular minister could not resist applying a pun from archery: "The first word of the Text is the *Cardinall* word, the word, the hinge upon which the whole Text turnes; The first word, *But*, is the *But*, that all the rest shoots at." Donne had opened his commentary with two paragraphs devoted solely to the title of the book of Acts; he then turned to the eighth verse of the first chapter, noting that Acts preserves twenty-two distinct sermons in its pages, "and yet the booke is not called the *Preaching*, but the *Practise*, not the *Words*, but the *Acts* of the *Apostles*."[37]

This love of teasing exegetical significance out of the smallest grammatical elements in a biblical passage formed the meeting point between the humanist and religious schools of reading that prevailed in William Bradford's lifetime. Donne's archery metaphor seems suggestively similar to the "right cutting of words" that Perkins, too, clearly sought to encourage—not as a barren display of ingenuity but as a demonstration of the way in which attentive reading could yield illuminating results, similar to those that Donne achieves when he pinpoints the equation of speaking with acting implicit in the form of the New Testament narrative or emphasizes the conditional impact of a particular conjunction on the sentences that follow it.

Contemporary congregations, as well as the sort of godly and judicious audience to which William Bradford immediately appeals in *Of Plimmoth Plantation*, respected the capacity of language to lend itself to surprising disclosures in the hands of an author or speaker who patiently undertook to open or unfold it. In the first pages of his book, Bradford indicates that the true pattern of his own words—even in the preliminary details of his title and preface—is assembled very much like "a weaver's web," requiring in turn a correspondingly meticulous untwisting. As Walter Ong has observed, a community of readers and writers steeped in Learned Latin (and habitually responsive to bilingual puns) will quickly identify the suggestive relationship that Perkins exploits between "weaver" and "textor," its Latin equivalent. *Of Plimmoth Plantation* immediately seizes upon this complex understanding of narrative fabric.

Principles of exegesis like those described by William Perkins or exemplified by Donne readily become guides to a writer. In William Bradford's experience, a lifetime of attending to such sophisticated interpretive performances, in sermons and in books, predisposed him to see his own work as a complex interlacing of parallel and sequential events—like the contrasting storms of his opening chapters—out of which subtle distinctions and startling differences could emerge almost of their own volition. The subordination of the preacher to biblical authority did not, in Perkins' view, absolve him of the responsibility for framing his sermon by calling upon all "the artes, philosophie, and varietie of reading" at his disposal. The Bible alone was the fountain of meaning, but the full apparatus of humanistic learning was required to tap it. At the same time, Perkins cautioned, "Humane wisdom must be concealed" in the literary product of these labors: "it is also a point of Art," as he put it, "to conceal Art."[38]

Similarly, the subordination of the historian to the circumstantial record does not preclude him from selecting and ordering the elements of his narrative in such a way as to expose patterns or to invite conclusions, even in the midst of composing work that is, ideally, dispassionate. The summary of ecclesiastical conflict with which Bradford begins *Of Plimmoth Plantation* prepares his reader to embrace the unique history of a village that he intends to offer by identifying just such an implicit structure in the oppositional course of the English Reformation. The "firie flames" and "cruell tragedies" of Queen Mary's reign produced a rich legacy of religious heroism, Bradford wrote, but they generated at the same time an equally rich legacy of persecution, for which the machinations of Satan are only metaphorically accountable. The true perpetrators of this new era of victimization, he carefully explains, prove to be the victims themselves:

> Mr. Foxe recordeth, how that besids those worthy martires and confessors which were burned in queene Marys days and otherwise tormented *many (both students and others) fled out of the land, to the number of* 800. *And became severall congregations. At Wesell, Franckford, Bassill, Emden, Markpurge, Strausborugh, and Geneva etc.* Amongst whom (but especialy those at Frankford) begane that bitter warr of contention and persecution aboute the ceremonies, and servise-booke, and other popish and Antichristian stuffe, the plague of England to this day, (which are like the highplases in Israell, which the prophets cried out against, and were their ruine) Which the better parte sought (according to the puritie of the gospell) to roote out, and utterly to abandon. And the other parte (under veiled pretenses) for their ouwn ends and advancements, sought as stifly to continue, maintaine, and defende. (6)

It was better to fly from persecution, Peter Martyr had reasoned, than to remain within reach of the savage legal apparatus of a sixteenth-century state and confront a stark choice between abjuration and agony.[39] But it was uniquely distressing, as well as humbling, for English dissenters to recall the rapid descent into bitter ideological conflict and mutual recrimination among the Frankfort exiles in 1554.

The dilemmas of disharmony in exile became familiar elements in the story of Plymouth as well, but for the purposes of Bradford's opening pages they serve to introduce the plight of nonconformists in England after the succession of Elizabeth to the throne. The contention over liturgical ceremonies "dyed not with queene Mary," Bradford noted. The refugees in the city states of Germany and

Switzerland had preserved their violent disagreements, as well as their lives and their faith, bringing "that inveterate hatered against the holy discipline of Christ in his Church" back to England with them. In this latest iteration of the Protestant struggle, it is the episcopal hierarchy of the Elizabethan settlement, rather than the papal Antichrist, pagan emperors, or Marian bishops that pits itself against the true church,

> incensing the queene, and state against it as dangerous for the common wealth; And that it was most needfull that the fundamentall poynts of Religion should be preached in those ignorante and superstitious times; And to winne the weake and ignorante, they might retaine diverse harmles ceremoneis, and though it were to be wished that diverse things were reformed, yet this was not a season for it. And many the like to stop the mouthes of the more godly. To bring them over to yeeld to one ceremoney after another, and one corruption after another; By these wyles begyleing some and corrupting others till at length they begane to persecute all the zealous professors in the land (though they knew little what this discipline mente) both by word and deed, if they would not submitte to their ceremonies, and become slaves to them, and their popish trash, which have no ground in the word of God, but are relikes of that man of sine. And the more the light of the gospell grew, the more they urged their subscriptions to these corruptions. So as (notwithstanding all their former pretences, and fair colures) they whose eyes God had not justly blinded, might easily see wherto these things tended. (8)

In this climate of beguilement and corruption, Bradford notes, the invidious coinage "Puritan" quickly emerges to stigmatize those whose pursuit of the "primative order, libertie, and bewtie" of religious life was so closely identified with the ideal of "anciente puritie" that they hoped to restore (8).

William Perkins' complaint in the sermon on Zephaniah deftly summarizes the results of the course that Bradford has traced and marks still another renewal of old antagonisms, this time from the close of the deeply troubled sixteenth century. "In England at this day," Perkins laments, "the man or woman that begines to profes Religion, and to serve God, must resolve with him selfe to sustaine mocks and injuries even as though he lived amongst the Enemies of Religion" (9). The hostility that Perkins describes is cast not against the expansive landscape of "the Christian world," with which Bradford had begun his account, but within individual men and women whose religious resolution has put them at odds with their neighbors. The fundamental contention within English culture, as Bradford presents it, is both repetitive and evolutionary; its opposing forces go "more closely to work" in successive periods, and the historian of the conflict must be prepared to follow suit: disentangling matters of vital principle from the seductive web of contingencies and justifications produced by one's enemies, exposing the true pattern of events amid the welter of details that threaten to blind even the most perceptive observer (4–5).

What Bradford terms "the mixture of men's inventions" with the laws of God was at the root of the bitter quarrel that had broken out within the English church. But men's inventions were also the historian's subject matter, a complex texture of "veiled pretenses," "fair colures," and sincere profession distributed throughout human affairs, to which the analytical methods that William Perkins had described in his manual for ministers were perfectly suited. Perkins offered a technology for the untwisting of twisted meanings that could be as readily applied to the disclosure of historical design as to the explication of obscure passages in the Bible. In structuring his opening pages, and in exploiting the physical possibilities of his manuscript, William Bradford immediately began to adapt the lessons of the rhetorical tradition in which he and his Plymouth associates had been most closely schooled.

In *The Arte of Prophecying* Perkins had reminded ministers of the first principles of exegesis that Augustine had emphasized centuries earlier: to begin examining their sermon texts by scrutinizing what Perkins termed "the circumstances of the place." At any given moment in the biblical narrative, he suggests, apply the following questions: "Who? to whom? upon what occasion? at what time? in what place? for what end? what goeth before? what followeth?"[40] Such rudimentary inquiries will sound surprisingly familiar to most modern readers who have had any exposure to a fiction textbook; indeed, they could serve as a reasonably complete guide to the opening pages of Bradford's history. Perkins' larger aim, however, is not to steer particular readers or writers through the architecture of a given story but to demolish the highly stratified, fourfold system of textual analysis endorsed by the "Church of Rome," which "maketh 4 senses of the Scriptures, the literall, allegoricall, tropological, and anagogicall." In Perkins' view, these four senses comprise a sequence of arbitrary interpretive layers that cut across the subtle flow of narrative and replace the fluidity of reading with the fixity of readings. This practice of imposing doctrinal authority upon narrative meaning, Perkins insists, "must be exploded and rejected."[41]

Following William Tyndale's memorable pronouncement in *The Obedience of a Christian Man* (1528), Perkins declares that "There is one onelie sense," to a given biblical passage, "and the same is the literall."[42] As with his great predecessor, Perkins' intent is to restore the primacy of scriptural "story"—to recover its primitive order and beauty by considering it first and foremost as a narrative unit, rather

than as a riddle capable of being decoded only by specialists. Though committed
to a conception of "literall" sense, Perkins is anything but a literalist. The preliminary questions that he recommends to ministers, as they investigate biblical language, point to his recognition of the artificial nature of writing. The Bible, like its
reader, is a created thing; the intentions of its Creator, Perkins believes, are most
readily discerned by those who, like Saul in Acts 9:22, treat words in the manner of
"Artificers." Such lexical technicians, Perkins observes, "being about to compact or
joyne a thing together," strive "to fit all the parts amongst themselves," in the hope
that they will "perfectly agree." In other words, it is the work of readers, as well as
that of writers, to assemble the written artifact. Humanist scholar that he is,
Perkins elicits this gloss on Saul's exegetical skill directly from the Greek Testament, in part to remind readers of *The Arte of Prophecying* that the vernacular Bible
must always be treated as a kind of comprehensive parallel text, simultaneously present in both its original and its translated tongues.[43]

This sort of linguistic alertness forms one aspect of what Perkins calls "the collation of places." In its traditional meaning, this term refers to the systematic examination of biblical language that has been imaginatively or physically reconstructed
in parallel columns, allowing widely separated passages to serve as commentaries
on one another—a process Augustine described as the use of clear passages to illuminate darker ones. To the sequential questions that Perkins had posed earlier—
"what goeth before?" and "what followeth?"—he now adds this extra dimension:
what passages sit "beside" a particular verse, and how might that collated language
assist in making meaning "evidentlie appear"?

Except in special circumstances, modern books strive to avoid printing text in
parallel format or surrounded by a halo of marginal comments circling the main
body of the page. Footnotes and endnotes have replaced the kind of copious marginalia for which the Geneva Bible is celebrated and with which readers in Bradford's day were familiar. A marginal note, even in the minute type to which the
Geneva translators were forced to resort, is a uniquely assertive presence on the
page. It stands beside the central field of print, where a reader's eye is unavoidably
drawn to investigate its contents as an immediate complement of the primary line.
The modern footnote, by contrast, seems a strictly academic province—an association that James Joyce exploits for the comic structure of the "Night Lessons" passage in *Finnegans Wake*.[44]

Although *The Arte of Prophecying* demonstrates "the collation of places" literally
by printing closely related biblical verses side by side, Perkins clearly views collation as part of the mental preparation of the minister, illustrating a kind of visual-
ized reading, rather than writing or printing. This cognitive process, however, is

clearly akin to the physical construction of the commonplace books that Perkins also urged beginning ministers to keep as a means of putting their reading to use. Collect "common-place heads" of every important point of "divinitie," or religious learning, Perkins recommended, and enter these heads on the top of every "formost" page in "thy paper booke," keeping the reverse side of the sheet empty. Divide every page with a head into two columns, he continued, presumably to double its capacity as well as to allow for the kind of direct textual collation that Perkins advocated as a critical reading strategy. The blank reverse sides of each page would provide for expansion or for the insertion of fresh material pertaining to the headed pages that they faced. Such a prebound "paper booke" would serve as a flexible collection site for passages from one's reading that could be employed in creating effective sermons, but it might easily be adapted as a storage vehicle for other sorts of composition as well.[45]

William Bradford seems to have worked with at least two such paper books as he wrote *Of Plimmoth Plantation*. The first was a bound collection of the colony's official letters, linked together by brief narrative bridges, that has survived only in a fragment, discovered near the end of the eighteenth century in Halifax, Nova Scotia.[46] The glosses that he provided for Plymouth's correspondence, as he maintained this Letter Book, may have suggested to Bradford the idea of embedding these records in a far more elaborate narrative, using the same model for assembling a commonplace book that Perkins had recommended. The bound paper sheets comprising *Of Plimmoth Plantation* use, for the most part, only the "formost page" of a leaf, its recto surface, reserving the blank sides for a variety of interpolated or collated text that is set beside the main narrative. It is to these blank pages that Bradford turns when he wishes to capture some feature of his own thinking as he rereads his book or to insert details or documents that he had overlooked. The "Late Observation" of 1646, on the verso of his third manuscript page, is the first indication of how Bradford plans to treat the resources of his paper book.

These comments are "worthy to be Noted," he insists, but they are in no sense a "note." Bradford places the "Late Observation" adjacent to, rather than beneath, his account of the plight of religious nonconformists during the early years of King James' reign. It parallels, but it does not interrupt, his deliberative movement from the citation of Perkins' sermon on Zephaniah to the history's main subject: the evolution of a small congregation of English dissenters into citizens of Leiden and settlers of New England. Although its tone is initially measured and informative—merely a collection of some recent thoughts, Bradford suggests, "as it were by the way"—he quickly gives vent to the excitement that he feels at the apparently successful termination of Parliament's struggle:

Full litle did I thinke, that the downfall of the Bishops, with their courts, cannons and ceremonies, etc. had been so neare, when I first begane these scribled writings (which was aboute the year 1630, and so peeced up at times of leasure afterward) or that I should have lived to have seene or heard of the same; but it is the Lords doing, and ought to be marvelous in our eyes! Every plante which mine heavenly father hath not planted (saith our Saviour) shall be rooted up. Mat: 15.13. I have snared the, and thou art taken, O Babell (Bishops) and thou wast not aware; thou art found, and also caught, Because thou hast striven against the Lord. Jer. 50.24. But will they needs strive against the truth, against the servants of God; what, and against the Lord him selfe? Doe they provoke the Lord to anger? Are they stronger than he? 1. Cor: 10.22. No, no, they have mete with their match. Behold, I come unto ye, O proud man, saith the Lord God of hosts; for thy day is come, even the time that I will visite the. Jer: 50.31 . . . Let all flesh be still before the Lord; for he is raised up out of his holy place. (10)

The proliferation of biblical citations alone indicates that such a passage is anything but casually written. Bradford's parallel page is itself a tissue of biblical parallels, which he happily assists his reader to appreciate by stressing the parenthetical identification of Babel with the fate of the fallen English bishops.

At the same time that he is responding to William Perkins' cry of dismay with his own outburst of triumphant vindication, Bradford also highlights the biblical basis for the metaphor of God's husbandry that is so pervasive in the first paragraphs of his book. The healthy plants of reformed religion are finally free of the invasive errors that Satan had sown. The "prophane mixture" of the Anglican settlement is "rooted up," and Bradford appears to exult at the outcome in a manner that is disquietingly similar to the "mocks and injuries" of which Perkins had complained, in his characterization of the Anglican establishment during its years of haughty triumph. When Bradford originally cited Perkins' sermon, in the main body of the history, he had coolly endorsed its portrait of those dark years. The conditions that had troubled Perkins so deeply, he wrote, were no more than "commone experience hath confirmed, and made too apparente" (9). In the impassioned language of the "Late Observation," his feelings are far less constrained: "And are not these great things?" he cries of the collapse of the Royalist cause. "Who can deney it?" How is a reader to understand the relationship between the antithetical voices simultaneously present at this point in the manuscript: the historian who, in conformity with the ideals of Bodin and Bacon, turns purposefully and calmly to his "intendmente" and the exultant "reader" on the facing page who directly assaults us with a strident display of partisan loyalty?

Much later in *Of Plimmoth Plantation,* Bradford allows himself an angry digression on the "vilanie" of Thomas Morton that remains in the main body of the history. "But I have forgott my selfe," he acknowledges, as his fit of temper seemingly runs its course, and he resumes the task of recording how the colony dealt with the threat posed by Morton's arms trade with the Indians (288–89). The containment of his own retrospective resentment subtly underscores the lack of all capacity for self-government in Thomas Morton—a sophisticated use of narrative juxtaposition in its own right, but quite different from the impact of a parallel passage that functions very much like an elaborate reader's annotation rather than an aspect of authorial design. Even if one assumes that Bradford's outrage at Morton's behavior is genuinely spontaneous, it is clear that the carefully collated language of the "Late Observation" is not similarly self-forgetful.

It is, instead, a dramatic aside, magnifying the account of patience, progressive enlightenment, and unanticipated costs that the main body of the history simultaneously addresses in the early experience of Robinson's small congregation of dissenters. This little handful of poor people, as Bradford describes them, ultimately find themselves the beneficiaries rather than the victims of events—survivors on a grand scale, enjoying a rich harvest of divine favor that complements but does not fundamentally alter the story that Bradford intends to tell. In this sense the "Late Observation" is precisely what its label suggests: a perception abruptly felt "by the way," reflecting a single psychological moment in a continuum of such moments, stretching across the thirty years that now separate Bradford from the experiences that he is recalling as he rereads his manuscript.

Of Plimmoth Plantation is necessarily a history of flux, partly stabilized by the retrospective control conferred on one's understanding of experience by the passage of time but partly unstabilized by that same temporal movement. Bradford emphasizes this progressive dimension to human awareness in his account of the rise of religious feeling among his English neighbors, who no sooner "discover" their ignorance and sin, and set out to "make conscience of their wayes," than their entire world is thrown into chaotic motion by the police apparatus of the English episcopacy and the scorn of the "prophane multitude." Gradually they come "to see further into things," Bradford records, and later still, when they frame a covenant and become a church "estate," they strive to provide not only for what they already believe they know but also for what they hope will one day "be made known unto them" about the proper structure of communal religious life.

In every feature of this initial description of the body of people who will become John Robinson's Leiden congregation, Bradford stresses the expectation of change in their inner lives: the new perceptions of their moral condition that impel them to reforge the links between what they believe and how they live; their deepening insight into Scripture, or history, or human character; their receptivity to fresh formulations of religious meaning. This portrait of the first stages of their communal journey, in the main text of the history, helps to underscore the provisional nature of the "Late Observation" that sits beside it in Bradford's paper book. The triumphal language and sentiments of 1646 are subject to the same transformative process for which Robinson and his devoted congregation had sought to provide in the conditional structure of their first church "estate" nearly half a century earlier.[47]

Bradford's chronicle of 1625, in the second book of the history, includes a reply to the colony's English investors in which he gives explicit form to this kinetic understanding of the religious and historical consciousness. The investors had written a self-exculpatory letter to Plymouth, hoping to justify their decision to break off economic ties to the colony by citing certain theological objections to the settlers' church practices. In his answer, Bradford restates the central impetus of the Reformation with memorable clarity:

> Wheras you taxe us for dissembling with his majestie and the adventurers aboute the french discipline, you doe us wrong, for we both hold and practice the discipline of the French and other reformed churches, (as they have published the same in the harmony of confessions,) according to our means, in effecte and substance. But wheras you would tye us to the french discipline in every circumstance, you derogate from the libertie we have in Christ Jesus. The apostle Paule would have none to follow him in any thing but wherin he follows Christ, much less ought any Christian or church in the world to doe it; the french may erre, we may erre, and other churches may erre, and doubtless doe in many circumstances . . . And it is too great arrogancie for any man, or church to thinke that he, or they, have so sounded the word of God to the bottome, as precislie to sett downe the churches discipline, without error in substance or circumstance, as that no other without blame may digress or differ in any thing from the same. (239)

Like the Frankfort troubles of 1554, this exchange involves the imposition of a book upon the heterogeneous and evolutionary nature of human experience: Jean François Salvard's *Harmony of Confessions* (1586). Bradford invokes Salvard's book to defend the ecclesiastical practices of Plymouth, but he immediately indicates that the particular "means" available to different groups of people, living under very different sets of circumstances, require a measure of latitude in the judgment of their religious conduct. Notwithstanding the hopeful implications of Salvard's title, Bradford endorses only an approximate harmony of church disciplines, not a close one—a harmony "in effecte and substance," allowing for the differences that will invariably distinguish individuals and communities without (one hopes) always dividing them.

The specific issue in this letter of 1625 involved some correspondence from eight years earlier, in which John Robinson and William Brewster had sought to assure the directors of the Virginia Company that the Leiden community was not a dangerous group of unstable schismatics. Bradford had copied these earlier letters into the history too, when he discussed the negotiations of 1617; the reader is free to make the necessary collation of places in order to test Bradford's claim that the Plymouth emigrants had never dissembled with anyone on the nature of their relationship to the practice of the French Protestant churches. But this clarification of the record is less important in itself than the statement that it prompts concerning the ubiquity of change in all human arrangements, particularly those arrangements which grow out of an attempt to sound the word of God to the bottom. William Perkins' account of textual analysis in *The Arte of Prophecying* is a practical guide to this "sounding" process, but Bradford makes clear that no interpretive results are ever final, not even results that are as richly buttressed with biblical collation as the exultant sentences of the "Late Observation."

Indeed, no interpretive technology is ever secure from interference by the prejudices of the interpreter. Jeremy Taylor's 1647 defense of liberty of conscience in religious matters surveys all of the reading strategies advocated by Perkins and other exegetical guides, disclosing their irreducibly subjective core. Men's "fancies" intrude at every level, Taylor notes, until "Scripture seems so clearly to speak what they believe, that they wonder all the world does not see it as clear as they doe."[48] Bradford's "Late Observation," linking its biblical texts with historical events, expresses precisely this degree of exultant self-confidence—"Who can deney it?"— in parallel with the deep suspicion of interpretive control that the Scrooby dissenters had imbibed from their enforced exile and that Bradford voices in his letter on the imputed harmony of all confessions. "The truth is," Jeremy Taylor would later declare,

> all these wayes of Interpreting of Scripture which of themselves are good helps are made either by design, or by our infirmities, wayes of intricating and involving Scriptures in greater difficulty, because men doe not learn their doctrines from Scripture, but come to the understanding of Scripture with preconceptions and idea's of doctrines of their own, and then no wonder that Scriptures look like Pictures, wherein every man in the roome believes they look on him only, and that wheresoever he stands, or how often soever he changes his station. So that now what was intended

for a remedy, becomes the promoter of our disease, and our meat becomes the matter of sicknesses.[49]

Passages such as this one explain Roger Williams' admiration for *The Liberty of Prophesying* and account for its presence in William Bradford's library, not long after its publication, at the same time that many members of the established English Church viewed Taylor with loathing. "It and you would make a good fire," Anne Coke Sadleir had snapped, when Roger Williams recommended to her the study of Taylor's book.[50] *Of Plimmoth Plantation* dramatizes just such exchanges as contesting elements within a single historical consciousness: impassioned belief coupled with a profound conviction of the ubiquity of human error. Together these attributes shape Bradford's literary sensibility across the full range of his history.

The "textor," or weaver, implied by Perkins' description of narrative art is necessarily a master of movement, out of which patterns may well emerge that disguise, as well as express, the kinetic processes that produce them. But no single book, or (in the case of the Bible particularly) no single reading, can legitimately function as a "tye," a restraint or a knot, binding all subsequent books or readers. Bradford makes evident in his pages how deeply committed he is to this contingent perception of experience: preserving the liberty to digress and differ, rather than fixing the precise limits beyond which communal religious life may not venture. This sharp repudiation of closure in the volatile theological or ecclesiastical debates of his day may well account for Bradford's decision to leave the manuscript of the history similarly unclosed. The textual record that forms *Of Plimmoth Plantation* remains hospitable to the amendments of time and experience, even to those that may be recorded by other hands.

૬ล

AS BRADFORD UNDERSTOOD IT, then, the historian's challenge is to recount the contending forces of human "arrogancie" without falling victim to one's own susceptibility to interpretive arrogance. This is the lesson that Bodin, Bacon, Perkins, and Taylor, in different ways, strove to teach. This struggle is not simply a professional liability of the historian. In some respects it is the theme of history as well—one that Bradford's reading and writing practices predisposed him to represent in the pages of his book. A few additional examples will illustrate how deliberately and effectively Bradford wove his narrative in order to expose this fundamental feature of experience.

In a detailed account of the closing months of 1623, *Of Plimmoth Plantation* reconstructs, on the main and facing pages of the manuscript, a series of events surrounding the last period of acute food shortages that the colony experienced. A key element in the underlying design of these pages is the arrival of two ships carrying officers from the Council for New England with instructions to extend the authority of that administrative body over the disorderly mixture of settlers, fur traders, and fishermen who had established themselves between Cape Cod Bay and the rivers of what is now southern Maine. The tug of war that ensues between the appetite for control and the appetite for liberty, in this marginal theater of the Atlantic world, mirrors a number of competing hungers at work among the colonists themselves, who are meanwhile maintaining a bare subsistence in the face of their English investors' frustrating policy of being generous with advice and with new boatloads of potential colonists but frugal with shipments of additional food and trading goods.

The first of the ships from the Council for New England arrived in June, commanded by Francis West, who had been ordered to protect the council's fishing and trading monopolies in the region. In addition to carrying out his administrative responsibilities, West had two hogsheads of peas that he was willing to sell at Plymouth, but seeing how desperate the colonists were for food, he set such an exorbitant price on them that the settlers (or at least most of them) declined to buy: "they tould him they had lived so long with out, and would doe still, rather then give so unreasonably" (170).

Shortly after West departed, a pair of small ships arrived from the English adventurers, containing ninety-three new settlers for the colony, many of whom were to be independent planters, on their own "particular," with no relation to Plymouth's collective economic life. About sixty of the new arrivals were intended to be part of the "generall," but some of them proved so "bad," Bradford rather cryptically observes, that the established colonists "were faine to be at charge to send them home againe the next year," much as they had sent Francis West off to Virginia with most of his surplus peas still on board (171). With this new accession of people—almost as large as the original *Mayflower* emigration—came very few provisions.

The strain on the colony's limited food supply was made considerably more acute by this human influx, and though the Providence of God "fedd them out of the sea for the most parte," the "old planters" (as Bradford terms the veterans of the *Mayflower*'s voyage three years earlier) were so alarmed by the profusion of hungry mouths to feed that they asked the governor to reserve their own crops strictly for their own use "and let the new-commers injoye what they had brought"—a policy equally satisfactory to the newcomers, who were likewise alarmed at the ragged appearance of the "hungrie planters." Within the space of a few pages, the noble self-denial of the colonists, when confronted by the opportunistic greed of Francis West, quickly shifts to anxiety and suspicion, prompted by an unexpected human increase that more than doubles their population.

On the facing leaf of his manuscript, opposite these events, Bradford recounts a memorable rainstorm that had been "overslipt" in its proper place in the narrative. He chooses to "inserte the same" at this point—though he does not indicate precisely where it should be inserted—in order to collate the miraculous generosity of God with the uncharitable expressions of selfishness that the main text contains. A great drought, from late May through the middle of July, had withered Plymouth's vital corn crop. The colonists decided "to seek the Lord by humble and fervente prayer, in this great distresse." After they spent a day in humiliation and watchful anxiety, the Lord sent "a gracious and speedy answer, both to their owne, and the Indeans admiration":

> For all the morning, and greatest part of the day, it was clear weather and very hotte, and not a cloud or any signe of raine to be seen; yet toward evening it begane to overcast, and shortly after to raine, with shuch sweete and gentle showers, as gave them cause of rejoyceing, and blessing God. It came, without either winde, or thunder, or any violence, and by degreese in that abundance, as that the earth was thorowly wete and soked therwith. Which did so apparently revive and quicken the decayed corne and other fruits, as was wonderfull to see, and made the Indeans astonished to behold; and after wards the Lord sent them shuch seasonable showers, with enterchange of faire warme weather, as, through his blessing, caused a fruitfull and liberall Harvest, to their no small comforte and rejoycing, for which mercie (in time conveniente) they also sett aparte a day of thanksgiveing. (170–71)

The incremental stages of this providential rain, its gradual approach to abundance by degrees, and the purposeful way in which it gently restores the earth's fruits, suggest an additional contrast to the dysfunctional apparatus of the human world. The clash of goals and appetites in the main narrative of the history had been, in some respects, as withering as the relentless summer heat. Captain West conducted himself as little more than a commercial police officer, with a commission to extract a "round sume of money" from any fishermen who encroached on waters claimed by the governing council in London. The fishermen, in turn, proved to be "stuberne fellows" who successfully resisted West's authority, much as the Plymouth settlers, too, repudiated his extortionate commercial practices, shortly before seeking to forestall any decision on the part of their governor to share the colony's drought-stricken corn crop with a shipload of newcomers. The systems of human interchange depicted in such passages seem all the more crippled in contrast to the beneficent "enterchange" of showers and sunshine that eventually produced a "fruitfull and liberall harvest" for the illiberal human wayfarers of New England (169–70).

Suggestive as this contrast may be, Bradford is careful not to claim too much for it. The quickening rains of 1623 were dramatic evidence of the Lord's swift response to a humble appeal, but even so, Bradford notes, he "overslipt" them in the course of composing his narrative—an inexplicable lapse for a historian who elsewhere seems so attentive to signs of providential care in the fabric of events. The astonishment of the Indians at the efficacy of English prayers would seem to be an especially significant feature of this episode, one that a narrator like John Winthrop or Edward Johnson could never have neglected until it belatedly occurred to him that it was "meet" to insert this detail into the story of Plymouth's early years. Bradford clearly recognizes the importance of including this brief passage in his book, but he sets it quite conspicuously to one side, muting its impact and diminishing the potential for the displays of cultural arrogance that such circumstances readily elicited from his contemporaries. In this sense Bradford's collating tactics can have more than one end in view. Habits of cultural arrogance find ample expression in these pages of the history, not in Bradford's claims of providential solicitude for Plymouth's crops, but in the conduct of the Council for New England and its imperious agents.

The second emissary from London, Robert Gorges, arrived at Plymouth in the middle of September with a written commission "to be generall Governor of the cuntrie," to oversee the efforts of his predecessor Francis West, to form a council of assistants, and to execute justice "in all cases, Capitall, Criminall, and Civill . . . with diverce other instructions" (178–79). This authorizing document was so unexpectedly sweeping in its assignment of civil powers that Bradford asked to take a copy of it, which he pointedly neglects to insert into the text of the history, recording instead the formal written conditions by which the colony arranged to coexist with the independent settlers whose untimely arrival had disturbed the Old Planters in the midst of the summer drought.

Strictly speaking, Bradford preserves an insignificant local record and ignores the grand, official commission of Robert Gorges, son of Sir Ferdinando Gorges, whose own designs on the political autonomy of New England, emerging later in *Of Plimmoth Plantation,* effectively convert the family name into a pun on the gluttonous human "gorge"—precisely the sort of fearful image that the Old Planters and the newcomers had seen in one another a few weeks (and a handful of pages) earlier. Bradford's principles of selection are not in themselves subversive, perhaps, but his calculated neglect of Robert Gorges's commission underscores both the

implicit resistance with which he greets this second imposition of English authority upon the complexities of colonial life and his awareness of the proliferation of
ominous conflicts in the web of this year's events.

The web has still further degrees of elaboration in its design. Robert Gorges
had been specifically instructed to apprehend Thomas Weston, one of the original
financiers of the *Mayflower* expedition who had withdrawn from the company of
investors and sent to New England a group of sixty "lusty men" out of whom he
intended to form a plantation in Massachusetts Bay. A number of financial abuses
related to this plan, as well as the misconduct and eventual dispersal of Weston's
advance party of settlers, had led the Council for New England to seek his arrest.
Weston himself had arrived in New England waters on a fishing vessel some
months before Gorges, traveling under an assumed name and disguised as a black-
smith—a dramatic transformation from the confident English merchant whose
offers of support in Leiden, four years earlier, had been largely responsible for shaping the terms and conditions under which Plymouth was originally founded. The
colonists "pitied his case, and remembered former curtesies," lending Weston a
quantity of beaver skins with which he hoped to retrieve his fortunes, but the arrival of Gorges with his formidable commission significantly complicated Weston's
predicament.

Taking the part of his old associate, in spite of Gorges's bill of complaints, Bradford mediated between the two and gained a temporary reprieve for Weston. Although the colonists were "yonge justices," Weston remarked in his bitterness, they
were "good beggars." Gorges, however, eventually seized Weston, along with his
ship and crew, and had the expense of feeding them through the early spring of
1624, for Weston too was nearly out of food at the time of his arrest. After these
summary actions, Bradford writes, "haveing scarcly saluted the cuntrie in his Gov-
ermente," Gorges abruptly sailed for home, "not finding the state of things hear to
answer his quallitie and condition" (184). New England was not, Bradford implies,
a suitable stage for the sort of presumptive arrogance that Robert Gorges and his
voracious family represent. Weston too disappears from the history; "He dyed
afterwards at Bristoll," Bradford records in a marginal note, "in the time of the
warrs, of the sicknes in that place." The year ends with the near loss of the colony's
trading pinnace, in a storm that struck "at the very entrance into ther owne har-
bore." "But her mast and takling being gone," Bradford writes, "they held her till
the wind shifted"—an evocative note on which to close a chapter that contains so
many telling shifts of wind in the fortunes of Plymouth itself (186).

Over the course of eight manuscript pages, Bradford develops a series of in-
terlinked scenes and themes addressing the authoritarian representatives of the

Council for New England and the stubborn resistance that they encounter, but incorporating as well recurrent varieties of hunger amid the settlers themselves, along with the miraculous rains that appear, in part at least, to assuage them. July's withering drought proves to be an atmospheric precursor to the ominous fire, in early autumn, caused by Thomas Weston's "roystering" sailors. Breaking out in some dry roof thatch, it consumes three or four houses and endangers the colony's common storehouse, "which if it had been lost," Bradford grimly notes, "the plantation had been overthrowne." An unidentified voice warns the colonists to guard their reserves of food during the "tumulte" of fighting the fire, confirming their vague suspicions that the fire was deliberately set. "But God kept them from this deanger," Bradford concludes, as the rain kept them from the loss of their corn, "what ever was intended." Like the mysterious voice "that bid [Plymouth's citizens] look well aboute them," the historian becomes a discerning observer, exposing through the less occult methods of narrative design the common thematic elements in a succession of circumstances that otherwise might, indeed, seem a meaningless tumult (182–83).

Bradford's narrative texture is not always so densely woven as it proves to be in these pages, but with surprising frequency he takes advantage of the interaction between collated passages and the main threads of the history to suggest levels of significance that he is unwilling or unable to fully explore. The fate of John Billington in 1630 is a comparatively straightforward instance of this narrative practice. Billington, his wife Ellen, and two young sons, Francis and John, had been among the heterogeneous complement of *Mayflower* emigrants recruited in London to fill out the original passenger list of Leiden "saints." Although the elder Billington, as a head of household, had signed the Mayflower Compact, promising "due submission and obedience" to the colony's authorities, his lawless temperament ultimately proved to be his downfall:

> This year John Billinton the elder (one that came over with the first) was arrained; and both by grand and petie jurie found guilty of willfull murder, by plaine and notorious evidence. And was for the same accordingly executed. This as it was the first execution amongst them, so was it a mater of great sadnes unto them; they used all due means about his triall, and tooke the advice of Mr. Winthrop, and other the ablest gentle-men in the Bay of the Massachusets, that were then new-ly come over, who concured with them that he ought to dye, and the land to be purged from blood. He and some of his, had been often punished for miscariags before, being one of the profanest families amongst them; they came from London, and I know not by what freinds shufled into their company. His facte was, that he way-laid a young-man, one

John New-comin, (about a former quarell) and shote him with a gune wherof he dyed. (329–30)

Like the account of the miraculous rainstorm of 1623, this passage is set beside the main narrative, on a verso page that faces a letter from Massachusetts Bay describing a virulent epidemic in Charlestown which was inexplicably afflicting the righteous and the wicked indiscriminately. The settlers at Salem wrote to ask Plymouth to join them in a day of humiliation "beseeching the Lord, as to withdraw his hand of correction from them."

The juxtaposition of this appeal with Bradford's interpolated account of Billington's execution helps explain the strange intensity with which the "gentlemen in the Bay of the Massachusets" had urged that the land "be purged from blood." The decision to hang Billington is one in which Plymouth and its immediate neighbors concur, but Bradford has framed the passage in such a way that the vindictive biblical language appears to emanate from the beleaguered people of Salem and Charlestown, whose judgment may be shaped as decisively by their own sense of communal crisis as by the circumstances of Billington's crime. Plymouth's independent judicial actions, in contrast, appear to be more measured, less closely tied to the grandiose apparatus of defilement and of purging. "Plaine and notorious evidence," two juries, all due legal means, and prudent counsel frame this "mater of great sadnes," as Bradford describes it. He is interested in Billington's "facte," the archaic term for his deeds, not in the metaphorical uses to which his death might be put.

This striking difference in verbal practice points to deeper issues that are the subject of a later chapter. Here it is important to notice only the subtle interpretive instructions that are implicit in this instance of narrative collation: the suggestion Bradford is able to convey that judicial procedures, like the crimes they are intended to address, are subject to the influence of the passions. These circumstances form a dramatic contrast to the murky financial activities of Isaac Allerton, which in 1630 had just begun to entangle Plymouth in a network of debts that would require nearly fourteen years of frustrating labor and bewildering correspondence to discharge.

On the pages immediately preceding his account of Billington's execution, Bradford acknowledges that Allerton "plaid his owne game," as the plantation's business agent in England, seeking to enrich himself, rather than the plantation or the English investors, in his various trading and fishing ventures. Bradford and his Plymouth associates sent letters to England that "renounsed Mr. Allerton wholy, for being their agente, or to have any thing to doe in any of their business" (329), but even this decisive step proves ineffectual. Allerton's "facte," unlike Billington's, proved stubbornly resistant to all the legal means at Bradford's disposal. Only notorious figures, exposed by the explosive nature of their appetites, are brought to justice. Devious ones must be left to the operations of Providence.

Billington's crime and punishment, then, illuminate both the legalistic piety of Massachusetts Bay and the furtive illegality of Isaac Allerton. The close conjunction of narrative threads dramatizes the interplay between unity and variety in Plymouth's experience and at the same time prompts Bradford's reflections on Billington's entire family. "He and some of his," Bradford recalls, had already played roles both in *Of Plimmoth Plantation* and in the 1622 *Relation or Journall* that Robert Cushman had conveyed to London in the first years of the colony's existence. Their prominence in Bradford's memory underscores the pattern of intratextual reference that binds the history together, not just in the interchanges that characterize particular episodes but across significant spans of time and narrative space.

Near the end of July 1621, Bradford notes in his account of that year's events, John Billington the younger had gotten lost in the woods for five days, "living on beries and what he could find," until he stumbled upon an Indian settlement at Manamet, twenty miles south of Plymouth. The Manamet people passed the seven-year-old boy along to the Nauset Indians, who had greeted the *Mayflower* emigrants the previous November with a shower of arrows as they sailed along the inner shore of Cape Cod looking for a place to settle. The Nauset viewed all European ships as potential enemies since Thomas Hunt had kidnapped seven of their people in 1614, intending to sell them as slaves in Malaga—another plain and notorious New England crime. Now governor for the first time, since John Carver's sudden death in April, Bradford ordered the missing boy "to be enquired for among the Indeans, and at length Massasoyt sent word wher he was." Bradford sent a shallop across Cape Cod Bay "and had him delivered" (124). The recollection of these events, perhaps, contributes to the peculiar sadness that Bradford associates with having to condemn the father of the boy whom he had helped to rescue nearly a decade earlier.

The younger Billington's sojourn among the Nauset proves to be the means by which the settlers at Plymouth are able to reestablish peaceful relations with this aggrieved people and to give "full satisfaction" for the corn that the English had taken from several of their storage pits the previous winter. In its way, his adventure creates the opportunity for a kind of impromptu diplomacy that is at least as successful as the formal visit that Edward Winslow and Stephen Hopkins had paid to Massasoit earlier in the same month. Bradford briefly describes this official embassy in the paragraph immediately preceding his account of young Billington's experience, creating just the sort of sequential narrative juxtaposition to which William Perkins had urged that readers pay heed. What initially appears to be a shift in focus, from the public business of the colony to an anecdote concerning a single individual who "lost him selfe in the woods," in fact draws public and private experience more closely together.

This hungry and bewildered English boy—perhaps because of his age alone, but perhaps for other reasons too—is not treated by the Manamet or Nauset people as an opportunity to exact revenge. One can hardly avoid drawing the obvious contrast with the elder Billington's murderous ambush nine years later—another intratextual reflection of the kind that Perkins' methods of exegesis are clearly designed to encourage. Instead, these earlier events become the basis for a friendly overture and a means by which Bradford can introduce the Indians' diplomatic agency into his narrative, describing how the "peace and acquaintance" of Plymouth came to be "pretty well establisht" with their immediate neighbors.

The 1622 account of John Billington's recovery in *Mourt's Relation* is in some respects more evocative than the treatment that Bradford gives it in *Of Plimmoth Plantation*. The earlier narrative stresses the four days that Hopkins and Winslow spend traveling to and from Plymouth to visit Massasoit, a journey that apparently occurs in early June, not July, as Bradford later recalls in the history. The "voyage" across Cape Cod Bay to retrieve John Billington takes place while Winslow and Hopkins are gone, not after their return, as Bradford implies, and is given a brief chapter of its own in *Mourt's Relation*, in which Billington himself is never specifically named. According to the earlier account, the boy is returned to the English "behung with beads," as a peace offering—a detail that *Of Plimmoth Plantation* neglects to preserve—and on the trip to fetch him the colonists meet an old Nauset woman whose three sons had been among the Indians kidnapped by Thomas Hunt seven years earlier. The implicit contrast between Hunt's predatory behavior and the Indians' generosity in saving and returning John Billington is at once painfully and beautifully vivid.

These particulars do not figure in Bradford's pages twenty-five years later, though he was almost certainly not dependent on memory alone when he retold the story in *Of Plimmoth Plantation*. Indeed, as chapter 2 makes clear, Bradford goes out of his way to remind the reader of the history that an earlier discussion of the colony's first months in New England is readily available for comparison with the less expansive version in *Of Plimmoth Plantation*.

Instead he emphasizes the "short commons" customarily endured by Massasoit's people in late spring and early summer, as their winter surpluses dwindled before a new season's crops could ripen: "For the Indeans used then to have nothing so much corne as they have since the English have stored them with their hows, and seene their industrie in breaking up new grounds therwith" (123). On their way to visit Massasoit, Bradford reports, Winslow and Hopkins encountered the "sad spectackle" of unburied "sculs and bones," scattered through the woods—the remains of Indians who had died in the "wasting plague" of 1616, an epidemic that left the Narragansett people unscathed and correspondingly aggressive with their demoralized and depleted Indian neighbors. An alliance with Plymouth (Bradford implies) may prove useful, not only as a source of hoes but also as a deterrent to Narragansett intimidation. Although Massasoit's people themselves are hungry, they do their best to feed Plymouth's official emissaries, much as the Nauset do young John Billington. Moreover, the adaptability and industry that the Wampanoag shortly display, with the help of English farm tools, will soon offer a striking contrast to the behavior of Thomas Weston's sixty "lusty men," who appear in New England the following April and swiftly begin the descent to starvation and social collapse that will destroy their fledgling settlement in Massachusetts Bay within a year (149).

In *Of Plimmoth Plantation,* Bradford positions John Billington's period of wandering and near starvation in the foreground of these events—a precursor to the desperate scavenging for food to which Weston's men will soon be reduced and a counterweight to the hostile exchanges with the Narragansett that draw the narrative of 1621 to a close. It is a decision on Bradford's part that perfectly reflects William Perkins' emphasis on the suggestive power of narrative sequence: "Who? To whom? upon what occasion? at what time? in what place? for what end? what goeth before? what followeth?" Fortuitous diplomacy is only one of several threads that incorporate this apparently trivial event into the increasingly complex texture of Plymouth's political relations.

The interval of peace brought on by John Billington's recovery does not last long—less than a paragraph in narrative terms. Corbitant, an ally of Massasoit but "never any good freind to the English to this day," abruptly threatens Hobomock and Squanto, Plymouth's Indian interpreters, prompting the colonists to respond with an expedition of fourteen armed men, led by Miles Standish. They were instructed to determine whether Squanto had been killed and if so to behead Corbitant in revenge. Bradford's skill at exploiting the effects of narrative sequence underscores this startling change in the face of things. Indeed, modern scholars are prone to recall only this outburst of militant anxiety on Plymouth's part and neglect the varied forms of diplomacy and cultural interaction that precede it.[51] The size of Standish's retaliatory party represents, at this point in the summer of 1621, nearly the entire surviving adult male population of Plymouth—a fact that speaks to the colony's acute sense of its vulnerability. But Bradford does not dwell on this point; the narrative history (unlike its English protagonists) is not defensive. Squanto, as it happens, is not dead, and Corbitant avails himself of "the mediation of Massasoyte" to make an uneasy peace with these explosive yet amicable Englishmen. The mixed portrait that Bradford offers of Anglo-Indian relations in these initial months of Plymouth's existence effectively resists a simplistic or reductive account of its significance. It is a persuasive example of the resilience and flexibility of the "textor's" narrative art (125–26).

CHAPTER TWO

Such Neighbors and Brethren As We Are

LIFE IN LEIDEN had made Bradford and his companions familiar with the mixture of latent hostility, provisional friendship, and diplomatic constraint that quickly came to characterize the tiny political theater of southern New England. Human "arrogancie"—the urge "to dominire and lord it over the rest," as Bradford put it in his characterization of the Narragansett—might be held in check for significant periods of time, much as the Spanish and the Dutch had succeeded in doing during the long years of their truce, but it could not be extinguished. The antagonistic interests of the European states dissolved into the chaos of the Thirty Years War in the same month that the *Mayflower* made its landfall. Against this background of tragic collapse and innocent suffering, Bradford implicitly casts the closing paragraphs of his account of 1621. Despite the understandings that they felt they had reached with Massasoit and Corbitant, as well as with the Manamet, the Nauset, and the Narragansett, the colonists determined, through that winter and spring, to "inclose their dwellings with a good strong pale," a log fortification complete with "flankers" and gates "in which evry family had a prety garden plote secured" (134). *Felix civitas quae in pace de bello cogitat,* reads the Latin aphorism on Peter Isselburg's admonitory engraving of 1614: Happy the city that in peace contemplates war.[1]

Within Plymouth's bucolic fortification, however, human differences persist. Bradford quickly acknowledges these in an account of the conflict over the observation of Christmas Day that he professes to introduce, precisely at this point in the history, as a matter "rather of mirth then of waight." Yet the collision of consciences that he describes, largely between the original party of colonists and a group of new emigrants who joined them in November 1621, all too palpably recasts the bitter contention at Frankfort in 1554, the "mocks and injuries" inflicted on religious dissenters that William Perkins had cited in 1593, the storms of opposition

that had prompted the emigration to Holland in 1608, and the forces that were pro-
pelling mercenary armies across central Europe during the years when Bradford
was writing his book. The relative proportions of mirth and weight in this passage
would not be a simple matter to determine:

> One the day called Chrismas-day, the Governor caled them out to worke, (as was
> used,) but the most of this new-company excused them selves and said it wente
> against their consciences to work on that day. So the Governor tould them that if they
> made it mater of conscience, he would spare them till they were better informed. So
> he led-away the rest and left them; but when they came home at noone from their
> worke, he found them in the streete at play, openly; some pitching the barr, and some
> at stoole-ball, and shuch like sports. So he went to them, and tooke away their imple-
> ments, and tould them that was against his conscience, that they should play and oth-
> ers worke. If they made the keeping of it mater of devotion, let them kepe their
> houses, but ther should be no gameing or revelling in the streets. Since which time
> nothing hath been atempted that way, at least openly. (135)

From the comparatively narrow viewpoint of the modern reader, this episode is
clearly an instance of the pious repression of pleasure associated with the stereo-
typic Puritan. But for Bradford the incident is just as clearly part of a much more
ambitious narrative fabric, embracing a century-long struggle to accommodate the
explosive forces of religious and cultural pluralism within a single political body.

Despite its apparent triviality, this disagreement over the proper manner of
observing a "holiday" has a rich, covert life in Bradford's pages. "He would spare
them till they were better informed," the governor told the Christmas revelers—a
striking formulation calculated to evoke the unsparing use of force, in religious,
national, or ethnic conflicts, that occurred across the broad canvas of seventeenth-
century history. The faint note of martial discipline that Bradford casts over the
colonists as they set off to work echoes this ominous allusion, though later, when
he confiscates the "implements" of play, Bradford implies that he acts alone rather
than at the head of a body of subordinates, more as a parent than a soldier. Even
so, he suggests, these concerns are confined to the street—to public rather than to
private places. How individuals choose to keep their houses is, in fact, a matter of
conscience. As William Perkins might have pointed out, interpreting these sentences evidently requires an aptitude for the right cutting of words. Indeed, without careful attention to the subtlest of verbal signals, the reader might easily overlook the degree to which Bradford strives to make allies instead of opponents out
of mirth and weight, in the complex exercise of political and literary "authority"
that this passage describes.

At the same time, Bradford's words underscore his intention to treat *Of Plimmoth Plantation* as part of a wider referential network, one that he repeatedly invokes during these earliest chapters. This additional dimension to Bradford's textual world helps expose the ethical and thematic unity of his book: its preoccupation with the recognition and the containment of human difference. Plymouth's log enclosure is at best an imperfect barrier against such a pervasive source of conflict. It is precisely this perception that Bradford explores in the complex of early narratives and documents to which his history is most closely tied.

☙

THE PAGES of the 1622 *Relation or Journall of the beginning and proceedings of the English Plantation setled at Plimoth* make clear that John Billington's symbolic beads were not the only ceremonial gifts exchanged between Indians and Englishmen in the early summer of 1621. Edward Winslow and Stephen Hopkins had presented Massasoit with "a Horse-mans coat, of red Cotton, and laced with a slight lace," on their visit to Pokanoket, along with a copper chain that Massasoit could use to establish the credentials of any future messengers he sent to Plymouth. On their way to recover John Billington, Plymouth's emissaries were so troubled by the Nauset mother who had been "deprived of the comfort of her children in her old age" by the treachery of Thomas Hunt that they "gave her some small trifles, which somewhat appeased her." The sachem of the village where this old woman lived, a man named Iyanough, was a particularly impressive individual (according to his English visitors), "very personable, gentle, courteous, and fayre conditioned, indeed not like a savage, save for his attyre." In contrast to the short commons that Winslow and Hopkins had encountered at Massasoit's town, Iyanough's "entertainement was answerable to his parts, and his cheare plentifull and various." His people told the Englishmen where they could find their missing child, and Iyanough accompanied them in the shallop to recover him.[2]

Almost immediately upon young Billington's appearance—escorted by the Nauset sachem Aspinet and "a great traine" of his followers—the English hear a rumor that the Narragansett had attacked some of Massasoit's men and captured Massasoit himself, an alarming breakdown in the system of peaceful relations that they had been attempting to construct in recent months:

> This strucke some feare in us, because the Colony was so weakely guarded, the strength thereof being abroad: But we set foorth with resolution to make the best hast home wee could; yet the winde being contrary, having scarce any fresh water leaft, and at least 16. Leagues home, we put in againe for the shore. There we met againe with

> *Iyanough* the *Sachim of Cumaquid,* and the most of his Towne, both men women and
> children with him. Hee being still willing to gratifie us, tooke a runlet and led our
> men in the darke a great way for water, but could finde none good: yet brought such
> as there was on his necke with them. In the meane time the women joyned hand in
> hand, singing and dancing before the Shallop, the men also shewing all the kindnes
> they could, *Iyanough* himselfe taking a bracelet from about his necke, and hanging it
> upon one of us.[3]

Like the ceremonial beads with which Aspinet had bedecked John Billington,
Iyanough's bracelet is a significant indication that the favorable impression that he
had made upon the English was, at least to some extent, a mutual one.

The rumored Narragansett attack proves to be a garbled version of Corbitant's
brief, and largely verbal, insurrection against Massasoit's authority—the event that
later prompts Miles Standish's retaliatory expedition. Kill Squanto and Hobomock, Corbitant had argued with Massasoit's people, and "the English had lost
their tongue," a threat that may well have provoked the colony's explicit instructions to cut off Corbitant's head in revenge. Fortunately, none of this politic mutilation takes place.[4]

Throughout the autumn of 1621, relations with their Indian neighbors preoccupied the settlers at Plymouth far less than the problems caused by the arrival of the
ship *Fortune* from England, late in the season, carrying thirty-five "lusty yonge
men, and many of them wild enough," sent by Thomas Weston, one of Plymouth's
merchant investors, "to remaine and live in the plantation." The barren New England coast so alarmed these newcomers when they first saw it that they briefly considered stripping their ship's sails from the yards, in order to keep the master from
leaving them in such a forbidding place—an outbreak of panic that reflected their
sense of how ill-equipped they were for wilderness life. Bradford noted that
Weston had provided very little in the way of support for this consignment of emigrants: "ther was not so much as bisket-cake or any other victialls for them, neither
had they any beding, but some sory things they had in their cabins, nor pot, nor
pan, to drese any meate in; nor overmany cloaths, for many of them had brusht
away their coats and cloaks at Plimoth as they came" (128). The new settlers would
have to be fed over the winter out of the plantation's first New England harvest.

The symbolic exchanges of the year were not over, however, for the Narragansett
did indeed send a direct challenge to the security of the colony in the form of a
"bundl of arrows tyed aboute with a great sneak-skine." As Plymouth's gift of a copper chain to Massasoit attests, the English were familiar with the utility of symbolic objects in diplomacy. After consulting with his advisers, Bradford replied to

the Narragansett with two messengers: one bearing a sharp verbal rejoinder, conveyed through the colony's interpreters, and the other carrying back the menacing snake skin, stuffed with bullets. This second, significant signal from Plymouth (Bradford terms it a "round" answer, venturing a pun on the shape of a musket ball) the Narragansett prudently declined to accept, bringing to a close the year's remarkable account of the initial conditions of coexistence that the colonists sought to establish with the native communities of southern New England (133–34).

Of Plimmoth Plantation records the bulk of these events but relegates much of the detail to the 1622 *Relation or Journall,* which preserves John Billington's beads. Massasoit's horseman's coat appears in Bradford's history, but not its color, its lace trim, or the impressive copper chain, all of which prompt Massasoit to deliver a "great Speech" in which he and his people jointly recite a list of at least thirty towns subordinate to his leadership, repeating for each place a formulaic confirmation of Massasoit's stature and of the good relations that they all consented to maintain with Plymouth: "Was not he Massasoyt Commander of the Countrey about them? Was not such a Towne his and the people of it? and should they not bring their skins unto us? To which they answered, they were his and would be at peace with us, and bring their skins to us." This mnemonic performance seals the written understanding that the colonists had earlier established with Massasoit's people, a fact that Plymouth's emissaries Winslow and Hopkins clearly appreciate but which does not prevent them from noting in the pages of the *Relation* that the recitation itself was as "tedious" as it was "delightfull."[5]

Once the necessities of oral record-keeping were over, Massasoit shared tobacco with his visitors "and fell to discoursing of *England,*" marveling at King James' lack of female companionship and offering advice on the containment of French ambitions in southern New England. None of this extraordinary encounter appears in the pages of Bradford's history, nor do Iyanough and the hospitable people of Cummaquid, though it is hardly likely that Bradford had forgotten them. Just before beginning his account of the events of 1621 in *Of Plimmoth Plantation,* he had referred his reader to the 1622 journal for a discussion of some "smaler maters" that the ambition and scope of the longer book would not permit him to address (120). At the end of this eventful section of the history, Bradford again points the reader to Winslow's more elaborate account of the Narragansett challenge, "already put forth in printe" in *Good Newes from New-England* (1624), the second of the two brief reports with which the colonists had sought to shore up their base of English support (134). These allusions to its complementary narratives effectively identify the continuous public record of Bradford's history with a network of intersecting texts, composed by at least three hands over a span of twenty-four years—a referential web that is as characteristic of Bradford's verbal world as Massasoit's great speech is of his.

The command that Massasoit exercises over the affairs of his people is sustained by the kind of oral administrative ritual that Winslow and Hopkins witnessed, a necessarily repetitive act of public remembering that seems (to his English visitors) strangely clumsy, particularly when compared with Massasoit's agile and wide-ranging curiosity. It is possible, too, that the dance of the Cummaquid women during the return voyage from Nauset is likewise a commemorative act, retelling the story of John Billington's rescue and the visit of the English boat to retrieve him. Bradford's verbal economy functions in a much different manner: relying not on repetition and memory but on clusters of complementary written records, frequently placed in immediate visual proximity to one another, highlighting differences and discrepancies as well as points of concurrence among competing literary authorities.

Groups of closely related books might be jointly consulted on a desk, while one wrote, or situated on a "reading wheel" for convenient cross-referencing and comparison. The audience of Indians at Pokanoket encircles Massasoit when he rehearses the political structure of his community, including all of its elements in the new economic relationship with Plymouth. But books effectively encircle the reader in the textual relations that Bradford invites us to consider as we read *Of Plimmoth Plantation.* The history relies on, rather than supersedes or simply repeats, its predecessors. This concept of textual interdependence is both thematically and practically important to Bradford's sense of Plymouth's significance in the larger historical narratives of which it is a part. The twice-told year of 1621 invites a joint consideration of textual as well as human neighbors in Bradford's book, stressing the depth and extent of the colonists' efforts to accommodate the human variety with which they quickly found themselves both surrounded and infused.

THE EMBLEMATIC READING WHEEL, with its freight of books, that Lisa Jardine and Anthony Grafton invoke to describe Gabriel Harvey's study habits would not have to be an ambitious piece of apparatus to satisfy the immediate needs of William Bradford's reader.[6] Once the history's initial battery of allusions to Eusebius, Foxe, or Perkins have been successfully assimilated, the story of the colony's early years is comparatively unencumbered. At most a handful of documents and titles play a role in augmenting Bradford's central narrative. In order to provide some context for appreciating Plymouth's diplomatic achievements, Bradford alludes to the predatory voyage of Thomas Hunt in 1614—an episode made memorable for English readers by the bitter marginal gloss that Samuel Purchas provides in *Hakluytus Posthumus* on "Hunts savage hunting of savages."[7] Purchas's copious volumes would quickly disclose how little reason the Indians of southern New England had to expect good faith or fair treatment from any European visitor.

Near the close of his discussion of the year 1620 in *Of Plimmoth Plantation,* Bradford quotes at length from a letter by another shipmaster, Thomas Dermer, demonstrating how futile Dermer's peacemaking efforts had been among Massasoit's people as late as the spring of 1620, a few months before the arrival of the *Mayflower.*[8] The legacy of hostility left behind by Hunt and others makes the success of Plymouth's early overtures among the Nauset and the Wampanoag all the more conspicuous—evidence, Bradford suggests, of how "the powerfull hand of the Lord did protect them" during their first months ashore (119). Evidence of more earthly reasons for the colony's diplomatic good fortune emerges most clearly, however, when one reads *Of Plimmoth Plantation* in close conjunction with the three printed works from these years that directly amplify Bradford's primary narrative.

Shortly after returning to England early in 1622 from his brief visit to the colony, Robert Cushman published the text of a sermon that he had delivered at Plymouth the previous December. This exhortation on "the danger of selfe-love, and the sweetnesse of true Friendship" does not add new details to the historical record, but it is an important index of the ethical necessities that Plymouth's leaders associated with their unique circumstances.[9] Though little more than a pamphlet, it clearly belongs among the important satellite documents that revolve around Bradford's history. More obvious in its importance, Edward Winslow's *Good Newes from New-England* (1624) reviews events in the colony from the arrival of the *Fortune* in 1621 through the drought of 1623, concluding with an account of the religion and customs of the Indians and a description of the New England climate. His growing familiarity with the Wampanoag people makes it possible for Winslow to correct some earlier statements that he had made about them, in the 1622 *Relation,* as well as to note another mnemonic practice that asserts the Indians' impressive command over their own past:

> In stead of Records and Chronicles, they take this course, where any remarkable
> act is done, in memorie of it, either in the place, or by some path-way neer adjoyning,
> they make a round hole in the ground, about a foote deepe, and as much over, which
> when others passing by behold, they enquire the cause and occasion of the same,
> which being once knowne, they are carefull to acquaint all men, as occasion serveth

therewith. And least such holes should be filled, or growne up by any accident, as men passe by, they will oft renew the same: By which meanes many things of great Antiquity are fresh in memory. So that as a man travelleth, if he can understand his guide, his journey will be the lesse tedious, by reason of the many historicall discourses [that] will be related to him.[10]

The tedium of oral record-keeping is only one dimension of Massasoit's verbal culture. Another is this penetration of the landscape by commemorative "places," like the imaginary loci in the classical arts of recall described by Frances Yates, to prompt the preservation of "many things of great Antiquity."[11]

Cushman's sermon and Winslow's narrative, along with the 1622 *Relation or Journall*, form, in turn, the mnemonic apparatus of Bradford's history. Collectively, they offer a picture of the colony's beginnings that emphasizes the interplay between religious principle and the pressing human contingencies of seventeenth-century New England. Of these three textual predecessors, the 1622 *Relation or Journall* is the most ambitious in the way that it seeks to structure the reader's movement. Its authors frame their account of Plymouth's first months of existence with two documents, offering interpretive perspectives that originate outside of colonial experience. Robert Cushman's defense of emigration against its English critics concludes this brief book, encouraging interested readers to consider joining an enterprise that blended material promise with high religious purpose. A prefatory "letter of advice," written before the original emigrants set sail, precedes the main body of the narrative. The voyage itself—an understandably key experiential element in many seventeenth-century emigration stories—simply disappears from the account, as these two mediating entities offer guidance directed as much at the reader of the *Relation* as at the potential emigrant to New England.

The prefatory letter, indicating the communal ideals to which these particular colonists sought to adhere, is, in fact, John Robinson's parting advice to the *Mayflower* passengers, sent in late July 1620 under the care of John Carver for a public reading before the ship sailed. Bradford copies this document into *Of Plimmoth Plantation*, identifying Robinson as the author, but for its first appearance in print, the 1622 *Relation or Journall* attributes it to a "discreete friend" who sought to offer "certaine useful advertisements" to the prospective settlers. The degree of discretion involved belongs as much to the *Relation*'s authors as to the "unfained well-willer of your happie successe," the enigmatic "I. R." who signs the preface. It may have been impolitic in 1622 to associate Plymouth too closely with the guidance of Robinson, a prominent theological opponent of the English establishment whose enemies were already sufficiently numerous and influential to prevent his own emigration to New England. Anonymous though it is, the letter establishes, at the beginning of the plantation's printed record, the relationship between civic and religious idealism that the colonists hoped to maintain.

Robinson was only too aware that members of his Leiden congregation were in the minority among the passengers on the *Mayflower*. Many of the doctrinal or liturgical issues that sharply divided seventeenth-century English Protestants were undoubtedly represented aboard the ship, as they would be the following winter in the colonists' differences over the significance of Christmas. Accordingly, Robinson opens his letter by emphasizing not these visible divisions but a strategically invisible one: the acute ideological anguish that many of his contemporaries felt at being caught between antithetical religious desires. "Make account of me," Robinson writes, "as of a man devided in my selfe with great paine," wishing desperately to be among the emigrants "in this first brunt" but "by strong necessitie held backe for the present." It is a disarming gesture made all the more effective by Robinson's confession that he is offering these few pages of written counsel "not because you need it, yet because I owe it in love and dutie." This initial conscientious mixture of humility and tact gives some indication of the personal qualities that enabled Robinson to inspire passionate loyalty among the members of his church for nearly twenty deeply contentious and difficult years.[12]

Repentance is the first task that his letter urged on the *Mayflower*'s passengers, not only for the sins they know of but for what Robinson terms "our unknowne trespasses" as well—an extraordinary demand made necessary by the emigrants' singular circumstances. Sin, like truth, was a matter of progressive revelation, in Robinson's mind, not a static or categorical list of proscriptions. One might discover oneself to have been in the wrong, to have sinned unknowingly, in light of subsequent worldly experience or religious growth. To admit such a possibility was immediately to chasten one's sense of spiritual certainty or moral complacency, and that is precisely the effect that Robinson seeks to promote among this compact body of people who were about to form a community by utterly artificial means. Conduct a "narrow search and carefull reformation" of your personal life and habits, he advises. An earnest repentance and divine pardon will produce a sense of individual security and peace "in all dangers." But this religious introspection, though vital, is only a preamble to its civic counterpart in Robinson's letter. After "this heavenly peace with God and our owne consciences," he continues, "we are carefully to provide for peace with all men what in us lieth."[13]

The words themselves are carefully chosen to evoke an ideal end without excluding all acknowledgment of psychological complexity and human limitation. It was, in fact, a limitation on the human capacity for peaceful coexistence that had originally driven Robinson and his fellow worshipers to Holland, that had incited the Spanish and the Dutch to four generations of war, and that was swiftly maturing the conditions for civil war in England. The peace that "in us lieth," from the historical standpoint of Robinson's day, as of our own, is often dwarfed by the capacity for conflict that is equally resident in the human constitution. Robinson emphasizes that "watchfullness" is a constant necessity of human community, "that we neither at all in our selves do give, no nor easily take offense being given by others." He underscores the urgency of this requirement by invoking the same verse from Matthew that Abraham Lincoln would cite in his second inaugural address, justifying the providential chastisements of his own time: "Woe be unto the world for offences," Robinson writes, "for though it be necessary (considering the malice of Satan and mans corruption) that offenses come, yet woe unto the man or woman either by whom the offense cometh."

As his parenthetical gloss on the verse makes clear, Robinson employs this biblical warning not as a retrospective justification for God's punitive intervention in history but as a psychological admonishment. The giving and the taking of offense, he believes, tend to be linked in human character, signaling a joint lack of grace and charity in individual lives. "Indeed in mine owne experience," Robinson observes, "few or none have been found which sooner give offence, then such as easily take it; neither have they ever proved sound and profitable members in societies, which have nourished in themselves that touchey humour." Irritable self-indulgence is all the more likely to break out among a group of strangers, Robinson cautions, who are unacquainted with one another's personal "infirmities." Conflicts will unavoidably occur, he assures his listeners (who are also, in some sense, his readers); it is "necessary" that offenses come. But "brotherly forbearance" and patience can quench them. "When such things fall out in men and women as you suspected not," he advises, do not "be inordinately affected with them." Startling disclosures are inevitable, given the mixed entity that is human nature, and "doth require at your hands much wisedome and charitie for the covering and preventing of incident offenses that way."[14]

The most "deadly plague" afflicting civil community, in Robinson's view, was not the touchy humor, however, but selfishness, an indifference to the general good or a "retirednesse of minde" that subordinates the well-being of the whole to some private end. "Let every man represse in himselfe and the whole bodie in each person, as so many rebels against the common good, all private respects of mens selves," Robinson urged. A new house should not be shaken before it is well settled; "unnecessary novelties" or quarrels at the outset of the settlement would originate all too readily from those who are "singularly affected any maner of way." Choose for leaders those who love the common good and strive to overlook "the ordinari-nesse of their persons" as they execute the duties of their offices: "the image of the Lords power and authoritie which the Magistrate beareth," Robinson argues, giving a democratic cast to Romans 13:1, "is honorable, in how meane persons soever."[15] With this final piece of counsel, he closes his letter, offering "these few things" in "few words" so as not to appear to impose his judgment or his authority on others—a dramatic enactment of the self-effacing principles by which he en-couraged the *Mayflower*'s passengers to live.

Bradford notes significantly, in *Of Plimmoth Plantation*, that when "the com-pany was caled togeather, and this letter read amongst them," it "had good accep-tation with all, and after fruit with many" (82). Robinson's ceremonial written benediction must have sounded quite familiar to those members of the *Mayflower* company who were used to the liturgical practices of the established church. In his "daily incessant prayers unto the Lord," Robinson asked "that he who hath made the heavens and the earth, the sea and all rivers of waters, and whose providence is over all his workes, especially over all his deare children for good, would so guide and guard you in your wayes, as inwardly by his Spirit, so outwardly by the hand of his power, as that both you and we also, for and with you, may have after matter of praising his Name all the days of your and our lives. Fare you well in him in whom you trust, and in whom I rest." These are reassuringly accessible formulas, from the oral traditions of English piety, that touch on none of the controversy that had led to Robinson's own religious exclusion and exile. They capture, in effect, an "ordi-narinesse" of expression that makes his voice particularly memorable under these distinctly extraordinary circumstances. If superhuman selflessness seems unattain-able, his letter offers the colloquial alternative that one might at least strive to be less touchy. Absolute harmony is not to be expected among this heterogeneous col-lection of English emigrants, but the peace "what in us lieth," properly nourished and guarded, ought to be adequate to the crosses and afflictions that almost cer-tainly lie ahead. This letter, like Robinson himself, is a divided entity, mixing real-ism with hopefulness, exalted callings with "meane" persons, who bear, neverthe-less, the "glorious ordinance of the Lord" (81). Its influence is evident both in the private effects on individual character that Bradford mentions in the history and in the thematic impact it has on the text of the 1622 *Relation or Journall*, over which Robinson's words seem to preside.

❧

THE MOST STRIKING FEATURE of the 1622 *Relation* is, in fact, its ordinariness. There is very little evidence in its pages of the intense religious feeling that had sustained many of the new colonists through twelve years of exile and a long and dangerous ocean voyage. They are appropriately grateful to God for bringing them safely to land, "after many difficulties in boysterous stormes," but it is the land itself that engages them. Far from the "hidious and desolate wildernes" that Bradford invokes at one memorable early moment in *Of Plimmoth Plantation*, New England impresses the authors of the 1622 *Relation* as a "goodly" place: its coastline forested "to the brinke of the sea" with "Okes, Pines, Juniper, Sassafras, and other sweet wood," much of which they promptly gather and begin to burn on board the *Mayflower*, savoring the "very sweet and strong" smell of juniper fires in particular, after the fetid air of a seventeenth-century ship during the dreary weeks at sea.[16]

Some indication of this deep physical pleasure enters into Bradford's account in *Of Plimmoth Plantation* as well. He notes there the satisfaction that an exploring party from the *Mayflower* takes in "the first New-England water they drunke of," finding it as pleasant as wine or beer had been in England (99). The Indian baskets they discover are "faire" and the brightly colored corn they contain "a very goodly sight," on aesthetic as well as utilitarian grounds. But to a significantly greater degree, the 1622 *Relation* is absorbed in the sensory immediacy of the experiences that it records.

Cape Cod Bay, the *Relation* reports, is full of whales, "playing hard by us" at the *Mayflower*'s first anchorage. The master of the ship and his mate predict that there is a small fortune in oil to be obtained there, for someone who has the proper tools for the fishery, but the only thing the passengers are able to catch, for the time being, are some "great Mussles, and very fat and full of sea perle" that give diarrhea to anyone who eats them. This experience is disappointing to say the least, but it does not elicit any comment from the authors of the *Relation* on the perils of earthly greed or gluttony. The mussels caused them "to cast and scoure, but they were soon well againe."[17] More serious colds and coughs begin to take a toll as the passengers wade back and forth through the freezing surf to get ashore.

The forests of Cape Cod are invitingly "open and without underwood, fit either to goe or ride in," but also prove to contain thickets of "boughes and bushes . . . which tore our very Armour in peeces," when a party from the ship try to follow a group of Indians that they have spotted on the beach. This potentially momentous encounter appears in *Of Plimmoth Plantation* as well, but the 1622 version develops into an expansive, seriocomic account that pictures the military formality of sixteen heavily armed Englishmen, with "Musket, Sword, and Corslet," moving cautiously down the beach in single file, when they abruptly spy "five or sixe people, with a Dogge, coming towards them, who were savages." It is a whimsical juxtaposition of extraordinary and commonplace occasions. At first Miles Standish and his companions (William Bradford among them) take these people to be some of the *Mayflower*'s sailors, who were also ashore at the time. But when the strangers "ran into the Wood and whistled the Dogge after them," they recognize that they are Indians and give chase. The heavily encumbered Englishmen are no match for the natives, who "ran away with might and mayne," while their singularly ill-equipped pursuers soon find themselves spending a night in the woods, with no water to drink, "only Bisket and Holland cheese, and a little Bottle of *aquavitae*."[18]

This excursion stretches through two days and two nights on shore, during which the English never see another Indian. They find abandoned cornfields, some ears of corn buried in baskets that are "very handsomely and cunningly made," an old fort or palisade, some Indian graves, and an extremely ingenious deer snare, which many of the exploring party pause to admire. As Bradford approaches ("being in the reare"), he inadvertently triggers the bent sapling that sets the snare: "it gave a sodaine jerk up, and he was immediately caught by the leg." Yet another demonstration of native ingenuity, the Englishmen conclude: "It was a very pretie devise, made with a Rope of their owne making, and having a noose as artificially made as any Roper in *England* can make, and as like ours as can be, which we brought away with us." They bring away also as much corn as they can carry from the Indian storage pits, along with a ship's kettle that they have found among the Indians' possessions. There was some "suspence" over this last decision, the authors of the *Relation* report, but they determine to return the kettle and pay for the corn, whenever they are able to make contact with the owners. They are equally in suspense over disturbing some Indian graves, "because we thought it would be odious unto them to ransack their Sepulchers," so they carefully restore most of the burial objects that they have removed during this ill-considered excavation "and left the rest untouched." This incident prompts the only religious reflection of any kind that impinges on the 1622 account of the colonists' "first Discovery" on shore.[19]

On a second and much larger expedition of discovery, involving thirty-four passengers and sailors led by the captain of the *Mayflower*, Christopher Jones, the English display considerably less compunction about investigating an Indian grave:

> when we had marched five or six myles into the Woods, and could find no signes of
> any people, we returned againe another way, and as we came into the plaine ground,
> wee found a place like a grave, but it was much bigger and longer then any we had yet
> seene. It was also covered with boords, so as we mused what it should be, and resolved
> to digge it up, where we found, first a Matt, and under that a fayre Bow, and there

another Matt, and under that a boord about three quarters long, finely carved and paynted, with three tynes, or broches on the top, like a Crowne, also betweene the Matts we found Boules, Trayes, Dishes, and such like Trinkets; at length we came to a faire new Matt, and under that two Bundles, the one bigger, the other lesse, we opened the greater and found in it a great quantitie of fine and perfect red Powder, and in it the bones and skull of a man. The skull had fine yellow haire still on it, and some of the flesh unconsumed; there was bound up with it a knife, a pack-needle, and two or three old iron things. It was bound up in a Saylers canvas Casacke, and a payre of cloth breeches; the red Powder was a kind of Embaulment, and yeelded a strong, but no offensive smell; It was as fine as any flower. We opened the less bundle like-wise, and found of the same Powder in it, and the bones and head of a little childe, about the leggs, and other parts of it was bound strings, and bracelets of fine white Beads; there was also by it a little Bow, about three quarters long and some other odd knacks; we brought sundry of the preatiest things away with us, and covered the Corps up againe.[20]

Much as the exploring party itself is a mixture of sailors and colonists, saints and strangers, so this remarkable passage mixes idle curiosity and wonder, desecration and reverence, in its meticulous and moving inventory. The grave proves to be a surprisingly mixed place in its own right, part Indian and part European, inexplic-able yet filled with evocative objects that suggest the cultural sophistication of its makers. Its "finely carved and paynted" crown and aromatic embalming powder hint at the stature of the dead man and testify to the scientific and artistic skill of the people who prepared him for burial. The diminutive bow and "odd knackes" that accompany the child's bones are equally telling evidence of the richness of their emotional lives. No ethnological barrier separates the Englishmen who are examining these objects from the story of parental tenderness and grief that they convey.

"There was a varietie of opinions amongst us about the embalmed person," the *Relation* reports, but no consensus on his origins, on what might have brought him there, or why he was buried with a child. This act is unquestionably invasive, but it is also an expression of deep curiosity, not indifference, greed, or bigotry. The pas-sage uncovers a mystery, rather than confirming established prejudices, and per-fectly captures the reciprocal humanity of its dead and its living participants. Here, too, is a meeting of strangers, much as Robinson had characterized the original gathering of passengers on the *Mayflower*, expressing both the infirmity and the charity of human nature.[21]

In wonderfully paradoxical fashion, the first extended encounter that the colonists have with living Indians also reflects this haunting mixture of mystery and familiarity to which Robinson's prefatory letter had pointed. On their circuit of the shoreline of Cape Cod Bay in early December, searching for a place to situate their settlement, the English catch a glimpse from their shallop of some Indians at a distance, cutting up a grampus that has been stranded by the tide. They find more abandoned cornfields and a "sumptuous" burying place, partly surrounded by "a large Palazado, like a Church-yard," according to the *Relation*'s authors, but encounter no native people during a long day's march through the coastal plain.

About midnight on their second night away from the *Mayflower*, they are awakened by "a great and hideous cry" that alarms their sentries, but the noise stops as soon as they fire a couple of muskets, and they conclude that it was made by wolves or foxes. The following morning, after a characteristic difference of opinion on the best procedure for loading the boat, they are interrupted at breakfast by a repetition of the midnight noises:

> Anone, all upon a sudden, we heard a great and strange cry, which we knew to be the same voyces, though they varied their notes, one of our company being abroad came running in, and cryed, *They are men, Indians, Indians;* and withall their arrowes came flying amongst us, our men ran out with all speed to recover their armes, as by the good Providence of God they did. In the meane time, Captaine *Miles Standish*, having a snaphance ready, made a shot, and after him another, after they two had shot, other two of us were ready, but he wisht us not to shoot, till we could take ayme, for we knew not what need we should have, and there were foure onely of us which had their armes there readie, and stood before the open side of our Baricado, which was first assaulted . . . The cry of our enemies was dreadfull, especially, when our men ran out to recover their Armes, their note was after this manner, *Woath woach ha ha hach woach:* our men were no sooner come to their Armes, but the enemy was ready to assault them.

Like the English, the Indians have a "captaine," a "lustie man and no whit lesse valiant," who stands behind a tree, well within musket range, and shoots his arrows into the English barricade. One especially well-aimed musket shot drives this bold assailant from his position, and the Indians run away, followed by a party of the English, who "shouted all together two severall times, and shot off a couple of muskets . . . that they might see wee were not afrayd of them nor discouraged."[22]

Bradford revisits these events in *Of Plimmoth Plantation* but does not mention Standish by name or attempt to reproduce the sounds of the Indian battle cry. The 1622 account, however, makes it impossible to overlook the peculiar symmetries that underlie this apparently hostile exchange: the matching captains whose personal examples give direction to their people, the matching shouts of defiance or insult, equally unintelligible to their intended targets, the wonderfully mixed effect of the English sentinel's initial warning cry: "They are men, Indians, Indians." This simultaneous acknowledgment of similarity and difference is in many respects a condensed expression of the meaning that the journal attaches to much of the apparently unrelated detail that it records.

A marginal note on the account of the battle refers to these events as "Our first combat with the Indians," but in the body of the *Relation* itself the English participants decide to call this spot "The first encounter"—a much more provisional indication of what the incident might portend for the future, as well as an instructive instance of the subtle influences that marginalia can be made to exert upon the text that it ostensibly glosses. Once the Indians are gone, the English carefully collect eighteen of their assailants' arrows to be sent back to England with the *Mayflower:* "some whereof were headed with brasse, others with Hartshorne, and others with Eagles clawes." These are clearly intended not as triumphant souvenirs but as eloquent testimony to the sophistication and ingenuity of their makers, much like the deer snare that Bradford encountered during their first excursion on Cape Cod. The Indians are already adapting European materials to their traditional technology of hunting and warfare. Despite the English reliance on muskets in 1620, they too came from a culture of skillful archers, capable of appreciating the craftsmanship behind these arrows. At the *Mayflower's* first, awkwardly shallow anchorage, near the tip of Cape Cod, the authors of the *Relation* had noted that they were often forced to wade "a bow shoot or two" to get to dry land after the ship's boat had run aground.[23]

For a book that clearly hopes to encourage at least some of its readers to consider emigrating to New England, the 1622 *Relation* is remarkably candid about the difficulties and the suffering that the first settlers endured. It does not specify in detail the daily and weekly deaths that, beginning early in 1621, eventually cut the English numbers in half, but neither does it conceal the progressive onset of colds and coughs that combine with poor nutrition and lack of shelter to take their toll: "Discoveries in frost and stormes, and the wading at Cape Cod had brought much weakenes amongst us, which increased so every day more and more, and after was the cause of many of their deaths." Bradford's poignant account of this period in *Of Plimmoth Plantation* takes note of the devotion of the few healthy colonists, who patiently nursed the sick and dying, and contrasts the mutual compassion of the emigrants with the selfish behavior of the sailors, who are equally afflicted with sickness. "O," one of the chastened crew of the *Mayflower* exclaims, "you, I now see, shew your love like Christians indeed one to another, but we let one another lye and dye like doggs" (113). The 1622 *Relation* does not draw such contrasts or point to any larger, providential end that this first, costly winter in New England could be said to serve.[24] Robinson's prefatory letter and, later, Cushman's closing reflections on emigration provide a broad moral framework for the several narratives in between, but the bulk of the *Relation* is devoted to the rich foreground of the colonists' experience.

Standish and a party of men on an excursion into the woods kill an eagle and pronounce the meat "excellent . . . hardly to be discerned from Mutton" (25). A whale sleeping by the side of the *Mayflower* proves indifferent to the awkward efforts of the ship's passengers to fire a musket at her, "but when the whale saw her time she gave a snuffe and away" (14). The first thunderstorm that the colonists experience is the highlight of an unusually mild, but characteristically changeable, New England day in early spring: "Saturday the third of *March,* the winde was South, the morning mistie, but towards noone warme and fayre weather; the Birds sang in the Woods most pleasantly; at one of the Clocke it thundred, which was the first wee heard in that Countrey, it was strong and great claps, but short, but after an houre it rayned very sadly till midnight" (31). This strange new world seems less remote, both in time and in distance, after reading such a passage. It is a reassuringly ordinary place.[25]

Even the alternation of remarkable and routine occurrences, in the pages of the *Relation,* is telling. Two of the colonists, John Goodman and Peter Browne, got lost in the woods while chasing a deer early in January 1621. They spent the night at the foot of a tree, terrified by what they thought were "two Lyons roaring exceedingly for a long time together." By the time they found their way back to Plymouth the next day, Goodman's feet were so badly swollen and frozen that his shoes had to be cut off. The following week, while hobbling about trying to recover, he had a second notable adventure:

> This day in the evening, John Goodman went abroad to use his lame feete, that were
> pittifully ill with the cold he had got, having a little Spannell with him, a little way
> from the Plantation, two great Wolves ran after the Dog, the Dog ran to him and
> betwixt his leggs for succour, he had nothing in his hand but tooke up a sticke, and
> threw at one of them and hit him, and they presently ran both away, but came
> againe, he got a paile bord in his hand, and they sat both on their tayles, grinning
> at him, a good while, and went their way, and left him.
> Saturday 20. We made up our Shed for our common goods.
> Sunday the 21. We kept our meeting on Land.

Munday the 22. Was a faire day, we wrought on our houses and in the after-noone
carried up our hogsheads of meale to our common store house.

The rest of the weeke we followed our businesse likewise.[26]

Goodman's encounter with the grinning wolves evidently provides some welcome
variety to the routine business of life in the new settlement. But precisely where one
might expect at least a formulaic acknowledgment of God's Providence in preserving Goodman from the jaws of death, the text of the *Relation* is silent.

The Sunday church meeting is duly noted, in a perfunctory line, and the tasks
of the next week are under way, without any effort to point to a moral or call attention to the uses that the colonist's presiding elders, John Carver and William Brewster, might have been able to make of Goodman's interesting experience as a Sabbath lesson. From the roaring of the lions to the grinning of the wolves, these
events would seem ideally suited for the application of a text from Daniel, perhaps.
But just as Robinson's letter mutes the sectarian passions that were largely responsible for the *Mayflower*'s voyage, this delightful passage appears willing to forgo an
opportunity for pious display that might risk giving even a mild degree of offense
to readers or colonists less steeped in the workings of the biblical imagination.

Throughout the 1622 *Relation*, Robinson's influence appears to extend itself in
the portrayal of differences and compromises among the settlers. Standish's first
small party of explorers heads off down the beach at Cape Cod without the full
consent of some influential leaders among the *Mayflower*'s passengers, who liked
the exploring party's willingness to embark but feared the dangers involved and so
"rather permitted then approved" the journey, offering an abundance of "cautions,
directions, and instructions." Standish himself is tentative about asserting his military authority among the colonists, until mid-February 1621, when the citizens of
Plymouth formally commission him as "our Captaine." The second party of discovery, which left the ship the previous November, was in fact commanded by master Jones of the *Mayflower*, "to gratifie his kindnes and forwardnes" (9), though
Standish was the only one of the passengers or the crew with significant military
experience, should the group in fact meet with a hostile reception. Differences of
opinion, or simple jealousy, among the English concerning how best to get themselves under way briefly give the Indians an advantage during their early morning
attack at First Encounter camp. Even the scope and duration of the search for a
settlement site "was controversall amongst us."[27]

A significant number of the passengers wanted to settle immediately on Cape
Cod. The harbor was adequate, it was clear that the soil would grow corn, and
whales "of the best kind for oyle and bone" seemed abundant. More urgently, per-

haps, winter storms had set in, many passengers already were racked with "vehement" coughs, and they were concerned about their dwindling supplies of food and diminishing physical strength. Others felt that the fresh water they had found on the Cape would prove insufficient or unreliable and wanted to explore twenty leagues farther north, on the mainland, where earlier voyagers had reported promising conditions for a colony. In the end the emigrants strike a compromise—one of many instances of resolving disagreements that reflect the "after fruit" of John Robinson's advice on the necessity of minimizing or "covering" differences. The Mayflower Compact is the most famous such covering, presented in the text of the *Relation* as a response to what its authors called "some appearance of faction" among the passengers shortly after landfall. Every male head of household is ultimately prevailed upon to sign the Compact, even the troublesome John Billington, whom Bradford will condemn to death for murder ten years later.[28]

The text of the Compact itself, with its formal profession of loyalty to "our dread sovereigne Lord King James," is in this respect a uniquely unconvincing effort at the covering of deep differences. It is difficult to imagine Brewster, Bradford, or the other passengers from Leiden acknowledging the sovereignty of the English king in anything but a technical sense. During the unsuccessful negotiations for a royal patent that Bradford described in the history, he noted James' reluctance to offer legal security to these English exiles under the protection of his great seal. But the king would "connive" at them, his informal messengers suggested, and permit an emigration that seemed potentially favorable to English interests. Neither James' great seal nor his aptitude for conniving finally inspire much confidence in the Leiden party, but Bradford may well have recalled the king's offer as he copied the equally conniving language of the Compact into *Of Plimmoth Plantation*.

The *Relation* closes with a letter from Edward Winslow to an English friend and an extraordinary defense of the ethics of emigration by Robert Cushman. Winslow comments on the physical progress of the colony, on crops, on the climate, and on the "Covenant of Peace" established with the Indians. He gives some specific advice on how future emigrants might best prepare to join the Plymouth settlement, including recommendations on the utility of fresh lemon juice and on the size of the musket shot that prospective settlers should provide, "most for bigge Fowles." In its immersion in physical particulars, Winslow's letter is an apt conclusion to the body of the journal itself. Cushman's address is a much more formal piece, clearly prepared after his return to England, with marginal glosses and scriptural citations that underscore his earnest indictment of the existential plight of the English reader and point to the remedy that emigration is able to supply. On broadly theological grounds, Cushman is impatient with sentimental attachments to "place," echoing the language from Hebrews 11 that Bradford will later, more famously invoke in the text of the history: "We are all in all places strangers and Pilgrims," Cushman writes, repeating even as he extends John Robinson's prefatory comment on the predicament of the *Mayflower*'s passengers: "Our home is nowhere" (66).

To the imaginary objections of a reader who contends that a man must remain where he is "born and bred," Cushman responds that only the ethical or spiritual quality of one's existence has any binding claim on human loyalty:

> I answer, a man must not respect only to live, and doe good to himselfe, but he should see where he can live to doe most good to others: for as one saith, *He whose living is but for himselfe, it is time he were dead.* Some men there are who of necessitie must here live, as being tied to duties either to Church, Common-wealth, houshold, kindred, etc. but others, and that many, who doe no good in none of those nor can doe none, as being not able, or not in favour, or as wanting opportunitie, and live as outcasts: no bodies, eie-sores, eating but for themselves, reaching but themselves, and doing good to none, either in soule or body, and so passe over daies, yeares, and moneths, yea so live and so die. Now such should lift up their eies and see whether there be not some other place and countrie to which they may goe to doe good and have use towards others of that knowledge, wisdome, humanitie, reason, strength, skill, facultie, etc. which God hath given them for the service of others and his owne glory.[29]

These words recapitulate, in passionate terms, Robinson's strictures against the deadly plague of selfishness in his prefatory letter, to which Cushman joins his own account of the deadly plague of emptiness in English life. The pages of the *Relation* that intervene between Robinson's and Cushman's appeals suggest the scope that New England might be able to offer to the knowledge, wisdom, humanity, and strength of the reader.

As one might expect, there is an acutely ethnocentric dimension to Cushman's resonant list of affirmative human powers. God's service, in his eyes, includes "the conversion of the heathens," as well as the populating and improving of a land that at one point Cushman seems to view as essentially empty—a "Chaos," in fact, inhabited by people who are little more advanced than wild beasts, not industrious, without art or sciences, and so without a claim to the land that ought to trouble the consciences of new, more energetic occupants. It is not particularly surprising that a seventeenth-century Englishman should appear to endorse so many of the notorious justifications for colonization that Washington Irving would later subject to withering attack in the opening chapters of his *History of New York*. Unlike many of his contemporaries, however, Cushman does not treat his prejudices as decisive.

Indeed, the profound ignorance and inhumanity that lie behind such attitudes are vividly exposed by contrast with the temperament expressed in Robinson's prefatory letter and the remarkable portrait of Indian intelligence, sophistication, and complexity that emerges from the body of the printed *Relation,* which precedes Cushman's remarks.[30]

Cushman himself appears to be aware of the glaring inadequacy of his appeal to imperial claims based on geographical emptiness or disuse. Shortly after invoking them, he abandons them. Massasoit rules a territory that is larger than England and Scotland combined, Cushman asserts (a statement likely to be of some interest to the conniving King James), and this substantial "Imperial Governor" (as Cushman terms Massasoit) has acknowledged fealty to England and peace with Plymouth, to which Massasoit ceded the land that the colony occupied "by common consent, composition, and agreement":

> neither hath this beene accomplished by threats and blowes, or shaking of sword, and sound of trumpet, for as our facultie that way is small, and our strength lesse: so our warring with them is after another manner, namely by friendly usage, love, peace, honest and just cariages, good counsell, etc. that so we and they may not only live in peace in that land, and they yeeld subjection to an earthly Prince, but that as voluntaries they may be perswaded at length to embrace the Prince of peace Christ Jesus, and rest in peace with him for ever.[31]

In a preface to the sermon that he published separately in 1622, Cushman (unlike many colonial apologists) specifies precisely what he means when he states that the wilderness of southern New England is "empty," noting the recent depopulation by plague among the Indians—without attaching any providential significance to that terrible catastrophe—and reporting that the nearest Indian town to Plymouth is eight or ten miles distant. Pokanoket itself, Massasoit's chief residence, is fifty miles away. These were significant distances by contemporary standards, particularly in the New England woods, and make evident Cushman's understanding of the local and provisional sense in which portions of southern New England might be said to be "empty." Far from a disorganized chaos, the region is (if anything) overadministered, with Massasoit's confederacy, Narragansett power, the Massachusetts alliances, and the newly arrived English all working out their complex interrelationships in the pages of these early narratives emanating from Plymouth.[32]

Cushman's language in the 1622 *Relation* would appear to suggest that the colonists had broadly applied what Anthony Pagden terms "the principle of attachment" in their adjustment to the unexpected complexity of Indian culture, incorporating Massasoit into a neofeudal system of subordination to the English crown and employing English legal terminology to characterize the understanding they had reached with the Indians concerning their occupancy of land made vacant when the Patuxet people were destroyed by disease.[33] But Cushman is writing for an English readership whose continuing support is essential for the survival of Plymouth Plantation. In the atmosphere of tactical duplicity that had produced the Mayflower Compact, it is difficult to assess the extent to which Cushman or the rest of the colony's leadership took seriously this nominal assertion of English hegemony.

As Edward Winslow later observes, southern New England is literally marked with evidence of the Indians' historical consciousness—with a structure of oral discourses that document an "antiquity" to their civilization in some degree commensurate with the antiquities that played a formative role in the development of English historiography in the closing decades of the sixteenth century. Moreover, Cushman speculates in the preface to his sermon that "God hath some great worke to doe" toward the natives of North America. The coldness, carnality, and conflict of Europe may even prompt the Lord to transfer his future favor to this "new" people, rather than to the small party of English exiles at Plymouth, even as Christ in rebuking the Pharisees claimed that he could "rayse up children unto Abraham" out of stones.[34]

It is unlikely that Cushman meant this possibility as anything more than an incitement to the well-disposed English reader to abandon the internecine conflicts of the Old World for a newer and less bitterly divided one. England is surfeited with people, Cushman argues in the closing pages of the 1622 *Relation:* "the straitnes of the place is such as each man is faine to plucke his meanes as it were out of his neighbours throat" (70). New England does not offer the "dainties" of Europe, perhaps, but neither does it contain overflowing hospitals or almshouses and a swelling population of beggars. For "honest, godly, and industrious" emigrants, Cushman affirms that there is "plainenesse and plentifulnesse" to be had across the sea, provided "they would learne to use the world as they used it not," as pilgrims rather than as possessors.[35]

These moral imperatives receive concentrated attention in the body of Cushman's sermon, printed in the same year as the *Relation.* Unlike his defense of emigration, which directed its energy toward English readers alone, the sermon is initially aimed at the new colonists to whom Cushman preached it on December 9, 1621. Its anonymous publication in London reflects his awareness that though its substance might conceivably attract the kind of emigrant whom the colonists were actively seeking, he was not in fact authorized to "preach," according to the lights of the established church. Cushman's comments fall into the category of lay prophecy—a theologically democratic practice of many dissenting congregations in England and in the Netherlands to which English ecclesiastical authorities strenuously objected.[36] Under the conniving title of "sermon," then, and shielded by anonymity, Cushman makes clear that the disease of self-love is not confined to the overcrowded shores of England. The settlers of Plymouth also need to be reminded of their obligation to live for a higher end. Employing as his text a verse from 1 Corinthians—"Let no man seeke his owne, But every man anothers wealth"—Cushman marshals a wide array of biblical citations to dramatize and to subdue what he terms the "belly-god" of human desire: the insatiable appetite for self-gratification that "shameth not to swallow all."[37]

This use of hunger in a sweeping metaphorical indictment of all human pride and willfulness must have struck home to a congregation of perpetually hungry English colonists in the early winter of 1621. Despite its heavy marginal apparatus of biblical references and rhetorical guideposts, Cushman's text was clearly intended for the ear rather than for the eye, for the listener rather than the reader. Its salient observations are conveyed by proverbs that easily lodge in the listener's memory: the selfish will readily give a penny "so as it may advantage them a pound"; they blow the bellows hard "when they have an Iron of their owne heating"; men write their own good actions in brass, those of others in ashes; a selfless man is a natural wonder, a black swan or a white crow; measure your own actions against those of the best, not of the most.[38] If in one respect self-love resembled hunger, Cushman suggests, in a still more traditional sense it was a disease—another relentless enemy of human happiness with which the Plymouth settlers were only too familiar. Indeed, Cushman asserts, "God himselfe hath cast all our waters, and felt all our pulses, and pronounced us all dangerously sicke" with self. The Lord is pictured as an intimate diagnostician, who does not hesitate to study his patient's urine in search of the cause of his ailment. Cushman draws his language from the most vivid and homely sources at his disposal.[39]

He draws too on the long Dutch background that many of the colonists shared, by condemning the "particularizing" appetites of selfishness in human character as emanations of Satan. The healthy subordination of the self to the communal good Cushman labels as "this generalitie," an imported coinage that sounds anomalous to a purely English ear but which a former citizen of Leiden might readily recognize as a version of the "generalitiets" that subsumed the individual autonomy of the seven states that formed the Dutch Republic. Less anomalous, perhaps, were Cushman's calculated echoes of Paul's incitement to charity in Romans 12, which echo in turn the preaching of Christ. "What then must you doe," Cushman asks his New England congregation, to restrain the appetite of the belly-god?

May you live as retired Hermites? and looke after no body? Nay, you must seeke still
the wealth of one another; And enquire as *David*, how liveth such a man? How is he
clad? How is he fed? He is my brother, my associate; we ventered our lives together
here, and had a hard brunt of it, and we are in league together, is his labour harder
then mine? surely, I will ease him; hath he no bed to lie on? why, I have two, Ile lend
him one; hath he no apparel? why, I have two suits, Ile give him one of them; eates he
course fare, bread and water, and I have better? why, surely we will part stakes: He is
as good a man as I, and we are bound each to other, so that his wants must be my
wants, his sorrowes my sorrowes, his sicknes my sicknes, and his welfare my welfare,
for I am as he is.[40]

A number of practical motives lie behind this ethical charge, in Cushman's view.
Unsolicited charity will prevent the loss of dignity and social cohesion associated
with begging. The equal bearing of economic burdens encourages all equally. Present need, prudent self-interest, and the example of Christ unite to recommend the
generous example that Cushman describes.

If others are idle, he suggests, then strive to "construe things in the best part."
Perhaps they have hidden physical or psychological weaknesses that hamper them:
"All men have not strength, skill, faculty, spirit, and courage to worke alike" (17).
Perhaps the fellowship of diligent neighbors will help cure them. In the case of
incorrigible and willful drones, he urges, do not nurse your resentments "whisper-
ingly" among yourselves, but "prove them idle" before the Governor, who will "keepe
back their bread" if they obstinately refuse to work: "And as you are a body together,
so hang not together by skins and gymocks, but labour to be joynted together and
knit by flesh and synewes; away with envie at the good of others, and rejoyce in his
good, and sorrow for his evill, let his joy bee thy joy, and his sorrow thy sorrow: let
his sicknesse be thy sicknesse: his hunger thy hunger; his povertie thy povertie: And
if you professe friendship, be friends in adversities; for then a friend is knowne, and
tryed, and not before."[41] Eight years after the appearance of Cushman's sermon,
John Winthrop would make a virtually identical application of religious ideals and
biblical texts to colonial experience in "A Modell of Christian Charity," exhorting
the Massachusetts Bay emigrants to remain "knitt together . . . in brotherly Affec-
cion." It seems likely that he modeled his own model, at least to some degree, on
Robert Cushman's fervent moral aspirations for life in Plymouth.[42]

℈

THE LAST OF THE FAMILY of texts to which Bradford alludes in his
chronicle for 1621 in *Of Plimmoth Plantation* is Edward Winslow's *Good Newes from*

New-England. Winslow had returned to London on the *Anne* in September 1623, to report to the colony's investors, to buy trading supplies, and to carry his manuscript account of recent events in the plantation to the same London bookseller, John Bellamie, who had arranged the publication of the 1622 *Relation.* Unlike the earlier work, Winslow's text is full of references to divine dispositions of Providence, intervening repeatedly in the destiny of the colony, but most of his attention in these pages is devoted to key turning points during the spring of 1623, when the colonists took their destiny directly into their own hands. Unlike Brewster or Bradford, Winslow never played a significant public role in Plymouth's religious life. He became, instead, the colony's most effective diplomat, an early student of Indian languages and culture, and a vigorous defender of New England political policy in the London press. Some of Winslow's emphasis on providential care, throughout *Good Newes from New England,* springs from these diplomatic instincts, reflecting his sense of an implicit conflict between the competing images of a self-reliant and a God-reliant community. He was, at the same time, only too aware that one of the most exacting readers of his narrative would be John Robinson, who chafed at the obstacles that continued to prevent him from joining his old neighbors at Plymouth.

The purpose of Winslow's brief book is to address the "vile and clamorous reports" about New England that had been brought back to London by some of the survivors of Thomas Weston's disbanded colony at Wessagusset—reports that apparently attacked the integrity of Plymouth as well as the peaceful intentions of the Indians living at Massachusetts Bay. Winslow makes clear that Weston's colonists were largely responsible for their own mistreatment. In the process of provoking the hostility of the Massachusetts people by pilfering corn and by begging, Weston's men had nearly precipitated a war of extermination against all the English living in the region, including the colonists at Plymouth. According to Winslow's official view of events, God "wrought our peace for us" when the colonists were "at the pits brim, and in danger to be swallowed up." But God works, in this instance, through a number of extraordinary scenes and human intermediaries that Winslow's pages bring to life, including Winslow himself, Miles Standish, and a group of individual leaders among the Indians who are both friendly and hostile to the English.[43]

Whereas the 1622 *Relation* incorporates an apparently heterogeneous range of episodes from the first years of the settlement, *Good Newes from New-England* concentrates the bulk of its attention on a single, dramatic action: Standish's preemptive attack on the Massachusetts Indians in late March 1623. As Plymouth's leaders must have anticipated, this blow prompts an agonized response from John

Robinson, in a letter that Bradford includes in *Of Plimmoth Plantation,* questioning whether Standish himself requires more stringent guidance from members of the colony's government who are less hardened by the mercenary experience that had shaped Standish's character. Once blood was spilled, Robinson lamented, the cycle of violence was often self-perpetuating. It had been their original intention (he forcefully reminded Plymouth's leaders) to convert the Indians, not to kill them. This moving rebuke has, to a significant degree, eclipsed the narrative that prompted it—obscuring, in the process, a number of features that Robinson's letter shares with, and may even derive from, the story that Winslow tells. Robinson is both a distant adviser to the colony, which he still hopes someday to join, and a reader of *Good Newes from New-England.* In many respects his reading is a clue to the subtlety and power of Winslow's account.

The impetus for Standish's aggression springs from Massasoit, who reveals to Hobomock a plot organized by the Massachusetts people to destroy Thomas Weston's plantation at Wessagusset. This claim is the central contention of Winslow's pages. A series of late-winter excursions to purchase surplus corn from the Indian settlements in Cape Cod Bay had already suggested to Plymouth's leaders that, for some reason, their reception and their treatment by the people whom they visited had grown markedly cool since the previous year. The reason for the change does not become clear until the colonists, hearing that Massasoit is dying, decide to send Winslow, Hobomock, and John Hamden (a temporary resident of the colony) to visit him, "it being a commendable manner of the Indians," Winslow writes, "for all that profess friendship to them, to visit them in their extremity." The decision is not strictly an act of charity. On the instructions of Bradford and others, Winslow also hoped to have an opportunity to confer with some Dutch traders, who would be paying their formal respects to Massasoit as well. But by the time Winslow arrives at Sowams, Massasoit's residence, the Dutch are already gone, and the delegation from Plymouth finds only the ailing chief, apparently near death, in a house crowded with Indians. Eight women are chafing Massasoit's limbs, while the native shamans are making a "hellish" noise, trying to drive his sickness from him.[44]

In the pages that follow, Winslow records his own medical treatment of Massasoit in striking detail. He begins with an exchange of greetings, once the Indians in attendance inform their leader "that his friends the English were come to see him." Massasoit has lost his vision, and when he asks who his visitor is "they told him *Winsnow* (for they cannot pronounce the letter l; but ordinarily n in the place therof) hee desired to speake with me; when I came to him, and they told him of it, he put forth his hand to me, which I tooke; then he said twice, though very inwardly, *keen Winsnow,* which is to say, Art thou *Winslow?* I answered, *ahhe,* that is, yes; then hee doubled these words, *Matta nean wonckanet namen Winsnow;* that is to say, *O Winslow I shall never see thee againe*."[45] This patch of dialogue marks the beginning of an extraordinary use of representational time. Winslow's brief narrative has a complex sequence of events to present, if he is to establish the circumstances prompting Miles Standish's attack and successfully refute the accusations of Weston's allies. He chooses, nevertheless, to dwell on this preliminary visit to Sowams, dramatically slowing the pace of his story in order to accommodate an absorption in the details of a sick chamber that greatly exceeds in scope Winslow's subsequent account of Standish's attack itself.

After the initial exchange of greetings, Winslow asks Massasoit if he would try to eat some food that he had brought from Plymouth, "a confection of many comfortable conserves" that Winslow has to insert through his patient's clenched jaws on the point of a knife—an excruciating picture that will acquire still more dramatic value once Winslow's reader advances to the account of the violence at Wessagusset a few pages later. When Massasoit is able to swallow this nourishment, his people, "much rejoyced" at such a promising sign, inform Winslow that Massasoit has not been able to eat for two days:

> Then I desired to see his mouth, which was exceedingly furred, and his tongue swelled in such manner, as it was not possible for him to eat such meat as they had, his passage being stopt up: then I washed his mouth, and scraped his tongue, and got abundance of corruption out of the same. After which, I gave him more of the confection, which he swallowed, with more readinesse; then he desiring to drinke, I dissolved some of it in water, and gave him thereof: within halfe an houre this wrought a great alteration in him in the eyes of all that beheld him; presently after his sight began to come to him, which gave him and us good encouragement."[46]

The inconspicuous "us" in the passage above suggests how quickly human alignments have begun to grow productively imprecise, as the narrative unfolds, allowing for the incorporation of Indians and English alike in a community of concern for the dangerously sick man in their midst. How has Massasoit slept, Winslow inquires of the people who have been tending him. When did he last have a stool? The Indians reply that he has not slept in two days and has had no stool in five. Winslow then administers more of his confection, mixed with water, and sends a letter by runner to Plymouth asking for additional "physic" from the colony's physician, Samuel Fuller, and for some chickens to make broth. Meanwhile he makes a vegetable stock out of bruised corn, strawberry leaves, and sassafras root, strains it through his pocket handkerchief, and gives it to his patient, with excellent results. Massasoit is able to get some sleep and "had three moderate stools."

The following morning a much improved Massasoit asks Winslow to treat a number of other people in Sowams who are also sick, and Winslow complies "with willingness," cleaning out their mouths and feeding them as he has Massasoit, "though it were much offensive to me, not being accustomed with such poysonous savours." The chickens from Plymouth had not yet arrived, so Winslow kills a duck for soup, but before Hobomock can skim away the fat from the kettle, according to Winslow's instructions, Massasoit "made a grosse meale of it" and experiences a relapse, vomiting up the broth and suffering an alarming nosebleed. Once the bleeding ceases, much to Winslow's relief, Massasoit is again able to sleep. Bleeding and purging were the most universally applied therapeutic techniques in seventeenth-century medicine, so Winslow feels some confidence that this apparent turn for the worse may prove to be beneficial in the end, and he reassures Massasoit's anxious friends:

> when he awaked I washed his face, and bathed and suppled his beard and nose with a linnen cloth: but on a sudden he chopt his nose in the water, and drew up some therein, and sent it forth againe with such violence, as he began to bleed afresh, then they thought there was no hope, but we perceived it was but the tendernesse of his nostrill, and therefore told them I thought it would stay presently, as indeed it did.
>
> The messengers were now returned, but finding his stomacke come to him, he would not have the chickens killed, but kept them for breed. Neither durst wee give him any physicke which was then sent, because his body was so much altered since our instructions, neither saw we any need, not doubting now of his recovery, if he were carefull.[47]

Massasoit is clearly himself again, taking abrupt measures to free his nose of clots from the previous day's bleeding and adopting a thrifty approach to the chickens that are no longer to be thoughtlessly squandered making soup.

His gratitude for Winslow's care leads him to reaffirm, in public, his loyalty to the English and to reveal the Massachusetts plot, in private, to Hobomock, with instructions for passing the information on to Plymouth. In conformity with the self-effacing standards of his day, Winslow dutifully apologizes to the reader of *Good Newes* for dwelling on these domestic scenes. Indeed, it would have been possible to account for Massasoit's disclosure much more quickly, sacrificing the wealth of intimate detail that Winslow provides, but at considerable cost to the circumstantial density and homely beauty of his prose. As with most complex narrative, the meaning is in the details. Albeit with some mixture of motives and of feelings, Winslow has enacted the religious ideals of charity and mutual support that Robert Cushman advocated in his 1622 sermon, that John Robinson invoked in his letter of advice to the *Mayflower*'s passengers, and to which Robinson would return in his critical response to Standish's preemptive attack. In key respects, this portion of Winslow's account, too, is preemptive. It offers in the form of his attentive nursing a persuasive counterweight to Standish's militancy. The physical conflict to come is significantly mitigated by the physical solicitude of the healing encounter that precedes it.

Massasoit's information is accompanied by the advice that the English strike first and "kill the men of Massachuset who were the authors of this intended mischief." His recommendation reflects his grasp of the psychology of Plymouth's leaders, as well as his familiarity with Indian policy in war. Once the Massachusetts people attack Weston's men, Massasoit explains, they will feel committed to striking at all the English in the region, who would otherwise (in conformity with Indian expectations) be compelled to revenge the initial, and perhaps justifiable, assault. Native warfare tended to be cyclic and to run through kinship networks in much this fashion, among the Algonquian peoples of southern New England as among their Iroquois neighbors to the west, whose Great League of Peace originated as an attempt to break just such a relentless linkage of conflict and revenge among the original tribes of their confederacy. This perceived necessity to assault both Wessagusset and Plymouth at once explains the attempts that the Massachusetts people have made to involve all the neighboring towns of the Wampanoag confederacy in their plan. Knowing that Plymouth's leaders were opposed to anything but a defensive war, Massasoit instructs Hobomock to stress that if Plymouth waits until Weston's settlement is attacked, it will be too late to save themselves. The mechanisms of a revenge cycle will have been set irrevocably in motion. Once blood has been spilled—as both Massasoit and John Robinson clearly understand—it leads almost inevitably to more bloodshed: "And therefore he counselled without delay to take away the principals, and then the plot would cease."[48]

The principals in question are two prominent individuals among the Massachusetts people, Wituwamat and Pecksuot, who are the first of Standish's victims in a trap that he sets, after the leaders of Plymouth agree to follow Massasoit's advice. Wituwamat in particular is (in Winslow's words) "a notable insulting villain," who liked to taunt the English with his knife, "on the end of the handle [of which] there was pictured a woman's face": "but sayd hee, I have another at home wherewith I have killed both *French* and *English,* and that hath a mans face on it, and by and by these two must marry: Further hee sayd of that knife hee there had; *Hinnaim namen, hinnaim michen, matta cuts:* that is to say, By and by it should see, and by and by it should eate, but not speake."[49] The phonetic accuracy of Winslow's Algonquin is less important than his determination to present Wituwamat in his own voice, expressing passions and intentions that are individual rather than collective or tribal. This is (Winslow implies) a conflict that is personal rather than cultural in origin. As if in conformity with Wituwamat's wishes, the battle that ensues shortly afterward is, indeed, largely speechless.

Standish strikes without warning at Pecksuot, a large man who has mocked Standish's height, and kills him with Pecksuot's own knife. Wituwamat and one other are killed by the rest of Standish's men, after a long and (Winslow emphasizes) grimly silent struggle. In all, seven Indians die, and the conspiracy dissolves. Standish disperses the remainder of Weston's men, giving them enough corn to reach the English fishing fleet, where they can find safe passage home. He and his companions bring Wituwamat's severed head back to Plymouth. Winslow reports that the Indians of Cape Cod Bay who had been parties to the Massachusetts plot were thrown into such a panic, when word of Standish's attack and its gruesome trophy reached them, that they abandoned their villages and fields, eventually falling victim to outbreaks of disease that killed, among others, Aspinet and Iyanough, the two sachems who had played memorable roles in the recovery of John Billington two years earlier.

This is in every respect an extraordinary narrative, not least in the suggestive disparity between the title that Winslow has chosen and the story that he tells. In what conceivable sense do these events amount to "good news from New England," and how could Winslow have hoped that his pages would ultimately encourage the kind of disciplined, spiritually earnest immigrant whom he and Cushman strove to reach? Winslow himself recognizes that many of his readers "wilt rather marvell that I deale so plainly, then in any way doubt of the truth of this my Relation, yea it may be tax me therewith, as seeming rather to discourage men, then any way to further so noble an action." His pages do nothing to disguise the chronic shortages of food that the colonists struggled with for the first years of their residence. The demoralization of Weston's men vividly displays how fragile the social fabric can become among these transplanted English. The example of Wituwamat indicates that the native people can sometimes articulate their anger as eloquently as the colonists do their well-intentioned Christian ideals. The ambush that Standish orchestrates, Winslow admits, lacks the spirit of open, frank defiance that characterized the colony's unambiguous reply to the Narragansett threats. Instead, the English choose to adopt what they consider to be the Indian practice of subterfuge: "to take them in such traps as they lay for others." It is not an ennobling picture of English valor.[50]

Such plain dealing, however—as Winslow clearly recognized—was also responsible for the impact of his narrative. "If any honest minde be discouraged" by this account, Winslow notes, "I am sorry." As he emphasizes in his dedicatory address, "To All Wel-willers and Furtheres of Plantations in *New-England*," his aim is to offer a "true" relation, not a euphoric one—to rebuke "the vaine expectation of present profit" in the merchants who financed English colonies hoping for rapid and lucrative returns, to chasten ambition in colonial leaders, to urge that prospective settlers be carefully screened to exclude "profane men, who being but seeming Christians, have made Christ and Christianity stinke in the nostrils of the poore Infidels." Such language briefly reduces the multiplicity and complexity of Indian life to little more than a trite epithet, but in fact Winslow's pages treat Weston's men in this dismissive fashion, not the Indians. Massasoit's individuality is a vivid presence in *Good Newes from New-England*, both during his direct contact with Winslow and through the eulogy that Hobomock delivers on Massasoit's behalf when the party traveling from Plymouth are initially misinformed that Massasoit has already died:

> In the way, Hobbamock manifesting a troubled spirit, brake forth into these speeches, *Neen womasu Sagimus, neen womasu Sagimus*, &c. My loving *Sachim*, my loving *Sachim*. Many have I knowne, but never any like thee: And turning him to me said; Whilest I lived, I should never see his like amongst the *Indians*, saying, he was no lyer, he was not bloudy and cruell like other *Indians;* In anger and passion he was soone reclaimed, easie to be reconciled towards such as had offended him, ruled by reason in such measure, as he would not scorne the advice of meane men, and that he governed his men better with few strokes than others did with many; truly loving where he loved; yea he feared we had not a faithfull friend left among the *Indians*, shewing how he oft-times restrained their malice, &c. continuing a long speech with such signes of lamentation and unfeigned sorrow, as it would have made the hardest heart relent.[51]

The marked resemblance between Hobomock's praise here and the values expressed in John Robinson's advisory letter at the beginning of the 1622 *Relation* suggests that Winslow, in preserving this speech, might also have modified it. Massasoit too appears to emphasize the charitable covering of offenses and the honoring of authority even in "meane" persons.

If this eulogy is indeed another instance of Pagden's principle of attachment, it is nonetheless remarkable for the glimpse that Winslow purports to offer of Massasoit's extraordinary gift for leadership, as well as of Hobomock's civic consciousness.[52] Attachment seems less an act of appropriation, in this passage, than a recognition of ethical reciprocity, commensurate with Winslow's recognition of the common physical bonds of humanity in the nursing scenes that follow. Even

Winslow's Indian "villains" in *Good Newes from New-England,* Wituwamat and Pecksuot, are formidable individuals, not generic "savages"; their physical vitality and courage, "not making any fearfull noyse, but catching at their weapons and striving to the last," earn a respectful tribute from their English enemies. Corbitant, Plymouth's antagonist among the Wampanoag people's subsidiary chiefs, entertains Winslow on the way back from his successful cure of Massasoit and proves himself "a notable politician, yet ful of merry jests and squibs, and never better pleased than when the like are returned againe upon him."[53]

The potential for some measure of community with the Indians seems, by the conclusion of Winslow's pages, to far exceed the menace posed by irreconcilable differences. Winslow himself shows considerable potential as a cultural go-between, the term that James Merrell has recently applied to those European and Indian figures who mediated the inevitable collisions among "strangers" in colonial North America.[54] Although not as superficially sympathetic to Indian life as Thomas Morton will prove to be, Winslow displays a capacity for personal friendship across profound ethnic barriers that is much deeper than Morton's and completely untainted by the libertine self-display associated with the host of Merry Mount. Moreover, as the text of Bradford's history repeatedly makes clear, it is not the treachery of Indians but the treachery of Englishmen that threatens the well-being of Plymouth.

John Robinson's response to Winslow's account, in the letter that Bradford transcribes into the history, stresses precisely this fact: the "provocations and invitments, by those heathenish Christians" at Weston's settlement had set the whole sequence of violent events in motion. The Indians may well have deserved their fate, Robinson admits, but the leaders of Plymouth "being no magistrats over them, were to consider, not what they deserved but what you were by necessitie constrained to inflicte." This recognition of independent sovereignties in New England suggests that Robinson has paid careful attention to Winslow's portrayal of Massasoit's character and authority. Indeed, Robinson echoes Massasoit's original advice to the Plymouth leadership, when he revealed the Massachusetts plot. An attack aimed at "on or tow principals" alone, Robinson insists, "should have been full enough, according to that approved rule, the punishmente to a few, and the fear to many" (197).

This grimly realistic view of the social efficacy of punishment indicates that Robinson's focus is more on the future than on the past. He addresses his letter to Bradford and Brewster jointly—the two magistrates of Plymouth, who are charged with the distribution of punishment and fear over their own constituency—and frames his comments on Miles Standish in such a way as to encourage Bradford, in particular, to apply them to himself:

> Upon this occasion, let me be bould to exhorte you seriously to consider of the dispossition of your captaine, whom I love, and am perswaded the Lord in great mercie and for much good hath sent you him, if you use him aright. He is a man humble and meek amongst you, and towards all in ordinarie course. But now if this be meerly from an humane spirite, ther is cause to fear that by occasion, espetially of provocation, ther may be wanting that tendernes of the life of man (made after Gods image) which is meete. It is also a thing more glorious, in men's eyes, then pleasing in Gods, or conveniente for Christians, to be a terrour to poore barbarous people; and indeed I am afraid least by these occasions, others should be drawne to affecte a kind of rufling course in the world. I doubt not but you will take in good part these things which I write, and as ther is cause make use of them. (197–98)

Robinson clearly fears that Standish's humility and meekness may prove as superficial as John Lyford's pious display shortly proves to be, not because Standish is (like Lyford) a hypocrite, but because he is human. Virtue that is not rooted in profound, religious change may buckle under provocation; one conspicuous model of pride or passion may seduce others to an equally destructive course. These observations are initially prompted by Standish's behavior, but they clearly apply to anyone who might be drawn to affect a ruffling course in the world, not only to the volatile temperament of Plymouth's "Captaine." Robinson's gift for offering tactful but penetrating advice is apparent in this letter. Equally apparent are the lessons that he has learned concerning how communities may be seduced or provoked into betraying their founding covenants. This larger contest between principled coherence and fragmentation is the story that Bradford chooses to emphasize in *Of Plimmoth Plantation,* a contest fueled by the terrifying inconsistencies of the human spirit.

THE YEAR FOLLOWING Winslow's return to England, carrying his account of Plymouth's wonderful "preservation and continuance," is marked by a range of disputes and disagreements that nearly shatter the small settlement. This interplay of contradictory forces—preservation and dissolution, "continuance" and collapse—is seldom far from the center of Bradford's design. The most dramatic of the challenges that the colony faces is John Lyford's attempt to subvert its leadership and to slander its reputation with Plymouth's financial backers in England.

But division and faction had broken out, both among the colonists and their investors, long before Lyford's appearance. Thomas Weston's first letter to Plymouth, in early July 1621, had accused the weak and disease-ridden new settlers of wasting time "in discoursing, arguing, and consulting" among themselves, rather than in loading the *Mayflower,* the previous winter, with a profitable cargo for her return voyage—an omission that, in Weston's graphic and revealing language, was "worthily distasted" by London's profit-hungry merchants (129).

Bradford convincingly refutes this ungenerous charge, but other parties to Plymouth's enterprise besides the London merchants were eager for personal profit. By 1624, despite broad satisfaction among the settlers with Bradford's leadership, some of the company who had been seduced by the example of Weston's independent planters and traders grew so discontented that "nothing would satisfie them, excepte they might be suffered to be in their perticular allso; and made great offers, so they might be freed from the generall" (188).

This initial, short-lived secession at Plymouth proves to be the harbinger of a more serious faction among the English investors themselves, which Bradford introduces through a letter from James Sherley, one of the company of merchant adventurers. It is the first of many messages from this correspondent, over the next eighteen years, that progressively disclose Sherley's duplicity and self-interest. God has stirred up the hearts of the investors (Sherley rather dramatically reports) to send the *Charitie,* the ship that carried his letter, with much-needed supplies and people to strengthen the colony. At the same time that he makes this announcement, Sherley also describes the actions of "malcontented persons and turbulent spirits" in England who opposed sending John Robinson to New England and who had initially appeared determined to thwart all efforts to help the colony thrive. These "restles opposers of all goodnes," Sherley calls them, and "continuall disturbers of our frendly meetings and love," in their "furie," have begun to circulate "scandale and false reports" to undermine confidence that Plymouth will ever be profitable to its backers (190–91).

These first signs of trouble are somehow smoothed over, and Sherley reassures his New England readers that he and his fellow merchant adventurers drank a friendly bottle of wine together, once their differences had been resolved. "Thus God can turne the harts of men when it pleaseth him," he concludes with some complacency (191). But the contrast between this formulaic expression and the rancor among the investors that Sherley had exposed is as striking as that between the name of the *Charitie* itself and the uncharitable sentiments that had very nearly prevented its voyage. Although Bradford copies Sherley's letter into the history a few pages before he adds John Robinson's response to Winslow's narrative—the two letters had arrived in Plymouth together—it is clear that the piety that Sherley so glibly expresses may well prove to be as fragile as Miles Standish's humility. Robinson's principled advice and Sherley's self-congratulatory report are carefully incorporated into the narrative sequence in such a way that they can illuminate one another at the same time that they point to deeper unities beneath the surface of events.

A letter from Robert Cushman, also delivered by the *Charitie,* introduces three new emigrants to the colony, whose mixed qualities underscore both the division of loyalties among the merchant adventurers and the temperamental opposition between James Sherley and John Robinson. The adventurers had sent to Plymouth a ship carpenter, a salt-maker, and (at long last) a minister, on all three of whom Cushman offers provisional but very telling judgments:

> This ship carpenter is thought to be the fittest man for you in the land and will no doubte doe you much good, Let him have an absolute comand over his servants and such as you put to him. Let him build you 2. catches, a lighter, and some 6. or 7. shalops, as soone as you can. The salt-man is a skillfull and industrious man, put some to him, that may quickly apprehende the misterie of it. The preacher we have sent is (we hope) an honest plaine man, though none of the most eminente and rare. Aboute chusing him into office use your owne liberty and discretion; he knows he is no officer amongst you, though perhaps custome and universalitie may make him forget him selfe. Mr. Winslow and my selfe gave way to his going, to give contente to some hear, and we see no hurt in it, but only his great charge of children. (192)

Cushman's unreserved confidence in the carpenter proves well-founded, but unfortunately this useful addition to the colony dies of a fever after finishing only two shallops and a lighter. The hewn timber that he carefully prepared for two catches went to waste in the absence of the carpenter's skills, both as a craftsman and as a manager of the workmen whom the colony put under his supervision. The salt-maker, Bradford reports, turns out to be an "ignorante, foolish, self-willed fellow," full of promises and excuses but finally incompetent (203). Cushman is mistaken in his praise for this man, but some hint of his true nature must have led Cushman to recommend that the colonists try to learn the "misterie" of his business, on their own, as soon as possible.

Cushman's and Winslow's joint doubts about the minister are fully borne out by Lyford's egregious abuse of the colonists' confidence over the next year. Of all the materials necessary to the ongoing support of a New England plantation, its human materials are the most unpredictable and unstable elements, a perception that Bradford quietly emphasizes by drawing his reader's attention to the transformation of hewn ship timbers into waste wood by the untimely death of Plymouth's new carpenter. Labor to be "joynted" together, Robert Cushman had advised the colonists in his 1621 sermon—an incitement to social carpentry in which the London financial partners were fully expected to participate. Bradford's chronicle of the events of 1623 and 1624 progressively exposes how imperfect that "labor" could prove to be.

Cushman's, Sherley's, and Robinson's letters all arrive on the *Charitie,* the verbal and human cargo of which grows increasingly complex and intricately interwoven the more Bradford unpacks it. Sherley attaches to his account of newly restored amity among the adventurers a long bill of objections against the colony and the country itself, which appears to belie his claim that God had put to rest the turbulent spirits and malcontents in London. Bradford replies to twelve of these objections, in the pages of the history that immediately precede John Robinson's pointed criticism of Standish's preemptive attack at Wessagusset. Indeed, the imaginary dialogue that Bradford stages with Sherley's complaints becomes at once a refuge from Robinson's more painful rebuke and an implicit reminder, before the fact, that those who live in European cities (whether London or Leiden) should not be too quick to judge those who have to cope with the exigencies of the American woods. The dialogue that he returned to James Sherley, Bradford reports, "did so confound the objecters, as some confessed their falte, and others deneyed what they had said, and eate their words." Still others eventually emigrated to New England "and here lived to convince them selves sufficiently, both in their owne and other men's judgments" that their criticisms had been unmerited (193).

John Robinson was destined never to be among those emigrants who lived to recognize their misperceptions, nor is it conceivable that Bradford meant these pages as an indirect attempt to make Robinson "eat" his words, as he hoped to make Sherley's colleagues eat theirs. But an unstable mixture of deference and resentment lingers in the narrative sequence that Bradford establishes, particularly as he addresses the last three objections that Sherley forwarded from the London investors:

> 10. ob: The cuntrie is anoyed with foxes and woules.
>
> Ans: So are many other good cuntries too; but poyson, traps, and other such means will help to destroy them.
>
> 11. ob: The Dutch are planted nere Hudsons Bay, and are likly to overthrow the trade.
>
> Ans: They will come and plante in these parts, also, if we and others doe not, but goe home and leave it to them. We rather commend them, then condemne them for it.
>
> 12. ob: The people are much anoyed with musketoes.

Ans: They are too delicate, and unfitte to begine new-plantations and collonies, that
cannot enduer the biting of a muskeeto; we would wish such to keepe at home, till
at least they be muskeeto proofe. Yet this place is as free as any; and experience
teacheth that the more the land is tild, and the woods cut downe, the fewer ther
will be, and in the end scarse any at all. (196)

It is difficult to overlook the darker implications that these spirited answers acquire
once Bradford links them (as he promptly does) to Robinson's recapitulation of the
bloodshed at Wessagusset the previous spring, when it seemed as if the colonists
might come to view the human and nonhuman inhabitants of New England as
indistinguishable. Having "despatcht" Sherley's complaints, like a cloud of mos-
quitoes, Bradford turns to Robinson's letter as if its concerns too might, for a
moment, resemble little more than another annoyance to be brushed aside. This
impression is a fleeting but unmistakable acknowledgment of Robinson's psychological acuity when he points to Miles Standish as an instance of how vulnerable
human virtue often proves to be to the sudden assaults of provocation.

Bradford numbers the twelve objections from the merchant adventurers in
roughly descending order of importance, from questions about religious practices,
at the beginning of the list, to these complaints about annoying mosquitos at the
end. This descent to peevishness makes the objectors appear to be quibbling or
insincere even in their more substantive worries, but Bradford's replies never seize
on this artificial tactical advantage to dismiss the criticisms wholesale. To the most
serious objections concerning "diversitie," or conflict, over religion, neglect of family duties on the Sabbath, and want of the two sacraments recognized by the
reformed churches, Bradford gives a variety of carefully measured replies, ranging
from positive denial to conditional agreement that emphasizes important mitigat-
ing circumstances. It is true, for example, that the colonists have lacked the sacraments of baptism and communion since their emigration to New England: "The
more is our greefe," Bradford pointedly observes, "that our pastor is kept from us."
Those who reported to the adventurers that the colonists neglected family religious
duties on the Sabbath "should have shewed their Christian love the more if they
had in love tould the offenders of it; rather then thus to reproach them behind their
baks." The colony countenances no such neglect, but "family duties" (Bradford
implies) are not always objects of public scrutiny (194).

To accusations that Plymouth's children were not properly educated or cate-
chized, Bradford replies that the parents "take pains with their owne as they can,"
though it is true that they have yet to find a "fitt person" and the adequate means
to maintain a common school. Many of the particular members of the plantation

do not work as hard as they might for the general benefit, Bradford concedes to one objection, but all do work, "and he that doth worst gets his owne foode and something besids." Criticism of Plymouth's water, soil, and fish gets rather curt treatment from Bradford: the water is wholesome enough, the cattle as fat as need be on the grass from Plymouth's meadows, and if the fish are deficient in any way (he wonders) why do "so many sayle of ships come yearly a fishing" to New England waters? The tone of the replies is conciliatory, oppositional, candid, and bemused by turns—handling these obvious attempts to disparage the colony with a measured and impressively humane display of temperamental and rhetorical resources.

Only once does Bradford permit any indication of anger in his replies. To the objection that many of the colonists are "theevish and steale on from another," he responds by directing the criticism to its source: "Would London had been free from that crime; then we should not have been trobled with these here; It is well knowne sundrie have smarted well for it, and so are the rest like to doe, if they be taken" (195). Bradford appears to have taken to heart John Robinson's endorsement of that "approved rule: The punishmente to a few, and the fear to many." He appears also to have noted Robinson's warning that provocation can lead people to violate the principles of self-restraint and charity by which they hope to live. The adventurers' objections are a protracted instance of just such provocation, to which Bradford's verbal composure appears more than equal. Even if these moments of self-realization were not immediate—as they undoubtedly were not—Bradford brings the relevant letters and replies into such close narrative proximity to one another that a patient reader can forge the necessary links among them.

In this sense, *Of Plimmoth Plantation* dramatizes its own retrospective construction. One cannot know how Bradford in fact reacted when he first opened James Sherley's unctuous letter, with its attached bill of complaints, or what mixture of feelings Robinson's sharp critique of the Wessasgusset attack may have originally aroused. But the sequence of documents that Bradford presents, as he begins his account of the events of 1624, is carefully and unobtrusively stitched together in the pages of the history, to emphasize what John Robinson too had stressed in his original letter of advice to the *Mayflower* emigrants: the moral imperative to mitigate rather than inflame the offenses that social experience inevitably entails. Repeated provocation must not be permitted to diminish what Robinson termed, in his review of Standish's excesses, "that tendernes of the life of man . . . which is meete" (198). This cautious phrasing itself—with its implication that tenderness must be "meete" rather than unconditional or limitless—suggests Robinson's acknowledgment of the ceaseless interchange, in individual and collective life, between the principled and the unprincipled dimensions of human character.

❧

BRADFORD TURNS from his examination of the literary cargo of the *Charitie* to describe an adjustment that the leaders of the colony had agreed to make, in the spring of 1624, to their original agricultural practices. Before getting drawn into his long account of John Lyford's treachery, he revisits this gradual movement from the ideal of common property in land, which the colony had set out to follow in 1621, to a system of private ownership that takes final form three years later. This evolution, in turn, sheds light on the most celebrated of the parallel interjections that Bradford records on the blank verso pages of his manuscript: his lament on the collapse of the original emigrants' sacred communal bond. Despite striking rhetorical differences between these widely separated passages in the history, change is their common subject. Old ideals of brotherly or neighborly communion appear to deteriorate with the passage of time, prompting Bradford in the first and most impassioned of these reflective moments to decry the signs of inevitable decay, much as John Robinson had decried the breach of faith represented by the killings at Wessagusset.

Faced with what he, in turn, regards as a lapse in "constante faithfullnes," Bradford inserts into the broad "margin" of his text a conventional complaint against the mutability of human hopes. Appearing as it does very early in *Of Plimmoth Plantation,* during Bradford's account of the negotiations with the Virginia Company in 1617, this complaint often strikes readers with apocalyptic force, but its tone and its implications are quite easy to misinterpret. Like the carefully interwoven pages that surround the arrival of the *Charitie,* this moment is a complex manifestation of deliberative reading—a specific instance in which the process of recapitulation briefly stops to allow the historian to compose a response to the page before him. Bradford's fictive "dialogue" with the London investors in 1624 depicts a similar exchange, recast as "speech" in order to bring a measure of dramatic life to the pages of his book. The elegy for Plymouth's lost social and spiritual bonds is likewise a piece of public marginalia—not an unguarded expression of private anguish but a natural consequence of the presence of Bradford's own narrative on his reading wheel. "When such things fall out in men and women as you suspected not," Robinson had written in his letter to the *Mayflower* passengers, "do not be inordinately affected with them" (80). By and large, Bradford follows this equable advice even where his affections and ideals appear to be deeply engaged.

The decisive shift in the colony's land policy in 1624 is an early sign of the diminishment in communal feeling that Bradford later comes to regret, but in this instance he clearly presents change itself as constructive rather than cataclysmic. It is part of a process of adaptation, not attrition, in which the social gains and losses fall into balance with one another. Of these two attitudes toward the outcome of historical forces, it is the second that Bradford most consistently incorporates into the pages of his book. With only rare exceptions, *Of Plimmoth Plantation* embraces transformation rather than stasis as its highest value, much as the original party of worshipers in Scrooby had done when they formed their uniquely provisional church "estate."

The triumph of private ownership, Bradford notes with considerable equanimity, "maks me remember a saing of Seneca's, *Epis:* 123. *That a great parte of libertie is a well governed belly, and to be patient in all wants*" (200). The colonists of Plymouth had discovered, from their first good harvest of 1623, that patience was far easier to come by, and the belly easier to govern, if each household were free to grow its own crops, rather than to work as parts of an agricultural collective. In that year every family had been allotted its own parcel of land, "only for present use," in response to widespread discontent with the earlier policy of common holdings and a common harvest. "Let none objecte this is mens corruption," Bradford admonished his reader, as he described this initial compromise—mindful, perhaps, of his own tendency to pen critical notes in the margins. "I answer seeing all men have this coruption in them, God in his wisdome saw another course fiter for them" (164). The conversational structure of "objection" and "answer," like Seneca's epistolary "sayings," sustains a sense of rich verbal community in this passage, even as Bradford proceeds to describe the further centrifugal adjustments that take place the following year, when the colonists decide that plots assigned for the duration of only a single growing season were also a discouragement to efficiency.

Corn had come to seem "more pretious then silver" to the settlers, both as a food crop and as a trading commodity. Accordingly they asked that land be assigned to each household "for continuance, and not by yearly lotte," so that the possessors would have an incentive to improve the soil (201). This step brings to a close the colony's brief experiment with what Bradford calls "that conceite of Platos . . . that the taking away of propertie, and bringing in communitie into a comone wealth, would make them happy and florishing" (163). In his *Six Bookes of a Commonweale*, Jean Bodin had flatly asserted that "Nothing can be publicke, where nothing is privat": "Neither [can there be] any harmonie, if the diversitie and dissimilitude of voyces, cunningly mixed together, which maketh the sweet harmony, were al brought unto one and the same tune." Communal property is "the mother of contention and discord," Bodin concluded, an observation that the experience of Plymouth had confirmed: "For that which thou shouldst dearly love must be thine owne."[55]

Plymouth's leaders agree to the proposal to make a permanent subdivision of farm land, stipulating only that the plots cluster as close to the town as possible, for mutual security, and that no further requests for expanded private holdings be made for seven years. This policy too prompts in Bradford a recollection of Pliny's nostalgic account of ancient simplicity, in the time of Romulus, when two acres and a pint of corn had satisfied the ambitions of Rome's people: "And he was not counted a good, but a dangerous man, that would not contente him selfe with 7. Acres of land" (202). Plymouth may well contain a number of potentially dangerous men, judging by this formula. Like the people of Romulus's time, however, the citizens of Plymouth, during the early years of the settlement, also had to pound their corn in mortars to make their own meal. It was, Bradford recalls with some satisfaction, "many years before they could get a mille." Plymouth's appetite for land, he observes, "did make me often thinke of what I had read in Plinie," but these thoughts are as much a source of consolation as of concern. Bradford is prepared to accommodate the lessons of experience and the consequences of growth, without abandoning all connection to the colony's sense of common religious purpose.

This common religious commitment had been the primary cultural capital that John Robinson was able to offer the members of the Virginia Company in 1617, when he sought a patent on behalf of the Leiden exiles to settle in North America. Bradford's description of these negotiations in *Of Plimmoth Plantation* triggers the lament that seems to belie the pragmatic spirit of his approach to the colony's hunger for private farms. In an exchange of letters with Edwin Sandys, Robinson had drawn the attention of the Virginia Company to five "instances of indusmente" that he hoped would convince the English government to support them. Robinson's first three points constitute a fairly brief characterization of the prospective emigrants. "The Lord is with us," Robinson firmly claims; we are already "enured to the difficulties of a strange and hard land" through years of exile in the Netherlands, and we are an industrious and frugal people. In the fourth inducement, Robinson describes in simple terms the core of their communal idealism: "We are knite togeather as a body in a most stricte and sacred bond and covenante of the Lord, of the violation wherof we make great conscience, and by vertue wherof we doe hould our selves straitly tied to all care of each others good, and of the whole by every one and so mutually" (42).

The original attempt to found a colony on the principle of communal property had its roots in the language of this covenant, with its sweeping assertion of the radical identity of interests among the Leiden emigrants. The collapse of Plymouth's agricultural collective by 1623, however, had already made it plain to Bradford, at least, that such idealism was inconsistent with human nature. In writing his account of the colony's early years, sometime after 1646, he had come to accept this realistic perception and to dismiss Plato's dreams as vain, but confronting Robinson's words on the page apparently reignites some lingering regret, and Bradford records his feelings of loss, much as any reader might record a vivid local response, on the blank page opposite his transcription of Robinson's letter. This appeal to the strictly covenanted nature of the Leiden emigrants, however, is not the last of the points that Robinson makes with Edwin Sandys and his fellow members of the Virginia Company.

The conscientious devotion to the collective good, in these potential colonists, is at once strengthened and chastened by the grim resolution that Robinson displays in his fifth, and final, inducement. Small discouragements and discontents, he affirms, will have no impact on a community whose experience has already exposed them to so much hardship. "We knowe our entertainmente in England, and in Holand," Robinson writes, in words that come quite close to being embittered. These emigrants will have no hope of starting life over if their American enterprise fails. Their material resources will be exhausted by the present effort, much as their very lives "are now drawing towards their periods." At the same time that they are a covenanted people, they are also, in some measure, a desperate one, with a realistic grasp of the sacrifices that inevitably accompany any attempt at a great social transformation.

A certain degree of tactical exaggeration marks this pose, but there is a considerable degree of truth in it as well. Moreover, Robinson acknowledges in the closing paragraph of his letter to Sandys that this candid disclosure of the mixture of strengths and weaknesses in the Leiden emigrants is a "bould" approach to attempt on behalf of a "despised" group of exiles who are appealing to their erstwhile persecutors for help. The relationship is at best a strained one, and Robinson's diplomatic and rhetorical skills receive a severe test over the coming months, as he equivocates with various English correspondents over the Oaths of Supremacy or Allegiance to the English crown that the emigrants might be required to take, or as he tries to cast his theological differences with the English establishment in the most innocuous light possible, in order to minimize official objections to settling such "radical" sectarians in the New World.

That such objections continued to persist in English government circles is apparent from the wary language that Edwin Sandys used in replying to the original overtures for support from Robert Cushman and John Carver. The "selecte gentlemen" from the Virginia Company had been impressed with the "good discretion" of the Leiden emissaries, Sandys observed, but they needed more time to consult with "interested" parties before coming to any decision on this unusual request.

Meanwhile, he advised Robinson and Brewster "so to directe your desires as that on your parts ther fall out no just impediments." If the Leiden petitioners were cautious and suitably deferential, Sandys went on to imply, then the English authorities (or at least "the best sorte" among them) would show "all forwardnes to set you forward," at least within reason (40). This discouragingly tentative language drew a dismissive pun from Bradford on the "sandie" foundation that such hedging support appeared to offer. John Robinson's five inducements represent an attempt to address the reservations of these select and influential gentlemen, without disguising the role that English intransigence had played in driving the Leiden exiles to seek refuge in New England. "We are well weaned from the delicate milke of our mother countrie," Robinson had observed in his reply to Sandys (42). Placed side by side with Sandys's shallow equivocations, in the pages of Bradford's manuscript, the metaphor is cutting.

Against this complex background of religious idealism and political compromise, hope and hopelessness—all incorporated into the fabric of the narrative as it treats events that took place three years before the *Mayflower* set sail—Bradford casts his famous lament on the deterioration of Plymouth's ancient fidelity and communion:

> O sacred bond, whilst inviollably preserved! how sweete and precious were the fruits that flowed from the same? But when this fidelity decayed, then their ruine approached. O that these Anciente members had not dyed, or been dissipated, (if it had been the will of God) or els that this holy care and constante faithfullnes had still lived, and remained with those that survived, and were in times afterwards added unto them. But (alass) that subtill serpente hath slylie wound in him selfe under faire pretences of necessitie and the like, to untwiste these sacred bonds and tyes, and as it were insensibly by degrees to dissolve, or in a great measure to weaken, the same. I have been happy, in my first times, to see, and with much comforte to injoye, the blessed fruits of this sweete communion. But it is now a parte of my miserie in old age, to find and feele the decay and wante therof (in a great measure), and with greefe, and sorrow of hart to lamente and bewaile the same. And for others warning and admonnition, and my owne humiliation, doe I hear note the same. (42)

Bradford links these words directly to Robinson's fourth inducement—his characterization of the covenant that binds together the Leiden church—but the structure of the passage as a whole incorporates elements from all five of Robinson's itemized replies to Edwin Sandys, with hints of Sandys's own "faire pretenses" carried over from the preceding letter as well. It is a carefully collated response not to a single instance of perceived historical change but to a densely textured passage in

Of Plimmoth Plantation. Bradford writes as both a principal witness and a reader. He is able to appreciate, in very personal terms, the impact of time upon a particular set of human bonds, but at the same time he depicts the uncanny parallel between his own immediate feelings, in all their complexity and ambivalence, and those to which Robinson was giving expression three decades earlier.

A sense of incipient decay marks Robinson's words as well as Bradford's. The sweet and precious fruits of community, for which Bradford grieves, resemble in some respects the delicate milk of mother England to which Robinson both regretfully and bitterly refers when he asserts that he and his companions have been harshly, not tenderly, weaned. The subtle serpent may have yet to invade the sanctity of Robinson's exiled congregation in 1617—as Bradford implies, through his interpolated complaint, that he has certainly invaded Plymouth—but Robinson clearly perceives himself to be entangled in subtleties that are forced upon him by the necessity of finding the money and the legal sanction to support a colony in New England.

Great changes clearly distinguish Bradford's circumstances in Plymouth plantation, near the middle of the seventeenth century, from those of John Robinson in Leiden thirty years earlier. But there are striking continuities as well, an appreciation for which leads Bradford to restrain the rhetoric of violation that he had initially invoked, in his marginal response to this episode in his book. The bonds that had seemed so irreparably broken among the New England heirs of Robinson's vision may in fact only be weakened—untwisted but not severed. The want of consolation is not complete, Bradford appears to concede, nor is the break with the past so decisive as to impair permanently the colony's prospects for a meaningful future. Something may yet be gained from warning, admonition, and humiliation—the critical experiences, recognized by all the reformed churches of Europe, that necessarily precede individual or collective renewal. In revisiting Robinson's prose, through the medium of his own pages, Bradford implicitly acknowledges that the "Anciente members" are in some measure still available for present guidance and present encouragement in the storehouse of history.

CHAPTER THREE

Artificial Persons

T HE INVIOLABLE BONDS of religious community, to which John Robinson had appealed in his effort to attract English support, were as much a rhetorical as they were a social or spiritual attribute of the Leiden exiles who hoped to establish a plantation in the "vast and unpeopled countries of America" (32). Bradford's history makes evident, in ways far less melodramatic than his retrospective lament for the loss of the colony's "sweete communion," that Robinson and his colleagues were only too aware of the compromises out of which their covenants were constructed.

On one memorable occasion, during the negotiations for an English patent, Robinson and William Brewster drafted two versions of a reply to some inquiries from the king's Privy Council and forwarded both to Sir John Wolstenholme, a sympathetic English correspondent. One version was "more breefe and generall," the other "something more large" (43). Would Wolstenholme review them, they wondered, and send on to the Privy Council the text that seemed to him most expedient? These scrupulous religious nonconformists, Robinson indicated, were quite willing to take either the 1606 Oath of Allegiance or the much older Oath of Supremacy, acknowledging King James' absolute authority over "all spiritual and ecclesiastical things or causes" in his realm, if that is what it took to secure the financial and political help that they required to prosecute their voyage.[1] Bradford prints both letters in his book—as well as a revealing account of how skeptically Wolstenholme received them—in order to recreate the pliable verbal world through which these prospective colonists were required to navigate, long before leaving home.

The initial decision to emigrate was founded upon equally pliable processes. Far from unanimous as it was, the conclusion that Robinson's congregation reached was based upon a heterogeneous collection of reasons, reflecting tactical as well as idealistic motives, and made particularly urgent by the prospect of renewed religious warfare in the Netherlands. A disorderly conjunction of cultural and historical forces came together to impel them to the decision to move. Accident finally placed them in New England, rather than in the Chesapeake or Hudson River regions, and delayed their voyage to the point where the urgencies of the season ultimately dictated the site of their settlement. If trust in Providence, operating in conjunction with conscientious religious bonds, played a vital psychological role in the early stages of Plymouth's history, equally vital roles were played by the kind of ideological and practical flexibility that Robinson and Brewster displayed in these preliminary negotiations and that Bradford later demonstrated in accommodating the colony's agricultural ideals to the demands of human nature.

The mixed character of Plymouth's experience, shaped by this collision between deep religious values and the pressures of historical circumstance, emerges most effectively and memorably from the abundance of letters that Bradford includes in his pages. Personal correspondence responds to the exigencies of the moment, exposing the processes of adaptation and compromise that Brewster and Robinson strove to practice as they wooed the support of John Wolstenholme, in the exaggerated, deferential language of the time:

> Right Worshipfull: with due acknowledgmente of our thankfullnes for your singular care and pains, in the bussines of Virginia; for our, and, we hope, the commone good. We doe remember our humble dutys unto you, and have sent inclosed (as is required) a further explanation of our judgments in the 3. points specified by some of his majesties Honorable privie counsell; and though it be greevious unto us that such unjust insinuations are made against us; yet we are most glad of the occasion of making our just purgation unto so honourable personages. (43)

Such a verbal performance, even in a good cause, must not have come easily to Robinson, who elsewhere in his work endorsed the observation of Diogenes that as tyrants were the worst of wild beasts, so flatterers were the worst of tame ones.[2] Although the tone of this letter clearly falls short of flattery, it nevertheless adopts the posture of courtly subordination that Robinson and Brewster believed to be necessary if they expected to have any success at removing what Bradford called the "many rubs that fell in the way" of their emigration plans. It does little good to rail against unjust insinuations; before an official forum like the Privy Council, a grasp of one's proper role is essential. To secure the cooperation of the English authorities, some oaths might well need to be spoken, much as a player speaks his lines, with sufficient outward conviction to satisfy the demands of an exacting audience.

Robinson and Bradford accommodated themselves to the requirements of this verbal climate, too, as well as to the holy care and constant faithfulness that their religious commitments entailed. A degree of artifice was a necessary element of civil life. Indeed, such an aptitude for judicious performance quickly proved to be vital to the political health of Plymouth Plantation. Unjust insinuations followed the emigrants to New England, most vividly in the person of John Lyford, whose own verbal capacities offered Bradford a considerable measure of dramatic scope with which to disclose the colony's simultaneous vulnerability to and dependence upon the artificial being of words.

&.

EVEN AFTER A LAPSE of two decades, John Lyford's character and behavior exercised a unique grip on William Bradford's imagination. Lyford spent only about a year in Plymouth, from the spring of 1624 through the spring of 1625, but in this brief period of time he had sought (by Bradford's account) to exploit existing resentments and disagreements among the colonists, to resist the authority of Plymouth's officers, to divide its church, and ultimately to overturn its government by urging his influential correspondents in England to flood the colony with pliant voters who would unseat Bradford and his assistants. Failing that, Lyford hoped to receive encouragement and support from at least some of the English investors to establish a competing plantation nearby.

To achieve these ends he wrote more than twenty letters to sympathizers among the merchant adventurers, presenting a distorted picture of life in the colony, accusing its leadership of operating a religious and economic monopoly, of playing favorites in the distribution of food, of wasting resources. Lyford acted so quickly that his bundle of accusatory correspondence was ready for shipment back to England by the time the *Charitie,* the vessel that had brought him to Plymouth, had completed a brief fishing excursion and was ready to make its return voyage. He was clearly following a preconcerted plan that reflected the bitter divisions among the merchant investors, which James Sherley had described. "One scabed sheep may marr a whole flock," Sherley had observed of these English malcontents in his report of their activities to Plymouth's magistrates. In John Lyford they appeared to have exported just such a scabbed sheep to New England.

By late August 1624, Lyford's threat was over. By the spring of 1625 he had left the colony, first moving to the settlements near Massachusetts Bay, where he served as a minister for a few years, and then to Virginia, where he died.[3] Two dramatic trials, one in Plymouth and one in England, had exposed Lyford's deceitful nature and vindicated the colony's decision to banish him, but the company of merchant investors, seizing on these events as a pretext, "broak in pieces" over the controversy

Lyford had caused. Plymouth's financial circumstances and its vital sources of supply from England remained uncertain for two anxious years, as first Miles Standish and then Isaac Allerton sailed to England to try to negotiate a new economic partnership. Meanwhile word arrived from Leiden that John Robinson had died; so too had "their anciente freind, Mr. Cush-man." Bradford's assessment of this series of blows emphasizes their profound, cumulative impact:

> All which things (before related) being well weighed and laied togither, it could not but strick them with great perplexitie; and to looke humanly on the state of things as they presented them selves, at this time, it is a marvell it did not wholy discourage them, and sinck them. But they gathered up their spirits, and the Lord so helped them, whose worke they had in hand, as now when they were at lowest they begane to rise againe, and being striped (in a maner) of all humane helps and hops, he brought things aboute other wise, in his devine providence, as they were not only upheld and sustained, but their proccedings both honoured and imitated by others; as by the sequell will more appeare, if the Lord spare me life and time to declare the same. (250)

In echoing the language that he had used to describe another memorable low point in *Of Plimmoth Plantation*—the storm at sea in 1608, during the abortive flight to Holland, when all human help and hope had also seemed lost—Bradford underscores the significance of this period of great perplexity in Plymouth's fortunes. Like the Dutch captain's beleaguered vessel nearly twenty years earlier, the colonists' spirits began to "rise againe" just at the point of greatest crisis.

Bradford tagged the word "lowest" in the passage above with a small asterisk in his manuscript and wrote in the margins the enigmatic admonishment, "Note," as an explanation of his mark. These circumstances were a prominent "place" in the textual landscape of Plymouth's history, like one of the small mnemonic holes that Massasoit's people maintained to commemorate the celebrated events of their past. Lyford's association with such a momentous turning point in the colony's experience explains some of his prominence in Bradford's memory. The inherent narrative appeal of a rogue's progress, and of a courtroom confrontation, surely influenced the decision to devote nearly twenty dense pages of manuscript to the story of Lyford's exposure. The bitter conjunction of this betrayal of trust with the loss of Robinson must have seared these events still more deeply into Bradford's mind. It was, after all, John Lyford whom the merchant adventurers had elected to send to New England in 1624, not Robinson, whose death in early March of the following year coincided almost exactly with the time of Lyford's banishment.

But this reprobate clergyman has a significance to *Of Plimmoth Plantation* that exceeds the import of the circumstantial "place" he occupies in the colony's story. His presence, for one thing, poses acute problems of elaboration and abridgment in Bradford's text. To a degree that Thomas Weston or Thomas Morton never quite achieve, Lyford seems to resist narrative containment, to overflow the boundaries that Bradford attempts to set for his presence in the book. He appears first in a marginal note attached to James Sherley's premature announcement of a resolution to the merchant adventurers' disagreements, in "the loveingest and frendlyest meeting that ever I knew." Divine Providence apparently seconded Sherley's powers of persuasion and turned the hearts of men. "But this lasted not long," Bradford comments, in his gloss on Sherley's extravagant optimism, for "they had now provided Lyford and others to send over" (191). The association of Lyford's name with Sherley's self-serving report of his diplomatic success is more telling than it originally seems, for Lyford, like Sherley, will quickly prove to be a construction of empty words. As Bradford presents him, he is a master of verbal abundance, employing his clerical gifts as a mask for ethical and spiritual poverty—an emblem, in some respects, of the paradox inherent in the Renaissance ideal of *copia*.

This Latin term refers to the cultivation of abundant reserves of language for use in public speaking and in writing, through the systematic collection and study of adages, exemplary stories, or memorable figures of speech. Such training was a central feature of sixteenth- and seventeenth-century humanist education, in the vernacular as well as the classical languages.[4] The institution of the commonplace book, with which *copia* is closely associated, and the kinds of reading and writing that it encouraged, invariably called attention to the constructed nature of verbal performance. Eloquence, whether in speech or in print, could be systematically cultivated by marshaling and rearranging the most memorable passages that one encountered in books, storing them under a variety of subject headings, and employing them as the need arose in one's own writing or speaking.

Feats of memory or of research might be required to sustain this process of textual recirculation, but it was not particularly dependent on depth of feeling or on inspiration. "Tudor exuberance of language and expression," Walter Ong observes, "was not accidental but programmed," an aspect of the contemporary verbal world that led Ben Jonson to complain about the occasional essay that it was little more than a variation on a scholar's workbook—a tissue of commonplaces, loosely strung together. When Polonius undertakes to instruct his son by reviewing a handful of his favorite precepts, in *Hamlet,* he embodies the imposition of this artificial verbal practice upon the intimate exchanges of speech.[5]

Polonius's familiar example is evidence of what Terence Cave has called "the essential duplicity of *copia*," the ease with which fullness of expression can come to be easily mistaken for a corresponding abundance of thought or feeling, when in fact it reflects neither.[6] The first intellectual "distemper" of the time that Francis Bacon addresses in his examination *Of the proficience and advancement of Learning, divine and humane* (1605) springs from "an affectionate studie of eloquence, and copi[a] of speech" that grew "to an excesse: for men began to hunt more after wordes, than matter, and more after the choisenesse of the Phrase, and the round and cleane composition of the sentence, and the sweet falling of the clauses, and the varying and illustration of their workes with tropes and figures, then after the weight of matter, worth of subject, soundnesse of argument, life of invention, or depth of judgment."[7]

The problem had arisen, Bacon believed, with Martin Luther's need for an arsenal of eloquent language with which to attack the Catholic Church. The reformers were compelled "to awake all Antiquity" in their struggle, "so that the ancient Authors, both in Divinitie, and in Humanitie, which had long time slept in Libraries, began generally to be read and revolved." Before long the processing of these verbal resources became an end in itself. Wind, according to Terence Cave, is a common metaphor for *copia* among early modern rhetoricians, both because of its associations with divine afflatus, or generative scope, and because of its simultaneous capacity to evoke emptiness.[8] The creative wind, or *spiritus,* of Genesis is the powerfully affirmative side of this figure; the association of wind with vanity and futility, in Ecclesiastes, is the negative side. Bradford applies this second sense, for example, to Thomas Weston, who was a purveyor of wind rather than words in the hollow letters of encouragement that he sent to New England in the summer of 1621. These first letters were addressed to John Carver, though Carver had already been dead for two months when Weston wrote them. Bradford relies on this accident of geography and time, as well, to emphasize the number of senses in which Weston's pages are affiliated with death (131).

John Lyford is nothing if not copious, but from the moment that he steps ashore, into the pages of Bradford's book, he is marked by a disturbing degree of verbal and dramatic excess, greeting the colonists with "that reverence and humilitie as is seldome to be seen," bowing and cringing in a way that made them vaguely ashamed, weeping, blessing God, and admiring the condition of the settlement "as if he had been made all of love, and the humblest person in the world." In retrospect, Bradford associates this performance with the treachery of the wicked man in Psalm 10, "That croucheth and boweth, that heaps of poore may fall by his might," but he notes in the margins of his manuscript that there were many witnesses who could confirm his account of Lyford's gratuitously staged arrival (205).

The challenge that Bradford faces, at the outset of this portion of the history, involves the presentation of his case against Lyford in a fashion that will seem evenhanded to his reader. Lyford's own "hand," in fact, must be turned against himself, in the form of the incriminating correspondence that Bradford is able to introduce at his trial. But for this scene, too, to be persuasive, it must appear to emerge naturally from what Thomas Hobbes called, in the preface to his translation of Thucydides, the "contexture of the narration."⁹ An appeal to witnesses with whom readers cannot speak, or to letters that they cannot read for themselves, entails certain risks. Lyford's correspondence would be "too long and tedious" to transcribe, Bradford explains, amounting to a small volume in itself (212). But on the face of things, such a claim is no more persuasive an argument for the justice of Bradford's actions than is Lyford's own assertion that he could easily make the innocence of his conduct "apeare planly to any indifferente men," if only an unbiased audience could hear him (222).

The contexture of Bradford's narration, accordingly, strives to identify Lyford with the negative associations of *copia*. He is fulsome in his professions of humility and tears of gratitude upon his arrival in Plymouth, but in a surprisingly short time, Bradford notes, "he desired to joyne himselfe a member to the church hear, and was accordingly received" (205). Lyford's confession of faith was "large," detailing the many "corruptions" of his past life, as well as his consciousness of God's blessing "for this opportunitie of freedom and libertie to enjoy the ordinances of God in puritie among his people, with many more such like expressions." Lyford was clearly adept at exploiting the potential for empty mimicry in Plymouth's religious vocabulary. "Such like expressions" in themselves disclose virtually nothing about the individual who happens to use them. When John Oldham makes a very similar profession of reconciliation with Plymouth's authorities, a few sentences after this confession by Lyford, Bradford seems inclined to think that Oldham was, at least briefly, sincere, though in the end "God only knows." He had been, Bradford writes, "a cheefe sticler in the former faction among the perticulars," before Lyford's arrival, but the appearance of the *Charitie* led Oldham "to open his minde to some of the cheefe amongst them heere" and acknowledge the blessing of God on Plymouth's efforts (206). Bradford credits Oldham with experiencing a "sudden pange of conviction," but his remorse, like Lyford's piety, is cloaked in a surprisingly full display of plausible "expressions."¹⁰

God only knows, too, the extent of the confidence that Bradford originally placed in these comparative newcomers to the community, who sought so precipitously and completely to "close" with them. With Oldham, as with Lyford, the colony's leaders elected to "shew all readynes to imbrace his love, and carry towards him in all frendlynes, and called him to counsell with them in all cheefe affairs, as the other, without any distrust at all" (206). A significant degree of reserve is more than perceptible in this "show" of readiness and friendliness, in the systematic stress that Bradford places on "all" the ways in which the colonists extend overtures of good faith, and in his cautious assertion of the absence of distrust in these new relationships. Unlike the elaborate verbal displays of Lyford or Oldham, this deeply inflected language captures the atmosphere of latent uncertainty that must have marked many of the encounters among strangers in a remote colonial village, where it was seldom possible to summon witnesses to vouch for one's past character. In such a context, the tactics of *copia* would be particularly suspect. Long before Lyford's letters become decisive exhibits against him in court, Bradford has made this more inclusive grasp of "letters" a key to understanding the significance of this section of the history.

Words take on a striking degree of material agency in these pages, both as the indispensable means of disclosing (or concealing) the thoughts of those who employ them and as key elements of what Bradford terms one's outward "carriage." In accordance with a long-standing figurative connection between speech and food, private whisperings become the verbal nourishment that sustains the spirit of faction in Plymouth. By Bradford's account, Lyford and Oldham devote themselves to "feeding" the colony's malcontents with promises of what Lyford's friends in England will accomplish, once his letters arrive, thus bringing "others as well as them selves into a fools paradise" (207). Lyford's written descriptions of the enormities that he claims to have witnessed in New England are intended to "choke" the colony's defenders by accusing Bradford and his colleagues of starving their political opponents. When this and all of Lyford's additional slanders are finally exposed, Bradford notes, he strove to "lick off" the blame through yet another accusatory letter, signed in suitably self-dramatizing fashion: "John Lyford, Exille." Food is seldom far from the center of Lyford's preoccupations. He brought to New England a large family and received a correspondingly large allotment from the colony's common store, but as Bradford's language strives to emphasize, he is copiously "oral" in many senses of the term (221–23).

In Bradford's treatment of these events, words retain their intimate connection to physical existence even when they are written down. Lyford's none-too-furtive correspondence with his English supporters has all the narrative vitality of Lyford himself. Like his powers of speech, the letters he writes are "large" and "full," not of formulaic religious profession but of "slanders and false accusations" on a scale calculated to ruin the colony. Bradford's suspicions had been sufficiently aroused to lead him to accompany the *Charitie* "a league or 2. to sea" on its return voyage, when he "caled for all Lifords and Oldums letters" and learned the extent of their misrepresentations. He discovered at the same time copies of two letters that Lyford himself had intercepted—one addressed to William Brewster from "a gentle-man in England" and one from Edward Winslow to John Robinson—the margins of which Lyford had filled "with many scurrilous and flouting annotations" before forwarding them to his friends among the merchant adventurers. Bradford and his associates take copies of Lyford's own letters but let "most" of them proceed to their destinations. In a few cases they keep the originals and forward "true copyes" to Lyford's recipients, "that they might produce his owne hand against him." After taking these extraordinary, time-consuming, and in some respects puzzling steps, they return in their shallop to Plymouth, determined to wait a bit longer to "let things ripen" before calling the conspirators to account (207–8).

To a modern reader, Bradford's reluctance simply to confiscate these damaging documents is at first confusing. If the powers of a seventeenth-century magistrate included, as Bradford subsequently argues, the authority to seize private correspondence when circumstances warranted it, then why not keep the letters in question to prevent the harm that they were intended to cause? The answer lies in the two trials that follow. *Of Plimmoth Plantation*, like the colony that it describes, inhabits two jurisdictions, addressing at least two juridical audiences, each of which requires some material display of Lyford's nature in order to vindicate the colony's leadership. Both moments of exposure play important, mutually reinforcing roles in the narrative. Bradford reconstructs the confrontation at Plymouth in great dramatic detail—incorporating elements of his opening accusation to which he was especially attached, comparing Lyford and Oldham to the ungrateful hedgehog in the fable, who drove the hospitable coney from her burrow, relishing Oldham's rage that the magistrates had dared to interfere with his letters, few as they were. Bradford notes with some complacency that Oldham "was so bad a scribe as his hand was scarce legible" (209).

It is Lyford who is uncharacteristically silent during these initial courtroom exchanges, recognizing that he has little basis for complaining about intercepted letters. The magistrates, in contrast, are copious in their own defense, proceeding methodically "from poynte to poynte" through Lyford's accusations, repeatedly requesting him or his supporters "not to spare them in any thing; if he or they had proofe or witnes of any corrupte or evill dealing of theirs, his or their evidence must needs be ther presente, for ther was the whole company and sundery strangers" (218). Lyford's attempts to attribute his errors to misinformation from various colonists prove futile; even the fractious John Billington, among others, "deneyed the thinges, and protested he wronged them." Once the circumstances seemed sufficiently ripe, Bradford and his colleagues sought to present their case before the most comprehensive audience that they could secure, in studied contrast to the secretive methods of their opponents. The results of their patience are gratifyingly complete.

Lyford's conspiratorial letters are the textual basis for this indulgence in judicial theater. Without them his duplicity, and Plymouth's vindication, could not have been staged as fully as it is. *Copia* at its best entails an appetite for fullness, and it is in part this same rhetorical predisposition, rather than private misgivings, that leads Bradford and his colleagues to allow the slanderous correspondence to pass on to England after going to all the trouble to intercept it. A performance like Lyford's requires to be answered rather than suppressed, unfolded in all its elements, point by point, as Bradford does both in written replies that accompany Lyford's letters to England, once they have been carefully copied, and in open court. He reproduces a lengthy portion of this polemical exchange in *Of Plimmoth Plantation,* despite justifiable fears that the whole controversy may strike his reader as being "tedious." The urge to amplify, however, is a trait that Lyford and Bradford clearly have in common.

In the end, the relentless verbal assault from his accusers prompts Lyford to not one confession but two. He is copious even in remorse. First he burst into tears, before the assembled colonists at his original arraignment, and "confest he feared he was a reprobate, his sinns were so great that he doubted God would not pardon them, he was unsavorie salt, etc." (219). Bradford's truncation of this initial outpouring has all the dramatic subtlety that Lyford's appeal clearly lacks. The confessional formulas (Bradford implies) are simply too familiar to bear repeating. All that he had written against the colony's leadership "was false and nought," Lyford continued, "both for matter and manner"—a distinction that touches on Francis Bacon's critique of the rhetorical tradition from which *copia* derives, and which Bradford strives to apply to the contrast between his own species of narrative "fullness" and Lyford's transparent mannerisms.

The second confession occurs "publikly in church, with tears more largely then before." The magistrates have agreed among themselves to consider remitting Lyford's sentence, provided that he "caried him selfe well" over the ensuing winter and "his repentance proved sound." Bradford notes this possibility, without further remark, before copying the church confession into the history:

> I shall here put it downe as I find it recorded by some who tooke it from his owne words, as him selfe utered them. Acknowledging "That he had don very evill, and slanderously abused them; and thinking most of the people would take parte with him, he thought to cary all by violence, and strong hand against them. And that God

might justly lay innocent blood to his charge, for he knew not what hurt might have come of these his writings, and blest God that they were stayed. And that he spared not to take knowledg from any, of any evill that was spoaken, but shut his eyes and ears against all the good; and if God should make him a vacabund in the earth, as was Caine, it was but just, for he had sined in envie and malice against his brethren as he did. And he confessed 3. Things to be the ground and causes of these his doings: pride, vaine glorie, and selfe love." Amplifying these heads with many other sade expressions, in the perticulers of them. (220)

It is not difficult to detect the point in this putative transcription when Lyford's words begin to swerve away from the true weight of the matter and come increasingly to be shaped by what Bacon had called, dismissively, "the sweet falling of the clauses." His extravagant identification with the transgressions of Cain is the first signal of Lyford's habitual verbal duplicity—the substitution of theatrical for actual being. His all-too-confident itemization of three formulaic "heads" of discourse marks the point at which the traditional powers of amplification begin to deploy, and all hope of sincere repentance disappears beneath a cloud of sad expressions.

The speech of Lyford's victims, when they are finally able to offer direct testimony regarding his conduct, is emotionally rather than verbally full. Sexual misconduct long preceded slander and political conspiracy in the list of his crimes. Lyford's wife talks "sparingly" and with obvious pain of her husband's predatory infidelity with the family's maidservants. A young Irish parishioner whom he seduced, as he was counseling her prior to marriage, eventually "discovered" her shame to her husband, but not before growing so "troubled in mind, and afflicted in conscience" that she "did nothing but weepe and mourne, and long it was before her husband could get of her what was the cause" (235). This disclosure emerged during an unusual meeting of the merchant adventurers in England, called at the instigation of Lyford's friends, who were incensed at his treatment by Plymouth's magistrates. Lyford's "faction" chose a lawyer to present his complaint; the interests of the colony's leadership were represented by Thomas Hooker and Edward Winslow, back in England for the second time in two years. A veiled accusation by Winslow, spoken "in some heate of replie" during these proceedings, resulted in an irate call for witnesses to support Winslow's assertion that Lyford had conducted himself "knavishly."

The witnesses to his pastoral misconduct in Ireland accordingly came forth, upon which "this matter broke out," as Bradford vividly puts it, much like a ruptured abscess. Their manner was "so grave, and evidence so plaine, and the facte so foule, yet delivered in such modest and chast terms, and with such circumstances, as struck all [Lyford's] freinds mute, and made them all ashamed" (236). He had not only "satisfied his lust" upon his young parishioner, Bradford reports, but had taken unspecified steps to "hinder conception"—a wonderfully apt phrase to apply to a man who has devoted himself to planting false conceptions in the minds of his English correspondents and his confidants in Plymouth. The measured syntax of this brief passage, the simplicity of its rhetorical elements, stands in for the gravity of the testimony itself, imposing a speechless dismay that closely resembles the effect of Lyford's letters when Bradford and his colleagues read them in open court. There too, Bradford wrote, in the face of incontrovertible exposure "all his freinds were blanke," like an empty page (212). As the dignified reticence of these Irish witnesses demonstrates, *copia* was understood to imply powers of expressive restraint as well as of excess.[11]

The scope and variety of verbal animation in these pages reflects Bradford's interest in the vexed relationship between language and character. One listens, and one reads, with the greatest care, in order to distinguish certain linguistic clues to the nature of a given "speaker." This interpretive process can be fairly simple in the case of someone like John Oldham, who repeatedly gives evidence of his inability to submit his "unruly passion" to the kind of discipline that Bradford dramatizes in his account of the grave and modest witnesses who silence Lyford's English supporters. Lyford himself is a more difficult problem.

His initial confession in court was sufficiently encouraging to prompt the magistrates to consider overlooking the evidence that they had so carefully gathered and give him a chance to redeem himself. The more expansive performance in church, Bradford reports, with its ample "signes of sorrow and repentance," caused Samuel Fuller "and some other tender harted men amongst them" to profess that "they would fall upon their knees to have his censure released" (221). These sympathetic listeners "all stand amased in the end," at Lyford's last incriminating letter, which he tried to smuggle out of the colony at some point after his compelling public acknowledgment of the pride, vainglory, and self-love that had led him to contemplate violence against Plymouth's leaders.

This final document Bradford transcribes in full, along with three manuscript pages of detailed rebuttal. "Though the filth of mine owne doings may justly be cast in my face," Lyford writes his English correspondents, "and with blushing cause my perpetuall silence, yet that the truth may not herby be injuried, your selves any longer deluded, nor injurious dealing caried out still, with bould out facings, I have adventured once more to write unto you." He may have been indiscreet in some of his earlier letters, Lyford acknowledges, but he has written "nothing but what is certainly true" about Plymouth's "audatious" leaders (220). These renewed slanders represent an especially startling reversal from his penitential identification with Cain. Such calculating hypocrisy, Bradford concludes, in a final, angry reference to Lyford's invidiously oral nature, "is to devour holy things" (225).

A hypocrite is, self-evidently, an artificial person, but in *Of Plimmoth Plantation* Bradford is acutely aware that all constructions of character are dependent upon artifice. The magistrates of Plymouth, too, adopt a verbal posture, which they "carry towards" Lyford and Oldham, much as Lyford and Oldham, in turn, adopted their initial poses of piety and accommodation toward Plymouth. The deportment that one maintains, the words one uses, or the letters one writes are all representational acts—indispensable media for the human beings who employ them to express or to conceal their thoughts, as well as to extend the influence of their presence in time and space. One of the most important features of John Lyford's story is the variety of ways in which it illustrates the narrative vitality of letters, both spoken and written, captured in a characteristic scribal "hand" or arranged in a body of correspondence intended to store some features of the writer's mind. It is peculiarly appropriate that Lyford's name first appear, in *Of Plimmoth Plantation,* in a marginal note that Bradford applies to a letter from James Sherley. So textual a being is uniquely suited to an introduction that is deeply imbedded in the visual construction of the page.

Moreover, Lyford himself is fond of conducting his business in the margins, adding flouting annotations to letters that he has intercepted and copied, whispering "to his intimats such things as made them laugh in their sleeves," as he was preparing his shipment of incriminating correspondence for England (207). "I pray you conceal me in the discovery of these things," Lyford had advised one of his confidential readers, even as he performed that act of "discovery" for the benefit of an admiring audience in Plymouth (218). The request vividly depicts the knotted conscience of its author—his determination to remain hidden while others circulate the substance of his accusations against the colony's leadership—but it likewise depicts the mixed nature of letters themselves in Bradford's culture. They have a semiprivate (or semipublic) identity that invites the provocative blend of disclosure and concealment to which Lyford alludes.

Few, if any, of the letters that Bradford includes in *Of Plimmoth Plantation* are directed to a single reader. They are intended by their authors to be put to use, in whole or in part, as the discretion of the recipient dictates: shown to others, read to groups, even collected in histories, where their presence recreates the vivid conjunction of private character and public experience out of which the historical narrative emerges. Letters are, Bradford affirms, "the best part of histories" because they capture as no other medium could the entanglement of circumstances and of consciousness that brings the dead record to life. Far from being simply documentary auxiliaries to the text, they are the essential, circulating medium of Bradford's story.[12]

THE "INDISCREET CHARM OF EPISTOLOGRAPHY," Claudio Guillen observes, derives from "the latent voyeurism" of the letter. The representation of immediacy and of human presence that correspondents construct through their words, in order to address the painful consequences of absence, has both an intimate and a public dimension.[13] It is both a performance and a personal message. This mixed nature is a key element in the social and dramatic roles that letters play in *Of Plimmoth Plantation*. When John Robinson sent his parting advice to the passengers sailing on the *Mayflower,* he reminded both John Carver and those who heard Carver read Robinson's letter that this document was a surrogate for his being. The Lord's pardon might be "sealed up unto a man's conscience," Robinson believed, by thorough self-scrutiny and repentance, but most other dimensions of one's character, whether weaknesses or strengths, were destined for wider circulation. Many of the emigrants were strangers to one another, Robinson suggested, like the contents of unread letters. Sooner or later, however, the sealed envelopes would open and their pages fall out for all to view. That moment would call for charity, not resentment or recrimination, in the reading of one another's "infirmities." This latent analogy in Robinson's message is particularly conspicuous, after considering the elaborate unsealing process that Bradford depicts with the correspondence and the character of John Lyford. But Robinson, too, had hinted at the processes of public recirculation and reuse of correspondence in the brief note to John Carver and his wife which had accompanied what he called his "large letter to the whole" in August 1620.

These two letters themselves are part of a family of related correspondence that Bradford carefully arranges, in the early chapters of the history, in order to expose the dense, mental texture that characterizes the emigrants' final weeks in England—the mingling of private and public anxieties, misunderstandings, and reconciliations that their complex enterprise entailed. Carver apparently enclosed, in a previous letter to Robinson, a "note of information" outlining some of these stubborn difficulties, which Robinson in turn promises that he will "carefully keepe and make use of as ther shall be occasion" (77). William Bradford similarly keeps and uses these documents, as precisely the kind of narrative enticements that Claudio Guillen describes. Not mythic clarity of purpose but human immediacy is the goal that Bradford strives to achieve by incorporating into the history, to the fullest possible extent, the epistolary voices of his Leiden and Plymouth colleagues.

The note from Carver to which Robinson refers was almost certainly a summary of the long letter that a number of the "cheefest" of the emigrant company had sent to the merchant adventurers in early August 1620, attempting to strike a compromise with them in the terms of their investment agreement. Those terms had been arbitrarily changed by the adventurers, with Robert Cushman's consent, after many of the emigrants had already sold their property in Holland and were preparing to travel to Southampton to meet the ships that would take them to New England. Now that they had actually arrived in an English port and had begun coping with the cramped conditions of shipboard life, their grievances grew particularly deep and personal. In *Of Plimmoth Plantation* Bradford transcribes the would-be emigrants' collective letter of complaint, in which they summarize their objections to Cushman's action and propose a solution that might "heale" the breach with their backers. Cushman had agreed, under pressure from Thomas Weston, to grant the merchant investors a share in the value of the colonists' houses for the first seven years of the colony's existence—a serious infringement of personal privilege, as Bradford and his colleagues saw it, as well a violation of their earlier understanding: "We never gave Robart Cushman commission to make any one article for us," they angrily insisted:

> But that it may appeare to all men, that we are not lovers of our selves only; but desire also the good and inriching of our freinds who have adventured your moneys, with our persons, we have added our last article to the rest, promising you againe by leters in the behalfe of the whole company, that if large profits should not arise within the 7. years, that we will continue togeather longer with you, if the Lord give a blessing. This we hope is sufficente to satisfie any in this case, espetialy freinds . . . We are in shuch a streate at presente, as we are forced to sell away 60 li. worth of our provissions to cleare the Haven, and withall put our selves upon great extremities . . . And yet we are willing to expose our selves to shuch eminente dangers as are like to insue, and trust to the good providence of God, rather then his name and truth should be evill spoken of for us. Thus saluting all of you in love, and beseeching the Lord to give a blesing to our endeavore, and keepe all our harts in the bonds of peace and love, we take leave and rest. (76–77)

The barely suppressed resentment in this language makes evident how difficult the covering of human infirmity could prove to be. Carver, Bradford, and their companions cannot refrain from underscoring the dramatic difference between those who have invested their lives in this extremely uncertain enterprise and those who have merely invested their money. "The bonds of peace and love" appear to be severely strained by the extraordinary circumstances in which the writers find themselves. From this contentious message, Bradford turns in the pages of the history first to Robinson's "private" reply to Carver and then to his public letter to the *Mayflower* passengers, exposing their thematic continuities.

"I have a true feeling of your perplexitie of mind and toyle of body," Robinson wrote to Carver, acknowledging the emotional and physical price that these final weeks of preparation had begun to exact. In words that are clearly meant to be made use of as Carver found occasion to do so, Robinson quickly reassured his old friend that "The spirite of a man (sustained by the spirite of God) will sustaine his infirmitie, I dout not so will yours." As a deacon of the Leiden church, Robinson reminded him, Carver had considerable experience helping others bear their burdens. Surely he could apply this experience to himself, particularly "when you shall injoye the presence and help of so many godly and wise bretheren . . . who also will not admitte into their harts, the least thought or suspition of any the least negligence, [or] least presumption, to have been in you, what so ever they thinke in others" (78). Robinson's admonishment is carefully phrased for the ears of those godly and wise colleagues to whom he evidently expects that Carver will read these words, much as he expects him to read Robinson's public exhortation on the charitable covering of infirmities to the whole of the *Mayflower* company.

"Now," Robinson continues, "what shall I say or write unto you and your good wife my loving sister?" This question indicates not a change in subject so much as a modulation in approach to the anxieties with which Carver finds himself beset. The letter "turns" from one reader (or group of implied readers) to another but continues to suggest Robinson's awareness of the fictions of speech that he is trying to maintain, in the interests of restoring Carver's energy and confidence. At one point even the syntax with which he addresses his beleaguered "Brother" seems to require that we imagine Robinson's bodily presence in order to grasp the implied gesture behind the parallel prepositions that emphasize Robinson's affection and support: "I desire (and always shall) unto you from the Lord, as unto my owne soule" (78).

Carver's godly brethren in Southampton may well have to struggle to exclude from their hearts the "least thought" of any blame for Carver's management of the emigration arrangements, but Robinson's letter extends this guarded level of support beyond all momentary contingencies or conflicts. He brings a degree of dramatic life to his advice, affirming a common bond that is as intimate as the familial terms that he applies to Carver and his wife, undercutting the superficial anxieties that will prove so destructive of Robert Cushman's peace of mind over the coming weeks. The taking and the giving of offenses engage Robinson's attention in these brief pages as well as in the long epistolary address that he offers to the "whole" of the *Mayflower* passengers, where Robinson assures the future residents of Plymouth that their powers of forgiveness and stores of patience will inevitably be tested. In the private letter to Carver, he gives a memorable indication of how such reserves of patience might express themselves in the intimacies of speech.[14]

As this sequence of documents suggests, Bradford clearly appreciated the ability of the letter to function as an artificial person in the pages of the history, capturing not just a given correspondent's thoughts and feelings but reconstructing a scene of reading in which small communities of people, other than the letter's immediate recipient, might be represented. Robinson's absence from Southampton forces him to picture Carver's mental exhaustion and the tense atmosphere of recrimination with which he is surrounded—to insert himself into his friend's experience, as well as into the experience of Carver's immediate colleagues and that of the rest of the *Mayflower* passengers, through the best means available to him, with the clear expectation that once his letter was delivered to its intended destination, it might be introduced, to good purpose, in other contexts as well. It would have a vitality in excess of its occasion, inviting its repeated reuse, both alone and in relationship to other letters that evoked their own scenes of writing and reading.[15]

Bradford notes that the long message John Robinson originally wrote for public delivery to the *Mayflower* emigrants had already been printed, for presentation to a distinctly different "public," some years before he transcribed it into the pages of his history. The "breefe leter" to Carver had also played its own complex social role long before Bradford chose to incorporate it, too, into the narrative, as evidence of "the tender love and godly care of a true pastor." The value of these records, for Bradford, clearly lies as much in their dramatic as in their documentary weight. "I thinke it best to render their minds in ther owne words," he observes at one point, as he transcribes some letters from Plymouth's unpredictable London investors.[16] In such instances, the rendering of the mind clearly engages him more than the circumstantial preoccupations of a given historical moment. The dramatic, psychological immediacy of letters offers the best opportunity of conveying the human significance of Plymouth's experience.

Among the minds that Bradford sought to capture in this fashion, none is more important than Robinson's, but none is more vividly presented than that of Robert Cushman. It was Cushman, more than Carver, who was subjected to considerable criticism and suspicion as the *Mayflower* and the *Speedwell* tried to get successfully to sea in the summer of 1620. Robinson himself expressed to John Carver some reservations about the choice of Cushman to represent their interests in England.

He was, Robinson thought, "a good man, and of spetiall abilities in his kind, yet most unfitt to deale for other men, by reason of his singularitie" (60). Some lingering frustration with Cushman may be reflected in Robinson's willingness to countenance accusations of negligence and presumption toward "others," even as he completely exonerates Carver of any responsibility for the friction that has already begun to develop with the merchant adventurers before the *Mayflower* has sailed. What Robinson might mean to imply by stressing Cushman's "singularitie" emerges from the series of five extensive letters that Cushman writes between May 1619 and mid-August 1620, all of which Bradford copies into *Of Plimmoth Plantation* in order to recreate in great detail the extraordinary psychological pressures surrounding these first stages of the emigration.

One can almost reconstruct the opening pages of Bradford's lost letter book from these early chapters of the history. Cushman's imagination becomes an extraordinarily sensitive emotional and narrative register, to which the historian is required to make comparatively few additions in order to draw the story together. Troubling as these conflicts over financial arrangements and shipping must have seemed at the time, in retrospect Bradford appears to have recognized how accurately they forecast the years of difficulty that Plymouth's leaders experienced with James Sherley, the struggles that they had containing the increasingly "singular" behavior of Isaac Allerton, the recurrent problems posed by "untoward persons" whose private appetites or personal weaknesses disturbed the social and ethical cohesion of the colony. Cushman's first letter, in fact, describes precisely the sort of communal nightmare that must have haunted the imaginations of the emigrants' leaders both long before and long after their arrival in America.

Cushman and Carver left Leiden for England sometime in the early autumn of 1617 to try to negotiate arrangements with the Virginia Company that would provide a patent for their American settlement, as well as some money to meet the expenses of the emigration. But eighteen months of careful (and in some respects devious) negotiation with company officials had produced no result.[17] William Brewster, in the meantime, had been forced to abandon his Leiden printing business and had joined Cushman and Carver in England, where it was easier for a well-connected Englishman whose activities had made him obnoxious to the government to conceal himself. Both Carver and Brewster wrote reports to Robinson on the state of their negotiations with the Virginia Company, but in May 1619 Cushman also wrote to explain the mixture of electoral contention and personal jealousy that had brought the business of the Company to a standstill. He reports as well on the fate of another emigrant ship, carrying some members of the Eng-

lish church at Amsterdam, which had sailed for Virginia as the previous winter had
approached and had encountered adverse winds.

During the protracted voyage, disease had broken out on the crowded ship. Out
of 180 passengers and crew, 160 died, Cushman reports:

> They had amongst them the fluxe, and allso wante of fresh water; so as it is hear rather
> wondred at that so many are alive, then that so many are dead. The marchants hear
> say it was Mr. Blackwells faulte to pack so many in the ship; yea, and ther were great
> mutterings and repinings amongst them, and upbraiding of Mr. Blackwell, for his
> dealing and dispossing of them, when they saw how he had dispossed of them, and
> how he insulted over them. Yea, the streets at Gravesend runge of their extreame
> quarrelings, crying out one of another, thou hast brought me to this, and I may thanke
> the for this. Heavie newes it is, and I would be glad to heare how farr it will discour-
> age. I see none hear discouraged much, but rather desire to larne to beware by other
> mens harmes, and to amend that wherin they have failed. (48)

Cushman undertakes to draw some lessons from this terrible story—"take heed of
being enthralled by any imperious persone" like Blackwell, "espetially if they be discerned to have an eye to them selves"—but he is more than a little shaken by Blackwell's fate and troubled by the inexperience of the Leiden church in managing such
a hazardous business. "We are," Cushman confessed, "all to learne and none to
teach; but better so, then to depend upon such teachers as Mr. Blackwell was" (48).
He closes this letter by reasserting his own "readiness" to continue with the emigration effort, but the seeds of anxiety are sown. By June 1620, under sharp criticism from Robinson, Bradford, Winslow, and others for agreeing to a change in the
financial terms of the prospective settlement, Cushman's passions flare up in a
series of three letters that strive to answer accusations that he had shown "too great
indifferencie" to his responsibilities (60).

Robinson's criticism is contained in a long letter to John Carver that Robinson
signs, in uncharacteristically curt terms, "Yours to use." He evidently intends the
observations on Cushman's "singularitie" which he makes in these pages to come
to Cushman's attention, perhaps through the fairly blunt means of having Carver
simply share the letter with his colleague. The delay in securing shipping, as well
as the lack of money to purchase supplies, was causing significant hardship among
the prospective emigrants who were still in Leiden. "Ther is in this some misterie,"
Robinson complained, that neither the English investors nor his own representatives could explain. Robinson is rather severe with himself also, for relying too
much on general assurances from the merchant investors, "without seeing the per-

ticuler course and means for so waghtie an affaire set down unto us" (60). He implicitly chastises Carver, too, for withholding a number of critical details: "Send me word what persons are to goe, who of usefull faculties, and how many, and perticulerly of everything. I know you want not a minde" (61). These questions point to Robinson's own anxieties about the nature of those passengers intending to sail on the *Mayflower* who do not come from Leiden—those to whose infirmities Robinson, too, was a stranger.

Bradford's willingness to include in his book such an outburst of frustration on Robinson's part suggests the extent of his determination to preserve a detailed portrait of the mixed emotions plaguing even the most disciplined and resolute mind among the Leiden community in the face of the grave uncertainties confronting the prospective colonists. Robinson's feelings were almost certainly aggravated by his awareness that he would not, finally, be sharing the risks that he was assisting others to take. Bradford and Winslow, along with Samuel Fuller and Isaac Allerton, also wrote to Carver and Cushman at the same time, expressing considerable exasperation on behalf of those still in the Netherlands who were directly implicated in the arrangements with the merchant investors that their agents were negotiating. They implored Cushman, in particular, to "exercise" his "brains" in an effort to protect their interests:

> Salute Mr. Weston from us, in whom we hope we are not deceived; we pray you make known our estate unto him, and if you thinke good shew him our letters, at least tell him (that under God) we much relie upon him and put our confidence in him; and, as your selves well know, that if he had not been an adventurer with us, we had not taken it in hand; presuming that if he had not seene means to accomplish it, he would not have begune it; so we hope in our extremitie he will so farr help us as our expectation be no way made frustrate concerning him. (62)

This letter too, from Carver's "perplexed, yet hopfull brethren," was open to inspection if its recipients "thinke good" to use it. What that inspection indicates, at least to a modern reader, is that Bradford's famous allusion to Hebrews 11 a few pages later in *Of Plimmoth Plantation*, picturing the quiet resignation of these "pilgrimes" as they left Leiden for Delftshaven, is set against a background of mental and verbal turmoil that is at best only briefly stilled before breaking out once more as the *Speedwell* and the *Mayflower* are repeatedly thwarted in their attempts to get to sea.[18] "Salute Mr. Weston from us," Bradford and his companions write from Leiden, ostentatiously dating their letter "June 10. New Stille," as if to underscore the extent to which the English investors and their partners in the Netherlands have yet to find common ground, any more than they share a common calendar (62).

The salute is equivocal at best, calculated to fix Weston, too, with a measure of responsibility for placing innocent people in economic extremity.

The extraordinarily open nature of this remarkable correspondence—the assumption on the part of its authors that their audience, like their message, is mixed—makes it extremely useful to a historian who is predisposed to find his human subjects to be of diverse minds, or to embrace diverse opinions, at nearly every point of his narrative. The original debates over the decision to emigrate had, Bradford reports, been characterized by the circulation of "many variable opinions amongst men" with "many fears and doubts" concerning the wisdom of the decision, despite the obvious perils associated with remaining in the Netherlands as war loomed or of trying to preserve their communal identity in the face of the economic pressures and temptations of life in a continental city (33). Once the determination to emigrate had been taken, other differences arose over the precise destination that they should aim for, with some of these pious exiles ("and none of the meanest," Bradford confesses) having apparently been enticed by Ralegh's sensuous prose to favor Guiana over Virginia. They were willing to risk proximity to the Spanish rather than proximity to a settlement of profligate Englishmen. These preliminary disagreements—at least as Bradford has represented them—prove comparatively easy to settle. The entanglements in which Cushman, Carver, and their Leiden constituents find themselves involved, as they prepare for the actual journey, are far more stubborn and have repercussions that extend across the full scope of the history. These too will entail the politic interception of letters.

Cushman replies to his critics in early June 1620 with an elaborate, ten-point address, reflecting the contents of a "paper of reasons" in which the Leiden party appear to have specified their objections to the merchant investors' new conditions. As these reasons "were delivered to me open," Cushman notes, "so my answer is open to you all" (64). The "many quirimonies and complaints" that he had received, accusing him "of lording it over my brethren, and making conditions fitter for theeves and bondslaves then honest men," had taxed his patience nearly to the breaking point. In the grounds of his reply, Cushman makes a convincing and energetic case for himself, accusing the Leiden party, in turn, of placing inordinate emphasis on the material ends of their enterprise. Whatever the adventurers' motives might be, those of the prospective colonists are not primarily about money, Cushman reminds his associates. If the new financial terms discourage the building of "good and faire houses," then so much the better: "Our purpose is to build for the presente such houses as, if need be, we may with litle greefe set a fire, and rune away by the lighte; our riches shall not be in pompe, but in strenght; if God send us riches, we will imploye them to provid more men, ships, munition, etc. You may see it amongst the best pollitiks, that a commonwele is readier to ebe then to flow, when once fine houses and gay cloaths come up" (64). People with an eye chiefly to self interest, Cushman snaps, "are fitter to come wher catching is, then closing"; they are more suited to live by their wits, than in civil society. Should profit indeed prove to be the main end of any of the colonists, he cautions, then take care "least you be like Jonas to Tarshis," a cursed human cargo on the upcoming voyage (65).

It is true, Cushman acknowledges, that the prospective colonists are risking far more on the success of their efforts than the English investors:

> but doe they put us upon it? doe they urge or egg us? hath not the motion and resolution been always in our selves? doe they any more then in seeing us resolute if we had means, help us to means upon equall termes and conditions; if we will not goe, they are content to keep their moneys. Thus I have pointed at a way to loose those knots, which I hope you will consider seriously, and let me have no more stirre about them . . . As for them of Amsterdam I had thought they would as soone have gone to Rome as with us; for our libertie is to them as ratts bane, and their riggour as bad to us as the Spanish Inquision. If any practise of mine discourage them, let them yet draw back; I will undertake they shall have their money againe presently paid hear. Or if the company thinke me to be the Jonas, let them cast me of before we goe; I shall be content to stay with good will, having but the cloaths on my back; only let us have quietnes, and no more of these clamors; full litle did I expecte these things which are now come to pass. (66)

Samuel Eliot Morison relegates this spirited language to the appendix of his edition of Bradford's book, submerging Cushman's vivid personality and with it Bradford's own suspicion that John Carver found a way to "stay" these pages from reaching their destination, while "forgiving" any offense that they contained.[19] Bradford must have discovered Cushman's outburst among Carver's papers when he succeeded him as Plymouth's governor. Like Bradford himself, Carver was capable of intercepting correspondence that he was clearly reluctant to destroy, however damaging its contents might be. Cushman's offense, perhaps, would have been all the greater in view of the disturbing degree of plausibility to his arguments, turning (as they do) the rhetoric of selfless idealism against some of its more accomplished and revered practitioners in the Leiden community.

Thinking better of his own vehemence, perhaps, Cushman followed up this vigorous self-defense almost immediately with a more even-tempered report of the efforts that he and Weston had made to hire a ship and an experienced pilot for the voyage. Rather than live "by clamours and jangling," Cushman confessed, he had much rather "study to be quiet," trusting that his "naturall infirmities" would not present an insurmountable barrier either to the accomplishing of the voyage or to the restoration of good will with his friends. On the previous day, however, Cushman had written John Carver concerning some difficulties that had arisen over provisioning the ships, complaining at the same time about the "wrangling" that was driving this band of fraternal pilgrims to what Cushman termed a "flatt schisme": "we are redier to goe to dispute, then to sett forwarde a voiage" (70).

The order of these letters in Bradford's manuscript apparently confused his early readers.[20] By following Cushman's politic effort of June 11, 1620, addressed to his Leiden critics, with this assertion of a flat schism in the June 10 letter to John Carver, Bradford clearly indicates that the wounds inflicted during this acrimonious exchange persisted even as Cushman tried to mend fences. Indeed Cushman seems to be adverting to the fate of Blackwell's expedition when he expresses some concern that the *Mayflower* party will consume the summer in quarrels before they finally set sail. "I have received from you some letters, full of affection and complaints," he writes to Carver, putting his finger squarely on the tangle of emotions expressed in the messages that he and his scattered colleagues had been circulating among themselves over the preceding weeks. Some measure of what Robinson termed Cushman's singularity certainly consists in the dramatic fervor that he displays in these passionate rejoinders: "Negligence, negligence, negligence," Cushman exclaims at one point, mimicking the complaints of his Leiden friends, "I marvell why so negligente a man was used in the business" (69).

Bradford steps back briefly from this series of transcriptions in the history, in order to explain his reasons for presenting such a detailed and extensive correspondence, covering what are at best only preliminary elements in Plymouth's story. "I shal labour to be more contracte" in future passages, he writes, punning on the effort required to give birth to his book. But it is important to be "the larger in these things." Bradford hopes, of course, that the letters he includes might prove useful to future parties of emigrants, but more importantly he intends them to convey to the children of the original settlers a sense of the difficulties with which "their fathers wrastled . . . in ther first beginnings" (71).

The familial metaphors are more than just conventional usage. Fourteen-year-old Thomas Cushman, Robert's eldest son, had accompanied his father to New England in 1621 and remained in Plymouth when Robert returned to London, living in the Bradford household for the next fifteen years, effectively as an adopted son, until his marriage in 1636. "Have a care of my son as of your own," Cushman had written in one of his last letters to Bradford; "I pray you let him sometime practice writing." Though evidently not a very reliable correspondent, Thomas would be certain to take a deep interest in Bradford's portrait of his father's role in these formative events.[21] Indeed, the presence of such a potential reader at Bradford's elbow suggests the degree of personal investment he almost certainly felt in the gestation of his historical "labour." Plymouth too was produced out of the bodies and minds of its founders. The difficulties that beset them as they planned their voyage, like the resources of character that enabled them to succeed, were part of their nature—part of what John Robinson had recognized as the inescapable infirmity of being human. Few figures in Bradford's book embody that human infirmity more completely or more articulately than Robert Cushman.

The fifth and final letter in the ambitious series that Bradford employs to relay the troubled story of their departure was written by Cushman from Dartmouth, on August 17, 1620, to Edward Southworth, an old Leiden friend then in London. "Though it discover some infirmities" in Cushman's character, Bradford writes of this strikingly candid confession, "I will hear relate it" for "it shows much of the providence of God working for their good beyonde man's expectation" (86). It shows, too, clear evidence of Bradford's appreciation for the expressive powers of Cushman's pen. More than any other principal participant in these events, Cushman is able to render what Claudio Guillen terms "the illusion of a vital present from the angle of the present"—a literary quality that Renaissance artists had recently come to prize in the vernacular prose letter. This representational vitality had encouraged novelists to adapt collections of letters to meet the needs of imaginative literature, as well as historical testimony, since the late fifteenth century.[22] Cushman's words, in particular, repeatedly invite Bradford to "relate" or "recite" them, as if to underscore the conflation of speech and writing that Cushman's language makes evident at moments of intense feeling.

The *Speedwell* and the *Mayflower* had barely put to sea, in the first week of August, when leaks in the *Speedwell* forced both ships to put in to Dartmouth for repairs. On a second attempt to embark, the two ships had gone "above 100. leagues without the Lands End" when the *Speedwell* again began to take on water, and they returned once more, this time to Plymouth, where the *Speedwell* was abandoned, some of its passengers sent home, and the *Mayflower* resupplied from the smaller ship's stores to sail alone. Cushman and his family were among those who remained behind, but Bradford returns to this Dartmouth letter because of the vivid picture that it provides of the "conceptions and fears" stirred up by these final ominous delays.

As Cushman writes, he believes that he is dying. An "infirmitie of body"—that ubiquitous term, in this portion of the history—has gripped him, which Cushman compares to "a bundle of lead, as it were, crushing my harte more and more, these

14. days, as that allthough I doe the acctions of a liveing man, yet I am but as dead" (86). He describes for Southworth the dilapidated condition of the *Speedwell*'s hull, the inroads that these long delays were making on their food supplies, and the provocative behavior of Christopher Martin, one of the emigrant "strangers," not of the Leiden minority, who had served as a purchasing agent for supplies while the two ships were being fitted out. Martin categorically refused to provide accounts for how he had spent the money entrusted to him. He had even succeeded in offending the sailors by meddling in the operations of the ship—possibly because, unlike Cushman, he suspected the *Speedwell*'s crew of trying to make their vessel appear to be unseaworthy, so that they would be released from their obligation to make a distasteful and risky late-season crossing of the Atlantic. "Freind," Cushman addressed Southworth, in the depths of his discouragement:

> if ever we make a plantation, God works a mirakle; especially considering how scante we shall be of victualls, and most of all ununited amongst our selves, and devoyd of good tutors and regimente. Violence will break all, wher is the meek and humble spirite of Moyses? and of Nehemiah who reedified the wals of Jerusalem, and the state of Israell; is not the sound of Rehoboams braggs daly hear amongst us. Have not the philosophers and all wise men observed that, even in setled commone welths, violente governours bring either them selves, or people, or boath, to ruine; how much more in the raising of commone wealthes, when the morter is yet scarce tempered that should bind the wales. If I should write to you of all things which promiscuously forerune our ruine, I should over charge my weake head, and greeve your tender hart; only this, I pray you prepare for evill tidings of us every day. (89)

Cushman had clearly taken to heart Robinson's farewell exhortation that a new house must not be shaken until it is well settled "and the partes firmly knit" (81). Such recurrent figures of speech link these letters still more closely to one another, emphasizing the collective nature of their readership and confirming Bradford's decision to use them as a means of recreating both a communal and an individual portrait of the stresses of their departure from England.

"What is of use to be spoken of presently," Cushman urged Southworth in his closing sentences, "you may speak of it, and what is fitt to conceile, conceall" (90). Even this deeply revealing piece of personal correspondence has a public dimension that its author is willing to commit to the judgment of its recipient. It is unlikely that a reader so alert to textual collation as William Bradford would have overlooked the telling contrast between Cushman's plaintive request, in the troubled summer of 1620, and John Lyford's calculating desire, four years later, to be concealed in the discovery of his damning letters. By entrusting such evidence of his own anxiety and fear to a friend's care, Cushman demonstrates both the strength and the weakness of this unusual emigrant band. His voice, more than any other, provides the background for Bradford's portrait of the colonists' emotional and physical isolation at the moment of landfall. The first nine chapters in *Of Plimmoth Plantation* are carefully structured to make the maximum use of this exemplary witness, who did not sail on the *Mayflower* and who did not live to join his son in New England. In recording the news of Cushman's death, in 1625, Bradford wrote that he had been "as their right hand" in dealings with the merchant adventurers "and for diverce years had done and agitated" all the colony's English business. These words perfectly capture the blended energies of Cushman's nature (249).

ALTHOUGH ROBERT CUSHMAN'S correspondence does not entirely dominate the first half of the history, it provides the most impassioned record of the difficulties that confronted the Leiden community as they attempted to coordinate the complex emigration effort. Human singularity posed obstacles at every turn: the disintegrative ambitions of the members of the Virginia Company, the evasiveness of Thomas Weston, Cushman's own impetuous character, the dictatorial arrogance of Christopher Martin. The settlers had been in New England for just over a year when Weston wrote that the adventurers wanted to break off their original agreement altogether and work out some new arrangement for supporting the colony (141). By April 1621 Weston himself had sold his economic interest in Plymouth and had begun intercepting correspondence from other English investors, who were seeking to warn the colonists not to trust Weston as a shipping agent. Cushman had to smuggle news to Bradford disguised as a letter from a wife to her husband, who opened his mail, found his expectations disappointed, and brought Cushman's pages to the governor. John Lyford's behavior seems less surprising, if no less objectionable, in such a context.

The most conspicuous epistolary voice in the second half of Bradford's book is the same correspondent whose confidence in the original group of merchant investors had proved to be so badly misplaced: James Sherley. Forty-two investors signed the new financial agreement with the colony that Isaac Allerton had finally secured in November 1626, but Sherley and four others were named as agents for the whole, with Sherley apparently serving as their secretary. After Bradford and a small group of Plymouth's leaders assumed responsibility for the colony's collective debt, in return for complete control over its trading enterprises, they asked Sherley to take on an additional role as their agent in England, supplying them with the trade goods that they needed in order to secure furs from the Indians. Plymouth would try to pay its expenses in animal skins, a practice that comes increasingly to trouble Bradford and of which he makes startling figurative use later in his book. As of the beginning of 1629, James Sherley seemed a congenial and reliable partner, able to secure good prices in the London market for the pelts that the colony exported and willing to help them reduce the exorbitant interest rates that they had to pay for English loans. Over the next decade, however, Sherley's appetite for profits and his inability to manage the colony's accounts kept Plymouth deeply in debt.

The first stages of this relationship, like John Lyford's initial weeks in New England, were promising. Sherley even implied that he might emigrate to Plymouth himself. Parliament and Charles I were at odds over taxation, the Petition of Right, and the king's judicial powers—conflicts that came to a head early in 1629, when Charles dissolved Parliament and embarked on the eleven years of personal rule that ended in civil war.[23] In a letter written to Plymouth late in 1628, Sherley concluded that "if the Lord should send persecution or trouble hear (which is much to be feared) and so should put into our minds, to flye for refuge, I know no place safer then to come to you" (277). Bradford transcribed this letter on a verso page of his manuscript, opposite a copy of the official document naming Sherley and another London merchant, John Beauchamp, the factors and agents of the Plymouth partners who had undertaken to pay the colony's debts.

But New England was already losing its character as a refuge from European and English disorders even as Sherley wrote. Indeed, the primary value of Sherley's correspondence for Bradford is its ability to dramatize the proliferation of economic ties that drew Plymouth imperceptibly closer to the predicament of Europe over the next fifteen years. The process begins shortly before Sherley expresses his concerns about England's future, with the establishment of the Dutch plantation at New Amsterdam. Isaac de Rasier, the secretary of the Dutch colony, sent a letter to Plymouth's leaders in the spring of 1627, offering to open trade relations between the two colonies. He cited as reasons for his proposal the proximity of England and Holland, the long-standing alliance between the two Protestant nations, and "the old contractes, and entrecourses" between them, "confirmed under the hands of kings and princes, in the pointe of warr and trafick; as may be seene and read by all the world in the old chronakles" (268). On this basis of ancient friendship, Rasier offers to buy any furs that Plymouth might be willing to sell, either for merchandise or ready money, at some mutually convenient meeting place between the two settlements.

This letter arrives at Plymouth in both Dutch and French versions, but Bradford carefully transcribes an English translation into the text of the history, thus highlighting this abrupt reemergence of the cosmopolitan past shared by so many of the colony's leaders. Rasier's overture comes at a timely moment, in some respects, for Bradford and his Plymouth partners have just established a trading post twenty miles to the south, at Manamet, on a small river flowing into Buzzard's Bay, where they can conduct business with the neighboring Indian tribes without having to transport supplies or furs around Cape Cod. This commercial expansion, and a similar one established on Kennebec River to the north a few months later, already represent an ominous enlargement of the colony's presence and an increase in its exposure to sources of friction with other European trading ventures.

The residents of Plymouth had spent the decade between 1618 and 1628 trying to get out from under the hands of the very kings and princes to whom Rasier so confidently alludes—to escape from the centers of war and traffic in the Netherlands that had appeared to jeopardize the survival of their community. In a small but prophetic way, however, they had already begun to evolve into just such a commercial and political center themselves. Accordingly, Rasier's language evokes considerable ambivalence in the pages of Bradford's history, a fact that Bradford emphasizes by stressing the "superfluous titles" of Rasier's Dutch salutation and noting in his official reply that the grandiloquent terms of address, which Rasier is accustomed to using in Europe, are "more then belongs to us, or is meete for us to receive" (270).

This extension of the world of the old chronicles into the woods of New England is the theme of the second half of the history. Its initial appearance, here, prompts a cautious but largely favorable response from Bradford, acknowledging to their neighbors in New Amsterdam the debt of gratitude that these former citizens of Leiden owe the Dutch for twelve years of "good and curteous entreaty" and expressing a willingness to trade at some point in the future, "if your rates be reasonable." A history of friendly intercourse, apparently, is not inconsistent with the instinct to drive a bargain (270–71).

Such scrupulous control in Plymouth's foreign relations proves impossible to maintain over the coming years. The Dutch have a number of tempting commodities for sale which Plymouth sorely needs, but more importantly, they introduce the English settlers to the commercial value of wampumpeag, which revolutionizes the economic climate of southern New England. Plymouth is able, within a few years, to cut off all Indian trade from English fishing vessels that do not have access to the precious shell money that the inland tribes increasingly covet. The Narragansett and Pequot originally monopolized the manufacture and circulation of wampumpeag. Soon the New England tribes north of Cape Cod begin to make it too, after Plymouth's traders introduce them to its value.[24] Very quickly, according to Bradford, this dramatic expansion in the money supply makes the neighboring tribes "rich and power full and also prowd therby," able to purchase firearms and ammunition, in increasing amounts, from the English, the Dutch, and the French, all of whom are now vigorously competing for the valuable furs to which Indian trappers and hunters have access (283).

Bradford introduces this remarkable transformation in the economic and military circumstances of New England in a handful of pages that form the preamble to his discussion of Thomas Morton. Morton's experiments in the American arms trade, in turn, are part of a larger, historical design that includes the initially benevolent incursion of the Dutch, signaled by Isaac Rasier's offer, and the rapid escalation of Plymouth's debts under the management of James Sherley and Isaac Allerton.[25] The antithetical experiences of sudden change and progressive disclosure form an intoxicating and bewildering blend through this portion of Bradford's narrative—not unlike the intoxicating atmosphere of Morton's licentious "nest" of runaway servants and malcontents at Merry Mount. Sherley's letters provide Bradford the means of exposing the full scope of Plymouth's commercial predicament, as well as displaying the uniquely insinuating methods by which various agents of the old political economy establish a presence in New England. The significance of Sherley's tactics is thrown into high relief by contrast with the dramatic clarity of Thomas Morton's arrest and deportation.

Discrete events have much less independence in these pages than might at first seem to be the case. Like the confusingly mingled consignments of trading goods that Isaac Allerton repeatedly imports from England—in which private "adventures" were "so intermixte with the goods of the generall" that it was impossible to tell whose debts (or whose profits) were whose—circumstances are tightly "pact up together" in this portion of Bradford's book. This narrative density in its own right underscores the figurative diminishment of the barriers insulating New England from the ailments of the Old World.

Morton's story comprises an especially compact mixture of narrative threads and historical forces. Bradford prepares his reader to appreciate this apparent digression by first introducing the flood of wampumpeag that had transformed southern New England into a luxury market. In such a context, it quickly becomes apparent that Thomas Morton himself is a figure of "luxury." He had originally come to Massachusetts Bay as part of another sort of speculative investment in expensive goods: people. A small group of propertied men, Bradford reports, led by "one Captaine Wolaston," brought a large number of bound servants to a small settlement just north of Plymouth in 1625, intending to form a plantation named after their leader,

Mount Wollaston. Morton was one of the party of investors connected with this enterprise, though not a particularly prominent one. When profits were slow in coming, Wollaston took a substantial portion of his servant labor to Virginia, where he sold their time, "at good rates," and promptly wrote back to his chief agents in Massachusetts, two men named Rasdall and Fitcher, asking for a second, equally lucrative human shipment to be sent to him.

Morton was not among Wollaston's salable servant commodities, but after this second batch had been shipped south, he exploited the understandable anxieties of the servants who remained and promoted a revolution. Bradford reconstructs Morton's subversive speech for the benefit of contemporary readers, who might be expected to identify Morton's behavior in 1628 with that of the Levellers two decades later. By the time Bradford began composing these pages, the Levellers had come to represent an extreme expression of radical Protestant ideology:[26]

> But this Morton abovesaid, haveing more craft then honestie, (who had been a kind of petifogger, of Furnefells Inne) . . . watches an oppertunitie (commons being but hard amongst them) and gott some strong drinck and other junkats, and made [the servants] a feast; and after they were merie, he began to tell them, he would give them good counsell; you see (saith he) that many of your fellows are carried to Virginia; and if you stay till this Rasdall returne, you will also be carried away and sould for slaves with the rest. Therfore I would advise you to thrust out this Levetenant Fitcher; and I, having a parte in the plantation, will receive you as my partners and consociats; so may you be free from service, and we will converse, trad, plante, and live togeather as equalls, and supporte and protecte one another, or to like effecte. This counsell was easily received, so they tooke oppertunitie, and thrust Levetenante Fitcher out a dores, and would suffer him to come no more amongst them; but forct him to seeke bread to eate, and other releefe from his neigbours, till he could gett passages for England. (284–85)

Bradford has framed Morton's appeal to Wollaston's remaining servants in such a way that it is impossible to overlook the parallel between these events and the original foundation of Plymouth itself. Morton's new plantation will be (according to this preamble) a consociation of equals, offering one another mutual support and protection, rather than a frightened remnant of exiles waiting helplessly for a grim future to overwhelm them. The predicament is strikingly similar to the circumstances surrounding the Leiden exiles a decade earlier—a parallel that Bradford has introduced into Morton's story through an act of narrative ventriloquism.[27] It would have been an easy matter to move from Morton's alluring feast, at the beginning of the account, directly to the establishment of his so-called school of atheism, which quickly follows Lieutenant Fitcher's expulsion, omitting the suggestive reference to egalitarian ideals with which Bradford briefly credits his libertine antagonist. This fictive speech complicates rather than simplifies the nature of the contrast between the two New England communities.

Moreover, Plymouth had recently reorganized its own political arrangements in a manner suggestively similar to Morton's consociation. In 1627, the year that Plymouth's new economic partnership with James Sherley and his colleagues had been confirmed, the colony had dramatically broadened its standards of citizenship to take in many of the "untowarde persons" who had gradually accumulated in their midst as a result of various independent emigration "adventures" over the last seven years. In the interests of "peace and union," the Old Planters agreed "to take in all amongst them, that were either heads of families, or single yonge men, that were of abillity and free, (and able to governe them selves with meet descretion, and their affairs, so as to be helpfull in the common-welth) into this partnership or purchase" (258). Plymouth's debts, as well as its profits, its land, and its livestock would now be more broadly distributed among its inhabitants, so that the distinction between "general" interests and "particular" ones would largely disappear. Women were not explicitly recognized in this partnership, except insofar as they counted as an additional purchase share, equal to that of their husbands, in the aggregate allotment of a household. Servants were entirely excluded from Plymouth's new arrangements, except as their masters or the company as a whole determined to reward them for "their deservings."

This plan differs as sharply from Morton's more radical proposal as it does from the crass exploitation of Captain Wollaston in marketing his vendible servants. Bradford's parenthetical emphasis on the importance of "meet" discretion in his single young men appears to invite the contrast with Morton's libertine practices, which will become clear a few pages later, as the Merry Mount episode unfolds. The potential for at least some upward mobility among Plymouth's servants is equally important to Bradford's careful positioning of the colony in between the political extremes represented by Mount Wollaston and Merry Mount. Morton's community of consociates, however, rapidly falls victim to the new luxury economy in Massachusetts Bay, much as Plymouth itself soon feels these transforming economic effects.

Emulating the Dutch, the French, and the traders in the English fishing fleet, Morton begins to exchange firearms for exotic furs among the Indians. The furs, in turn, provide him with the highly profitable commodity that he needs to acquire more weapons to sell and to support his prodigal way of life. Morton never directly admits, in any surviving documents, to conducting this trade, but neither does he ever deny it, perhaps because it simply seemed superfluous to him (or to his English sympathizers) to confirm or deny one individual's participation in a profit-generating activity that was so universally familiar to all the European trading communities.[28] On a small but suggestive scale, Morton is only repeating in New England the exhilarating commercial experience that Lisa Jardine has described as the basis of the luxuriant urban economies of the fifteenth century.[29]

Indeed, like the Hungarian and German ballistics engineers whom Jardine notes servicing the Ottoman court, Morton provides both tools and technical support for his Indian customers. Bradford presents the process of technology transfer in some detail, specifying the stages by which Morton appears to have developed Indian demand for his guns:

> first he taught them how to use them, to charge, and discharg, and what proportion of powder to give the peece, according to the sise or bignes of the same; and what shotte to use for foule, and what for deare. And having thus instructed them, he imployed some of them to hunte and fowle for him, so as they became farr more active in that imploymente then any of the English, by reason of ther swiftnes of foote, and nimblnes of body, being also quick-sighted, and by continuall exercise well knowing the hants of all sorts of game. So as when they saw the execution that a peece would doe, and the benefite that might come by the same, they became madd (as it were) after them, and would not stick to give any prise they could attaine too for them; accounting their bowes and arrowes but bables in comparison of them. (286–87)

The result of such merchandising efforts is that the Indians gradually succeed in acquiring not only firearms of all sorts but also generous supplies of lead, molds in which to cast their own shot, and even screw plates and other tools to keep their weapons in good working order. "Some," Bradford vaguely asserts, "have tould them how gunpowder is made . . . and I am confidente could they attaine to make saltpeter, they would teach them to make powder" (288).

Morton's villainy (as Bradford terms it) involves much more than just an excessive devotion to *The Book of Sports,* coupled with some dubious trading practices. He is an agent of cultural and historical acceleration who is quickly helping to erode the distinction between "old" and "new" worlds, creating the technological conditions by which the nexus of war and traffic, to which Isaac de Rasier had referred, might establish itself firmly in New England. Indeed, Bradford structures his account of Morton's activities in order to imply a measure of similarity between the emergence of Merry Mount and the second generation of Stuart monarchs, emphasizing Morton's blunt repudiation of the proclamations of James I against selling arms to Indians. The old king was dead, Morton had asserted, and his proclamations with him (290). Merry Mount is a case study in highly personal misrule—like that of James' successor—against which Bradford pointedly appeals to the joint authority of "princes and parlements" for help in suppressing the American arms trade (288).

Like the current English king, Morton is scornful, both of friendly verbal admonishments and of more serious warnings that "the countrie could not beare the injure he did." He answers the letters of the neighboring settlements in "scurrilous termes full of disdaine" that finally force them to arrest him and ship him to England, where (much like his royal double) Morton proves to be an elusive prisoner. This intriguing relationship to the fate of Charles I, however, is less pronounced, and finally less important, than Morton's narrative relationship to the history of Plymouth—as its emblem more than as its opposite. The evolution of Merry Mount is a highly compressed version of Plymouth's own evolution, over the years immediately after Morton's arrest, as the commercial practices of Plymouth's English partners follow their own trajectory of profuse excess.

The most vivid evidence of this thematic link in *Of Plimmoth Plantation* is Isaac Allerton's surprising relationship with Thomas Morton. After his role in renegotiating the colony's economic arrangements with James Sherley and the remaining merchant adventurers, Allerton continued to travel between London and Plymouth on an annual basis, delivering the colony's shipments of fur for sale and buying new supplies of trade goods to take back to New England. Bradford and his Plymouth partners gave Allerton a written commission authorizing him to act as their purchasing and receiving agent, a position Allerton was able to exploit as he began to finance private trading ventures of his own.[30] Although he was clearly aware of Plymouth's firm response to Morton's "misdemenors," Allerton nevertheless employed him as a "scribe" (or clerk) shortly after Morton's deportation and brought him back to New England, within a few months of his original arrest, lodging him "at his owne house," directly across Plymouth's main street from the Bradford home (302).

When Bradford records this incident on a verso sheet of his manuscript, facing an account of the events of 1629, he professes to have almost forgotten this extraordinary affront to the colony's authorities. Morton's return as Allerton's protégé, however, caused "great and just ofence" at the time (302). Plymouth's leaders quickly compelled Allerton to evict his new scribe, though Bradford is mysteriously silent concerning the details of what must have been an extremely uncomfortable confrontation. Even more mysterious are the reasons that might have prompted Allerton to risk offending his colleagues and trading partners in the first place. Bradford does not speculate on these, either, in the pages of the history, though it is difficult to believe that he and Allerton did not discuss them.[31]

Equally difficult to credit is Bradford's claim that he had almost forgotten this profoundly disquieting incident. "Covetousness never brings ought home," Bradford knowingly observes in the main text of the book, as he outlines Allerton's and Sherley's mishandling of the colony's Kennebec patent (302). As if to echo this proverb, he records his brief account of Thomas Morton's unexpected New England homecoming, under the wing of Isaac Allerton, on the manuscript sheet that faces his pointed comment on the barren nature of greed. This act of authorial collation underscores the intricate nature of the economic web in which Bradford and his trading partners increasingly find themselves snared. Morton's mix of egalitarian rhetoric, scandalous verse, and irresponsible commerce poses a fairly simple challenge to the safety of New England's fledgling English communities. Isaac Allerton and James Sherley operate behind verbal screens that are far more difficult to penetrate. Sherley's correspondence offers Bradford the opportunity to dramatize how this pervasive, and costly, texture of deception was developed and maintained through the apparently confidential medium of letters.

In his detailed account of Plymouth's affairs between 1625 and 1643, Bradford incorporates lengthy excerpts from fifteen of Sherley's letters, describing the increasingly "large and intreate" nature of the commercial ties between the colony and its London agents (344). Indeed, the frustrating interplay between commercial scope and economic intricacy becomes the theme of this portion of the history.[32] The copious documentary record that Bradford provides is unevenly distributed among the principal actors in the affair. For reasons that become clear as the story unfolds, Isaac Allerton is curiously silent in these exchanges. *Of Plimmoth Plantation* contains no letter of which he is the sole author, and on the rare occasions when Bradford does mention Allerton's response to direct criticism from Plymouth's leaders, the potential for confrontation evokes no corresponding dramatic effort on Bradford's part. Instead he turns his attention away from the kind of vivid personal antagonisms that characterized events at Merry Mount to focus on a dramatized act of reading. Letter after letter from James Sherley progressively reinforces lessons that the colonists have been learning, through their extensive correspondence, since 1617: "even amongst freinds, men had need be carfull whom they trust" (335).

In a particularly critical sequence of pages, Bradford dissects a single elaborate letter that captures this dramatic process. On March 19, 1629, Sherley and one of his English colleagues, Timothy Hatherley, wrote a long report to Plymouth on the activities of the colony's London agents. Bradford transcribes the full text of the letter in three parts, separated by long comments of his own, emphasizing the complex interplay between Sherley's verbal strategies, their immediate reception by the reading audience in New England, and Bradford's retrospective analysis, based on twenty years of subsequent experience with Sherley's commercial and rhetorical practices. Earlier in the book, Bradford effectively permits the correspondence of Robert Cushman to speak for itself, as he reconstructs the anxieties of the original emigration. But this memorable report from James Sherley becomes virtually a physical antagonist in the text. Bradford repeatedly arrests its progress, with all the figurative energy that Miles Standish had applied to Thomas Morton, calling Sherley directly to account for activity that is ultimately far more damaging to the colony's interests than Morton's sensational displays.[33]

The first part of the March 19 letter addresses the progress that Sherley claims he and Isaac Allerton had made that year in their attempt to improve the terms of Plymouth's trading patent on the Kennebec River. This process involved negotiating a bureaucratic labyrinth in order to obtain what Sherley called "the love and favore of great men in repute and place," gaining the endorsement of the king, the Lord Keeper, the Lord Treasurer, and the Council for New England, through the services of a number of well-connected solicitors—all "locks," as Sherley noted, which required silver and golden keys. The metaphor itself is a suspiciously worldly one, coming from a correspondent so prone to embrace the colonists' overriding religious mission, but veterans of the *Mayflower*'s voyage were only too aware that bribery was an unavoidable feature of public business.[34] Even so, the Kennebec patent request bogged down when the Lord Treasurer balked at issuing a customs warrant that Allerton and Sherley had independently added to the colony's initial request. This feature of the patent, Sherley assured Plymouth's leaders, would make them politically and economically "compleate," but Bradford notes in the commentary with which he follows Sherley's account that these grand ends were "never accomplished," despite "a great deale of money veainly and lavishly cast away" on a long list of English officials (302).

This pattern of incomplete completion persists throughout the long relationship that the colony maintains with Sherley and his associates. Many locks will prove resistant to golden keys, including most prominently the final resolution of the size of Plymouth's debt. At the same time, Bradford proves adept at exploiting Sherley's own language to expose the contrast between Plymouth's conduct and that of its commercial agents. To Sherley's euphemistic reference concerning the efficacy of golden keys, for example, Bradford responds with the proverbial saying that collates so effectively with Allerton's patronage of Thomas Morton: "covetousness never brings ought home."[35] To Sherley's assurances that this expensive new patent will "stope the moueths of base and scurrulous fellowes" who are eager to slander the colony among its English supporters, Bradford juxtaposes a reference to Morton's "infamouse and scurillous booke," *New English Canaan*, that was still damaging Plymouth's reputation over a decade after Morton's original arrest (303). Transcribing Sherley's letter in segments allows Bradford to scrutinize its language from every conceivable angle, as a reader and as an annotator, exposing Sherley's glib assumptions at the same time that he discloses the unexpected contrasts and parallels that give order to the unfolding story.

To make the emerging profusion of economic detail palatable to the reader, Bradford relies (in part) on the aphoristic vitality of proverbs. His comment on the futility of covetousness, for instance, aptly nullifies Sherley's wry tolerance for bribery among government officials. "Love thinkes no evill," Bradford originally explains, as he notes Isaac Allerton's tendency to mingle shipments of trading goods in a manner that appeared to work to Allerton's private advantage (293). This adaptation of language from 1 Corinthians quickly accounts for Plymouth's vulnerability to such devious practices by a trusted member of the community. Near the end of Bradford's extended exploration of the colony's economic plight, he draws this "tedious and intricate" business to a close with another proverb: "They that will be rich fall into many temtations and snares . . . for the love of money is the roote of all evill" (341). At strategic moments in the discussion, he incorporates Sherley's commercial aphorisms in order to expose the sharp contrast between the practical policy of a cunning investor and the ethical and religious culture of Plymouth. In the second section of the March 19 letter, Sherley admonishes the colonists against fiscal timidity: "let us not fulfill the proverbe, to bestow 12d. on a purse, and put 6d. in it." The merchant investors, he insists, have "been at great charg" to support the settlement of Plymouth; correspondingly great risks are required on the colony's part if the investors are to make their profits (304).

Proverbial reassurances and incitements alone do not exhaust Sherley's persuasive resources. He employs John Robinson's religious vocabulary as well, urging the colonists to "bear one an others infirmities" and resist those "discontents and factions amongst your selves" that might imperil Plymouth's ability to conduct an effective trade. By "joyning in love," Sherley assures Bradford and his colleagues, shortly before instructing them on the perils of expensive purses, we can overcome all our debts, but "we must follow it roundly and to purpose" lest competitors "step in and nose us" (304). Piety and the main chance blend, in Sherley's language, quite as closely as they do in the exhortations of the Quaker whaling captains Bildad and Peleg in the opening chapters of *Moby-Dick*. The Plymouth partners were troubled at the time by the mysterious "concurrence" between Allerton and Sherley, but Sherley's astute appeals to the bonds of love effectively suppressed this cautionary instinct (305).

Yet another "more secrete cause was herewith concurrente" as well, for Allerton had married one of William Brewster's daughters, and the remaining economic partners in Plymouth (Bradford, Standish, and Winslow) were reluctant to hurt Brewster's feelings by questioning the credibility of his son-in-law. To the influence of this quite palpable bond of love Bradford adds an extraordinary portrait of the external and internal forms of coercion that conspired to make the colony comply with the economic strategies of their London agents. In his commentary on the second part of Sherley's letter, Bradford describes how Allerton and Sherley together worked on the sentiments of Brewster, much as John Lyford had earlier worked on Samuel Fuller and Plymouth's tender-hearted magistrates. Allerton in particular "carried so faire with him, and procured such leters from Mr. Sherley to him, with shuch applause of Mr. Allerton's wisdom, care, and faithfullnes in the bussines," that Brewster's judgment was apparently swayed (306). The tactics of *copia* once more prove successful at sustaining a persuasive if hollow ethical "carriage."

Immediately before transcribing the final section of Sherley's letter, Bradford elaborates on his proverbial allusion to 1 Corinthians a few pages earlier, in order to account for the complex mixture of motives and feelings that these circumstances have increasingly exposed, both in Isaac Allerton and in his historian:

> Besids, though private gaine, I doe perswade my selfe, was some cause to lead Mr. Allerton aside in these beginings, yet I thinke, or at least charitie caries me to hope, that he intended to deale faithfully with them in the maine, and had such an opinion of his owne abillitie, and some experience of the benefite that he had made in this singuler way, as he conceived he might both raise him selfe an estate, and allso be a means to bring in such profite to Mr. Sherley, (and it may be the rest) as might be as lickly to bring in their moneys againe with advantage, and it may be sooner then from the generall way; or at least it was looked upon by some of them to be a good help ther unto; and that neither he nor any other did intend to charge the generall accounte with any thing that rane in perticuler; or that Mr. Sherley or any other did purpose but that the generall should be first and fully supplyed. I say charitie makes me thus conceive; though things fell out other wise, and they missed of their aimes, and the generall suffered abundantly hereby, as will afterwards apear. (306–7)

Faith, hope, and charity are not quite adequate to overcome the misgivings that Bradford expresses in this carefully phrased passage. He conceives that it may have been vanity as much as greed that led Allerton and Sherley to overreach themselves. Their intentions were not openly culpable, though in the end the colony's suffering is much the same either way. These nominally generous conclusions, however, spring from an inversion in the traditional order of Christian graces.

Charity carries Bradford to hope that these old colleagues remained faithful to their trust. In reordering the familiar Pauline sequence, Bradford suggests the struggle between religious idealism and disillusion that these bitter experiences continue to evoke.

In the final section of the March 19, 1629, letter, Sherley introduces a surprising variation to the colony's economic ties. "We have thought good," he wrote, "to joyne with one Edward Ashley" in a completely independent trading investment on the Penobscot River, roughly fifty miles northeast of Plymouth's outpost on the Kennebec and in direct competition with it. Hearing that Ashley was about to receive financial backing from some Bristol merchants, Sherley explains, he and Allerton had decided to step in and support him themselves: "and he, on the other side, like an understanding yonge man, thought it better to joyne with those that had means by a plantation to supply and back him ther, rather then strangers, that looke but only after profite" (307). Plymouth too, Sherley hastens to add, is welcome to join in the Penobscot venture, though he acknowledges the confusion that is likely to result from this layering together of multiple partnerships and recommends that the colonists "keep the accounts apart, though you joyne with us," to avoid the "mingling" of debts. The strategic mingling of debts later proves to be a chief device by which Sherley and Allerton themselves manage to hold Plymouth liable for expenses that the colony never had any knowledge they were incurring (307–8).

By this point in his analysis of Sherley's letter, Bradford has indicated in a number of ways that his correspondent's emphatic devotion to the bonds of love and unity is related to Bradford's formal decision to divide and closely scrutinize the document in which Sherley makes these appeals. By the time the letter itself draws to a close, with the entirely conventional wish on Sherley's part "that our loves and affections may still be united, and knit together," it is clear that such customary metaphors have lost all power of reassurance (309). Indeed, they have become little more than a mask for the commercial tactics that lead Sherley and his colleagues to support two identical trading enterprises on the northern New England coast, in the hope that one of them, at least, will enable the English backers to recover their costs.

Edward Ashley may well have been the understanding young man that Sherley claims—Bradford acknowledges that he has "wite and abillitie"—but the colonists also knew him to be "very profane," a wilderness go-between of the most unsettling kind, for (according to Bradford) he had "lived among the Indians as a savage, and went naked amongst them, and used their maners (which time he got their language), so they feared he might still rune into evill courses (though he promised better), and God would not prosper his ways" (309). A confusing and liminal figure

at best, Ashley is by no means an unequivocally degenerate one. For all his ambivalence, Bradford emphasizes Ashley's talents and his promise more than the preco-
cious commercial instincts that James Sherley finds so appealing. He represents a
mingling of cultural identities and of personal attributes, as well as a mingling of
monetary accounts. In most respects, Ashley is better adapted to the New England
trading economy than Thomas Morton was, for he has accommodated himself to
Indian customs and language, rather than following Morton's course of assimilat-
ing Indian women, primarily, into Old World rituals of sexual license.[36] But like
Morton, Ashley will shortly be arrested by the Massachusetts Bay Colony for
allegedly trading arms with the Indians. Through Sherley's opportunistic designs,
however, he first becomes the means by which Plymouth finds itself abruptly
drawn into an improbable partnership.

Bradford and his colleagues have little option but to support the Penobscot venture, despite its prejudicial impact on their Kennebec trade, since a refusal to join
(Bradford believes) will only encourage Isaac Allerton to "swime, as it were, between both" trading partnerships, ultimately to the detriment of Plymouth (310).
This facility at swimming between opposite camps (like Ashley's cross-cultural
identity) is a form of unity in its own right, but it is also a self-interested debase-
ment of the lofty ideal of cohesion to which Sherley's language so frequently appeals. In taking Sherley's long letter apart, Bradford has exposed the ways in which
it is knit together by commercial ends to which Plymouth is little more than a convenient means. Sherley's principles, in many respects, prove closely related to those
of Captain Wollaston, whose impatience for profit led him to convert his indentured servants into cash. Sherley, too, hoped to capitalize on Plymouth's economic
dependence in order to supply Ashley's far less elaborate and (he hopes) far more
lucrative business.

Isaac Allerton quickly demonstrates aspirations in the international arms trade
that eclipse those of Ashley and Morton. Among the purchases that he made in
England, drawing on Plymouth's account with the merchant investors, was a small
ship named the *White Angel,* intended for service in supplying Ashley's Penobscot
trading post. When Timothy Hatherley travels to New England in 1630 to help
address the growing financial confusion between the colony and its creditors, Bradford learns that Allerton eventually planned to sell the *White Angel* as a warship to
the Portuguese, "she being wel fitted with good ordnance, and known to have made
a great fight at sea" (326). The colonists briefly delay this particular transaction in
illegal luxury goods, but with Sherley's help, Allerton is at last able to sell the ship
in Spain, "and who had, or what became of the money," Bradford notes, "he best
knows" (358).

The Plymouth partners never succeed in having the *White Angel*'s expenses removed from their account. Allerton's own books prove "so large and intrecate" that the colonists can never make sense of them, particularly in the absence of Allerton himself, who is increasingly "hard to gett amongst them" (344). By 1631 Sherley's records put Plymouth almost six thousand pounds in debt, an extravagant sum that Allerton has managed to keep hidden from his New England colleagues by persuading Sherley and Hatherley to blot out two lines of an earlier letter, which might have warned them of Allerton's fiscal excesses. "Thus were they kept hoodwinckte," Bradford concludes, and "abused in their simplicitie, and no better then bought and sould" (348). The parallel to Captain Wollaston's traffic in human beings, which Bradford had introduced into the history thirty manuscript pages earlier, is complete.

ᵍ❧

BY 1633 Sherley too had lost faith in Isaac Allerton's commercial ventures and business ethics. "Oh the greefe and trouble that man, Mr. Allerton, hath brought upon you and us!" he exclaims, "I cannot forgett it, and to thinke on it draws many a sigh from my harte, and teares from my eyes" (368). In transcribing the letter that contains these words, Bradford must have relished the striking similarity between Sherley's copious expressions of regret and those of John Lyford nearly a decade earlier:

> By Mr. Allertons faire propositions and large promises, I have over rune my selfe; verily, at this time greefe hinders me to write, and tears will not suffer me to see; wherfore, as you love those that ever loved you, and that plantation, thinke upon us. Oh what shall I say of that man, who hath abused your trust, and wronged our loves! but now to complaine is too late, nither can I complaine of your backwardnes, for I am perswaded it lys as heavie on your harts, as it doth on our purses or credites . . . the Lord I hope will give us patience to bear these crosses; and that great God, whose care and providence is every where, and spetially over all those that desire truly to fear and serve him, direct, guid, prosper, and blesse you so, as that you may be able (as I perswade my selfe you are willing) to discharge and take off this great and heavie burthen which now lyes upon me for your saks. And I hope in the ende for the good of you, and many thousands more, for had not you and we joyned and continued togeather, New-England might yet have been scarce knowne, I am perswaded, not so replenished and inhabited with honest English people, as it now is. (368–69)

This is Sherley's last effort to resuscitate the fiction of loving unity between the London merchants and Plymouth Plantation. Even so, it is Sherley's own financial obligations that clearly preoccupy him, not the role that he played in assisting Isaac

Allerton to run up the colony's debts. The strain on his purse and his credit is at the center of Sherley's concerns, not the heavy hearts of the people whom he has misled. Bradford's comment on the letter is terse, and though ten more years will pass before the partnership is formally dissolved, its role in Bradford's narrative is largely finished: "But I leave these maters," he summarily notes, after pointing out the self-interested nature of Sherley's rhetoric, "and come to other things" (369).

The remainder of the history addresses conflicts and crimes of a far more vivid and concrete sort. Allerton's financial maneuvering was perpetually "foulded up in obscuritie, and kept in the clouds" (329). By contrast, there is all too little obscurity associated with the events that Bradford explores in the last thirteen years that he chronicles in *Of Plimmoth Plantation*. An intimation of this change is contained in two brief episodes that Bradford records on the facing pages of his manuscript during the long account of the events of 1631, the year in which Isaac Allerton finally abandoned all pretense of serving as Plymouth's agent.

In the first of these interpolated incidents, Bradford describes the robbery of the Penobscot trading post by the French. Thomas Willett—"an honest yonge man" from Leiden whom the Plymouth partners originally sent to Penobscot to help keep Edward Ashley "within bounds"—had remained after Ashley's arrest to run the trading post on his own. While Willett and some of his men were on a trip to Plymouth to get a fresh supply of goods, a small French ship visited the harbor and, finding "but 3. or 4. simple men, that were servants," left in charge:

> they fell of comending their gunes and muskets, that lay upon racks by the wall side, and tooke them downe to looke on them, asking if they were charged; and when they were possest of them, one presents a peece ready charged against the servants, and another a pistoll; and bid them not sturr, but quietly deliver them their goods, and carries some of the men aborde, and made the other help to carry away the goods; and when they had tooke what they pleased, they sett them at liberty, and wente their way, with this mock, biding them tell their master when he came, that some of the Ile of Rey gentlemen had been ther. (351)

This is the first of two such raids by the French within the space of four years, both involving many "complements," "congees," and fine words but resulting in the loss of several hundred pounds worth of goods and furs and finally in the loss of the post itself.

After the second incursion, in 1635, which resulted in Thomas Willett's eviction from his fortified trading house, the colonists attempted to retaliate, with disappointing results. They hired an armed ship whose captain expended all his powder in a furious assault on the French from such a cautious distance that his cannon were useless. This ill-fated expedition plays a minor role in Plymouth's growing differences with Massachusetts Bay, but the first robbery seems to offer Bradford a measure of dramatic relief from the opaque nature of the colony's struggles with Allerton and Sherley. French mockery and deceit, however unwelcome, were in some respects less offensive than the record of juggled accounts, overcharges, and shoddy goods with which the Penobscot events are directly collated in the main body of the narrative.

The final interpolated episode fills the blank reverse sides of three pages in Bradford's manuscript—the longest such parallel narrative in *Of Plimmoth Plantation*. In it Bradford offers a detailed account of the misadventures of Sir Christopher Gardiner, a self-proclaimed "Knight of the Sepulcher" at Jerusalem and a relative of Stephen Gardiner, one of Mary Tudor's inquisitorial bishops, who came to New England in 1630, a month before the Winthrop fleet, and later settled near Boston "under pretense of forsaking the world, and to live a private life, in a godly course" (352). Among his entourage was "a comely yonge woman" whom Gardiner called his cousin, though the Massachusetts authorities suspected her of being his concubine, "after the Italian maner," as Bradford puts it. Italy was the stereotypical hotbed of irregular sexuality, in the seventeenth-century English imagination. These suspicions were aroused in part by letters arriving from London describing Gardiner's unsavory past, but before the officers of the Massachusetts General Court could seize him, Gardiner escaped, taking refuge in the vicinity of Plymouth's Indian neighbors, who soon inquired of Bradford whether they might kill Gardiner and collect the reward for his capture offered by Winthrop's government.[37]

Bradford dissuades the Indians from this drastic step but encourages them to capture Gardiner alive and bring him to Plymouth:

> And so they did, for when they light of him by a river side, he got into a canowe to get from them, and when they came nere him, whilst he presented his peece at them to keep them of, the streame carried the canow against a rock, and tumbled both him and his peece and rapier into the water; yet he got out, and having a litle dagger by his side, they durst not close with him, but getting longe pols they soone beat his dagger out of his hand, so he was glad to yeeld; and they brought him to the Governor. But his hands and armes were swolen and very sore with the blowes they had given him. So he used him kindly, and sent him to a lodging wher his armes were bathed and anoynted, and he was quickly well againe, and blamed the Indeans for beating him so much. They said that they did but a litle whip him with sticks. (353)

During Gardiner's recovery at Plymouth, "a litle note booke" discovered in his bedding reveals that he is in fact a Catholic, who had taken his scapular, an order

Fig. 8. From John Foxe, *Actes and Monuments of matters most speciall and memorable . . .* (London, 1583), STC 11225, 2:1493. By permission of the Houghton Library, Harvard University.

of monastic confraternity, in a European university. Bradford forwards this document to John Winthrop, when he returns Gardiner to the custody of Massachusetts Bay. The notebook, along with other evidence of Gardiner's criminal behavior, and his ill-concealed hostility to the colony's leadership, prompt Winthrop and his assistants briefly to imprison him. Rather than forcibly deport Gardiner, however, as they did Thomas Morton the previous year, they allow him to join some English settlements in the Androscoggin region before his voluntary return to England in the summer of 1632. Both Morton and Gardiner quickly became willing assistants in Ferdinando Gorges's efforts to have the Massachusetts Bay Company charter revoked.[38]

It is easy to see how a figure such as Gardiner might have caught Catharine Sedgwick's eye, nearly two centuries later as she was assembling a list of characters for *Hope Leslie*, her 1827 novel set in seventeenth-century Massachusetts. Along

The burning of M. Iohn Hooper, Bifhop at Glocefter.   An. 1 5 5 5. Februarie 9.

Lord Iefu receiue my foule.

Fig. 9. From John Foxe, *Actes and Monuments of matters most speciall and memorable . . .* (London, 1583), STC 11225, 2:1510. By permission of the Houghton Library, Harvard University.

with Morton, Gardiner offers promising possibilities for treatment in historical fiction.[39] *Of Plimmoth Plantation,* however, was not available to Sedgwick as a source for her book, so the curious detail of Gardiner's capture by the Indians makes no appearance in her story.

It is, nevertheless, a suggestive event for Bradford. Christopher Gardiner's famous relative, the grimly vindictive bishop of Winchester, had presided over the opening phases of the Marian persecution, personally interrogating a number of England's most distinguished martyrs and overseeing the inhumane conditions of their imprisonment before sending them to the stake.[40] The woodcuts of their executions in John Foxe's *Actes and Monuments* were vivid reminders of the brutality of Mary's reign and of the legendary courage of many of its victims. Arms and hands played a prominent role in this iconography of suffering. John Rogers—whose last request to see his wife and ten children before he died was callously rebuffed by Bishop Gardiner—washed his hands in the flames as they rose around his body. The woodcut accompanying the account of his execution in Foxe's pages depicts

Rogers reaching his arms toward the fire (fig. 8). Thomas Cranmer famously held in the fire the hand with which he had originally signed an abjuration of his Protestant beliefs, so that this offending member would be the first part of his body to suffer. John Hooper slowly struck his chest as he died, until one of his partly consumed arms fell into the flames at his feet and his remaining hand fused to the chains with which his body was bound to the stake (fig. 9). Foxe's description of this gruesome death, and its accompanying illustration, are among the most graphic in his book.[41]

In describing the swollen hands and arms of Christopher Gardiner, William Bradford may well have had these celebrated images in mind. Indeed, the long pole with which one of John Hooper's tormentors prods the logs at his feet, in Foxe's illustration, seems uncannily to prefigure those with which the Wampanoag had prudently disarmed Christopher Gardiner before taking him prisoner. Bradford was undoubtedly familiar with this famous woodcut. One of the first and most celebrated victims of the Marian persecution, John Bradford, had grown up in Lancashire and gone to school in Manchester, some thirty miles west of William Bradford's Yorkshire birthplace. Their common north-country surname must have made Foxe's account of John Bradford's repeated examinations by various Catholic interrogators, his many letters smuggled from prison, and his agonizing death at the stake in July 1555 especially prominent in William Bradford's memory of the "cruell torments" associated with Mary's reign. When his own son was born in Leiden, Bradford broke with three generations of family tradition to give him the martyr's name.

A copy of Foxe's book was available to Bradford as he began writing his history, though it is likely that he was so steeped in its vivid images and anecdotes from a lifetime of study as to require little reminder of the dramatic essence of Foxe's story. Christopher Gardiner's lineage, as well as his injuries, could hardly have failed to prompt Bradford's comparative instincts. The contrast between justice as it was administered in Plymouth and the judicial corruptions of the English past must have alternately consoled and troubled him as he drafted the final chapters of his book. The Indians' wary (if oddly clumsy) manner of approaching their violent antagonist, coupled with Bradford's kind usage of his prisoner, form a suggestive turning point in the colony's story, as its leaders increasingly find themselves implicated in, rather than suffering from, the grave injustices of their time.

CHAPTER FOUR

Here Is the Miserablest Time

IN THE LETTER that John Winthrop sent to Bradford, acknowledging Plymouth's role in apprehending Christopher Gardiner, he offered some assurances concerning his attitude toward this latest candidate for deportation from New England. "I never intended any hard measure to him," Winthrop wrote, "but to respecte and use him according to his qualitie, yet I let him know your care of him, and that he shall speed the better for your mediation" (354). Apparently, in addition to shielding Gardiner from the violent intentions of the Indians and providing for his bruised arms after his capture, Bradford had also interceded on Gardiner's behalf with the Massachusetts authorities, for reasons that the pages of the history do not make immediately clear.

These actions are intriguingly inconsistent with the vehemence of Bradford's response to John Lyford's hypocrisy or the "villanie" of Thomas Morton, both of whom appear to prefigure important features of Gardiner's character. Like Lyford, Gardiner disguises libertine habits beneath what seems to be a superficial pretense of religious feeling. Like Morton, he proves adept at deflecting the intentions of the Massachusetts General Court, joining forces with the colony's enemies, once he returns to England, in order to bring charges of misgovernment against Winthrop and his colleagues before a committee of the Privy Council. In retrospect, Bradford acknowledges the "means and malice" that Gardiner brought to bear against the plantations of New England and guardedly concurs with Winthrop's opinion that Providence played a role in thwarting this attempt to discredit the officers of Massachusetts Bay. But the account of Gardiner's behavior in *Of Plimmoth Plantation* remains more complicated than its brevity might initially suggest.

Unlike Winthrop, Bradford does not display any particular interest in Gardiner's gentlemanly "qualitie," nor does he elaborate on the nature of the specific offenses that prompted Gardiner's flight to the woods. Most of these details, including the disposition of the petition of complaint that Gardiner and his allies present to the Privy Council, directly concern Winthrop's government rather than Bradford's. The historians of Massachusetts Bay, whoever they might prove to be, would undoubtedly explain that colony's treatment of Christopher Gardiner as fully as Bradford tried to do in the case of John Lyford. Plymouth is able to assume the role of good physician, rather than judge, in the face of this particular expression of human infirmity—seeing to it that Gardiner's injuries were "bathed and anoynted," as well as soothing the resentments of his pursuers. Bradford clearly hopes to strike a balance between the medicinal and the punitive roles that Plymouth plays in these events. This perception of the mixed obligations of civil authority shapes the final third of his book.[1]

A critical index to the judicial temperament expressed in *Of Plimmoth Plantation* is the matter-of-fact tone that Bradford adopts toward Christopher Gardiner's devotional notebook. In the hands of many a contemporary historian or clergyman, such a document would amount to a sensational discovery—damning evidence of some dark, conspiratorial intent behind Gardiner's self-serving pose as a religious recluse hoping to escape the liturgical infection of the English Church. John Lyford's letters create just such a sensation in Bradford's book, but only because they are pointed acts of misrepresentation, aimed at tumbling Plymouth into a political crisis. Gardiner's Catholic piety, however, is a matter of conscience, not dramatically different from the quarrel over the Christmas holiday that occurred briefly in the streets of Plymouth in 1621. Bradford confiscates Gardiner's notebook, as he did the implements of play ten years earlier, and turns it over to Winthrop's officers, but that is the end of the matter. Even a libertine Catholic hypocrite may expect to have his wounds anointed rather than his flesh consumed, in Plymouth Plantation. Bradford is clearly aware of the rich legal and punitive history that this trivial incident evokes. He uses it to help portray Plymouth's struggle to remain independent of the entrenched religious hostilities that marked seventeenth-century life.

THE SUGGESTIVE CIRCUMSTANCES surrounding Christopher Gardiner's capture indicate, on a concise dramatic scale, the narrative course that Bradford hopes to pursue. The entire incident occupies little more than a month, in the early spring of 1631, beginning with the arrival of letters in Boston accusing Gardiner of bigamy. According to Thomas Dudley, Winthrop's deputy governor, two women identifying themselves as Gardiner's abandoned wives had found one another out and joined forces in London to seek redress, "his first wife desiring his return and conversion, his second his destruction for his foul abuse." Gardiner himself had been in New England a little less than a year when these accusations surfaced, living seven miles outside Boston with a third woman whom his aggrieved wives identified as Mary Grove, "a known harlot." These are the "miscarriages" (as Bradford tactfully calls them) for which the Massachusetts General Court orders Gardiner's arrest, but his wariness in settling so far from town permits him to escape to the north (as Dudley thought), "hoping to find some English there like to himself."[2]

However, instead of going north and dying of hunger and cold, as Dudley vaguely hoped, Gardiner flees southward into the vicinity of Plymouth. Neighboring Indians—probably from Massasoit's Wampanoag confederacy, though Bradford does not specify their identity—bring Gardiner to Bradford's attention, initially as a kind of legal problem. Does the offer of a reward for this fugitive mean that it is permissible to kill him, as the safest and easiest way to satisfy the authorities at Boston? The Massachusetts Indians are inclined to think so. Does the governor of Plymouth agree? Bradford notes these preliminary consultations in part to stress the entangled earthly jurisdictions that Gardiner represents. He is, in conceptual as well as literal terms, a "great traveller": descended from the house of a notorious English bishop, a Knight of the Sepulcher at Jerusalem, steeped in Italian "manners" with his dubious paramour, a would-be citizen of Massachusetts Bay, and an unwelcome but potentially profitable transient in the territory of two New England native peoples.

Gardiner is a dispositional challenge of some complexity. His London wives agree that they want him returned to England, along with his current romantic partner, to face the consequences of his acts, but they differ sharply on the nature of the penalty that they envision for their deceiver. The Indians are willing to help their English neighbors capture Gardiner, but he is heavily armed and poses risks that the monetary reward does not necessarily justify. Bradford cooperatively turns his prisoner/patient over to the Massachusetts officers sent to retrieve him, sending along the provocative "litle note booke" of religious memoranda that casts further doubt on Gardiner's character and motives, but he counsels Winthrop against treating Gardiner with undue severity—partly for political reasons, perhaps, but partly too out of some sympathy with his plight.

The tangle of emotions and interests surrounding this equivocal figure suggests that no one will be able to take complete satisfaction in the resolution of his story. Thomas Dudley relishes the prospect of Gardiner's bones bleaching in the New England woods, but instead this apparent reprobate falls into the distinctly gentle custody of William Bradford. Despite the antithetical wishes of Gardiner's wives, neither his conversion nor his destruction is a very likely outcome for these events. The potentially promising details of Gardiner's actual capture are marked, in Bradford's account, not by the triumph of native woodcraft or martial prowess but by a nearly comic conjunction of accidents.

The Indians do not set out to trap their quarry but simply "watch their opportunitie," as Bradford advised, and happily "light" on Gardiner at an awkward moment, as he is trying to flee in a canoe. When the canoe strikes a rock, Gardiner gets a dunking and loses his gun and his rapier, retaining only a "litle dagger" with which to keep the Indians briefly at bay. Like the "litle note booke," discovered "by accidente" in Gardiner's bedding at Plymouth, this ineffectual weapon seems a wistfully diminutive prop with which to sustain any large dramatic claims. The Indians likewise "did but a litle whip him" before packing Gardiner off to Bradford's care. Nothing in this episode, as Bradford presents it, invites John Winthrop's grand declaration that a "spetiall providence of God" had brought Christopher Gardiner, along with suggestive evidence of his popish sympathies, safely into "our hands" (353–54).

Throughout Bradford's circumstantially vivid account, hard measures appear to mingle, in productive but ambivalent ways, with gentler ones—much as Gardiner's English wives share a common predicament but reflect very different views of the social and moral purposes of punishment. The memory of Mary Tudor's great persecutor serves to emphasize the absence of persecutorial fervor in Bradford's language. Gardiner's religious notebook seems no more formidable than his dagger; indeed, the fact that Gardiner kept these potentially damaging personal memorials, and tried to conceal them, suggests that his religious feelings were not simply matters of pretense, though it is questionable whether he ever sincerely intended to forsake the world, as he claimed he did when he first arrived in Massachusetts. Such a determination in itself is a way of taking hard measures with earthly temptation and human weakness. By contrast, a susceptibility to moral failings usually elicits Bradford's patience and restraint, rather than his judgmental instincts, even as such failings occasionally tax these personal resources to their limits.

Four years before Gardiner's appearance in New England, Bradford had dealt with a very similar, problematic figure in equally forbearing fashion. In the winter of 1626, Bradford reports, a ship bound for Virginia with a cargo of trading goods and indentured Irish servants was crippled and run aground at Manamoyake Bay, south of Cape Cod. The shipmaster's sickness and his crew's incompetence had protracted their voyage until the passengers had begun to believe that they would starve or die of disease at sea. Although they had been able to save their lives and most of their cargo, as they came ashore, the survivors were "strucken with sadness" at their desolate predicament, until some Indians addressed them in English and informed them that they were near the settlement at Plymouth. Bradford took the castaways a boatload of necessary supplies, and when their ship eventually proved unsalvageable, settled them at Plymouth until another vessel could be found to take them south, assigning some land to the two most prominent passengers, "one Mr. Fells and Mr. Sibsie," on which their servants could raise a crop "to help bear their charge" (265).

Much like the suspicious partnership between Christopher Gardiner and his "cousin" a few years later, Mr. Fells was accompanied by a maid whom his other servants alleged to be his "concubine." "Both of them were examined ther upon," Bradford wrote, "but nothing could be proved, and they stood upon their justification, so with admonition they were dismiste." The maid, however, became pregnant and, "for fear of punishmente," Fells "ran away with her" in a small boat to Massachusetts Bay, hoping to take passage on a fishing ship. Partly by the absence of a suitable refuge and partly by the danger of the sea, he was eventually forced to return to Plymouth and "submite him selfe."

Bradford does not make clear what this submission entailed, or whether the magistrates at Plymouth would have felt authorized to punish an involuntary and temporary resident exactly as they punished their own citizens for sexual offenses. He simply writes that they "pact" Fells away "by the first oppertunity," along with "those that belonged unto him." Fells was not, in any case, the only "untoward" person among this group of would-be Virginians, "though ther were allso some that caried them selves very orderly all the time they stayed" (266). Before the rest of this party of emigrants finally sailed south, late in the summer of 1627, Bradford confessed that "the plantation had some benefite by them," selling them surplus corn and other food in return for clothing, cloth, hose, and shoes, all highly desirable commodities at Plymouth. "So they both did good, and received good one from another," Bradford concluded, "And sundrie of them have acknowledged their thankfullnes since from Virginia" (266).

Although not a perfect parallel to Christopher Gardiner's circumstances, this episode, too, suggests the absence of much appetite for hard measures in Bradford's judicial practice. Gardiner's transgressions appear in the pages of the history on a series of verso sheets that face Bradford's detailed summation of Isaac Allerton's "grosse miscarrages" in managing the colony's business affairs over the course of several years—a contrast that further tends to mitigate the extent of the insult that Gardiner has offered to the public well-being. Gross as they were, Allerton's offenses never prompted either the government or the church at Plymouth to a decisive repudiation, though Allerton repeatedly "broke his bonds, kepte no covenante

. . . nor was ever like to keep covenants" with his old companions from Leiden (358). Christopher Gardiner's revealing notebook, in contrast, suggests that some covenants, at least, were meaningful to this otherwise faithless character. In these passages, too, the boundary between transgressors and good neighbors appears intriguingly blurred.

By contrast with Bradford's forbearance, John Winthrop's attitude toward Gardiner's behavior seems far more legalistic, even conspiratorial, in nature. In his initial letter of thanks to Bradford, in early May 1631, he asks that Plymouth's officers keep secret the existence of Gardiner's religious notes, urging Bradford to "speake to all that are privie to them, not to discovere them to any one, for that may frustrate the means of any further use to be made of them" (354). Like Lyford's intercepted letters, perhaps, these notes may be put to some dramatic purpose in court, but under any circumstances it is difficult to see the necessity for such secrecy. Bradford clearly implies that Gardiner's private memorials concern only himself and have little direct bearing on the legal charges that lead the Massachusetts authorities to imprison him. The energies of religious persecution appear to stir beneath Winthrop's request—an ominous suggestion that Bradford handles very cautiously, perhaps because at the time that he recorded Gardiner's story in *Of Plimmoth Plantation,* Winthrop had recently died.

Two concluding documents bring this long, interpolated narrative to a close. First Bradford transcribes a second letter from Winthrop written more than a year after Gardiner's return to England, describing Winthrop's immense relief at the conclusion of the Privy Council investigation in which Gardiner and Thomas Morton had played key roles. Bradford follows this letter with the Privy Council report itself, explaining that he will take "a litle libertie" to discuss the outcome of Christopher Gardiner's vengeful efforts, "though I doubt not but it will be more fully done by my honourd [Boston] friends, whom it did more directly concerne, and have more perticular knowledge of the matter." Nevertheless, Bradford continues, he will offer a "hinte" of "Gods providence in preventing the hurte" that Gardiner sought to inflict.

What follows, however, is much more than a hint. Bradford copies onto the verso sheets of his book the full text of a Privy Council resolution from January 1632, concerning the "great distraction" and "disorder" in Massachusetts Bay that had prompted the formation of "a comitie of this bord, to take examination of the matters informed" (356). After hearing from the "principal adventurers" in the plantation, as well as from Gardiner and his fellow "complanants," the committee determined that it would be too expensive to bring the necessary witnesses from New England to resolve the charges and that a long inquiry might cripple important lines of credit and bring the trading projects of the English merchants to "a stand." Making a vague but disquieting promise to investigate the faults of "some perticular men . . . in due time," the committee declared that since "the appearances were so faire, and hopes so greate" for New England's future commercial contribution to the kingdom, they would urge the investors concerned in Massachusetts Bay "to go on cherfully with their undertakings," adding that "if things were carried as was pretended when the patents were granted, and accordingly as by the patentes it is appointed," the king would continue to support them (357).

This less-than-reassuring language is a texture of pretense, not unlike the well-traveled Knight of the Sepulcher with whose exploits Bradford's brief narrative had begun. The goodwill of the Privy Council is little more than a superficial mask for the economic influence brought to bear by a group of English merchants who are sensitive to any disruption in the management of New England affairs and only too prone to "take suspition" of the true intentions of the government toward their precarious investments (356). The council, in turn, implicitly recognizes that the terms of the colonial patents are likewise "pretended" accounts of how the colonists intend to conduct themselves. Should this network of fair appearances ever cease to be mutually beneficial, the interest of the Privy Council might easily take a much less favorable turn for the current magistrates of Massachusetts Bay. If anything at all is merely hinted in this portion of Bradford's text, it is the long-term threat contained in this deceptively satisfactory short-term result.

In contrast to Bradford's tentative hints, John Winthrop greets this troubling memorandum from Whitehall with a cascade of providential rhetoric, all incorporated into a letter that Bradford carefully transcribes. In Winthrop's eyes these proceedings signal the success of the Massachusetts cause and the "blame and disgrace" of their adversaries, making "it evident to all that the Lord hath care of his people hear." Though God "hath humbled us by his late correction," Winthrop admits, "so he hath lifted us up, by an abundante rejoysing, in our deliverance out of so desperate a danger; so as that which our enemies builte their hopes upon to ruine us by, He hath mercifully disposed to our great advantage" (355). This divine disposition, in Winthrop's mind, entirely supplants the more ominous implications of the Privy Council report—the text of which Bradford immediately juxtaposes to Winthrop's ecstatic claims.

Perhaps no feature of Bradford's narrative in *Of Plimmoth Plantation* is more striking than the distance that he consistently maintains between the subtle, analytical registers of his own prose and the kind of broad religious fiction to which Winthrop's heavily biblical language gives expression. Christopher Hill has commented perceptively on Walter Ralegh's inability to resolve the contradiction between his faith in providential causality and his clear perception of the interplay of earthly contingencies in human affairs. Ralegh's *History of the World* is marked by the tension between these interpretive poles.[3] This tension forms an equally prominent part of William Bradford's subject, as he consistently exposes the disparity between what Francis Bacon termed the poetic appeal of "fained history" and the stubborn, circumstantial resistance of actual experience. It is the work of the imagination, Bacon argued, to submit "the shewes of things to the desires of the Mind," much as Winthrop subsumes the tactical equivocations of the Privy Council beneath his account of divine correction and abundant deliverance. Unlike these gratifying shadows, the work of memory must adhere to the discipline of fact and seek its account of historical significance there, even in the story of such "meane concordances" to Bacon's great city of the world, as Plymouth Plantation.[4]

෪

J O H N   W I N T H R O P ' S brief epistolary psalm, rejoicing in the ruin of New England's enemies, resembles many passages in Bradford's book where he permits other portraits of historical causation or design to compete with his own, sometimes employing the verso sheets of his manuscript book to sharpen the contrast. A few pages after the interpolated story of Christopher Gardiner, for example, Bradford records the wreck of William Peirce's trading vessel, the *Lyon*, in the winter of 1632, as it was carrying a shipment of furs and important documents from Plymouth to London. Peirce had intended to stop in Virginia before setting out across the Atlantic. Instead, Bradford notes, "it pleased God" that the ship "was cast away on that coast" (365). Peirce and his crew saved themselves, along with the colonists' letters, and eventually got "safly home" to England, but most of the valuable cargo was lost, including an annotated set of Isaac Allerton's accounts, which Bradford and his colleagues had labored over in an attempt to clear up lingering disagreements between themselves and the merchant adventurers on the extent of the colony's indebtedness. They had kept a copy of this important record in Plymouth, however, and promptly sent on a replacement. "And thus much of the passages of this year," Bradford dutifully observes, ending his chronicle of 1632 (365).

The note of the routine in this last sentence effectively captures the spirit in which Bradford recounts the misfortune of the *Lyon*. It pleased God, perhaps, to bring this ship to grief, but prudent men prepare for such unexpected blows by keeping duplicates of irreplaceable records that have to run the hazards of the sea. Peirce and his men, at least, were safe.[5] The loss of the furs, Bradford remarks, was the first such disaster that they had experienced "in that kind" in twelve years of conducting transatlantic commerce. On the whole, Bradford would appear to emphasize that Plymouth had very little cause to complain of dramatic setbacks. William Peirce, however, reports these events in very different terms in the letter that he sends to Plymouth announcing the wreck. Bradford transcribes Peirce's letter on the verso sheet that faces his own comparatively dispassionate account:

> Dear freinds, The bruit of this fatall stroke, that the Lord hath brought both on me and you all, will come to your ears before this commeth to your hands (it is like) and therfore I shall not need to inlarg in perticulers, &c. My whole estate (for the most parte) is taken away; and so yours, in a great measure, by this and your former losses . . . It is time to looke aboute us, before the wrath of the Lord breake forth to utter destruction. The good Lord give us all grace to search our harts and trie our ways, and turne unto the Lord, and humble our selves under his mightie hand, and seeke atonemente, &c. Dear freinds, you may know that all your beaver, and the books of your accounts, are swallowed up in the sea; your letters remaine with me, and shall be delivered, if God bring me home. But what should I more say, have we lost our outward estates? yet a hapy loss if our soules may gaine; ther is yet more in the Lord Jehova than ever we had yet in the world. Oh that our foolish harts could yet be wained from the things here below, which are vanity and vexation of spirite; and yet we fooles catch after shadows, that flye away, and are gone in a momente. (365–66)

Peirce, of course, is writing from Virginia in late December 1632, with the harrowing experience of a shipwreck fresh in his mind, much as John Winthrop was reporting to Bradford his relief at the decision of the Privy Council shortly after learning the result of Christopher Gardiner's complaint. Compositional immediacy accounts for part of the striking contrast between Bradford's muted, retrospective presentation in both cases and the passionate language of these contemporary records.

But it is notable that Bradford makes little effort to close this emotional distance. His description of Thomas Morton's behavior is written almost two decades after the fact, much like his report of Christopher Gardiner's malice or the wreck of the *Lyon,* but where Morton is concerned, Bradford's anger is swiftly revived. Retrospective and contemporary levels of feeling readily blend in the pages of his narrative, when it suits Bradford's purposes to have them do so. That is not the case in the way that he has chosen to present Winthrop's vision of providential intent in the deliverance of Massachusetts from its English enemies or Peirce's fervent attack on the deceitful vanities of earthly life. In both of these instances, the rhetorical separation is distinct and suggestive, stressing the propensity of the mind to get caught up in figurative structures of meaning at the expense of reason and judgment.

Winthrop and Peirce were old and tested friends, whose words, however strongly colored by the biblical imagination, captured the intense anxieties of the colonial world that Bradford sought to preserve in his book. If the piety that they express in their letters is unquestionably sincere, Bradford leaves little doubt that it is also, in some measure, opportune. It is language that could easily serve hypocrites well, as it had John Lyford a few years earlier in Plymouth's experience. Christopher Gardiner's professed determination to forsake the world in favor of a godly private life is at least briefly persuasive to a New England audience precisely because it appears to echo William Peirce's longing to be weaned from a dependence upon earthly things, to discipline his foolish heart under the Lord's corrective hand.

James Sherley takes a very similar line with his Plymouth partners, in a letter of September 1636 in which he explains his inability to make a better financial report concerning the colony's latest shipment of furs to England. Bradford and his colleagues had sent that year, by two ships, more than a ton of beaver pelts and more than two hundred otter skins—a small fortune in commodities that Sherley was unable to sell because plague had virtually closed the London exchanges. His explanation is perfectly plausible: "when the Lord shall please to cease his hand," Sherley observed, "I hope we shall have better and quicker markets" (410). In the meantime, Plymouth's furs "shall lye by."

But this shipment, and an equally valuable one from the preceding year, had failed to ameliorate the demands and disagreements of the London investors, who continued to complain of the heavy debts that they had incurred in supporting the colony and to accuse one another of bad faith. Sherley is able to explain none of this ongoing strife:

> You will and may expect I should write more, and answer your leters, but I am not a day in the weeke at home at towne, but carry my books and all to Clapham; for here is the miserablest time, that I thinke hath been known, in many ages. I have known 3. great sickneses, but none like this. And that which should be a means to pacifie the Lord, and help us, that is taken away, preaching put downe in many places, not a sermone in Westminster on the saboth, nor in many townes aboute us. The Lord in mercie looke uppon us. In the begining of the year was a great drought, and no raine for many weeks togeather, so as all was burnte up, haye, at 5 li. a load; and now all raine, so as much sommer corne and later haye is spoyled. Thus the Lord sends judgmente after judgmente, and yet we cannot see, nor humble our selves; and therfore may justly fear heavier judgments, unless we speedyly repente, and returne unto him, which the Lord give us grace to doe, if it be his blessed will. (411)

Bradford's reaction, after transcribing this apocalyptic passage into the history, is a remarkably curt observation: "This was all the answer they had from Mr. Sherley." Although Sherley's account of London's dire condition in the troubled summer of 1636 was a reasonably accurate portrayal of one of the worst plague outbreaks in decades, Bradford clearly treats it as a formulaic lament—language so conventional as to arouse suspicion that the person who uses it is attempting to disguise some purely material interest or motive beneath a cloud of religious metaphor and spiritual angst.[6]

Sherley's performance is in every sense an extreme case, made all the more conspicuous by his pattern of questionable financial practices in handling the colony's affairs. Bradford's treatment of the outbreak of disease at Charlestown in 1630, however, is marked by an equally striking determination to preserve the emotional and rhetorical distance between his retrospective presentation of events and the religiously charged language of the letters that he uses to introduce key circumstances into his history. Shortly after the arrival in Massachusetts Bay of John Winthrop's small fleet of emigrant ships, disease broke out among the newly landed settlers, much as it had with the Plymouth emigrants during the early months of 1621. Bradford includes in *Of Plimmoth Plantation* two lengthy reports from Salem and from Charlestown in the summer of 1630 that prefigure London's plight in James Sherley's 1636 letter, declaring "the hand of God to be upon them, and against them . . . visiting them with sicknes, and taking diverse from amongst them, not sparing the righteous, but partaking with the wicked in these bodily judgments" (331).

The authorities at Charlestown designated a special day of humiliation to appease the Lord's wrath, beseeching him "to withdraw his hand of correction from them," though neither letter that Bradford transcribes from his Massachusetts correspondents identifies any particular area of religious or moral failing that might have prompted this inexplicable assault. The sense of mystery only appears to intensify the urgency of the public response. The second of the letters that Bradford preserves is from Samuel Fuller, Plymouth's physician, who was sent to Charlestown to help during the epidemic. Fuller has fallen in with the anxieties of his hosts, expressing to Bradford his concern that Plymouth too might invite the Lord's retribution without being conscious of a precise cause: "We have a name of holines," Fuller wrote, "and love to God and his saincts; the Lord make us more and more answerable, and that it may be more then a name, or els it will doe us no good" (332).

Partly as a result of Fuller's pointed reminder, perhaps, the parallel to Plymouth's "generall visitation" of disease in 1621 could not have been far from Bradford's mind as he copied these letters into his book. But he introduces them with language that seems calculated to forestall any comparison between the experiences of the two colonies until he can draw it on his own terms. When he does so, at the conclusion of Samuel Fuller's report, he ignores the spiritual anxieties that both letters from the Bay Colony reflect. Indeed, Bradford's preamble to the first letter that he transcribes, announcing the Charlestown epidemic, appropriates the dramatic convention of God's judgmental presence in human affairs—the powerful explanatory narrative to which the afflicted people of Massachusetts Bay had appealed—and reduces it to a quite unremarkable level: "Having by a providence a letter or to that came to my hands concerning the proceedings of their Reverend freinds in the Bay of the Massachusets, who were latly come over, I thought it not amise here to inserte them, (so farr as is pertenente, and may be usefull for after times) before I conclude this year" (330). The modest bibliographic operations of Providence to which Bradford points in this passage involve a considerable contrast in dramatic force to the cry of a scourged and wayward people in the disease-wracked year of 1630. Some of the material in the Massachusetts letters does indeed concern their initial political "proceedings" and their division into several distinct churches—useful and pertinent information that it might not be amiss to record. But the religious crisis precipitated by the epidemic eclipses these administrative details in the minds of Bradford's correspondents. It is precisely this crisis, and the language it evokes, that Bradford strives, in an almost offhand fashion, to isolate in the body of the letters themselves, as if he were placing them (as well as their authors) in quarantine.

When Bradford does undertake to draw religious instruction from these documents, his emphasis is on gratitude and on growth, not on the puzzling operations of divine justice. After copying Samuel Fuller's letter into the history, he elects to stress not the "sadd news" of sickness and death that Fuller reports but the extraordinary future that this latest emigrant enterprise indicated for New England: "Thus out of smalle beginings greater things have been produced by his hand that made all things of nothing, and gives being to all things that are; and as one small candle may light a thousand; so the light here kindled hath shone to many, yea in some sorte to our whole nation; let the glorious name of Jehova have all the praise" (332). Although the impact of such a passage—intensified by its strategic placement at the very end of a chronicle year—is quite different from Bradford's dismissive approach to James Sherley's 1636 letter, the degree of historical detachment in the two instances is quite similar. The surrounding narrative that Bradford constructs for these letters carefully and visibly separates itself from the intense preoccupations of the historical moment. *Of Plimmoth Plantation* depends on its reader to take note of this separation and recognize in its effects Bradford's determination to maintain a measure of objectivity by carefully observing the obligation of the historian to be wary of the shaping influence of his own "conceits," as well as of those he might detect in his sources. Bradford's deference to the will of Jehovah is as marked as that of his correspondents, but it is largely free of circumstantial passion—sealed off from the dramatic context of chastisement, atonement, and implicit recovery of divine favor that the language of Massachusetts Bay strives to impose on that colony's collective experience. Bradford offers his own sense of larger significance as an addendum (but only "so farr as is pertenente") to the course of the year's events.

Such wariness in the student of nature and culture was a key element of Francis Bacon's prescription, in *The Advancement of Learning*, for developing a mature body of secular knowledge: learning that could "minister to all the diseases of the mind" in its search for historical, scientific, or religious truth.[7] Bacon's brief but extraordinary book—a copy of which William Brewster had brought with him to Plymouth—applies the traditional biblical trope of the good physician with great enthusiasm to all of the "peccant humors" of the human intellect. Among the most pervasive of these, Bacon believed, was the tendency of the mind to be "peremptory" or "magistral" in its convictions, much as John Winthrop, for example, appeared to be in the peremptory conclusions that he was eager to draw from the ambiguous text of a Privy Council memorandum. "Men have used to infect their meditations," Bacon complained, with fixed and settled ideas—"with some conceits which they have most admired, or some Sciences which they have most applyed"— that tended to preclude rather than nourish productive inquiry. "Hast[e] to assertion without due and mature suspention of judgement" and a crippling "impatience of doubt" were the results of such premature certitude, hardening the understanding in its own defects, rather than predisposing it "still to be capable and susceptible of growth and reformation."[8]

Writing as he was, in 1605, with the express intention of flattering James I into offering him a lucrative government appointment, Bacon was careful not to extend his critique too freely to the fixed theological conceits of his monarch. The peremptory convictions of kings posed special problems for the humanist scholar in search of patronage. In one of the most gratuitous authorial dedications of a sycophantic age, Bacon had declared James to be a particularly appropriate patron for *The Advancement of Learning*, because he was invested with what Bacon called the "triplicitie" of attributes traditionally associated with Hermes Trismegistus: "the power and fortune of a King; the knowledge and illumination of a Priest; and the learning and universalitie of a Philosopher." James was (Bacon asserted) the most intellectually distinguished earthly ruler since the time of Christ, not excluding Marcus Aurelius.[9]

This degree of excessive praise comes perilously close to a suicidal mockery of its object, but however spurious the language of Bacon's dedication may seem to a modern reader, he was clearly sincere in the attempt that he makes, in the pages that follow, to remove many of the prejudices against intellectual accomplishments that contemporary politicians and men of affairs frequently expressed in their complaints that learning made men idly curious and irresolute, dogmatic and quarrelsome. These were precisely the stereotypical qualities that Thomas Weston had associated, in 1621, with the scrupulous but argumentative band of sectarian colonists at Plymouth and which had elicited from Bradford a suitably caustic and argumentative reply.

Bacon acknowledged that many of these temperamental deficiencies were indeed to be found in learned men, but they were counterbalanced, in a fully trained mind, by important benefits: "learning ministereth . . . greater strength of medicine or remedie" in public affairs than it causes indisposition or weakness. Properly applied, it makes "the mindes of men gentle and pliant to government," Bacon argued, whereas ignorance makes them churlish and mutinous. The disciplined pursuit of knowledge instructed men how to "turn back the first offers and conceits of the mind," how to wait for evidence, how to assess it patiently, "how to carrie things in suspence without prejudice, till they resolve":

> If it make men positive and reguler, it teacheth them what thinges are in their nature demonstrative, and what are conjecturall; and as well the use of distinctions, and exceptions, as the latitude of principles and rules. If it mislead by disproportion, or dissimilitude of Examples, it teacheth men the force of Circumstances, the errours of comparisons, and all the cautions of application: so that in all these it doth rectifie more effectually, than it can pervert. And these medicines it conveyeth into men's minds much more forcibly by the quicknesse and penetration of Examples.[10]

Bacon's interest in the training and progress of the intellect is not confined to a single academic discipline; indeed, one of his complaints about the organization of knowledge in the first decade of the seventeenth century is that it was already too subdivided and specialized. But his defense of the application of "learning" to the business of government, coupled with his own aphoristic method, has a particular bearing on the reading and writing of history. Among other things, *The Advancement of Learning* offers a deft reformulation of Cicero's platitudes on the stature and utility of historical inquiry, portraying it as the training ground of a specific mental posture, uniting skepticism and faith in a complex, therapeutic collaboration. William Bradford is able to achieve just such a collaboration in his careful presentation of the rhetoric of providential causality in the 1630 letters from Massachusetts Bay.

If Bradford's cautious treatment of these documents, along with the scrupulous distance that he preserves from John Winthrop's or William Peirce's facility with religious metaphor, does not quite amount to skepticism, it nevertheless provides vivid evidence of his determination to turn back the first conceits of a deeply religious temperament and to carry more things in "suspence" than many of his fellow emigrants or historians found themselves able to do, under the extraordinary pressures of colonial life. "I dare not be bould with God's judgments," Bradford prudently observed, in recording some "crosses" that befell the Bay Colony's early efforts to compete with Plymouth's profitable fur trade in the Connecticut valley (415). Despite a few familiar instances, early in *Of Plimmoth Plantation,* in which Bradford appears quite willing to exercise such boldness, the pages of the history are remarkably free of the interpretive reflexes that Winthrop and Peirce display— or that James Sherley is able to deploy with such facility as he depicts himself prudently carrying his account books to Clapham, awaiting the "better and quicker markets" that he confidently believes will follow the passing of God's judgmental London plague (410).

As *Of Plimmoth Plantation* moves toward its conclusion, Bradford explores a number of notable occurrences in the colony's history that seem to invite the exercise of the religious imagination in precisely the ways that Winthrop, Peirce, and Sherley have wielded it. Like Sherley's London, though on a much smaller scale, Plymouth experiences a number of figurative and literal plagues that Bradford situates carefully in his narrative, allowing them to resonate with the surrounding circumstances that he records but seldom offering to decode their providential significance with the kind of confidence that his contemporaries so readily displayed.

By the middle of 1632, for example, the population expansion to the north, in the newly settled towns of Massachusetts Bay, had begun to expose Plymouth's farmers to what Bradford called "the disease" of prosperity. Crops and cattle increased in value to such an extent that the settlers of Plymouth began to strain against the landholding policies that were intended to foster a compact community:

> For now as their stocks increased, and the increse vendible, ther was no longer any
> holding them togeather, but now they must of necessitie goe to their great lots; they
> could not other wise keep their katle; and having oxen growne, they must have land
> for plowing and tillage. And no man now thought he could live, except he had catle
> and a great deale of ground to keep them; all striving to increase their stocks. By

which means they were scatered all over the bay quickly, and the towne in which they lived compactly till now, was left very thine, and in a short time allmost desolate. And if this had been all, it had been less, thoug to much; but the church must also be devided, and those that had lived so long togeather in Christian and comfortable fellowship must now part, and suffer many divisions. (361–62)

These divisions coincided with William Peirce's unfortunate shipwreck, as well as with the ongoing controversy between Plymouth and its London investors.

At this sensitive juncture, sometime between the summer and early fall of 1631, Roger Williams brought his perplexing mixture of "unsetled" judgment and great religious gifts to the colony. Williams had arrived in Boston in February 1631 but had refused a call to the church there unless the congregation would agree to declare its formal separation from the Church of England, a politically drastic act that the Massachusetts magistrates (among others) would not permit. The church at Salem was more receptive to Williams' radical convictions, but the General Court prevented them from offering him a pulpit.[11] Williams then sought a living at Plymouth, in a church that had already met his separatist criteria and where, according to Bradford's brief account of his residence, his teaching was "well approved" at first, until he "begane to fall into some strang oppinions, and from opinion to practise; which caused some controversie betweene the church and him, and in the end some discontente on his parte, by occasion wherof he left them some thing abruptly" (370).

Bradford does not elaborate on the differences that led to Williams' fateful return to Salem, except to imply that they were religious in nature, having little to do with the opinions that Williams held concerning the validity of colonial land titles. While he was at Plymouth, Williams apparently put in writing the grounds of his opposition to all territorial grants in North America originating with the English crown. The native peoples alone, in Williams' view, possessed sovereign title to the regions that they inhabited. English settlers could only arrange for legal rights to the land by purchase from its native owners.[12] Plymouth had long accepted this principle. Indeed, Bradford forcefully asserted it in a letter that he sent to John Winthrop in April 1638, concerning a boundary dispute with Massachusetts Bay. Plymouth staked its claim to the lands in question, Bradford wrote, "by compossision and anciente compacte with the natives to whom the right and soverainitie of them did belonge." Only when the native title was legally acquired did Plymouth seek to confirm its holdings "by patente from his Majesties authoritie"—scruples with which Winthrop apparently had little patience.[13]

Although Williams' convictions on native sovereignty sorted well with those of

Plymouth's magistrates, his uncompromising separatism made him a theologically divisive presence in a small community that was already beginning to suffer the strains of many divisions. The regenerate could not pray with the unregenerate, Williams believed, even if they were man and wife, parent and child. Women, he thought, ought to wear veils in public, in order to conform to Paul's apostolic passion for separating the spheres of the sexes. Members of the colony like Edward Winslow or Miles Standish, who took trips to England on public business, could not be readmitted to the church at Plymouth, Williams held, if they had polluted themselves by attending services in the Church of England during the long periods that they were absent from home. Stern admonishment and sincere repentance were necessary to cleanse them from the episcopal contagion.[14]

Under Williams' earnest guidance, a few months after his return to Salem in 1633, John Endecott sought to eradicate all religious corruption from public life by mutilating the English flag to remove its offensive papal cross. By early 1636, according to John Winthrop's journal, the magistrates of Massachusetts Bay had, in turn, come to view Williams as an agent of "infection," a judgment with which Bradford appeared at least partly to sympathize.[15] The church at Plymouth, Bradford reports in the history, had written to their colleagues at Salem on the occasion of Williams' departure in 1633, "with some caution to them concerning him, and what care they ought to have of him," though on the whole Bradford concluded that Williams was "to be pitied, and prayed for," rather than made the object of any harder measures (370).

In the midst of this conjunction of stresses, Plymouth found itself on the verge of armed conflict with the Dutch over trading rights in the Connecticut valley. Bradford's brief but crowded account of this sequence of troubling events, throughout 1632 and 1633—beginning with the diseases of prosperity among the colony's farmers and ending with a clash of acquisitive passions in the Connecticut woods—draws to a close with his description of an outbreak of infectious fever at Plymouth in which more than twenty people died, including the colony's "surgeon and phisition," Samuel Fuller, who had served as their medical emissary to Massachusetts Bay two years earlier. The warlike displays of the Dutch end peacefully, thanks to the speed with which Plymouth's traders fortified their trading house, but the casualties at home from sickness are heavy for this small community.

Like their Massachusetts neighbors, Bradford wrote, the settlers at Plymouth resolved "to humble them selves, and seeke the Lord" in their predicament, "and towards winter it pleased the Lord the sicknes ceased" (374). But unlike the detailed religious anxieties expressed by the Massachusetts authorities in 1630, this strikingly brief observation marks the extent of Bradford's application of providential meaning to the suggestive figurative potential of this epidemic. Instead he stresses that the neighboring Indians, too, suffered greatly in this outbreak of fever—an acknowledgment that appears to emphasize naturalistic, rather than divine, grounds for this particular visitation, and which does not exclude the Indians from a measure of participation in the collective "sadnes and mourning" that these losses bring. The Indians, in fact, offer a naturalistic account for the origins of the fever, which Bradford carefully records, noting that in the previous spring a great hatching of "flies, like (for bignes) to wasps, or bumble-bees" came out of the ground "and replenished all the woods, and eate the green-things; and made shuch a constante yelling noyes, as made all the woods ring of them, and ready to deafe the hearers." The Indians told the English at the time that sickness would follow this infestation of what appear to have been seventeen-year locusts; "and so it did," Bradford acknowledged, "in June, July, August, and the cheefe heat of sommer."

A quick collation of places, across this compact portion of Bradford's book, makes clear that the rhetorical and liturgical tactics of Massachusetts Bay during the 1630 epidemic give place, at the close of 1633, to Bradford's personal interest in the curious predictive accuracy of the Indians' natural science. His own deployment of religious conceits is negligible by comparison to the extraordinary emphasis that Winthrop and his colleagues place on their efforts to pacify the Lord's wrath. In the same year that "it pleased the Lord" to strike Plymouth with disease, Bradford notes, it also pleased Him to enable the colony to ship over three thousand pounds of "coat beaver" and 346 otter skins to London, paying their expenses and immediate debts and for once placating their profit-hungry English investors. *Of Plimmoth Plantation,* however, makes no effort to claim this windfall as evidence of heavenly favor or to link it to the instructive outcome of the summer's feverish struggle. The metaphysical patterns of chastisement and reward have very little opportunity to take hold in the wonderfully commingled narrative that Bradford presents (375).

The following year Edward Winslow escorted another huge shipment of furs to England: two additional tons of beaver pelts, "a great part of it, being coat-beaver, sould at 20s. per pound," and 234 otter skins. The value of the whole consignment, Bradford observed, came to "a great sume of money" (385). These commercial details are part of the protracted argument that Bradford conducts in the pages of the history with James Sherley and his London colleagues, who repeatedly complain about the disappointing nature of the colony's economic return. But in his account of the year 1634, Bradford immediately follows this inventory of fur exports with a vivid account of a smallpox outbreak among the Indians living around Plymouth's Connecticut trading house. "I am now to relate some strang and remarkable passages," he announces, a narrative alert of sorts that makes it difficult for Bradford's reader to overlook the suggestive and terrible conjunction between Plymouth's increasing dependence on the English market for animal skins and the catastrophic effects of smallpox on the native population.

A small party of Dutchmen, possibly carrying the disease, had gone up the Connecticut River in the winter of 1633 to trade at a large Indian town farther north and discourage them from bringing their supply of spring pelts downriver to the English. Before the trading season arrived, however, a great sickness broke out among the Indians: "of a 1000. above 900 and a halfe of them dyed," Bradford wrote, "and many of them did rott above ground for want of buriall" (387). Although unaffected by the disease itself, the Dutch, too, nearly died of hunger and cold, amid the breakdown of this Indian community, until they were able to retreat to Plymouth's outpost, in midwinter, for food and shelter. The following spring, the Indians settled around Plymouth's trading house were, in turn, attacked by smallpox "and dyed most miserably," Bradford reported, "for a sorer disease cannot befall them." In the ensuing description, he graphically depicts their misery.

The Indians, Bradford explains, usually erupt in an "abundance" of infected blisters—the characteristic pox—which "breaking and mattering, and runing one into another, their skin cleaving (by reason therof) to the matts they lye on, when they turne them a whole side will flea of at once, (as it were) and they will be all of a gore blood" (388). It is, Bradford confesses, a "fearfull" sight: "They dye like rotten sheep." But it is at the same time a haunting, as well as a fearful, spectacle. The descriptive sequence in *Of Plimmoth Plantation* makes all too evident the nightmarish similarity of such excruciating details to the processes of trapping and flaying the thousands of beaver and otter whose extraordinarily valuable fur was making it possible for the English at Plymouth to pay their relentless debts:

> The condition of this people was so lamentable, and they fell downe so generally of this diseas, as they were (in the end) not able to help on another; no, not to make a fire, nor to fetch a litle water to drinke, nor any to burie the dead; but would strivie as long as they could, and when they could procure no other means to make fire, they would burne the woden trayes and dishes they ate their meate in, and their very bowes and arrowes; and some would crawle out on all foure to gett a litle water, and some times dye by the way, and not be able to gett in againe. But those of the English house (though at first they were afraid of the infection) yet seeing their woefull and sadd condition, and hearing their pitifull cries and lamentations, they had compastion of them, and dayly fetched them wood and water, and made them fires, gott them victualls whilst they lived, and buried them when they dyed. (388–89)

By "the marvelous goodnes and providens of God," Bradford dutifully notes, the English entirely escaped infection, despite the close contact which their nursing "offices" required them to have with the afflicted Indians. These efforts earned the Plymouth traders a reputation for mercy, as well as the generous praise of the colony's magistrates. But Bradford's conspicuous decision to link his account of this epidemic with his portrait of Plymouth's economic reliance on the fur trade, and on the native trappers who furnished the pelts, suggests that the English immunities are at best superficial. Plymouth is deeply implicated in commercial practices that are filling the New England woods with flayed corpses. The history implicitly insists on this dark subtext to Bradford's strange and remarkable passage.

Less probing but equally suggestive accounts of the hurricane of 1635 and the earthquake of 1638 underscore Bradford's determination to hold in a kind of fruitful suspense the imputed relation between striking natural occurrences and providential design to which his contemporaries freely appealed. As the competition for Indian trading partners and for rich farmlands in the Connecticut region intensifies in the pages of the history, Bradford punctuates his narrative with an account of a tremendous storm that struck New England in August 1635, "like (for the time it continued) to those Hauricanes and Tuffons that writers make mention of in the Indeas" (401). The winds and the tidal surge destroyed many houses and "would have drowned some parte of the cuntrie" if the storm had not repeatedly shifted direction: "tall yonge oaks and walnut trees of good biggnes were wound like a withe, very strang and fearfull to behould." This ominous language alone invites comparison to the Indian epidemic of the previous year, or to the great dangers that Bradford perceives in the continuing willingness of European traders to supply the Indians generously with "gunes and munishtion" in return for their furs. But he carefully avoids attaching any implication of providential warning to this deluge or to the "great eclips" of the moon that follows the storm two nights later (402).

In the summer of 1638, among a number of "enormities" that Bradford associates with that year, "a great and fearfull" earthquake struck the colony: "It came with a rumbling noyse, or low murmure, like unto remoate thunder; it came from the norward, and pased southward; as the noyse aproched nerer, they earth begane to shake, and came at length with that violence as caused platters, dishes, and such like things as stoode upon shelves to clatter and fall downe; yea, persons were afraid of the houses them selves." It seemed, Bradford speculated, "as if the Lord would herby shew the signes of his displeasure" at the departure of so many families from their old homes at Plymouth to outlying settlements, where they could cultivate more land and earn greater profits from corn and cattle.

But this tentative providential reading passes almost as quickly as the tremor itself. Bradford acknowledges the "mighty hand of the Lord," who makes earth, sea, and mountain "tremble before him," but he expresses an equal measure of interest in a hypothesis that he offers about the potential relationship between the earthquake and the local climate: "It was observed, that the sommers, for divers years togeather after this earthquake, were not so hotte and seasonable for the ripning of corne and other fruits as formerly; but more could and moyst, and subjecte to erly and untimly frosts, by which, many times, much Indean corne came not to maturitie; but whether this was any cause, I leave it to naturallists to judge" (438). The vocation of naturalist was quite new in English culture at the time of Bradford's writing, an extension of the new science to which Francis Bacon hoped to direct the energies of seventeenth-century thought. The word *naturalist* itself does not appear in English much before the last decade of the sixteenth century; many early-seventeenth-century users of the term continue to associate it with heresy or atheism. Very few of Bradford's New England contemporaries would have blended biblical and scientific structures of thought with the freedom that Bradford displays in this passage or would have shared his evident willingness to mingle the old interpretive tradition with a new one.[16]

The year 1638 was characterized by a number of human enormities as well as by the spectacle of this extraordinary geological one. Rumors reached Plymouth early in the spring that Anne Hutchinson, a relentless critic of the clerical establishment in Massachusetts Bay, had given birth to a monster. Bradford wrote to John Winthrop in some skepticism, asking him to confirm the report and describe the "forme" of this "prodigious" creature.[17] Samuel Gorton—a "proud and pestilent seducer," as Nathaniel Morton described him—continued to plague the Plymouth community with his blasphemous religious opinions, stirring up discontented citizens "to mutynie in the face of the court."[18] Samuel Hickes, a member of the church who may have been influenced by Gorton's example, submitted fourteen theological challenges to Plymouth's leaders, sometime in 1637, that they undertook to answer at great length, perhaps out of the anxiety associated with their recent expulsion of John Cook, a former deacon, for Anabaptist convictions.[19] These religious and political controversies, like those triggered by Anne Hutchinson in Winthrop's government, almost certainly spilled over into the following year, exacerbated by Samuel Gorton's disruptive presence.

Surprisingly, Bradford chooses to address none of this considerable official turmoil in *Of Plimmoth Plantation*. He turns his attention instead, as he begins his account of 1638, to the executions of three Englishmen for killing an Indian. In many respects this incident recapitulates the experiences of Christopher Gardiner seven years earlier, though few of the details of this latest crime appear to invite a similar exercise of Bradford's judicial charity.

Like Gardiner, the three offenders in 1638 are fugitives from the English settlements, led by one Arthur Peach, "a lustie and a desperate yonge man," Bradford remembers, who had fought in the Pequot War "and had done as good servise as the most ther, and one of the forwardest in any attempte" (432). Out of money and "loath to worke" at a peacetime occupation, Peach convinced three bound servants and apprentices to run away from their masters and accompany him to the Dutch plantations.[20] It later appeared that Peach had also impregnated a servant girl, "and fear of punishmente made him gett away." The governments of New England took a very dim view of this affront to public morals, even when the sexual partners in question later married and undertook to raise their child. The magistrates of Plymouth ordered Thomas Boardman "severely whipt" in August 1638 for fathering a child out of wedlock with a woman who had subsequently become his wife.[21] Arthur Peach apparently did not intend to assume Boardman's risks or responsibilities.

On their journey through the woods, Peach and his runaway companions encountered a Narragansett Indian—Plymouth Court records give his name as Penowanyanquis—returning from a trading visit to Boston: "Peach called him to drinke tobaco with them, and he came and sate downe with them; Peach tould the other he would kill him, and take what he had from him, but they were some thing afraid; but he said, hang him, rogue, he had killed many of them; so they let him alone to doe as he would; and when he saw his time, he tooke a rapier and rane him through the body once or twise, and tooke from him 5. fathume of wampam, and 3. coats of cloath, and wente their way, leaving him for dead" (433). Penowanyanquis, however, "made shift to get home" and lived long enough to identify his murderers, to the satisfaction both of his own people and of Roger Williams, whom the Indians had immediately summoned in order to get medical help and to demand justice.

The Narragansett quickly captured Peach, along with two of his companions, and with Williams' encouragement turned them over to the English settlement on Aquidnett Island. But the victim's "freinds and kindred," Bradford writes, "were ready to rise in armes, and provock the rest therunto, some conceiving they should now find the Pequents words trew: that the English would fall upon them" (434). Because the crime had occurred in Plymouth's jurisdiction, the Massachusetts Bay authorities referred the trial to Bradford and his colleagues but "pressed" for a quick resolution "or els the countrie must rise and see justice done, otherwise it would raise a warr." Against this coercive political background, Plymouth's magistrates begin their work. "Some of the rude and ignorante sorte" among Plymouth's population, Bradford recalls, had already begun to complain "that any English should be put to death for the Indeans (435)."

Confronted with the evidence against them, and under repeated questioning, Peach and his companions "all in the end freely confessed in effect all that the Indian accused them of." A delegation of the Narragansett, including some of Penowanyanquis's friends, witnessed the subsequent triple execution, "which gave them, and all the countrie good satisfaction." Counting John Billington's hanging eight years earlier, this was the second disposition of a capital crime in Plymouth's brief history and, like the first, Bradford wrote, "a matter of much sadnes" (435). Arthur Peach, according to at least one observer, died very penitently. The pregnant servant girl, whom Peach had decided to abandon—Dorothy Temple, according to the colony's court records—worked for Stephen Hopkins, who apparently kept a kind of tavern in Plymouth. The magistrates arranged for Temple's punishment, too, once her condition became apparent, and for her support after Hopkins refused to keep her or her child in his household.[22]

Roughly half of William Bradford's chronicle account of 1638 in *Of Plimmoth Plantation* is taken up by the crime and punishment of Arthur Peach, despite the range of public "enormities" that might otherwise have claimed his attention. Anne Hutchinson and her associates consumed John Winthrop's journalizing efforts for over two years, requiring many pages to detail the confrontation. Samuel Gorton's heresies and mutinous behavior, at Plymouth and elsewhere in New England, prompted Edward Winslow to a book-length rebuttal that he published in London in 1646.[23] It may indeed have been the comprehensive nature of Winslow's response that permitted Bradford to ignore Gorton almost completely in the pages of his history.

The narrative decision to focus on the fate of Arthur Peach, rather than on some more prominent theological or political threat, reflects Bradford's pattern of deliberate disengagement from the highly charged religious contests of his time, as well as the caution with which he approaches the pervasive judicial metaphors that shaped the conventional understanding of providential governance. Such conceits (as Francis Bacon implicitly recognized) had an ominous propensity to cloak earthly magistrates with a dangerous confidence in the grounds of their own authority. Examining private crime rather than public heresy gives Bradford scope for his human sympathies as well as a narrative framework for depicting the complex interactions among different peoples that prove necessary to the exercise of justice in seventeenth-century New England.

Peach himself, as Bradford portrays him, is not a simple figure to dismiss—corrupted by the violence of the Pequot War into a callous indifference to life, more than equal to the dangers of a wilderness fight but afraid of punishment for seducing a servant girl, "a desperate yonge man" rather than a hardened reprobate, who freely confessed to his crime once it was clear that he could no longer hope to escape its consequences. Bradford goes to some lengths to explain Peach before passing judgment on him, much as Roger Williams and the Narragansett people appear to have explained to one another the complementary legal necessities of the English and the Narragansett communities in the face of such a cold-blooded crime.

Neither body of people is without its troubling divisions, after Peach and his companions are captured. Some of the Indians, mindful of the horrors of the recent war between the Pequot and the English, are deeply suspicious of English motives; some rude and ignorant inhabitants of Plymouth make clear that these suspicions are not without basis. Bradford carefully weaves all these elements into a concise but dramatically rich portrait of the social and political mixtures that marked seventeenth-century New England life, conditioning as well as complicating the process of government. At no point does his narrative succumb to the kind of crude, categorical distinctions that lie behind Arthur Peach's casual racism, the Indians' growing distrust of the English, or the sharp animosities of class among the English themselves, to which Peach was clearly able to appeal in convincing three bound servants to join him in his attempted escape to the Dutch plantations.

Instead, Bradford's account carefully exposes all these potentially explosive forces—carrying them in suspense without prejudice, as Francis Bacon might have observed—until the waste of life surrounding the figure of Arthur Peach can be in part redeemed by the dispassionate operation of law. "Both Just and Gentle, Merciful and Just / And yet a Man, and yet compos'd of Dust" was the concise description of Bradford's character that Josiah Winslow offered in a 1657 funeral acrostic.[24] The account of this complex matter of sadness in 1638 gives substance to Winslow's poignant words.

THE JUDICIAL CULTURE of Plymouth plantation, as Bradford depicts it in the history, is by no means tender-minded. Christopher Gardiner's battered arms call for treatment, perhaps, but not for an apology from the magistrates who cooperated with their Indian neighbors to return him to his captors in Massachusetts Bay. Plymouth's court records report that Dorothy Temple, Arthur Peach's lover, was sentenced to be whipped, in two stages, for conceiving a child out of wedlock, though when she collapsed under the first phase of her punishment, the magistrates remitted the second, perhaps out of some appreciation for the emotional, as well as physical, suffering that she had already undergone.[25] The gentle and merciful face of justice seems at best disfigured by such circumstances—as it will yet again in Bradford's discussion, in the pages of the history, of the third capital crime that the colony confronts, some years after the execution of Peach and his companions.

Bradford's portrayal of civil judgments, however, is marked by the same caution and complexity that he brings to the process of attaching interpretive significance to the mysterious judgments of Providence. Even a crime like the one that Peach so callously commits does not receive peremptory treatment in *Of Plimmoth Plantation*. The sin itself may be all too evident and cry out for the kind of swift retribution that the Massachusetts Bay authorities clearly urge on Bradford and his colleagues, but the narrative that the history provides emphasizes "all the cautions of application" that Francis Bacon had recommended in restraining the precipitate urges of the human mind. There are good reasons for caution. The English colonial governments are understandably eager to prevent the outbreak of another Indian war so close on the heels of the Pequot conflict. Guilty or not guilty, Peach and his companions are convenient scapegoats with which to placate the powerful and suspicious Narragansett. Penowanyanquis is dead, and the identification of his killers is dependent on intermediaries, who may easily be mistaken in their transmission of the victim's testimony. There is, apparently, more than one English settler who does not believe in the sanctity of Indian life or Indian property. The bigoted elements of Plymouth's population must be brought to recognize that their magistrates' verdict was deliberate and fair, rather than merely expedient.

In reconstructing the murder itself, Bradford pointedly implies that Peach is a product of the organized militance of Massachusetts Bay, as well as a criminal—a double identity, of sorts, that does not mitigate his guilt but hints at a degree of culpability in the communities that had helped to shape him. The appropriate sentence for Peach's crime is ultimately clear to Plymouth's court, but Bradford's pages effectively distinguish between the agent and the deed, following the best traditions of humanist jurisprudence. In his essay on judicature, Francis Bacon formulated this elusive goal in terms that any of his contemporaries would have found familiar: "In causes of life and death," Bacon wrote, "judges ought (as far as the law permitteth) in justice to remember mercy, and to cast a severe eye upon the example, but a merciful eye upon the person."[26] It is not immediately obvious how such an adage is to be followed in actual experience, but Josiah Winslow certainly based his assessment of Bradford's judicial practice on the ideals that Bacon expressed.

These problems of civil judgment reflect broader ethical and religious perplexities, with which Plymouth's leaders had grown familiar long before their emigration to New England. Bacon's judicial ideal is founded upon dilemmas of amalgamation and separation that are suggestively similar to those with which John Robinson's Leiden followers had struggled, during their protracted legal controversy with the English church. Separatism—the oppositional posture that Robinson and his congregation had adopted with respect to the English episcopal establishment—implied a sharp distinction between pure and impure forms of ecclesiastical government. Fixing the precise nature of that distinction, however, often proved as fraught with cautions of application as the judicial task of dividing persons from examples. The ethical and religious experience of dissenting congregations was largely shaped by this entanglement of spiritual questions with legal ones. Indeed, John Robinson's printed legacy of theological polemics and moral essays is equally a school for magistrates as for communicants. Bradford's own performance as a judge, as well as his depiction of judgment, springs from his acquaintance with the detailed portrait of the ethical intelligence preserved in Robinson's books.

Numerous figures, throughout the turmoil of the Reformation, migrated back and forth across apparently absolute theological frontiers during the course of their lifetimes, as they wrestled with the status and significance of the sacraments or the form of church organization that seemed most closely to follow biblical models. Even Robert Browne, the English exile whose name became synonymous with radical opposition to the episcopal hierarchy, ended his life a repatriated Anglican clergyman.[27] Distinguishing between a true and a false church was every bit as urgent a social necessity, for Browne and his successors, as the absolute legal separation between individual guilt and innocence that civil courts strove to preserve— and, in many instances, every bit as problematic. Indeed, the seemingly endless printed debates between advocates and critics of episcopacy in seventeenth-century England were structured like complex legal briefs, appealing to Scripture for relevant precedents in divine law that might endorse or exclude the wearing of clerical vestments, the practice of kneeling during the Eucharist, or the authority of bishops over individual congregations or of the civil magistrate over the church.

Carried to extremes, the separatist instinct could appear arrogant and judgmental in the eyes of its opponents: "What communion hath light with darkness?" was the provocative Pauline epigraph from 2 Corinthians that John Robinson selected for an elaborate defense of English Separatism, which he published the year after he had fled to Holland.[28] In many respects this verse is the classic exclusionist aphorism—one that Bradford or Winthrop might have been tempted to apply to Christopher Gardiner, John Lyford, Thomas Morton, or Arthur Peach in the opening decades of New England colonial life, just as Robinson had invoked it in the tumultuous opening decade of the seventeenth century. The painful disruptions of exile and the attacks of colleagues from within the English Church, many of whom Robinson knew personally, had exasperated him to the point where his zeal could occasionally overwhelm his reason, much as passion or prejudice might occasionally threaten the composure of the civil magistrate. But even at the beginning of his long residence in Leiden, Robinson's judgment, both in theological and in civil matters, was governed by an appreciation for the impure nature of human understanding and its institutional or literary products.

Passionate conviction and fervent language, Robinson recognized, even in a good cause were not necessarily evidence of a disinterested love of truth. "Fyery zeal for these frozen times of ours," as he put it, called for a corresponding degree of care that one's inner fires be kindled at heavenly rather than hellish altars. Indifference on matters of great religious importance Robinson dismissed as a "bastardly disposition," but he was equally wary of the pretense of deep religious or ethical commitment: "all men," he noted, "have taught their tongues in generall to speak goodly words"—a realistic recognition of the problem of hypocrisy that so preoccupied religious thinkers in the first decades of the seventeenth century.[29] The result of such widespread religious fluency, Robinson felt, was "a thick mist" of nominally pious language, clouding all theological and political controversies. Readers or listeners of goodwill had to negotiate this atmosphere with some care. Precipitous temperaments were suspect, Robinson felt, particularly in times of great upheaval, "for all thing[s] ordinarily whither in grace, or nature, are wrought by degrees, and the passage from one extreme to another without due means, as it can hardly be sound so can it not possibly be unsuspected." The theological and legal debates with which Robinson found himself surrounded fostered many minds "which are violent in all things but constant in none."[30]

These strictures are part of Robinson's preface to *A Justification of Separation from the Church of England* (1610), a book that he must have begun drafting within a few months of his arrival in Leiden and which Brewster and Bradford both brought with them to Plymouth. Although he had fled the jurisdiction of England's ecclesiastical courts, Robinson nevertheless reentered what he called "the lists of contention" in print, out of a mixture of resentment at his human antagonists and suspicion of human authority. Like Francis Bacon, Robinson was unwilling to allow Pilate's skeptical question "What is truth?" to go unanswered, but he was uneasy about precisely who should answer it. "To accept the person in judgement is not good," Robinson wrote, citing Proverbs 24 to explain his inability to accede to mere opinions about religious life and church government that he could not find biblical evidence to sustain. "The naked and simple truth is to be inquired after," Robinson hoped, "with an unpartiall affection. And then the Lord which gives a single heart to seek after it, will give a wise hart to find it out."[31] But the Lord did not always provide human inquirers with a "single," unmixed, or undivided, heart. Affections were the natural catalysts of partiality.

"Good and evil are ought times so intermingled," Robinson observed, "as that men cannot touch that which is good, but some evil wil cleave unto their fingers."[32] Vice too often wears the livery of virtue and finds "the more free passage in the world." Even a desire for the peaceful resolution of theological or political antagonism can all too easily blend with ulterior motives, becoming a "politick pretense" that the stronger employ "to beat the weaker" (13). "Men plead custom," Robinson confesses, "when they want [lack] truth" and suffer from doubt out of "weakness of fayth" or "want of knowledge" (40). Individual scruples can bring spiritual growth to a state of painful suspension that calls for patience rather than coercion or conformity: "Weak and tender consciences do oft tymes stick at a very strawe, and there must they stand, til the Lord give strength to step over" (28).

Robinson's recognition of the incremental development of all things, "whither in grace, or nature," necessarily led to the conclusion that human convictions are at best merely provisional, subject to a variety of internal and external checks. His own early and intense attraction to Separatist doctrine, Robinson recalled, was temporarily "quenched" by an "overvaluation" of the learning of his teachers that left him "blushing in my selfe to have a thought of pressing one hayr bredth before them":

> Even of late tymes, when I had entered into a more serious consideration of these things and (according to the measure of grace received) serched the scriptures, whether they were so or no, and by searching found much light of truth, yet was the same so dimmed and overclouded with the contradictions of these men and others of the like note, that had not the truth been in my heart as a burning fyre shut up in my bones *Jer. 20.9.* [I] had never broken those bonds of flesh and blood, wherein I was so streytly tyed, but had suffered the light of God to have been put out in myne owne unthankfull heart by other mens darknes.[33]

Even the most all-consuming hunger for truth is beset by shadows comprised of one's own and of other men's darkness; but this predicament never led Robinson to repudiate the fire in his bones, even as he strove to prevent his thoughts from being "conjured into the circle of any mortall man or mens judgment" (48). This extraordinary capacity to unite a skeptical intelligence with passionate faith is at the root of Robinson's own profound pedagogical appeal.

Of Plimmoth Plantation makes evident, quite early in the narrative, William Bradford's admiration for Robinson's ability to yoke together public roles and in-

tellectual aptitudes that would seem at first to form incongruous partnerships, cel-
ebrating in particular Robinson's unique mixture of gifts for both "able ministrie
and prudente governmente" (24). When Bradford offers historical parallels as a
means of conveying Robinson's significance to the Leiden church, he chooses the
Roman emperor Marcus Aurelius or the celebrated Hussite general Ziska from
fifteenth-century Bohemia, rather than a famous preacher or theologian. Robinson
played a central role in promoting the spirit of "peace, love, and holiness" with
which the diverse body of Leiden exiles managed to live together for twelve stress-
ful years before the departure of a portion of the congregation for New England.
But he apparently did so through means that were not inconsistent with the kind
of political astuteness and personal force associated with two quite improbable
models for a seventeenth-century clergyman.

When differences did break out within the congregation, Bradford writes in his
praise of Robinson's leadership, "they were ever so mete with, and nipt in the head
betims, or otherwise so well-composed, as still love, peace and communion was
continued." This mixture of tactics suggests a productive combination of flexibility
and firmness in Robinson's pastoral character. "Incurable and incorrigible" members of the community were "purged" from the social body, Bradford recalled, but
only "when after much patience used, no other means would serve, which seldom
came to pass" (24). The good physician or chastising parent was Robinson's preferred model of social discipline, though even his skills were not always capable of
rendering the offices of a stern judge unnecessary.

This relationship between personal attributes and communal well-being is at
the core of Bradford's tribute to Robinson's remarkably blended nature:

> His love was greate towards them, and his care was all ways bente for their best good,
> both for soule and body; for besids his singuler abilities in devine things (wherein he
> excelled), he was also very able to give directions in civill affaires, and to foresee dan-
> gers and inconveniences; by which means he was very helpfull to their outward estats,
> and so was every way as a commone father unto them. And none did more offend him
> then those that were close and cleaving to them selves, and retired from the commone
> good; as also shuch as would be stiffe and riged in matters of outward order, and invey
> against the evills of others, and yet be remisse in them selves, and not so carefull to
> express a vertuous conversation. (25)

This impassioned and articulate Separatist could not abide those who withdrew
from the community at large into enclaves of narrow self-interest or who indulged
in unrelenting judgments of others while extending unwarranted charity toward

themselves. "Matters of outward order," Robinson recognized, were the preoccupation of hypocrites. He was, Bradford concluded in suitably concise and memorable fashion, a "leader and feeder" of his people (25). His death in 1625, at the age of fifty, was a blow both to the portion of the church that had remained at Leiden and to the settlers at Plymouth, whom Robinson had hoped to join. But the feeding did not completely come to an end. Both Bradford and Brewster brought copies of all of Robinson's published work to New England. One title in particular captures the full range of Robinson's personal example—his gift for both divine and civil counsel—conveying these complementary attributes to his reader in a context that is completely free of the theological and legalistic acrimony that shaped the highly polemical world in which Robinson lived.

Unlike his defense of the Synod of Dort in its proceedings against the Dutch Arminians or his extensive reply to Richard Bernard's detailed "invective" against the English Separatists, Robinson's *Observations Divine and Morall. For the Furthering of knowledg, and vertue,* published in the year of his death, is addressed simply to the "Christian Reader," with no effort to distinguish particular sectarian camps among its audience. The divisions of the book carry titles that make clear the religious calling of its author but which also suggest Robinson's broad secular reading in the tradition of Plutarch's *Moralia,* Seneca's moral letters, or the essays of Montaigne and Bacon: "Of Authoritie, and Reason," "Of Wisdom, and Folly," "Of Examples," "Of Counsell," "Of Envie," "Of Anger," "Of Death." Robinson opens the book with a series of reflections on religious subjects, beginning with man's knowledge of God and moving through an enumeration of divine attributes to a consideration of the unique stature of the Scriptures, but even these signs of his calling are offered not as sermons or homilies but as commonplace entries. The first edition of the *Observations* characterizes the opening twenty-four essays (more than one-third of the contents) not as "chapters" but as "heads," invoking the customary term for the sections of a commonplace book, the Latin *caput,* to distinguish the contents of each observation from more formal didactic or polemic genres.[34]

These are humanist exercises as well as clerical ones, embracing all that Robinson has been able to glean from what he calls his "pilgrimage" among a wide range of learned authors as well as his lifelong immersion in "the great volume of men's manners." He has had, he notes, "speciall opportunitie of conversing with persons of divers nations, estates, and dispositions, in great varietie" over the course of his life. This knowledge of mankind mingles with his knowledge of books in the pages of the *Observations.* There is method in the arrangement of the text, but, Robinson claims, "I have been neyther curious, nor altogether negligent" in its application. A degree of order and a degree of disorder blend in its pages, just as secular and sacred learning do, or as the world of books does with the world of men's affairs. "This kind of study," Robinson concludes in his preface, "hath been unto me full sweet, and delightful," a consolation "amids many sad, and sorrowful thoughts unto which God hath called me" (ODM, A2v). Amid the various matters of sadness with which William Bradford, too, had frequently to deal, it would be surprising indeed if he had not turned regularly to these humane and hospitable pages for instruction and reassurance. Robinson explicitly invites just this use of his book.

To a significant degree, in fact, Robinson's essays become an elaborate manual for readers, more broadly focused than William Perkins' *Arte of Prophecying* but equally absorbed by the challenges that all human interpretation confronts. Human nature itself is partly responsible for these challenges, but so too are the media of expression. Unlike Perkins, who stresses the oral tradition of the sermon, Robinson's interest lies in the legible "volumes" of print and of character. "Writing is the speech of the absent," he reminds the reader of the *Observations,* offering a measure of conventional consolation to those settlers at Plymouth who felt his absence most acutely. But at the same time Robinson develops a surprising modification of this familiar claim, putting to one side its sentimental or nostalgic implications—writing's role in overcoming the pain of physical separation—in order to emphasize the instructive advantages that the written word possesses for an author whose "personall presence and speech may endanger either contempt, or offence" (ODM, 135).

Speech, Robinson emphasizes, is the foundation of religious faith. Like all nonconforming Protestants, he is committed to a tradition of vigorous preaching. The tongue is the index of the mind and the heart, Robinson agreed, "And so the Second Person in Trinitie is not called the Work, but *The Word of God*" (ODM, 127). But the tongue was also a notoriously unruly member, and human speakers were notoriously prone to indulge in flights of "affected" eloquence, and "pompous, or plausible speech," out of vanity rather than deep feeling or profound knowledge. Robinson clearly shares his culture's growing suspicion of verbal fluency. Writing, however, taught "the truth in its kind . . . both more fully, and more simply, and more piously, then by speech." Men generally take greater pains with what they write, Robinson thought, than with what they say. Writing is less subject to the influences of momentary passion in the author and less likely to be molded by a "partiall respect of others" among its audience than the words of a public speaker or a preacher. "Men of more unquiet, and stiffe spirits" got more benefit from the reading of books than from oral instruction or dispute: written arguments on contentious issues "will not be the provocation to inordinate anger, and passion, which in speech often falls in." One cannot possibly hear in a lifetime, Robinson added, "the tythe" of what one could read (ODM, 127, 135–36).

These sensible and perceptive claims, like virtually every ethical or psychological observation that Robinson offers in the *Observations,* are immediately subject to important cautions of application. Pious writing can often mask terrible impieties in its author: "Who shall ever finde a black-mouthed blasphemer cursing and swearing in his *Books?*" Habits of "great reading," Robinson feared, in conformity with Plato's celebrated complaint in the *Phaedrus,* might be neutralized by a "slipperie memorie" that is prone to lose knowledge as quickly as it is acquired, "like Water-conduits, which what they continually receav in at one end, they let out as fast at the other" (ODM, 136–37). Indiscriminate retentiveness, however, could produce only "those great Book-men, that know better the most other men's judgments, then their own." Guiseppe Arcimboldo's composite portrait *Il Bibliotecario*—a human figure constructed out of books—reflects this contemporary scorn for the compulsive scholar who systematically obscures his humanity beneath the apparatus and appurtenances of voracious reading.

Individuals whose memory and judgment were "answerable" to the demands of relentless study, Robinson thought, were likely to be "singular" and "rare." People of "ordinarie capacities" were well advised "to travell in some few Books . . . as it is best for weak stomacks to eat of few, and wholesom dishes." Even such consumers, however, were not by any means encouraged to view themselves as uncritical receptacles for an author's meaning: "Indeed he reads a *Book* ill," Robinson wrote, "that understands not something more either in, or, at least, by it, then the Author himself did in penning it" (ODM, 137–38).

The use of the Bible as the ultimate ethical and religious guide is hedged about with similar complexities, in Robinson's view, derived from the analysis of reading that he, along with most of his Protestant contemporaries, inherited from William Tyndale and William Perkins. Human concerns and human affairs often mingle with divine truth in a biblical text, partly as a consequence of historical circumstances, Robinson recognized, but partly too as a result of the conditions of composition. Not all that the prophets uttered was "spoken by the Spirit," he acknowledged, nor were all of their inspired words invariably written down. Translators and expositors were necessary but imperfect instruments in conveying the Bible's meaning to a broad audience; but even so, obscure words and phrases required considerable interpretive ingenuity, not just in the collation of places or in the eliciting of significance from narrative sequence, but also in the reader's continuing effort to remain alert to the "largest sense" that the words might suggest. If the authority of

Scripture itself was beyond dispute, its message was at the same time entangled in lesser authorities, of purely human origin. These impurities Robinson approached with considerable sophistication and distrust (ODM, 54–62).

Throughout the *Observations* Robinson blends the most useful ethical and religious aphorisms that he has culled from his reading with the contingencies and cautions that experience has taught him to invoke, whenever the question arises of applying absolute standards of thought, belief, or behavior to human life. Heresy and schism, for example, as Robinson presents them, reflect particularly obstinate errors in the religious imagination, the first arising "from want of Faith" and the second from "want of Love." Salvation, however, does not depend "upon the perfection of the Instrument, Faith; but of the Object, Christ." Who can say how little or how imperfect one's faith might be and still leave the error-prone believer eligible for unconstrained mercy? Heresy, in Robinson's judgment, was largely a human construct that had no relation to Christ's privileged knowledge of the integrity of the soul. "And for *schism*," he noted, that too had its roots in the limitations of human knowledge. Some people may well appear to be schismatics and yet still feel "truly disposed to union" with their opponents. Such individuals (Robinson claims) possess a "Superfedeas" from the Lord—a kind of metaphysical, legal immunity from being "attached" for schismatical behavior (ODM, 88–89).

"Counsell" is a sacred thing, the *Observations* advises its reader, perhaps with a measure of self-interest on its author's part, noting that Solomon himself kept "his Counsellors about him." But Robinson's comments on the taking and the giving of advice—unlike those of Francis Bacon, for example—are intended as a guide not for princes but for common neighbors and friends in the ordinary course of life: "No one man but stands [in] need of another; and if for little els, yet for *counsell*." Too often, however, those who ask for advice have no intention of following it. Advisers, in turn, frequently offer earnest recommendations that are too vague to be useful. Moreover, those most in need of good advice will frequently fail to ask for it, either because they are too proud or too simple to do so, or because they have grown so "melted in their miserie" that, like wax, they are "too soft to retain any impression." Astute advisers, therefore, wisely refrain from advising altogether, at least at first. Stall for time, Robinson suggests, "By which course we shall have our friends both ear, and heart more open to receav *advice* from us; as conceiving, that we neither are forward to crosse his designe, nor caried against him, or it, in passion, contempt, or unadvisednesse" (ODM, 119–22).

Cautions of application prove necessary and illuminating at every turn in the *Observations*. Robinson concurs with Tertullian, for example, that perseverance in "well-doing" is "the consummation, and store-house of all vertue," but even good and godly people are subject to moral lapses, sometimes into "grosse evills": "We are not therefore to measure a person's state by some one or few acts, done, as it were, by the way, and upon instance of some strong temptation, but according to the tenour, and course of his life. Els what wise man should not be a fool also?" (ODM, 30–31). Sobriety is an essential ingredient in a godly life, Robinson unsurprisingly affirms, but he nevertheless endorses the "special use" of strong drink that is acknowledged in Proverbs 31: "that the heavy of heart, and readie to perish might drink, and forget his povertie, and miserie" (ODM, 164).

Natural affections "are common to us with bruit beasts," Robinson notes in the *Observations,* and consequently must be carefully ordered by the understanding, in order to keep men from becoming brutish. Yet he takes a psychologist's keen interest in the interaction of human appetites and in the therapeutic utility of the passions as the means of counterbalancing one another. Human emotions are created faculties, Robinson observes, and so, like all created things, are good in and of themselves. Indeed, "they are the greater the better, if rightly ordered": "And so it is not unprobably sayd by some, that Christ had the greatest fear, sorrow, anger etc. upon him, that ever man had, or could have. But as the stronger the horses in the waggon are, though the better, yet the more dangerous; so are those *horses of the soul* in us, lest by misguidance they overthrow all" (ODM, 275). Even fear, which Robinson categorically terms "a base affection," is in some respects sublime: "In the law, God's sacrifices were to be offered of lambs, and kids, and doves, and pigeons (*fearfull* creatures, and innocent withall); and not of Lyons, and Eagles; though they be the Kings of beasts, and birds." God, Robinson asserts, loves a good heart, more than a great one (ODM, 279).

The margins of his book are filled with citations to the learned or sacred authorities that Robinson drew upon in framing his moral digest, but his attitude toward "authority" is mixed. Men of experience were "not lightly to be gainsaid," but experience alone was a "dull Mistresse," a "plodding guide" that could only distinguish "the beaten way to which it hath been used" (ODM, 113). Moral aphorisms, even from the most venerated sources, were sometimes too "peremptorie" for Robinson's taste and always required great caution in their application to human beings. In one of the most surprising heads of his book, Robinson offers a brief celebration of discretion as the critical skill that enables a man to adjust to the "variable circumstances and occasions" of life, preserving honesty, sincerity, and good intentions but doing so in a way that takes careful account of the dictates of circumstance, as much as those of principle. "Discretion is to be preferred before wit, or art, or learning," Robinson thought, "and only comes after goodnesse in worth" (ODM, 110–11). This is a surprising acknowledgment from a preacher whose powers of discretion appeared at times to desert him in his conflicts with the English Church, but even in his most forceful assaults on entrenched privilege or the prestige of high place, Robinson preserves a balance of fervor and skepticism that is, in many respects, self-correcting:

> The credit commending a testimonie to others cannot be greater then is the *Authoritie* in it self of him that gives it; nor his *Authoritie* greater then his person. The person then being but a man, the *Authoritie* can be but humain; and so the faith but humain, which it can challeng. *The custom of the Church is but the custom of men: the sentence of the Fathers but the opinion of men: the determination of Councels but the judgments of men,* what men soever . . . We are therefore to beware, that we neither wrong our selvs by credulitie; nor others by unjust susption. *To receav without examination mens sayings, is to make of men God: to reject them lightly, is to make of men Divels;* or fools, at the best. The latter hath pride, and uncharitablenesse for the ground: the former either argues men to be simple, which cannot; or idle, which will not; or presumptuous, which think they need not; or superstitious, which dare not judg; or (which is worst of all the rest) desirous in a kinde of humble hypocrisie to shelter an evill conscience before God under the shadow of great mens *Authoritie. (ODM, 70)*

Robinson himself is clearly restive in this shadow, even as he recognizes the perils of unjust suspicion and the folly of nourishing a blind preference for our own convictions or conclusions over the inherited sayings of great predecessors and hallowed tradition.

Robinson's *Observations Divine and Morall* brings under scrutiny the nature of moral observation itself, much as Stanley Fish has persuasively and elegantly demonstrated that Francis Bacon's essays repeatedly do. In this respect, Robinson's performance amply sustains Christopher Hill's decision to list him among the first generation of Baconians. The result of Bacon's penetrating analysis of motives and behavior finally impresses Fish as "merely self-regulating" rather than self-consuming, but this diminishment in metaphysical status would not have mattered much to Bacon himself, or to John Robinson, whose literary purposes were not directed toward fostering moments of ecstatic religious insight but toward leading a religious life. Robinson's humane embrace of the moral psychology of human beings, as he found them, equipped him with a mixture of sympathy and discernment ideally suited to the role of pastoral guide for a congregation of independent religious seekers who were negotiating the psychological and social labyrinths of Reformation England and Dutch exile.[35]

In describing Robinson's debates with Simon Episcopius, the leader of the Dutch Arminians in the second decade of the seventeenth century, Bradford appears mindful of the ethical example captured in the *Observations Divine and Morall.* He is careful not to cast Robinson as a victor in the lists of contention, despite the eagerness of many in Leiden at the time to proclaim this event to be a "famous victory" for the orthodox Calvinist cause. The Arminians, Bradford wrote in *Of Plimmoth Plantation,* had "greatly mollested the whole state" and divided the faculty and students of the university at Leiden into hostile camps, with their dramatic emphasis on the adequacy of Christ's sacrifice to redeem virtually all genuine believers, not merely an elect few, and with their insistence on subordinating the Dutch Church to the civil government. "Dayly and hote disputes" had finally so fragmented the intellectual community that the antagonists and their "disciples" (as Bradford termed them) would no longer attend one another's lectures (28). This was, in effect, a textbook clash between human authorities mired in human passions.

Robinson, however, continued to attend the lectures of both theological camps—"though he taught thrise a weeke him selfe," Bradford noted, "besids his many fould pains otherwise, yet he went constantly"—becoming "well grounded" in the arguments and in the "shifts" of the adversary. As a result of this patient preparation, his presence "begane to be terrible to the Arminians," prompting Episcopius "to put forth his best strength," both in speech and in writing, offering "sundrie Theses, which by public dispute he would defend against all men" (28). On two or three such public occasions, despite the vigorous efforts of his opponent, Robinson put Episcopius "to an apparent nonplus," as Bradford recalled in *Of Plimmoth Plantation.* The curiously inconclusive nature of that description would have pleased John Robinson. "*Disputations in Religion* are sometimes necessarie," he wrote in his *Observations,* "but alwaies dangerous; drawing the best spirits into the head from the heart; and leaving it either emptie of all; or too full of fleshly zeal and passion if extraordinarie care be not taken still to supply, and fill it a new with pious affections towards God, and loving towards men" (ODM, 44). It is important to inquire after truth with a single and wise heart, Robinson might well have observed, but it is likewise important to keep open possibilities of community that zeal or passion could otherwise destroy: "As the boar whets and sharpens his tuskes in his own foam, so doth a proud person whet, and sharpen his heart . . . in the frothy and foamish imagination of his own worth" (ODM, 288). The potent combination of anger and pride makes men into brutes, a metamorphosis to be resisted with particular energy in matters of religious antagonism but pertinent to disputes in civil law as well.

Strive as much as possible, Robinson advises in the *Observations,* "to accord with all," a principle that he derives from the recognition that "there is hardly any

Sect so Antichristian or evill otherwise, in Church profession, in which there are not divers truly, though weakly *led with the Spirit of Christ* in their persons, and so true members of his mysticall body." Convictions such as these form the basis for the comparatively liberal approach of both the Leiden and the Plymouth churches to the admission of new members. Evidence of the operation of saving grace in a particular individual was never a requirement for participation in the sacrament of Communion at Plymouth, as it was for the churches in Massachusetts Bay. Robinson's successors shared his uncertainty concerning the ability of human beings to determine the nature and the scope of the religious faith required for salvation. Our "propertie" as men is to err, Robinson admits in these same pages of the *Observations*. Few principles of ecclesiastical exclusion, other than those based on outward, ethical conduct, could be safely or justly built upon such an imperfect foundation. William Pynchon subsequently found himself driven from New England by the government of Massachusetts Bay in part for his public embrace of a similar latitudinarian posture. Bradford and Brewster, however, successfully preserved in Plymouth an enclave for dissent that was modeled on John Robinson's measured example (ODM, 47–48, 52).[36]

Nearly twenty consecutive chapters of the *Observations Divine and Morall* address questions arising from social existence rather than from the government of one's private character: "Of Societie, and Freindship," "Of Credit, and good name," "Of Envie," "Of Appearances," "Of Oaths, and Lots," "Of Hipocracy." To these Bradford could have turned repeatedly for reminders of Robinson's skill at managing civil as well as divine matters. In particular, the brief chapter "Of Rewards, and punishments by men" clearly shaped Bradford's conduct as a magistrate and his practice as a historian of the judicial activity of Plymouth Plantation.

In these pages Robinson cites once again the advice that he offered Bradford and Brewster privately in the letter that expressed his deep reservations about the attack on the Massachusetts Indians in 1623. Punishments should by nature be narrow in their immediate scope, Robinson repeated, "reaching to one, or a few; and the fear and warning to many." For the worst members of society, Jean Bodin had insisted, fear is the only effective restraint on vice or villainy. Robinson reluctantly agreed, citing Bodin in the margins of his own book. Human laws do not "make men good," he conceded, they simply "keep them from such outrages, and extremities of evill, as into which otherwise they were in danger to break." In this sense, then, severe punishments were a "mercifull crueltie," Robinson observed, saving others (as well as the criminal who suffers them) from future crimes. By remitting such punishments, the magistrate risks practicing "a cruell mercie," much as the fond love of parents sometimes ruins a child (ODM, 270–71).

Having offered these blunt concessions to a dark account of human nature, Robinson promptly reverses his course, much as Josiah Winslow's funeral couplet on Bradford's judicial behavior does, blending the antithetical attributes of justice and mercy into a complex whole:

> Yet considering both mans frailtie, and pronenes to offend; and miserie in *suffering* for offences: all in authoritie should still encline to the more favourable part, and rayther to come short, then to exceed measure in *punishing* even where the offence is evident; and where it is doubtfull, to forbear, at any hand. He that *punisheth* another, whether as judg, or excequutioner eyther, must know legally, that he hath done evill, and deserved it: otherwise the authoritie of the whole world cannot bear him out, from being a murtherer before God. The law which sayth, *Thou shalt not murther,* forbids specially violence in judgment. Besides, *punishments* must be administered with sorrow, and commiseration; as *rewards* with joy and gladnes. It is pittie men should deserv *punishments;* and deserving them, pittie but they should have them: yet are we to pitty them in their miserie also: which he that doth, remembers himself to be a man. (ODM, 272)[37]

The best spirits of both the head and the heart are necessary partners in the exercise of law. Bradford tries as much as possible, in the pages of his history, to frame the legal performance of Plymouth's magistrates in terms that John Robinson would recognize and endorse.

&.

THE EXECUTION OF THOMAS GRANGER in 1642 for the crime of bestiality poses acute historical and ethical difficulties for William Bradford and his reader. The murderous greed of Arthur Peach and the violent social circumstances that encouraged the expression of his passions form a comparatively straightforward narrative challenge. But the extravagant disorder of Granger's sexual appetites would seem to exceed ordinary powers of understanding. John Robinson's exhortation to remember man's frailty and misery in dealing out punishments presupposes bonds of identification between a criminal and the legal agents who punish him—bonds that make the process of distinguishing the actor from the act if not simple, at least conceivable. Mercy blends with justice and may even transform it, whenever these common bonds can be recognized or reconstructed, as Bradford clearly attempts to do with Peach and his accomplices. The circumstances of Thomas Granger's plight appear to make this process of recognition and reconstruction next to impossible.

That Bradford chooses to address Granger's fate at all in *Of Plimmoth Planta-*

tion is something of a puzzle. "The truth of the historie requirs, it," Bradford explains, as he introduces the outlines of the case: "Ther was a youth whose name was Thomas Granger; he was servant to an honest man of Duxbery, being aboute 16. or 17. years of age. (His father and mother lived at the same time at Sityate.) He was this year detected of buggery (and indicted for the same) with a mare, a cowe, tow goats, five sheep, 2. calves, and a turkey" (474). Seventeenth-century court records in England and America are full of criminal indictments not much less sensational than this one, but it is difficult to see why the truth of Bradford's history in particular requires Thomas Granger's presence in his pages. Bradford felt no compunction about excluding Samuel Gorton almost completely from his narrative, though Gorton directly and repeatedly attacked Plymouth's political and religious institutions. Other sexual crimes of a less spectacular nature, committed during the period covered by *Of Plimmoth Plantation*, make no appearance in its pages.[38] Thomas Granger's offense, however, like his punishment, is extreme, and this fact alone may account for Bradford's determination to include it.

The history touches on each capital crime over which the colony's magistrates deliberated between 1620 and 1646, in some measure because capital punishment itself was a vexed issue for many radical Protestants. Among the books in Bradford's library, Peter Martyr's *Common Places* addresses at length Saint Augustine's reservations about executing criminals and thereby depriving them of a chance for repentance and restitution through a subsequently sanctified life: "We (saith he) doe imitate God, when we would not have the guiltie to bee destroyed but to be kept unto repentaunce." The unpredictable operations of grace made irrevocable human punishments seem unjustifiable, even dangerous, though Martyr finally set Augustine's scruples aside and concluded that the voice of the Lord in the Old Testament was "the welspring of punishments." He, along with most of his Protestant and Catholic contemporaries, accepted the necessity of putting criminals to death.[39]

The religious and political persecutions of the sixteenth and seventeenth centuries, however, had offered dramatic evidence of the insane excesses to which the punitive instincts of human justice could lead, particularly in capital cases. Mary Tudor's officers had exhumed Martin Bucer's corpse during the 1557 visitation of Cambridge University and burned it in its coffin, along with many of Bucer's books, in order to carry out the obligatory sentence for heresy, even against the dead.[40] The body of Peter Martyr's wife was disinterred during the same official purgation of Cambridge and reburied in a dunghill. There were many distinguished precedents for such perverse acts. The Council of Constance had ordered John Wycliffe's body exhumed and burned for the same reasons, more than forty

The order and maner of taking vp the bodye of John Wickleffe and burning hys bones xli.yeares after hys death.

Fig. 10. From John Foxe, *The First Volume of the Ecclesiasticall History . . .* (London, 1570), STC 11223.2, 1:552. By permission of the Folger Shakespeare Library.

years after his death. John Foxe devotes one of the most grotesque and fascinating illustrations in the *Actes and Monuments* to this macabre event (fig. 10). Three years after William Bradford's death, at the restoration of Charles II, royal officials ordered Oliver Cromwell's corpse to be disinterred, hung in its burial shroud at Tyburn, beheaded, and the head exposed on the facade of Westminster Hall, where it remained at least through 1684, a gruesome monument to the unlimited scope of human vindictiveness.[41]

Against such a mixed background of ambivalent theology and judicial barbarity, Thomas Granger's story takes on new dimensions. Bradford goes to some lengths to remind his reader of this legal and punitive context before presenting Granger's story, but the most important modern edition of the history obscures these efforts. Samuel Eliot Morison prints among the appendixes to *Of Plymouth Plantation* (1952) the three ministerial letters on sexual crimes that Bradford and his colleagues had asked Plymouth's clergymen to supply to the Massachusetts General Court in the same year that Granger came to trial. The magistrates in Boston were unsure how to deal with a complex case of child sexual abuse that had come before the General Court and sought advice from their neighbors. The most important of these clerical responses is by Charles Chauncy, formerly the minister at Plymouth itself but more recently established at Scituate, as a result of some religious differences with his first New England congregation. Chauncy's letter is the longest such document that Bradford transcribes into *Of Plimmoth Plantation,* exceeding even James Sherley's most extensive epistolary performances. Its contents, and the ethical sensibility of its author, immediately precede Bradford's discussion of Thomas Granger, creating one of the most complex exploitations of narrative sequence in the history.

Bradford lays the groundwork for that sequence by introducing a belated account of the quarrel over baptismal practices that had led to Chauncy's departure for Scituate. Shortly after his arrival in the colony in 1638, "ther fell out some differance about baptising" between Chauncy and the Plymouth church, "he holding it ought only to be by diping, and putting the whole body under water, and that sprinkling was unlawfull" (457). The church was willing to concede the efficacy of immersion, in deference to their new minister's opinion, but thought that the practice was not very "conveniente" in a cold climate. They would not accept his argument that sprinkling was "a human invention," however, and offered a compromise, allowing Chauncy to practice immersion while his teaching colleague, John Reinor, baptized by the traditional, less extreme method. Chauncy proved unamenable to compromise. The Plymouth congregation asked virtually every other minister in New England to try to persuade him to adopt a less doctrinaire position, but the effort was unsuccessful, and Chauncy finally "removed him selfe" to Scituate, where his convictions, though not entirely welcome, met with less opposition (456–58).

Bradford inserts this story at the close of his chronicle for 1641, claiming that he had forgotten to incorporate it in its proper place, at the beginning of the controversy three years earlier. But as his discussion of the eruption of "wickedness" in 1642 unfolds, it becomes evident that Chauncy's intransigence, like the sexual excesses of the following year, is in many ways additional evidence that "our corrupte natures" are, indeed, "hardly bridled, subdued, and mortified" (459). These words apply directly to Bradford's account of the "incontinencie" and other "notorious sins" that will culminate with Thomas Granger's trial, but they are also a strikingly apt description of Chauncy's stubborn refusal to bridle his own opinions, in the face of widespread disagreement, and accept a workable accommodation of differences, in the interests of peace. Bradford offers some possible reasons for the disturbing epidemic of vice in 1642—one religious, one psychological, and one social—but in pointed contrast to Chauncy's peremptory and magisterial temperament, he gives preference to none of them before turning to Richard Bellingham's letter from Boston, asking for Plymouth's help in addressing certain "heinous offenses in point of uncleannes" that had recently come to light in Massachusetts Bay (461).

At some point before *Of Plimmoth Plantation* came into the possession of Thomas Prince, early in the eighteenth century, someone excised a leaf from the manuscript on which Bradford had apparently copied Bellingham's account of the offenses in question. John Winthrop's journal, however, preserves the details. In the autumn of 1641, Dorcas Humfrey, a daughter of John Humfrey, one of the Bay Colony magistrates, brought accusations of abuse against three men, who had forced her to participate in a variety of sexual acts, occurring over a period of years, beginning when she was six years old. The testimony and the evidence made it unclear whether rape had actually taken place and to what degree Dorcas herself was a completely reliable witness. The three accused men, however, "presently confessed all but entrance of her body," Winthrop wrote, and were held in prison while the General Court tried to determine their punishment.[42] This was the point at which Bellingham consulted with his Plymouth colleagues.

Before copying the opinions of the colony's three ministers into the history, Bradford transcribes his own reply. "You know our breedings and abillities," he writes to his Massachusetts counterpart, expressing some reluctance "to presume to give our judgments in cases so difficulte and of so high a nature" (462). Nevertheless, he offers a few thoughts that reflect John Robinson's strictures against judicial excess. On the whole, Bradford doubted "whether it may be safe for the magistrate to proceed to death" if any uncertainty remained concerning the accomplishment of a capital crime. The New England colonial governments considered rape a capital offense. Even sodomy and bestiality, Bradford thought, did not deserve the death penalty "if there be not penetration," though he admitted that the "foulnes of circomstances" in the Massachusetts case left him "in the darke" concerning an adequate judicial response to such a series of aggravated assaults against a child (463).

Bradford follows his own letter, in the text of the history, with transcriptions of those from the three ministers currently established in Plymouth colony churches: John Reinor, Ralph Partrich, and Charles Chauncy. Reinor's reply to Bellingham's inquiry deals at some length with the question of whether various circumstances attending a sexual crime call for the death penalty regardless of whether bodily penetration had occurred. A magistrate "might" entertain the death penalty in such cases, especially where they involved "the foulest acts," Reinor thought, but like Bradford's, his judgment is inconclusive (464–66).

What Reinor does emphatically prohibit is the use of extreme means to "extracte a confession" from a criminal, as well as the administering of a death sentence on the evidence of fewer than two witnesses (465). On the manuscript leaf that was excised from *Of Plimmoth Plantation,* Bellingham may have inquired about the possibility of torturing one or more of Dorcas Humfrey's persecutors to secure a confession of rape that would clarify these troubling legal issues. Ralph Partrich, the minister at Duxbury, was not confident concerning which sexual crimes were adjudged to be capital in Levitical law, the standard to which the New England courts appealed, but he agreed with Reinor that it was "against the rule of justice" to compel a criminal to be his own accuser or to issue a death sentence on the testimony of only one witness (467). Taken together, Bradford, Reinor, and Partrich are distinctly cautionary voices, urging moderation and care on the part of the Massachusetts General Court.

Charles Chauncy offers a remarkable contrast to all three preceding opinions. He begins his elaborate letter by framing the legal issue in Latin (an ominous sign in itself) and then offering to expand his consideration of the particular case in question to take in the appropriate sentences for all cases of rape, incest, or bestiality, as well as other "unnatural" and "presumtuous" sins—disquietingly vague categories to entertain as possible capital offenses. In doing so, Chauncy emphasizes that he will "lay downe" a positive answer to the judicial problems that have prompted such caution in his colleagues (467–68). It is an entirely appropriate promise to issue from the peremptory dogmatist who had been unable to tolerate doctrinal differences with the Plymouth church.

Citing Luther, Melancthon, Calvin, Bucer, and Beza, Chauncy resoundingly affirms "the judicials of Moyses" and lists the Old Testament's capital offenses, as he interprets them: adultery, incest, bestiality, rape, sodomy, "and all presumptuous sins," by which Chauncy appears to mean any offense committed "with an hie hand" (according to the Geneva translator's gloss on Numbers 15:30), indicating that the sinner in question "blasphemeth the Lord." Any "evidente attempts" at these same crimes also deserve the death penalty, Chauncy believes, including the "discovering of [one's] nakednes" or merely "burning with lust," toward various forbidden partners, without necessarily putting lust in action. Abortion and masturbation were probably capital offenses as well, though Chauncy confesses that he draws these conclusions "by analogicall proportion," in the absence of a clear biblical directive (470).

In legal matters "of higest consequence," Chauncy endorses the use of racks and hot irons to obtain a confession, "espetially wher presumptions [of guilt] are strounge," but such techniques probably did not apply to private sexual crimes: "God sometims hides a sinner till his wickednes is filled up," Chauncy reluctantly but philosophically concedes (473). On the question of the necessity of witnesses to a capital crime, however, his principles are more flexible. When a man witnesses against himself, "his owne testimony is sufficente" to send him to his death, Chauncy believes. Sure and certain circumstances alone might suffice in the complete absence of either witnesses or a confession. In "waighty matters," such as those where Chauncy is willing to admit the legitimacy of torture, judges might have "recourse to a lott" as "the last refuge," when attempting to assign guilt for a particularly serious crime. He concludes this extraordinary legal disquisition by expressing his hope that the magistrates of Massachusetts Bay might carry out their judicial duties with "wisdom and largnes of harte" (474).

Chauncy himself is clearly oblivious to the irony of these closing words in comparison with the ruthless pages that precede them, but the telling sequence of transcriptions in *Of Plimmoth Plantation* makes equally clear that William Bradford is not similarly oblivious. He immediately follows the presentation of Chauncy's letter with the story of Thomas Granger's execution—a sentence that also conforms to Levitical law, but that law was applied to Granger's case with none of the merciless zeal so evident in Chauncy's detailed brief for the Massachusetts General Court.[43] Bradford's account of Granger's fate seems structured as a deliberate enactment of the mingling of pity and justice that John Robinson had urged upon the readers of his *Observations*.

By twentieth-century standards, of course, Thomas Granger's punishment is cruel, but it was not so by those of Bradford's time. In France, people found guilty of "unnatural" sexual acts were burned at the stake.[44] Sodomy and "buggery" (the official term for Granger's offense) were capital crimes in England, associated with considerable public ridicule and contempt. English dissenters, such as John Robinson's Leiden exiles, were often stigmatized by their opponents as sodomites and buggers; Richard Bernard hinted at these accusations in the attack on English Separatism that prompted Robinson to write his 1610 *Justification*, repudiating such "boyles and botches of reproch." The gallows and gibbets of England, Robinson noted, exhibit numerous members of the established English Church, in every county, executed "for treason, witchcraft, incest, buggery, rape, murders, and the like."[45]

In 1641, David Cressy observes, a pamphlet titled *The Brownists Conventicle*, published in London, associated Separatism with the cult of Adamites, religious radicals who were said to insist on conducting their worship services completely naked, "with men and women promiscuously mingled." The popular English press was quick to exploit the pornographic potential of this sensational news, depicting "nests" of Adamites in a state of mixed religious and sexual arousal.[46] Religious and erotic license had long been entangled, in the public imagination of Reformation England, in ways calculated to encourage a volatile mixture of prurience and bigotry. It is not difficult to imagine the reception that Thomas Granger is likely to have received in open court from "the rude and ignorante sorte" among Plymouth's population, who had already displayed an inclination to sympathize with the manly violence of Arthur Peach (434).

Indeed, it seems at least a possibility that Granger extravagantly exaggerated the circumstances of his offense in order to overawe those who might be tempted to mock him. Bradford's account traces the stages by which Granger comes first to acknowledge and then, quite unexpectedly, to expand on the scope of his crime. Initially "he strived to deny it," Bradford wrote, but in the end he offered a "free-confession" of his "lewd practise," not only in the single instance of which he was accused, but with a ludicrous and wholly improbable list of animal partners. The episode suggests a suicidal fantasy of defilement so startling in nature that Granger was required to offer his confession four times: "in private to the magistrates," then to the colony's ministers, then to the "whole court and jury" at his trial, and finally at his execution, where Granger, along with his executioners, participated in a bizarre parody of the Last Judgment, separating the animals that will die with him from those that will be allowed to live (475).

It was, Bradford acknowledges, "a very sade spectakle," but one that conferred a haunting, theatrical authority upon the young man at its center. Bradford apparently held conversations with Granger during the ten weeks that he spent in Plymouth's prison, trying to determine where he had first learned about "such wickednes." Puzzlement rather than inquisitorial zeal seems to motivate these interviews; Bradford draws no sweeping theological or legal conclusions from them. Nor does the appearance of such crimes in New England strike him as evidence of the Lord's singular disapproval or anger. Earthly envy, opportunism, lust, and greed were, in Bradford's view, more than adequate to the task of accounting for the presence of wicked, profane, or unworthy people in New England. In the pages of his history, particularly at moments of great discouragement, bewilderment, or sorrow, Bradford strives to look "humanly" on the individual and collective failings that a commitment to historical truth obliged him to record.

CHAPTER FIVE

Controller of Stories

I**N APRIL 1643** William Brewster died—or so the reader of William Bradford's history of Plymouth would conclude. "I am to begine this year whith that which was a mater of great saddnes and mourning unto them all," Bradford wrote: "Aboute the 18. of Aprill dyed their Reverend Elder, and my dear and loving friend, Mr. William Brewster" (487). April was the first full month of the year in the Old Style calendar, which Plymouth's settlers had adopted when they left Leiden to establish an English colony in territory claimed by the English crown, administered under English time. It would seem only sensible, then, to begin the chronicle for 1643, as Bradford does, with this momentous death, a point of emotional transition between the sad spectacle of Thomas Granger's execution the preceding September and the sweeping changes that impelled the New England colonies to take their first steps toward political union and political independence the following May.

Nathaniel Morton, in *New England's Memoriall,* appears to accept Bradford's date for Brewster's death, though his transcription of Bradford's eulogy for Brewster in the Plymouth Church Records shows some indication of uncertainty on Morton's part—a struggle, perhaps, between his reverence for Bradford's text and his own unclouded memory of events.[1] The colony's official records, however, are quite clear. William Brewster died without leaving a will. At its meeting of June 5, 1644, Plymouth's General Court granted letters of administration for Brewster's estate to his two eldest sons, Jonathan and Love, a legal necessity that would ordinarily occur as soon as possible after the date of death, not almost fourteen months later, as Bradford's account in the history implies.[2] It is quite unlikely that the passage of a handful of years would have resulted in such a material lapse of memory when Bradford undertook to record the last moments of his dear and loving friend. In *Of Plimmoth Plantation* he revises the date of Brewster's death in order to place it at a critical turning point in the colony's history and to position it in a suggestive relationship to the troubling religious and political controversies, the murders and executions, of the surrounding years.

Resituated in time, much like a passage of collated text might be transported from one point in a continuous narrative to another, this event has a strangely soothing effect on Bradford's story—an antidote, in some measure, to the disturbing reflections prompted by Thomas Granger's execution. Twice during his chronicle of the "sundrie notorious sins" that had marked the year 1642, Bradford struggled to account for the disquieting eruption of so much wickedness in Plymouth and in Massachusetts Bay. Perhaps the Devil resents with special intensity the commitment of the New England emigrants "to preserve holynes and puritie amongst them": "I would rather thinke thus," Bradford concedes, "then that Satane hath more power in these heathen lands, as some have thought, then in more Christian nations" (459–60). His speculative tone indicates that the demonic explanation is clearly unpersuasive. Perhaps passions that are dammed up by religious discipline "flow with more violence" once they overwhelm external cultural restraints. Bradford emphasizes, too, the number of untoward servants and "unworthy persons" who had emigrated to the colony in recent years and "crept into one place or other," bringing their moral infections with them (476–77). But none of these interpretive expedients address the challenge to New England's moral stature represented by the behavior of what Bradford termed the "mixed multitud" of its inhabitants. William Brewster's life becomes the decisive rhetorical counterweight in Bradford's narrative design.

This medicinal relationship, however, is more complex and more fraught with paradox than it seems. During his account of crime and punishment in 1642, Bradford suppresses the fact that Thomas Granger's fate had touched directly on the Brewster family. The young man was a servant in Love Brewster's household in Duxbury at the time of his arrest, a fact that Bradford glosses over by introducing Granger in the history simply as a "servant to an honest man" in the small settlement across the harbor from Plymouth, to which William Brewster had moved ten years earlier, joining his two youngest sons, Love and Wrestling, after his wife's death.[3] Granger's passions, in other words, do not break out in an ill-governed or obscure household of newcomers to the plantation. William Brewster's implicit involvement in Granger's trial had disturbing as well as reassuring implications. It both invited and required precisely the kind of ameliorative contrast that Bradford turns to in the chapter following Granger's death, through his eulogy for the man whose guidance had proved so critical in Bradford's own youth. "Some times it is good to buy peace," James Sherley observed, in a final letter from 1642 touching on the colony's financial quarrel with the merchant adventurers (486). The peace into which William Brewster's life subsides, within a few sentences of Sherley's calculating adage, seems briefly to purchase a moment of reflective satisfaction for William Bradford, after the troubling moral and economic quandaries of the preceding year.

These ethical and narrative complexities, in fact, along with the repositioning of Brewster's death in the historical record, play a significant role in the condensed history of political transformation in New England that Bradford's closing chapters explore. Brewster's character and, by implication, Brewster's library will help explain the larger significance of Thomas Granger's appearance in *Of Plimmoth Plantation*, but they also expose an unexpected conceptual dimension to Bradford's narrative. Beginning with an apparently local crisis in 1634, involving Plymouth, Massachusetts Bay, and the small trading plantation of Pascataway, Bradford gradually depicts an improbable but suggestive link between contemporary circumstances in the New England colonies and one of the most influential models of Renaissance historical thought available to him.

Among the books in Bradford's library was Francesco Guicciardini's celebrated story of the French invasion of Italy in 1494, along with Guicciardini's expansive account of the political and military repercussions that followed the initial act of French aggression over the next thirty years. This series of profoundly disruptive historical events, as Guicciardini presents it, was originally triggered by the death of Lorenzo de Medici in 1492 and by the mutual suspicions unleashed in the leaders of Florence, Milan, and the Kingdom of Naples by the loss of Lorenzo's considerable diplomatic skills. The emergence of a Florentine republic, free of Medici domination, that continued for eighteen years was one result of the French presence on Italian soil in the closing decade of the fifteenth century. The nearly complete degradation of the papacy formed a second, closely related element in Guicciardini's story, which made it particularly appealing to Protestant readers.[4]

The extraordinary range of character and events that Guicciardini portrays has no equivalent in the tiny communities of New England. The world that he describes is the same dense network of mutually antagonistic secular and ecclesiastical princes that produced Machiavelli's stark analyses of politics and war. No Borgia or Medici popes, no Savonarola, no impetuous and willful Julius II—"one of the demonic personalities of his age," in Felix Gilbert's words—no sack of Rome color the pages of Bradford's history.[5] The erotic excesses of New England pale in comparison to the legendary depravity of Pope Alexander VI and his family, which Guicciardini presents in suggestive detail. But two broad features of Guicciardini's historical design do have a surprising pertinence to Plymouth's experience: the threatened intrusion of a powerful monarch among a balanced system of much smaller communities and the attempt to address that invasive challenge by means of political confederation. Guicciardini's great book is, in one respect, a record of successive "leagues," beginning with the alliance of Florence, Milan, and Naples, forged by Lorenzo de Medici in the late fifteenth century, and ending with the League of Cognac in 1526, each of which proves ineffectual in providing stability and unity to the fragmented sovereignties of Italy.

Charles I of England plays the precipitating role in Bradford's story that Charles VIII of France plays for Guicciardini; the necessity that the New England communities recognize to provide for their own security, in light of the disruption caused by civil war in England, prompts New England's experiment with the formation of a political "league." In *Of Plimmoth Plantation,* Bradford relies on this instructive connection between Guicciardini's expansive historical canvas and his own far more modest one in order to draw the apparently diffuse incidents of the history's closing chapters into a meaningful order. It is a textual relationship that he is able to signal most conspicuously by moving the time of William Brewster's death. Placed before, rather than after, the mid-1643 formation of the United Colonies of New England, Brewster's death, like that of Lorenzo de Medici, marks the end of an irrecoverable period in colonial life. A preoccupation with the local affairs of Plymouth alone had been slowly yielding place, in Bradford's pages, to the demands of a more expansive social framework. A new perception of the general interest was absorbing the particular stories of individual colonies, just as Plymouth itself had sought to assimilate its diverse group of particular settlers over the first ten years of its existence.

With Brewster's death, the most potent symbol of the colony's local origins was gone: the man in whose private home the Scrooby congregation had first taken shape and planned its flight to the Netherlands. Immediately after commemorating Brewster's formative role, Bradford sets out to describe the most ambitious experiment in drafting large social covenants that took place in New England for at least a century. The retrospective impetus that produces Bradford's extended tribute to Brewster springs in part from the sense of decisive cultural change that Bradford came to associate with the death of the man who had exercised the deepest personal influence on his intellectual growth.

❧

IT WAS A QUIET END to what had been, in some respects, an unquiet life. Brewster "had bore his parte in well and woe with this poore persecuted church above 36. yeares," Bradford wrote, giving up a comparatively comfortable existence in England, as a manorial officer of the archbishop of York, for prison and then an impoverished exile. These changes were made all the more difficult for Brewster "in regard of his former breeding" and affluence, as well as his age (487, 490). He was in his midforties when John Robinson's congregation fled to Leiden, in his mid-fifties when he was forced to abandon the modest prosperity that he had achieved as a printer in Holland and sail to New England. Brewster was by far the oldest passenger on the *Mayflower*—twenty-three years older than Bradford, twenty years older than John Carver, eighteen years older than Miles Standish. Only Francis Cooke, a member of the original Scrooby congregation who was also among the *Mayflower* emigrants, was close to being a contemporary, and Brewster was his senior by ten years.[6]

For the rest of his life, Brewster professed to feel particular empathy for those of "good estate and ranke" who had lost their fortunes either for the sake of religion "or by the injury and oppression of others." In his youth, Bradford reported, Brewster had been a trusted servant of William Davison, Queen Elizabeth's principal secretary and the principal scapegoat for the execution of Mary Stuart in 1587. Brewster remained loyal to his master, Bradford recalled, even "in the time of his troubles" (489). Davison spent eighteen deeply anxious months in the Tower of London for his role in Mary's execution before the queen quietly consented to his release.[7] This early example of the instability of fortune, along with the subsequent course of Brewster's own life, clearly taught him that peace was not a commodity to be purchased, as James Sherley had cynically suggested, but an inner attribute to be carefully nourished in the face of outward vicissitudes.

Brewster's personal troubles never disturbed his remarkable equanimity, Bradford claimed, or dampened the "cherfull spirite" and sociable nature that endeared him to his friends. Despite his age, he contentedly took his part in the hard physical work of colonial life "as long as he was able," in addition to preaching twice every Sabbath during the many years in which the colony had no minister. "He had a singuler good gift in prayer," Bradford remembered, that was especially effective "in ripping up the hart and conscience before God," but this ability to penetrate the psychological defenses of his listeners did not entice Brewster to abuse his power: "He always thought it were better for ministers to pray oftener, and devide their preyars, then be longe and tedious in the same." Weak spirits, Brewster believed, could not stand "bente" toward God for very long before "flagging" (493). Like John Robinson, his old colleague in Leiden, Brewster was deft at suppressing "errour or contention," but he did so less through force of mind or personality than through the example of "a peaceable disposition" so "inoffencive and innocente," Bradford wrote, that he could deal very frankly with the "faults and evills" of others "in such a maner as usually was well taken from him" (492). Bradford ventures no comparisons to princely or militant figures in his long discussion of Brewster's traits. Unlike the charismatic Robinson, he was no Ziska, whose death orphaned his people.

The great age that Brewster had managed to attain, along with the longevity of many of his colleagues among the *Mayflower* passengers, seemed exhilarating evidence of God's favor toward Plymouth. "Man lives not by bread only," Bradford reminded his reader: "It is not by good and dainty fare, by peace, and rest, and hart's ease, in injoying the contentments and good things of this world only, that preserves health and prolongs life" (495). These sentiments are identical to those that Robert Cushman expressed twenty years earlier in the observations on emigration with which the 1622 *Relation or Journall* had come to a close. The apparent comfort and security of European or English life, Cushman had insisted, was ultimately a deceit. William Brewster's last hours suggest the kind of personal destiny that the Leiden emigrants originally envisioned for themselves and their children when they left the wars and plagues of the Netherlands behind:

> He had this blesing added by the Lord to all the rest, to dye in his bed, in peace, amongst the mids of his freinds, who mourned and wepte over him, and ministered what help and comforte they could unto him, and he againe recomforted them whilst he could. His sicknes was not long, and till the last day therof he did not wholy keepe his bed. His speech continued till somewhat more then halfe a day, and then failed him; and aboute 9. or 10. a clock that evning he dyed, without any pangs at all. A few howers before, he drew his breath shorte, and some few minuts before his last, he drew his breath long, as a man falen into a sound slepe, without any pangs or gaspings, and so sweetly departed this life unto a better. (487)

Brewster's sweet departure has narrative as well as personal importance for Bradford, confirming biblical assurances of the influence that virtue exercises over memory: "What though he wanted the riches and pleasures of the world in this life, and pompious monuments at his funurall?" Bradford asks, citing Proverbs 10:7, "yet the memoriall of the just shall be blessed, when the name of the wicked shall rott (with their marble monuments)" (488). This abrupt expression of latent resentment seems curiously out of touch with Brewster's own contented withdrawal from the "monumental" world of courts and princes. Bradford's reference to the hypocritical grandeur of marble monuments springs not from a sense of Brewster's private wrongs but from the complex network of public ones with which his eulogy in *Of Plimmoth Plantation* coincides, beginning with the crime of Thomas Granger but radiating steadily outward to more pervasive forms of personal and institutional wickedness.

It would be a mistake to assume that Bradford is at all defensive about the connection between Granger's dramatic sexual outburst and the household of William Brewster. He is prepared to account for the occurrence of such behavior in New England in a number of ways that absolve colonial life or colonial leadership of any direct responsibility for the young man's startling moral deterioration. More importantly, perhaps, Bradford and Brewster shared a psychological outlook on the potential for corruption in human nature that prepared them to absorb the most spectacular evidence of human failings without recoiling in horror or stigmatizing individual weakness. These attributes of moral resilience and humane understanding clearly structure Bradford's account of Brewster's character, but they derive also from the books that the two men had available to them as they dealt with notorious private crimes and equally egregious public affronts to justice or to charity.

Three or four manuscript pages before recording Brewster's death, Bradford closes his consideration of Thomas Granger's execution by offering a few reasons why New England's religiously earnest colonies attracted such a "mixed" multitude of settlers. Tares inevitably mingle with good seed, he suggests. The labor-intensive work of settlement led merchants and investors to send any available emigrants "when they could not have such as they would." Others, perhaps, were sent to the colonial plantations by their friends "under hope that they would be made better," or at least "kept from shame," by the discipline of New England life (476). Thomas Granger's parents, at Scituate, may have hoped that their son would benefit from the best domestic and religious examples that Plymouth had to offer, in the Brewster household.[8] Why, then, were William Brewster's incisive powers of prayer and influential personal qualities so inefficacious in Granger's case? The "great licentiousnes of youth" in Holland and the "manifold temptations" of Leiden had been among the reasons that prompted the original decision to emigrate (32). But licentiousness and temptation could apparently emigrate as well and take up lodging in the most pious of New England homes.

Of Plimmoth Plantation all but invites such observations by modifying exact chronology in order to juxtapose Brewster's personal sanctity with Thomas Granger's inexplicable vice in a fashion that dramatizes the striking psychological vision captured in a contemporary analysis of human nature that both Bradford and Brewster owned: Daniel Dyke's *The Mystery of Selfe-Deceiving, or A Discourse and Discoverie of the Deceitfulnesse of Man's Heart* (1628). The Augustinian explication of human depravity was a popular Calvinist subject in the seventeenth century, but

Dyke's title suggests a special interest in the methods of rationalization that might disguise the consequences of this familiar perception even from those who nominally share it. Dyke takes his text from Jeremiah 17:9–10, "The heart is deceitfull above all things, and evill, who can know it? I the Lord search the heart and try the reynes, that I may give to everyone according to his wayes, according to the fruit of his workes." A similar searching of the heart, Dyke insists, is crucial for every Christian who hopes eventually to withstand the Lord's exacting scrutiny. The chapters of his discourse undertake to prepare his readers for what they might expect to find.

The heart, Dyke declares, is a labyrinth of "close lurking holes . . . more than the largest and wastest Cities." It is a "stinking river," a corrupt temple, a "darke Cloyster," a filthy stable. "Taking then the anatomizing knife of the Word, and ripping up the belly of this Monster," Dyke urges his reader to "make havoc" of the sin contained at the core of human nature.[9] His language is surprisingly close to the terms in which Bradford celebrates William Brewster's extraordinary powers of prayer—his ability, in comparatively short order, to rip up the heart and conscience of his auditors before God. Self-deceit, Dyke asserts, leads us to believe ourselves to be much better than we actually are. A corrective meditation is necessary: "There is no baggage so filthy but my heart is a fit sinke to receive; no monster so hideous but it is a fit wombe to conceive, no weede so poysonfull, but it is a fit soyle to bring forth."[10] The student of Dyke's pages would expect to find vice lurking in virtue's household, self-interest or corruption at the center of power and privilege. Indeed, the names of William Brewster's two sons, Love and Wrestling, whom he joined in his old age in Duxbury, epitomize the struggle that Dyke's images vividly present between a higher and a lower nature within the soul. Measured against such a background, William Brewster's exemplary life and painless death are particularly significant, the well-deserved fruits of self-examination and self-discipline maintained against extraordinary odds.

Dying in particular had distinctive dramatic meaning for Bradford and his contemporaries, beyond the sensational fates depicted in John Foxe's famous book. John Robinson's fatal "ague," for instance, was so remarkably "free from infection" that he was able to receive his friends and perform his pastoral duties without pain and "sensible to the very last," throughout the brief period of his sickness (248). Such peaceful circumstances were invested with their own, potent mystery. The suggestive rhythms of William Brewster's respiration, as his condition rapidly declined—a few hours of short breaths, followed by a few minutes of long ones, drawn "as a man falen into a sound slepe"—imply the final victory of inward peace over the insignificant succession of earthly troubles. The deaths of reprobate and saintly figures alike were equally meaningful indexes of providential design. John Foxe famously enjoyed recording the most spectacular instances of God's anger falling upon Mary Tudor's inquisitors and executioners. The queen herself, with her false pregnancy and premature death, fit beautifully into the judgmental narratives of the Protestant opposition, much as Anne Hutchinson's medical history would later serve John Winthrop.[11] Bradford's efforts to confer narrative significance on the executions of Arthur Peach and Thomas Granger are part of this contemporary predisposition to scrutinize the act of dying, but in his hands the self-exonerating dimension of such passages, so conspicuous in Foxe or Winthrop, is almost completely absent. Even his eulogy of Brewster reflects Bradford's appreciation for the element of self-deceit that unavoidably insinuates itself into the most private moments of introspection or mingles with the most exemplary lives.

Brewster himself is not directly tainted with Daniel Dyke's "mystery," but in the brief portrait of his character that Bradford offers, it is clear that Brewster appreciated the ubiquity of self-deceit in human life. His strictures against long and tedious praying, for instance, reflect his sympathy for spiritual rather than physical limitations in the worshiper. The body was probably more than capable of standing bent toward God as long as the most exacting minister might require in order to deliver an impressively thorough and elaborate prayer. But such a performance, on the part of both the congregation and the officiating clergyman, was likely to have only an earthly audience in mind. The heart and the spirit, Brewster recognized, could not mimic sincere devotion in the publicly visible posture of a humble suppliant. Long prayers invited the falling off of inward feeling, becoming rehearsals for hypocrisy rather than exercises in contrition. This grasp of the psychological dynamics of public worship may have played a key role in Brewster's success as a preacher, despite his lack of formal university credentials. "He did more in this behalfe in a year," Bradford wrote, "then many that have their hundreds a year doe in all their lives" (492).

The external trappings of religious authority—generous church livings or ecclesiastical titles—were part of the institutional apparatus of self-deceit. The radical Protestant critique of clerical vestments in the English Church is rooted in the kind of sentiments that Bradford expresses concerning the efficacy of William Brewster's unpretentious and unadorned religious leadership. But Brewster also recognized the crippling effects that could result when people who had come to rely on the stability and the significance of such external signs of status or sanctity suddenly found those signs stripped away. Those fugitives from religious persecution who had abruptly lost their good estate and rank, then, were "to be pitied most," Brewster believed, not because of some residual entitlement or privilege that they retained, but because they had been rudely startled out of a particularly decep-tive dream. Bradford confirms that Brewster's greatest displeasure was reserved for "such as would hautily and proudly carry and lift up them selves, being rise from nothing, and haveing litle else in them to commend them but a few fine cloaths, or a litle riches more than others." Brewster's displeasure, however, gave place to ten-der-hearted compassion, once the deceit of wealth and status was painfully exposed (492).

The ubiquity of self-deceit may well have been part of the lesson that William Davison sought to teach his young servant in the waning years of the sixteenth cen-tury, when he consigned to William Brewster's care first the ceremonial keys of Flushing that Davison had accepted from the Dutch provinces on Elizabeth's behalf and then the gold chain with which the Dutch had honored Davison him-self at the end of his diplomatic mission. Bradford records this anecdote from Brewster's youth in *Of Plimmoth Plantation* in part to illustrate the unusually close relationship between Davison and his protégé. "He esteemed him rather as a sonne then a servante," Bradford wrote of Davison's feelings (489). But this level of intimacy makes the older man's unusual gestures of trust all the more intriguing. They suggest, on the one hand, Davison's personal determination to distance him-self from the kind of material props that sustain earthly pride; on the other hand, they have an implicitly instructive design on the young man whom Davison re-quires to present himself to the public gaze in borrowed honors.

When he commanded Brewster to wear the gold chain after they had arrived in England, "as they ridd thorrow the country, till they came to the courte," Davison may have hoped that the experience would impress upon Brewster the inherently deceptive nature of such displays—a perception that would have been greatly strengthened a little over a year later, when Davison himself went to prison for car-rying out the queen's warrant of execution on her royal cousin (489). Power and place are a double imposition on human credulity, or so the spectacle of William Davison's servant wearing the rich gift of the Estates General would suggest. Such prestigious symbols readily deceive those who appear to possess them, as well as those who defer to their authoritative appearance or who simply suffer their effects. A conclusion such as this one would account for Brewster's deep suspicion of class pretensions and his lifelong sympathy for those whose pretensions were cruelly exploded.

These inherently generous lessons in human weakness extend even to an indi-vidual like Thomas Granger, whose behavior would seem to illustrate perfectly Daniel Dyke's most invidious similes for the heart. A reader of *The Mystery of Selfe-Deceiving,* such as Bradford or Brewster, would have found Granger's sexual habits far less startling or deviant than a modern audience might suppose. Recounting Granger's arrest and subsequent confession to multiple acts of buggery, Bradford wonders where the young man first acquired "the knowledge and practice of such wickednes," but he is not surprised by Granger's remarkable aptitude for self-degradation (475–76). Human character is a perfectly suitable medium for the nourishment of every conceivable vice. Excesses belong to a familiar continuum of behavior that William Brewster surely illustrated on this same occasion by appealing to still another book in his library, a commentary on Ecclesiastes written in 1621 by a clergyman from Lincolnshire, on the English coast near Boston, who shared the same name as the young man soon to be executed for his notorious sexual practices in Plymouth.

The clerical Thomas Granger chose Solomon's grim meditation on earthly vanity as his subject, in the hope that he might be able to "withdraw men from the transitory world, and the perishing lusts therof." In his dedicatory epistle to *A Familiar Exposition or Commentarie on Ecclesiastes*, Granger makes clear that these lusts included "Belly-Idolatry, spiritual Mastupration, [and] Selfe-harlotry"—all outgrowths of what he identifies, in vivid anatomical terms, as the rebellious "plasme" or "sperme" of our brutal nature.[12] Writing in the closing years of the reign of James I, from the point of view of the established English Church, Granger is vulgarly dismissive of sectarian criticism; he associates it with illicit sexual practices, much as Richard Bernard did in his attack on John Robinson's Separatism a decade earlier. But Granger shares with his sectarian opponents a deep suspicion of "the deceitfulnesse of the heart," its ability to shelter "unknowne and unfelt corruption," which the Lord occasionally permits "to runne out into extremities of vice . . . that all men may see what horrible filth lyeth in the heart of every man."[13]

Like Daniel Dyke, Granger is adamant that "whatsoever vanity and vile abhomination of evill is in one man, is in the nature of all, and that which breaketh out of the skinne of one, lieth in the bones of another . . . For all is but man."[14] The corporeal intensity of Granger's prose, as well as the strange coincidence of names, makes it seem likely that either Bradford or Brewster sought out his book as a means of helping both the colony's magistrates and their terrified young prisoner come to grips with what they understood to be the larger significance of his crime. All is but man, Granger's biblical commentary assured them. Radical similarities, mixed with radical differences, form the basis of this ethical tradition—the same conjunction of antithetical perceptions to which John Robinson had tied the humane administration of justice in his *Observations Divine and Morall*. Young Thomas Granger's connection to the Brewster household, then, is more than simply circumstantial, just as his presence in *Of Plimmoth Plantation* is more than a fortuitous consequence of the necessity that history be truthful. He both challenges and embodies the compound vision of human nature upon which Plymouth's ethical experience was built—the mixture of self-deceit and potential for self-transcendence captured in Bradford's suggestive account of William Brewster's life.

᠅

THE BREVITY of the Brewster eulogy appears to have aroused some concern in its author: "I should say something of his life," Bradford acknowledges, by way of introducing this biographical digression, "if to say a litle were not worse then to be silent" (488). But this narrative ambivalence is deceptive. He has room in *Of Plimmoth Plantation* to discuss only a few features of Brewster's character and experience—touching only "the heads of things," as Bradford puts it—but in doing so he constructs a remarkable commentary on the sordid operations of power and appetite that had culminated with the "heinous offenses" of 1642. As Bradford explores the subtle relationship between Brewster's personal example and the immediate historical context in which he places it, he has in mind Richard Bellingham's provocative letter on the Dorcas Humfrey case, Charles Chauncy's strikingly punitive reply, and Thomas Granger's fate. The words of Bellingham and Chauncy, in particular, suggest how vital Brewster's skilled dissection of the human conscience might be to the preservation of public well-being and how clumsy the available judicial alternatives were in comparison to the ethical and psychological authority that Brewster's words were often able to wield. Indeed, the multiple inhumanities of Chauncy's extensive letter, like the long and tedious prayers that William Brewster deplored, overflow with evidence of its author's blind self-absorption—a spiritual disorder strikingly similar to the sexual excesses that Chauncy is so eager to condemn.

More is at stake, however, in Bellingham's letter than the kind of spiritual and ethical perplexity to which William Brewster's religious gifts most directly applied. Even in its truncated form, Bellingham's request for Bradford's advice points to the thickening network of interests and antagonisms that required some formal institutional response from New England's collective leadership. One governor might privately consult another on the best means of dealing with a common administrative difficulty, just as separately covenanted churches might seek one another's advice on how to manage doctrinal differences or congregational discipline. Charles Chauncy's baptismal convictions had triggered just such wider consultation. But the increasingly complex nature of New England's political landscape required that secular governments devise mechanisms of mutual cooperation and support that were not dependent on the moral authority or wisdom of remarkable individuals like William Brewster.

The Dorcas Humfrey case is in some respects a pretext for Bellingham's 1642 appeal to his colleagues at Plymouth. The letter as a whole addresses more extensive social and political concerns, involving the operations of avarice and spiritual pride in addition to lust. The heart, as Daniel Dyke had noted, was a fit womb to conceive a stunning variety of crimes against both public and private well-being. This disconcerting form of human fertility, in turn, provides a remarkably useful means of projecting the local tragedies of New England life upon a much more expansive psychological and historical canvas. Bradford employs Bellingham's fortuitous correspondence for just this purpose.

The governor of Massachusetts had some complaints about the conduct of the fur trade. In the absence of an effective system of mutually supportive trading policies in the various jurisdictions of English settlement, the Indians apparently found themselves able to exploit a significant commercial advantage, pitting numbers of unscrupulous English buyers against one another in order to drive up the price of their furs. Bellingham proposed to Bradford the formation of an informal trading company among the English colonies, in response to this comparatively sophisticated seller's cartel. Plymouth had tried to maintain "an orderly course" in its own trading practices, Bradford replied, but he was receptive to Bellingham's proposal, expressing a willingness "to advise and concure with you in what we may" to bring the fur trade under more uniform control. This response falls just short of an unqualified endorsement of common interests—Plymouth had already suffered the effects of Massachusetts's acquisitive energies—but it is at least encouraging. A second complaint raised in Bellingham's message elicits a more guarded response (462–63).

The "Ilanders at Aquidnett," as Bellingham called them, continued to plague the government in Boston. This settlement in Narragansett Bay had originally been composed of exiles from Massachusetts who left the colony's territory, either willingly or unwillingly, as a result of the Antinomian controversy five years earlier. Since then, Samuel Gorton and a handful of his followers had briefly joined them, igniting such political and religious discord that Gorton had been publicly whipped and expelled. He next sought refuge in Roger Williams' settlement at Providence, but there too Gorton provoked a number of prominent residents, formerly from Massachusetts, into requesting Boston's help in suppressing Gorton's anarchic temperament, perhaps by annexing the Narragansett region altogether.[15]

Gorton soon secured a grant of land from the Narragansett sachem, Miantonomo, and established his own small settlement just south of Providence—a calculated gesture on Miantonomo's part that particularly antagonized the Massachusetts leadership, who characterized all the English castoffs in the Narragansett Bay region as anti-Christian heretics. Any material assistance to them might encourage schismatic temperaments still remaining among the older colony's population. "We are not willing to joyne with them in any league or confederacie at all," Governor Bellingham wrote of this cluster of theological renegades, in the hope that Plymouth would help contain the dangerous social and religious "infection" that the Islanders represented (461). Mindful of the barely suppressed hostility of the Massachusetts position, Roger Williams shortly sailed for England in an attempt to obtain a colonial patent from the Long Parliament as protection for the Rhode Island communities.

Bradford's response to Bellingham's tentative overture for concerted action against these religious incorrigibles is masterfully brief. As to the Islanders, he replies, "we have no conversing with them, nor desire to have, furder then necessitie or humanity may require" (463). Gorton and Williams had already given ample evidence of their disruptive effects on communal harmony in Plymouth, but this concise (and discouragingly vague) statement is all the answer that Bradford provides to Bellingham's angry indictment of the "publick defiance" that he associates with the residents of Aquidnett or his request that Plymouth's magistrates would "consider and advise with us how we may avoyd them" (461). Avoidance plays no part in Bradford's carefully articulated neutrality. His message preserves a considerable social and political margin within which mutual intercourse might take place between Plymouth and its more radical neighbors; the bonds of humanity and necessity exert decisive claims on Bradford's loyalty.

The suggestive texture of Bellingham's letter, coupled with Plymouth's complex response, both from William Bradford and from the colony's three ministers, draws together themes of sexual, economic, and religious misgovernment in the increasingly volatile political circumstances of New England. Indeed, Bellingham introduces into the history the idea of a commercial and military confederacy among the English colonies, which at least in some measure reflects the disorder of affairs in revolutionary London as well as the troubling developments on Narragansett Bay or at the various trading outposts on New England's western and northern frontiers. The struggle to frame acceptable institutions and to identify acceptable methods for collective action gradually asserts itself as the dominant theme of Bradford's closing pages, one that he is content to allow to emerge from this unexpected and unpromising source. Bellingham invokes a history of local conflict that reaches back into the vexed relationship between Plymouth and Boston and extends forward, past the death of William Brewster, toward a temporary resolution of mutual antagonisms among the English colonial governments themselves, in order to confront the challenge of an especially deft and observant native leader who had recently shown himself capable of exploiting ideological divisions within the English communities.

Taken together, these are the ingredients of traditional "politic" history—res gestae, or great affairs, the implications of which are surprisingly large though the events themselves are conducted on a diminutive, colonial scale. Francesco Guicciardini's elaborate narrative, on Bradford's bookshelf, embraced many of these same provocative elements: the deep jealousies and contaminated loyalties that shape political competition, the ubiquitous religious hostility of the age, the uncontained lusts of human nature. These entangled narrative threads in Bradford's story, as in his Italian predecessor's, are closely associated with the death of an exemplary public figure whose passing could be made to symbolize a point of momentous civic transition. If the synchronization of individual fate with communal change is not quite close enough in actual fact, then facts might readily be adjusted to accommodate the requirements of historical art.

Bradford surely realized that the effect of doing so would inevitably jar contemporary readers, who vividly remembered the actual year of William Brewster's death. But from the perspective of two or three generations—the posterity that Bradford envisioned himself addressing through the medium of his book—a measure of productive ambiguity concerning dates would prove far less significant than the impact of a meaningful narrative design, embracing the broadest possible scope of Plymouth's experience. Beginning with the legal complexities immediately preceding the outbreak of the Pequot War and moving through the judicial assassination of Miantonomo, the Narragansett leader, *Of Plimmoth Plantation* dramatically expands its thematic and explanatory ambitions.

೭

THIS THEMATIC EXPANSION, over the last decade that Bradford treats in his book, is framed by transcriptions of the two longest documents that he decides to preserve in his pages: King Charles' commission for regulating plantations, issued from the Privy Council in 1634, and the full text of the Articles of Confederation creating the United Colonies of New England in 1643. Francesco Guicciardini gives dramatic immediacy to his sixteenth-century account of Italian affairs by composing extensive speeches, in imitation of Sallust or Livy, that he attributes to key agents in the development of his story: the incursion of a great power among the fragmented civic domains of Italy.[16] Bradford's decision to use carefully selected letters and documents for a similar purpose reflects both his confidence in the richness of the archive at his disposal and his appreciation for the capacity of contemporary language to communicate the indeterminate nature of experience before retrospective interpretation can impose meanings upon an apparently haphazard series of incidents.

At the same time, the events that Bradford carefully interweaves in these closing chapters of his book are anything but haphazard. They dramatize in the broadest terms a struggle that Plymouth's leaders had confronted since their first months in New England, when the encroaching ambitions of the Narragansett, along with the equally disquieting appetite for dominion on the part of the Council for New England, had threatened Plymouth's fragile autonomy. King Charles' creation of a governing commission for plantations in 1634 represents a considerable escalation in these threats, but it is not different in kind from the grand commission that Robert Gorges had brought to Plymouth eleven years earlier, in an abortive attempt of the commercial boards in London to impose a "generall Governor" on the country. The king's newest incursion remains a verbal, rather than a physical, invasion, but its effects contribute to the recognition of important collective interests, as well as the evolution of a collective identity, among the New England colonies.

This sensitivity to wider contexts marks Bradford's narrative at every turn. *Of Plimmoth Plantation* continually prompts its reader to recall the larger historical plots that circumscribe the story of the Leiden emigrants, beginning with the expiration of the fateful truce between the Dutch and the Spanish that threatened their original refuge in the Netherlands. Such immediate geopolitical developments exercise far more influence over Bradford's grasp of historical causation than the mythic struggle between Satan and the Saints that he invokes in the opening pages of his narrative. Isaac de Rasier's courtly overture of 1627, for example, alerts Bradford's reader to the familiar nexus of European war and traffic, beginning to take root in New England soil only seven years after Plymouth's settlers had sought to escape its influence. James Sherley's complex, manipulative nature—vividly preserved in the letters that Bradford subjects to withering analysis in the pages of the history—reflects the systematic impingement of London's sophisticated, commercial culture upon the colony's marginal, subsistence economy.

The excruciating details of the Pequot War inevitably evoke the increasingly routine horrors of the European conflict that is entering its third decade as Massachusetts Bay and Connecticut orchestrate their invasion of Pequot territory in the spring and summer of 1637. As Bradford makes evident, John Winthrop's colonial militia quickly shows itself to be brutally adept in the tactical exercise of slaughter—a calculated strategy of military ruthlessness all too familiar to observers of the Thirty Years War. Bradford's Dutch correspondents kept him informed of the shifting fortunes of Protestant and Catholic armies, as they maneuvered through the Rhine Valley on their way toward the eventual stalemate of 1648. C. V. Wedgwood summarizes what she terms the "morally subversive, economically destructive, socially degrading" outcome of that stalemate. For her the Thirty Years War remains "the outstanding example in European history of meaningless conflict." In the closing chapters of his book, William Bradford anticipates critical elements of Wedgwood's crushing judgment in his assessment of the Pequot War, making astute use of the letters of his English colleagues to expose the layers of equivocation in English policy.[17]

Letters, formal proclamations, and legal documents repeatedly offer Bradford dramatic evidence of the complicated interlacing of New England affairs with the menacing climate of European politics. This wider and increasingly unpredictable historical framework emerges most vividly as Bradford begins his account of what he calls "one of the sadest things that befell them since they came" to New England: the death of an English fur trader named Hocking, from the plantation of Pascataway, who was shot by one of Plymouth's Kennebec agents in an altercation over trading rights. Citing the official language of the Kennebec patent as a preface, Bradford briefly explains the circumstances that led to a double killing on the Kennebec River in 1634.

With the approach of the spring trading season that year, a bark loaded with commodities, under the charge of "one Hocking," passed upriver, beyond Plymouth's permanent trading post, in an effort to intercept the Indian hunters bringing their winter furs to the coast. Despite warnings that the Plymouth men would enforce their legal right "to take, apprehend, seise, and make prise" of all who tried to encroach on the trading rights that the Council for New England had granted them, Hocking persisted. Rather than attempt to capture him, Plymouth's agents decided to cut the anchor cable of his boat "and let him drive downe the river with the streame," but as Hocking's small craft turned in the current, he abruptly presented a musket to the head of the Plymouth man who had cut the cable and killed him. A companion of the dead man, in turn, "could not hold" and immediately shot Hocking in revenge. He "fell downe dead and never speake word," Bradford vividly if colloquially reports, but an abundance of angry words, both in England and in America, almost immediately springs from this event (377–78).

"The truth of the thing," Bradford insists, was simply as he had described it: Hocking's own intransigence, his "ill words," and finally his murderous assault had brought about his death. It is equally clear from Bradford's carefully constructed account, however, that the language of the English patent—and the expensive political process that lay behind such commercial grants—set the stage for the Kennebec killings:

> The said Counsell [for New England] hath further given, granted, bargained, sold, infeoffed, alloted, assigned, and sett over, and by these presents doe clearly and absolutly give, grante, bargane, sell, alliene, enffeofe, allote, assigne, and confirme unto the said William Bradford, his heires, associates, and assignes, All that tracte of land or part of New-England in America afforesaid, which lyeth within or betweene, and extendeth it selfe from the utmost limits of Cobiseconte, which adjoyneth to the river of Kenebeck, towards the westerne ocean, and a place called the falls of Nequamkick in America, aforsaid; and the space of 15. English myles on each side of the said river, commonly called Kenebeck River, and all the said river called Kenebeck that lyeth within the said limits and bounds, eastward, westward, northward, and southward. (376)

When Bradford copies this legal language into *Of Plimmoth Plantation,* a few sentences before the Hocking murder, he effectively places before the reader the entire ill-considered effort, on the part of commercial trading boards in London, to parcel out watersheds, trading rights, and police authority over the complex cultural and physical geography of the New England woods. The redundant legal terminology of the patent points to the great expense involved in securing such formal authority—the lawyers and the bribes that the colony's agents had been required to pay—which in turn accounts for the sense of urgency that Plymouth's Kennebec agent had felt to defend a legal privilege "which had cost them so dear." Bradford knowingly discloses, at the same time, his personal interest in Hocking's behavior, since he and his associates among the small band of trading partners at Plymouth had bound themselves, through equally daunting legal instruments, to pay the colony's extensive debts through the profits from its fur trade. Hocking's violent but speechless end takes place in a dense, circumstantial network of costly words.

These "sad tidings" from the Kennebec woods (as Bradford terms them) quickly produce a highly selective letter of protest from the settlers at Pascataway to their influential English patrons, along with equally imperfect rumors within New England itself. The "bruite" of the killings—literally, the noise that they produce—soon reaches Massachusetts Bay, whose magistrates grow "so prepossest with this matter," Bradford reports, that they seize John Alden from Plymouth's coastal trading vessel, on its next visit to Boston, and put him in prison (379). Although he had been at Kennebec, Alden was not involved in Hocking's death. He was, however, one of the elected assistants to Plymouth's governor in 1634, so his arrest took on the appearance of a well-calculated official assault on Plymouth's commercial and political independence.[18]

Plymouth's initial contact with members of the Massachusetts Bay Company, in 1629, had contained hints of latent difficulty between the two communities. Bradford transcribes into the history a letter from John Endecott, written shortly after his arrival in Naumkeag, expressing Endecott's relief at learning that Plymouth's religious practices were not so objectionable as English rumor had made them out to be. Surely there could be no discord between servants of the same heavenly master, Endecott wrote hopefully to Bradford: "God's people are all marked with one and the same marke, and sealed with one and the same seale, and have for the maine, one and the same harte" (315). Bradford thought it "not unmeete" to include this letter in his book, though he must have done so with misgivings. Similar appeals to underlying religious unity, beginning with the fervent Christian pacifism of Erasmus a century earlier, had proved conspicuously useless as a means of containing Europe's sectarian hostilities. The underlying harmony of God's people had not prevented the officers of James I from harrying English dissenters from their homes. Endecott's words are steeped in an atmosphere of formulaic impotence conferred by a century of ethical failure.

Discord between the emigrant neighbors in New England was not long in materializing. The Massachusetts seizure of John Alden "was thought strang here," Bradford writes, but this sense of understated bewilderment soon yields to stronger sentiments as the Bay Colony authorities seem increasingly determined to assert rights of legal jurisdiction over a citizen of Plymouth, for a crime alleged to have been committed outside of Massachusetts's borders. Bradford copies two letters from Thomas Dudley, then governor of Massachusetts Bay, into the text of the history in order to indicate how swiftly public roles could ensnare the passions and loyalties of private individuals, how readily the elaborate reverberations triggered by comparatively minor historical acts could be amplified by their context. The death of "one Hocking" on the New England frontier occurs at a place and time that are perfectly suited to such effects. Bradford does not even record the name of the Plymouth trader whom Hocking kills—Moses Talbott—in order to stress the disproportionate social and political consequences that these otherwise obscure deaths precipitate.[19]

Governor Dudley originally addresses Bradford as a personal friend, inquiring with apparently genuine concern about Bradford's health before proceeding to distinguish his private opinions on the Kennebec killings from the "frequente speeches" of others, in the Massachusetts General Court, who felt less compunction about "inter medling in the mater" (379–80). Perhaps because Bradford had recently yielded the governorship of Plymouth to Thomas Prence, he apparently initiated the exchange of letters with Dudley on an equally personal note, but he must have also made some spirited complaints about John Alden's treatment. At Bradford's urging, Dudley reports that he "sett Mr. Alden at liberty." At the same time, to placate his political critics at home, Dudley bound Miles Standish, who was serving as Plymouth's official emissary at Boston, to appear before the Massachusetts General Court to defend Plymouth's "innocencie" in the Hocking killing. "If any unkindnes hath ben taken from what we have done," Dudley wrote, "let it be further and better considred of, I pray you; and I hope the more you thinke of it, the lesse blame you will impute to us" (380).

Dudley's circumstances are in many respects similar to those that Plymouth's chief trading agent on the Kennebec, John Howland, had faced as he "prayed" and "entreated" the irascible Hocking to appreciate Howland's administrative predicament. Bradford's careful juxtaposition of narrative and letters makes this parallel all but inescapable. In the end, Dudley is only slightly more successful than Howland was in cooling the explosive passions by which he is surrounded. These passions are themselves exacerbated by the apparent determination of the king of England to force a similar confrontation over jurisdictions and legal privileges with the New England colonies as a whole.

This third layer of jurisdictional provocation appears in the extensive supplement that Bradford offers to the second of Thomas Dudley's letters. Miles Standish had apparently conducted himself in his customary, confrontational manner before the magistrates of Massachusetts Bay, forcing Dudley to produce Bradford's private letter on the Hocking killings, so that the court could formally answer it. Bradford's language, however, "made the breach soe wide" between Massachusetts and Plymouth that Dudley feared only time could heal it. A measure of embarrassment, perhaps, leads Bradford to suppress this provocative letter, but the account of its effects, in Dudley's correspondence, makes its nature clear enough. On this occasion at least, Bradford's literary composure appears to have deserted him.

"Set your wisdom and patience a worke," Dudley chides Bradford, in his report of the untoward results of Standish's mission, "and exhorte others to the same, that things may not proceede from bad to worse" (381). The basis for these fears is only partly the local jealousies and antagonisms between Plymouth and Boston. Dudley had recently learned of a threat emanating from London that dwarfed "this unhappie contention between you and us." "A comone danger to us boath approaching," he wrote Bradford, "will necessitate our uniting againe." On the facing page of the history, Bradford identifies the cause of Dudley's anxiety, transcribing on two verso sheets of his manuscript the complete text of the king's 1634 Commission for Regulating Plantations.[20]

Just as Hocking sought to encroach on the Kennebec patent and Massachusetts implicitly extended the sway of its General Court over the government of Plymouth, so the king now undertook "to provid a remedy for the tranquillity and quietnes of those people" who had settled in "large Collonies of the English Nation" throughout the world by dramatically extending the Crown's direct control of colonial life. Despite the comprehensive language of its preamble, the scope of the king's commission is directly aimed at the dissident churches and governments of New England. The terms of the commission itself immediately invite comparison to the fairly trivial privileges of the Kennebec patent that Bradford had woven into the history a few paragraphs earlier. Addressing himself to a dozen of his "beloved and faithfull Counselours," including the archbishops of Canterbury and York, along with an array of secular lords and officers, Charles declares his intention to commit the full power of colonial government into the hands of this body of commissioners.

Any five or more of these twelve men, in conjunction with the archbishops of York and Canterbury, could meet together to make laws, control trade, and establish institutions for "the cure of soules" among the English colonies. They were charged to organize a system of "tithes, oblations, and other things," in order to support an established clergy in New England. They were authorized to stipulate penalties, up to "the deprivation of member, or life," for violations of their decrees and "to remove, and displace the governours or rulers of those colonies, for causes which to you shall seeme lawfull" (542). All New England judges and magistrates were subject to the appointment of these commissioners, for both civil and ecclesiastical courts, and the commission itself would sit as a supreme tribunal over "all maner of complaints" arising between the colonies and their local "rulers" or among the several colonies themselves (541–42).

All boundary and jurisdictional disputes would hereafter be settled by Charles' commissioners rather than by local authorities, who were familiar with local geography. All new colonial patents would originate with the king's commission, and all old ones were subject to being revoked if the commission found them to have been "surrepticiously or unduly" obtained (544). In a closing gesture of imperial determination, the king charged New England's population to be obedient to the commission's warrants "at their peril." This extraordinary document clearly expresses the depth of frustration and anger that the king and his closest advisers felt over the intractable nature of his own kingdom during the years that Charles was attempting to govern without a parliament. What he could not do in Great Britain, he could at least dream of doing in North America.[21] At the same time the creation of the commission puts into effect the implicit threat of the Whitehall memorandum of 1632, which had brought the affair of Christopher Gardiner to a close. Indeed, this momentous document amounts to a complete restructuring of the political circumstances that lay behind Bradford's entire history. It provides for the exportation to New England of the same civil and ecclesiastical apparatus from which the Scrooby exiles had originally fled in 1608. In retrospect, Bradford acknowledges that Thomas Dudley was right to be alarmed.

The king's actions (or at least his will to act) made it seem particularly vital that the New England colonies do nothing to alienate potential allies among the British aristocracy, such as the patrons of the Pascataway settlement, who had been angered upon receiving distorted accounts of Hocking's death. Dudley's caution in handling Plymouth's complaint before the Massachusetts General Court is directed toward this broader conciliatory end, or so he tries to tell a hot-tempered William Bradford: "I hope the more you thinke of it," he writes, of New England's complicated predicament, "the lesse blame you will impute to us." Such geopolitical concerns were certainly not the only motives influencing Massachusetts Bay to meddle in Plymouth's affairs, but they proved sufficiently convincing to Bradford and his colleagues to prompt them to "appease" the Boston magistrates and "mollifie their minds" (382).

Following John Winthrop's advice, Plymouth's leaders undertook to arrange a conference among all the neighboring plantations to settle the question of right and wrong surrounding the Kennebec affair. "And for the clearing of conscience," Bradford wrote, "it was desired that the ministers of every plantation might be presente to give their advice" (383). This expedient struck some members of Plymouth's government as "dangerous," perhaps because it appeared to invite the same entanglement of civil and ecclesiastical power represented in the ominous provisions of the king's Commission for Plantations. Nevertheless, Bradford notes, "they put themselves upon it" out of confidence in "the justice of their cause, and the equitie of their freinds." Within a year Edward Winslow learned how misplaced such confidence could be, when he met directly with Charles' newly impaneled commissioners. Bradford's immediate purpose in Of Plimmoth Plantation is to dramatize how this network of encroachments progressively expands, like the invisible concussion of a shock wave, from the Kennebec woods to the Privy Council and back again, resonating through all the provincial authorities in New England.

The place that Plymouth names as the site of the intercolonial conference in which they propose to settle all these differences is Boston:

> But when the day and time came, none apered, but some of the magistrats and ministers of the Massachusets, and their owne. Seeing none of Passcataway or other places came, (haveing been thus desired, and conveniente time given them for that end,) Mr. Winthrop and the rest said they could doe no more then they had done thus to requeste them, the blame must rest on them. So they fell into a fair debating of things them selves; and after all things had been fully opened and discussed, and the oppinione of each one demanded, both magistrats, and ministers, though they all could have wished these things had never been, yet they could not but lay the blame and guilt on Hockins owne head; and with all gave them shuch grave and godly exhortations and advice, as they thought meete, both for the presente and future; which they allso imbraced with love and thankfullnes, promising to indeavor to follow the same. And thus was this matter ended, and ther love and concord renewed. (383–84)

This long train of incidents had begun four manuscript pages earlier, with Bradford's detailed description of what "fell out" on the Kennebec River in the spring of 1634. In the end, the two parties most deeply interested in these events, finding themselves alone at the conference called to resolve the story of Hocking's death, "fell into a fair debating of things." Bradford imposes a measure of verbal symmetry upon his story by implying that just as chance was largely responsible for the circumstances leading to the Kennebec killings, so chance dictates this initial experiment in forming an intercolonial consensus.

But chance is not in the least responsible for the careful layering of narrative, letters, and official documents that Bradford employs to expose the larger forces behind this abortive attempt at a federation of New England interests. Boston was also the site, nine years later, where representatives from the four major colonies met to frame the confederation that would help to strengthen their immediate negotiating position with the Narragansett. Within the larger symmetries suggested by these two meetings, Bradford offers, in quick succession, accounts of three additional events demonstrating the necessity for some broad, institutional restraint on what he calls at one point the restlessly "hankering" minds of men. These events, in turn, form the background for his carefully constructed treatment of the Pequot War.

The first of these illustrative historical cases immediately follows the copy of the King's Commission of 1634, on the verso sheets of Bradford's manuscript. In the same year as the Kennebec killings, Plymouth's trading bark had also visited New Amsterdam. An English sea captain named Stone, from the West Indies, was visiting the Dutch as well and managed to persuade their governor, on some pretext, to allow him to seize Plymouth's vessel, along with its valuable cargo, "and carry her away towards Virginia" (385). According to Bradford, some Dutch sailors, remembering the kindness of their Plymouth friends, thwarted this barely concealed attempt at piracy. On a later visit to Plymouth, Stone tried to revenge himself on the colony's governor, "but by God's providence and the vigilance of some was prevented." Later still, this violent figure so antagonized the Pequot people on a trading expedition that the Pequot killed him, along with his partner, Walter Norton, and seized their pinnace and trading goods.[22] Though clearly criminal in nature, Stone's attitudes are not entirely unlike those expressed in the king of England's piratical commission, a comparison underscored by Bradford's textual juxtaposition of the passages.

The Dutch and the French also are given to appropriating the rights and property of others in New England—a pattern of behavior that Plymouth tries to address by sending Edward Winslow to London in order to explain the colony's defensive needs to the king's newly impaneled commission. In 1635 Winslow appears before the commissioners to request that the English government intervene directly "with those foraine states" on New England's behalf, in order to restrain their respective colonial governments, or that they grant a special warrant to the English colonies "to right and defend them selves against all foraigne enimies" as the colonies themselves see fit (391). The granting of this second request would amount to a delegation of sovereignty that suggests how far some of the English colonial leadership had progressed toward a de facto recognition of their political independence.

Most of the king's commissioners, by Bradford's account, were not alarmed by such comparatively abstract implications. They were simply concerned that New England find a way to defend its interests "without any either charge or trouble to the state." Archbishop Laud, however, "crost" Winslow's petition—Plymouth's iconoclastic historian undoubtedly relished this modest pun—and turned the conversation toward religious questions, interrogating the petitioner about the management of church services and the administration of the sacraments in Plymouth (392). Edward Winslow apparently shared some of Miles Standish's blunt approach to diplomatically sensitive matters, at least in the presence of such an abrasive antagonist as William Laud. In the course of his questioning, Bradford reports, the archbishop grew increasingly vehement and ultimately succeeded in getting Winslow committed to Fleet Prison for nearly four months.

On a small scale, this encounter reenacts scores of similar interrogation scenes presented at great length in John Foxe's *Actes and Monuments,* but more importantly it links Laud's behavior with the series of usurpations (small and large) that Bradford first introduced with Hocking's infringement of the Kennebec patent, the previous year. Just as the French take delight in raiding Plymouth's trading posts, or the Dutch comply with Captain Stone's larcenous desires, so Laud's appetite for religious dominion leads him to appropriate the occasion of Winslow's petition and New England's needs to his own ends.

Even "some of their neighbours in the Bay," Bradford observes, "had a hankering mind," as they contemplated Plymouth's successful trading establishment on the Connecticut River. These commercial hankerings, in turn, result in the third of Bradford's sequential exhibits in the history, demonstrating the profusion of competitors seeking power and property in New England. "The Masschuset men are coming almost dayly," Jonathan Brewster reported to Plymouth's magistrates from his Connecticut outpost in July 1635, complaining that many emigrants from the settlements around Boston had begun to arrive in the Connecticut valley, clearly intending to appropriate land that Plymouth had recently purchased from the local Indians: "I shall doe what I can to withstand them. I hope they will hear reason; as that we were here first, and entred with much difficulty and danger, both in regard of the Dutch and Indeans, and bought the land, (to your great charge, allready disbursed,) and have since held here a chargable possession, and kept the Dutch from further incroaching, which would els long before this day have possessed all, and kept out all others . . . I hope these and shuch like arguments will stoppe them" (403–4). The Massachusetts settlers, however, professed to view any soil not immediately under some form of cultivation as "the Lords wast[e]," a term that Bradford and his colleagues clearly regard as scarcely more plausible a pretext for theft than Captain Stone's motives for seizing Plymouth's trading bark (405).

Forcible resistance to these English invaders was out of the question, Bradford confesses: "they had enough of that about Kenebeck" (407). In the end Plymouth simply sold most of its Connecticut land to the emigrants from Massachusetts Bay, rather than attempt to resist the pressure of numbers, but Bradford's pointed allusion to the Hocking killings signals his intent to stitch these episodes together, across a span of sixteen manuscript pages, disclosing a feverish outbreak of acquisitive passions that, in various forms, embraces the English community from Boston to London. Like the concurrent smallpox epidemics among the Connecticut Indians, these appetites for power and profit threaten to dissolve the social fabric. At the same time, however, they bring the New England colonies into such repeated collision with one another that their leaders are forced to confront, in the starkest terms, the nature of the social contract that will govern them. This confrontation takes its most Hobbesian form during the diplomatic and military exchanges of the Pequot War.

"A STOUTE AND WARLIKE PEOPLE," as Bradford calls them, the Pequots were competing, during these same years, with the English, the Narragansett, and the Dutch for commercial control of the lower Connecticut River.[23] Recognizing the unusual challenges posed by this four-way contest, and hoping to avoid having to contend with "over many enemies at once," the Pequot concluded a "peace and freindship" with Massachusetts Bay in 1634. Bradford's brief account of these negotiations frankly portrays the mixture of ambition, vanity, and diplomatic sophistication that shapes Pequot policy—a blend of attributes that would have been quite familiar to a student of Francesco Guicciardini's discussion of the complex political motives shaping civic behavior in fifteenth- and sixteenth-century Italy.

John Winthrop, however, brusquely assures Bradford that, despite the recent agreement established with the Pequot leaders, Massachusetts Bay's traders had found them to be "a very false people, so as they mean to have no more to doe with them" (417). A policy of nonintercourse is the same weapon that Richard Bellingham proposes against the Aquidnett Islanders in 1642. Plymouth's position with respect to the Pequot is less markedly neutral than the reply that they make to Bellingham five years later. Once the Pequot openly attack the Connecticut settlements, in 1637, Plymouth's leaders indicate, in reply to a request from Henry Vane, that they are "cordially willing" to join the Bay Colony in retaliating (420). But this cordiality is mixed with a degree of opportunistic caution that is closely akin to the atmosphere of diplomatic contingency that fills Guicciardini's history of the sixteenth-century Italian leagues.[24]

Bradford and his colleagues frankly exploit the urgency that the leaders of Massachusetts Bay feel in the face of the Pequot threat, answering Vane's request with an expression of support that, at the same time, itemizes a number of recent instances in which the government at Boston failed to come to the aid of Plymouth. As he did in presenting Thomas Dudley's 1634 correspondence concerning the Kennebec murders, Bradford omits from the pages of the history his own contribution to this written exchange, allowing the nature of Plymouth's official complaint to emerge indirectly through a long, revealing reply from John Winthrop. This narrative decision has the double advantage of leaving Winthrop's tactics and emotions fully exposed to Bradford's reader.

Writing shortly after the removal of Henry Vane from the governorship of Massachusetts Bay—an election marked by the tensions of the Antinomian crisis—Winthrop gratefully acknowledges Plymouth's "good affection" toward the proposal for a joint military campaign against the Pequot. He displays, however, a telling flicker of irritation at Plymouth's assertion that the war was largely of concern to Massachusetts Bay alone—and perhaps, by implication, largely of the Massachusetts General Court's own making.[25] "We suppose," Winthrop snaps, "that in case of perill, you will not stand upon shuch terms, as we hope we should not doe towards you; and withall we conceive that you looke at the Pequents, and all other Indeans, as a commone enimie, who though he may take occasion, of the begining of his rage, from some one parte of the English, yet if he prevaile, will surly pursue his advantage, to the rooting out of the whole nation" (420).

The internal political stresses of the Boston government almost certainly influenced the militant posture of this letter, but its language captures a strain of English thinking that will later express itself in the bigotry of Plymouth's rude and ignorant sort during the prosecution of Arthur Peach the following year. Winthrop's extraordinary disclosure makes immediately clear that he and his colleagues view contemporary political circumstances in New England in strictly racialized terms. Moreover, Winthrop attributes an equally racialized consciousness to the "Indeans," crediting them with the same ruthless appetite for rooting out entire peoples that the English militia will itself display in a subsequent assault on a Pequot fort, an assault that Bradford describes in considerable detail in the pages immediately following his transcription of Winthrop's letter.

In stark contrast to Winthrop's position, Bradford portrays Plymouth's understanding of the Pequot conflict as part of a broader system of sharply competitive relations between the English and the French, as well as among the various English communities themselves. One of the objections that Bradford and his colleagues lodge against the government at Boston, in their message of "cordial" compliance with the Pequot campaign, is the Bay Colony's ongoing "trade and correspondancie with the French" (421). Another is the refusal of Massachusetts Bay in 1635 to aid Plymouth in its attempts to recover their Penobscot outpost. Bradford and his colleagues want some assurance that such a lack of support will not recur, before fully consenting to participate in the Pequot war. Apparently, too, they took strong exception to the way in which Massachusetts Bay had embroiled the English colonies as a whole in armed conflict with a formidable native people without first consulting the opinions of its neighbors. The text of Winthrop's reply makes all of these grounds of complaint quite clear.

Like Plymouth, the Pequot view their diplomatic predicament in a complex light, incorporating a variety of clashing interests that, taken together, supersede the narrowly racial argument that John Winthrop invokes. In Bradford's account of these events, however, the more conspicuous and intriguing resemblance that he explores links the behavior of the Pequot leaders with that of the magistrates of Massachusetts Bay. The mixture of letters and interpolated narrative in *Of Plimmoth Plantation* clearly demonstrates that the Pequot adopt diplomatic arguments with potential Indian allies that are every bit as coercive as those that Winthrop employs with Plymouth. As they had two years earlier in their overtures to Massachusetts Bay, the Pequot try to reduce the number of their enemies in 1636, by enticing the Narragansett to join with them in their English war. Immediately following the text of Winthrop's reply to Plymouth's conditional offer of military support, Bradford describes what he has been able to learn (probably through Roger Williams) about the parallel negotiations among the Indians, using language that emphasizes the instructive resemblance between the political instincts of the Pequot leaders and those of their primary English antagonist:

> In the mean time, the Pequents, espetially in the winter before, sought to make peace with the Narigansets, and used very pernicious arguments to move them therunto: as that the English were stranegers and begane to overspred their countrie, and would deprive them therof in time, if they were suffered to grow and increse; and if the Narigansets did assist the English to subdue them, they did but make way for their owne overthrow, for if they were rooted out, the English would soone take occasion to subjugate them; and if they would harken to them, they should not neede to fear the strength of the English; for they would not come to open battle with them, but fire their houses, kill their katle, and lye in ambush for them as they went abroad upon their occasions . . . The which course being held, they well saw the English could not long subsiste, but they would either be starved with hunger, or be forced to forsake the countrie; with many the like things; insomuch that the Narigansets were once wavering, and were halfe minded to have made peace with them, and joyned against the English. (424)

The Pequot argument, in Bradford's retelling, is virtually identical to the case that John Winthrop tries to make with Plymouth—a relationship that the reader of the history can hardly overlook, since Bradford has so closely linked Winthrop's letter with his description of the Pequot appeal.

Your own safety, too, is at stake in this conflict, Winthrop insists to Plymouth's magistrates. The Pequot likewise assure the Narragansett that their own overthrow will be the inevitable result if they fail to form a united front against the English. Should the Bay Colony succumb to Pequot attacks, Winthrop warns, Plymouth would eventually have to face a formidable Indian enemy on its own—precisely the fate that the Pequot predict for the Narragansett, if they allow their natural allies to be "rooted out" by the English. The Narragansett, in turn, see an opportunity "by the help of the English" to take revenge on an old and presumptuous enemy. Bradford's deft collation in these pages underscores not the racial or cultural practices dividing the English and the native communities but the analytical intelligence and rhetorical resources that unite them (420–24).

Winthrop makes a point-by-point attempt to refute all of Plymouth's objections to the past behavior of Massachusetts Bay. Edward Winslow "can certifie you," he writes, that traders from the Bay have not been encroaching on Plymouth's Kennebec territory. Nor (he insists) have Boston's agents been trading with "the French, your enemise," though Winthrop's choice of words in making this denial is disconcerting at best. Bradford bluntly contradicts this claim, in the margins of his manuscript, inscribing the intractable nature of these deep disagreements among the English colonies in the appearance of his page. Like the Narragansett and the Pequot, the English have deep internal differences.

In the closing sentences of Winthrop's long and crucial reply to Plymouth's lukewarm expression of military support, he drops all pretense of trying to mollify Plymouth's leaders. "It concerns us much to hasten this warr to an end," he admits, before news of large-scale conflict with the Indians could discourage further English emigration. Self-defense is clearly not the only motive behind Massachusetts Bay policy in pressing for Plymouth's energetic cooperation.[26] Moreover, Winthrop continues, "if the Lord shall please to blesse our endea[v]ours, so as we end the warr, or put it in a hopefull way without you, it may breed shuch ill thoughts in our people towards yours, as will be hard to entertaine shuch opinione of your good will towards us, as were fitt to be nurished among shuch neighbours and brethren as we are" (423). Bradford immediately juxtaposes these words with the "pernicious" appeal of the Pequot emissaries to the Narragansett, with the result that his direct disparagement of Pequot motives appears to address Winthrop's coercive tactics as well.

Confronted with this barely concealed threat from their English neighbors, Plymouth prepares to send a militia company of fifty men to the Connecticut frontier to participate in the joint military campaign; but before they can depart, a decisive English assault on a large Pequot fort makes their presence unnecessary. Bradford's account of this slaughter captures the newly awakened ambivalence of the Narragansett, who had guided the English to the Pequot camp, as well as the contorted mixture of blessings and threats that marked the last lines of John Winthrop's letter. Approaching the Pequot fort at night, the English break into the enclosure, quickly setting fire to the woven mats and wooden frames of the Pequot houses, "and therby more were burnte to death then was otherwise slain":

> Those that scaped the fire were slaine with the sword; some hewed to peeces, others rune throw with their rapiers, so as they were quickly dispatchte, and very few escaped. It was conceived they thus destroyed about 400. at this time. It was a fearfull sight to see them thus frying in the fyer, and the streames of blood quenching the same, and horrible was the stinck and sente ther of; but the victory seemed a sweete sacrifice, and they gave the prays therof to God, who had wrought so wonderfuly for them, thus to inclose their enimise in their hands, and give them so speedy a victory over so proud and insulting an enimie. The Narigansett Indeans, all this while, stood round aboute, but aloofe from all danger, and left the whole execution to the English, except it were the stoping of any that broke away, insulting over their enimies in this their ruine and miserie, when they saw them dancing in the flames, calling them by a word in their owne language, signifing, O brave Pequents! which they used familierly among them selves in their own prayes, in songs of triumph after their victories. (425–26)

The devastating nature of the English attack, however, soon prompts the Narragansett to grow "very could and backward in the bussines," Bradford notes, perhaps out of recognition that the Pequot arguments a year earlier were all too prophetic (427).

Important as this moment of self-realization proves to be for the Narragansett, Bradford is still more concerned to expose the terrible implications of the blessing that Winthrop invoked on behalf of the English forces. The "hopefull way" that Winthrop envisioned as ushering in the end of the war leads directly to the potent iconography of burning human flesh—the vivid sights and smells, along with the mockery of unimaginable suffering, that no English reader of Bradford's day could have failed to associate with the scenes of martyrdom in John Foxe's book. The grotesque decision to term this military outcome a "sweete sacrifice" appears to originate with the English assailants rather than with Bradford, whose third-person pronouns repeatedly emphasize that he is reporting these events at second hand. The equivocal use of "seemed," however, is suggestive. Sacrificial victims in biblical tradition, as John Robinson reminded the reader of his moral essays, were invariably innocent and harmless creatures—doves rather than eagles or lions. When Mary Tudor's bishops sentenced many of their old clerical colleagues to the stake, they strove to characterize these brutal executions in sorrowful terms, as sacrificial acts conducing to the salvation of their victims and "the unity of the Catholic faith."[27] Bradford singles out this evocative term from the euphoric battlefield reports and situates it between vivid pictures of the "ruine and miserie" that the English have inflicted. The effect is profoundly disquieting—a subtle association of this seeming victory with the "stinck and sente" of persecution.

A month later, Winthrop wrote again to Plymouth, describing the final battle of the war, an attack on "a small Indean towne, fast by a hideous swamp," where about "80. strong men, and 200. women and children" had taken refuge. Winthrop's wording suggests at least some degree of discomfort over the disproportionate suffering of noncombatants in the English campaign. The Providence of God had guided the militia to this town, Winthrop declared, for their Narragansett scouts were gone. Over the course of a night-long siege, all but twenty of the Pequots in the English trap were killed or captured. Most of the prisoners were women and children, whom the English enslaved, sending the boys to the West Indies on a ship commanded by William Peirce, whose earnest religious reflections on the wreck of the *Lyon* had already appeared in the pages of Bradford's book. The Pequot women and girls were distributed among the New England towns. "Our people are all in health," Winthrop gratefully concluded, in acknowledgment of the Lord's "great mercies," "and allthough they had marched in their armes all the day, and had been in fight all the night, yet they professed they found them selves so fresh as they could willingly have gone to shuch another bussines" (430).

Bradford is mindful of this language, too, when he incorporates the letter that contains it into the pages of the history. The "business" to which the English forces brought such tireless enthusiasm, in Winthrop's account, proves to be a gruesome narrative residue that Bradford can only bring himself to introduce into *Of Plimmoth Plantation* through transcription: "For the rest of this bussines," he notes, effectively underscoring his correspondent's word, "I shall only relate the same as it is in a leter which came from Mr. Winthrop" (427). Gratitude for the Lord's great mercies clashes, in Winthrop's sentences, with the coldly utilitarian term that he applies to this final, merciless assault. Bradford does his best to ensure that the reader of his history will not overlook the ugly disparity at the heart of Winthrop's account. Morison's modern edition of Bradford's book places both of Winthrop's letters to Plymouth concerning the Pequot War in an appendix, making the implications of Bradford's striking critique of his colleague's behavior difficult to reconstruct.[28] Once Bradford's original orchestration of narrative and documents is restored, however, no acquaintance with the figurative treatment of sixteenth-century martyrdom is necessary in order to sense the deep psychological chasm that divides Bradford's perception of these events from the unslaked appetite for destruction in the Massachusetts militia.

The closing pages of the history are dominated by the repercussions of the

Pequot War, which draw Plymouth into a series of military displays and diplomatic initiatives aimed at providing a permanent framework for adjusting the interests of all the political communities of New England. It was clear that without some comprehensive mechanism for arbitration, retaliation and revenge would continue to embroil the English and Indian peoples of the region. The familiar business of war and traffic would run its course, exacerbated by the grim capacity to conceive monsters that Daniel Dyke had identified in the human heart. In dramatizing the equivocal role played by Massachusetts Bay during the prosecution of the Pequot War, Bradford exposes the relentless nature of this destructive cycle, exercising through his narrative the same complex purging and healing discipline that William Brewster strove to impose on individuals whose "faults and evills" he undertook to correct—or whose hearts and consciences he forcibly opened—without sacrificing the possibility of amicable relations in the future. In the second of the extensive documents with which *Of Plimmoth Plantation* concludes, Bradford undertakes to counter the dark picture of English motives and English conduct that emerges from his depiction of the Pequot conflict by stressing not the differences that divide Plymouth from the political and moral behavior of its neighbors but the collective success of the New England colonies in establishing a measure of peace, during a period when the states of Europe were distracted by a pattern of intractable conflict.

ɕ•

AFTER 1634, with the introduction of King Charles' provocative commission, attacking the sovereignty of the English colonies, *Of Plimmoth Plantation* increasingly resembles a diplomatic history of the region as a whole, rather than the story of an individual settlement. The documents and letters that Bradford weaves into his text gradually make plain the profusion of hankering minds and ambitious communities that sought to control the collective fortunes of New England. In this respect, William Brewster's early exposure to the diplomatic complexities of Elizabeth's court, through the medium of William Davison's career, is both a prophetic and an instructive anecdote. Indeed, Davison's involvement in the execution of Mary Stuart prefigures the equivocal role played by the agents of the United Colonies of New England in the execution of the Narragansett leader Miantonimo by his Mohegan rival Uncas. Bradford's tactical revision of the date of Brewster's death, once again, permits this historical relationship to emerge almost effortlessly from the sequence of events that *Of Plimmoth Plantation* records in its final chapters.

According to Bradford's account, following the catastrophe of the Pequot War

Miantonimo had sought to form his own political league, uniting a number of Indian communities in "a generall conspiracie against the English" (496). Through French or Dutch traders, perhaps, the Narragansett learned of the outbreak of the English Civil War and concluded that the time was propitious for driving the English out of their coastal enclaves, while they were unable to count on any support from their distracted countrymen. Only the diplomatic skill of Roger Williams had prevented just such a general conspiracy from taking place during the Pequot War. By the mid-1640s, however, the Narragansett had become practiced at exploiting differences among the English, just as the English had often exploited differences among the Indians. By 1645, Bradford reports, Miantonimo had concluded a formal "newtrality" with the settlers at Providence and Aquidnett Island, in order to concentrate Narragansett energies on Massachusetts Bay, Plymouth, and Connecticut.

This extraordinary evolution of Indian diplomatic ambition and skill prompts the formation of the United Colonies of New England.[29] Bradford copies the complete text of the Articles of Confederation creating this political body into *Of Plimmoth Plantation* in large part because of the implicit narrative that the document contains. Much like the language of King Charles' Commission, ten years earlier, these Articles respond to past anxieties and differences, as well as to the future threats that the parties to the confederation hoped to forestall. The preamble, in particular, marks the changes that have occurred in New England since the authors of the Mayflower Compact drafted the first social contract among English emigrants in "the northerne parts of Virginia":

> Wheras we all came into these parts of America with one and the same end and aime, namly, to advance the kingdome of our Lord Jesus Christ, and to injoye the liberties of the Gospell in puritie with peace; and wheras in our setling (by a wise providence of God) we are further disperced upon the sea coasts and rivers then was at first intended, so that we cannot, according to our desires, with conveniencie comunicate in one govermente and jurisdiction; and wheras we live encompassed with people of severall nations and strang languages, which hereafter may prove injurious to us and our posteritie; and for as much as the natives have formerly committed sundrie insolencies and outrages upon severall plantations of the English, and have of late combined them selves against us; and seeing by reason of those distractions in England (which they have heard of) and by which they know we are hindered from that humble way of seeking advice or reaping those comfurtable fruits of protection which at other times we might well expecte; we therfore doe conceive it our bounden duty, without delay, to enter into a presente consociation amongst our selves, for mutuall

> help and strength in all our future concernments. That as in nation and religion, so in other respects, we be and continue one, according to the tenor and true meaning of the insuing articles. (496–97)

By convention, a preamble is a summary account of the motives and occasions that prompt the resolutions that it introduces. It is not intended to reflect the full historical complexity from which legislative documents invariably emerge. Even so, this language is a particularly intriguing mixture of history and fiction, a hybrid identity that its setting in Bradford's pages unavoidably exposes.

The harmony of ends and intentions that this introductory language depicts is completely at variance with the diversity and disorder, the conflicts and disagreements, attending the actual process of settlement. Only a few sentences before introducing the text of the Articles into his book, Bradford had brought his eulogy of William Brewster to a conclusion with a long review of Plymouth's unique experience, emphasizing the perils and persecutions that had beset them at every turn, from "false brethren" among the English as well as from "the heathen," across the span of Brewster's life—a barrage of assaults that "God's vissitation" alone had been able to stave off (495). There is no sign of this volatile blend of triumphal and resentful piety in the cool assertion of English unity with which the 1643 Articles of Confederation begin. Plymouth's distinct religious origin and its historical priority in the settling of New England are subsumed by the fictive "we" that the Articles undertake to proclaim.

In a similar fashion, the comfortable fruits of English protection to which the Articles regretfully allude must have seemed as imaginary to the colonists themselves as they did to their surprisingly well-informed Narragansett opponents. Charles I's 1634 Commission for Regulating Plantations had given memorable form to the nature of English solicitude for colonial welfare. The Articles as a whole constitute a striking rejoinder to the intentions expressed in that ominous royal document. Equally deceptive is the portrait of domestic conditions that the preamble offers. The complex, twenty-three-year history of Anglo-Indian relations in New England is completely obscured by the simplistic oppositions postulated in this opening portrait of a homogeneous community of English settlers "encompassed" by an equally homogeneous body of hostile peoples, who have "of late combined them selves against us." Diplomatic fictions were widely understood to be part of the formal apparatus that made political agreements possible, but the language of this preamble in particular provides a uniquely wishful foundation for New England unity. The full document immediately proceeds to describe, through a sequence of twelve provisions, the ways in which the colonial governments proposed to handle all their dangers and differences in the future.

The invidious example of the King's Commission lies behind several features of the new colonial confederation. The local sovereignty of the four signatory plantations—Massachusetts Bay, Plymouth, Connecticut, and New Haven—is carefully secured from any interference by the United Colonies as a corporate body. The commissioners of the confederation were expected to "establish agreements and orders in generall cases of a civill nature" to help preserve harmony among the member colonies, but no centralized system of legislation or of justice was instituted (501). Each plantation was expected to honor the arrest warrants and legal requests of its neighbors and to inquire no further into the nature of their internal affairs. The Articles are completely silent on the vexed question of religion, except in the nominal assertion that the four confederated partners are "one" in matters of faith, and they go to great lengths to avoid the danger inherent in the appropriation of authority by an aggressive plurality. Each annual meeting of the eight commissioners of the confederation—two from each colony—will elect a president who has no special powers whatever, beyond those of a parliamentary chair, and no substantive action can take place on behalf of the confederation as a whole without the approval of six commissioners. In cases of significant disagreement during these annual meetings, public authority and initiative simply revert to each colony's General Court.

Military cooperation dominates the text of the Articles, but here too its authors are mindful of recent colonial history. No single colony can embroil the rest in war without the "consent and agreemente" of the commissioners as a whole. When one member of the confederation is attacked, the entire body of commissioners reserves the right to inquire into the origins of the conflict, and if the party attacked is found to be at fault, the other members of the confederation will require "that jurisdiction or plantation [to] make just satisfaction both to the invaders whom they have injured, and beare all the charges of the warr them selves, without requiring any allowance from the rest of the confederates towards the same" (499). The Articles frankly envisioned the New England colonies offering one another military assistance "for offence and defense," but not for unjust aggression. Plymouth's doubts about the prosecution of the Pequot conflict find indirect expression in these cautionary provisions.

If similar doubts about New England's latest confrontation with the Narragansett occur to Bradford as he describes these military arrangements, he gives no sign of them as *Of Plimmoth Plantation* draws to a close. One outcome of the

Pequot War had been a peace agreement imposed by the governments of Connecticut and Massachusetts Bay on Uncas, the Mohegan leader, and Miantonimo of the Narragansett, both English allies during the Pequot campaign.[30] According to Bradford, the Narragansett "thought to have ruled over all the Indeans aboute them," after the destruction of Pequot power, much as they had hoped to dominate the Wampanoag confederation after the devastating epidemics that had crippled Massasoit's people immediately before the arrival of the *Mayflower*. Uncas's influence with a number of English leaders, however, thwarted the goals of Miantonimo—an "ambitious and politick man," in Bradford's reckoning—who sought by poison and by treachery to remove his Mohegan rival (505).

Failing in his attempts at assassination, Miantonimo tries open warfare, despite preventive covenants that the English have tried to impose on their former allies. When Uncas has the good fortune to prevail in these attacks and takes Miantonimo prisoner, he consults with the newly seated commissioners of the United Colonies on the proper disposition of his prisoner. Perhaps sensing an opportunity to rid themselves of an implacable and clever opponent—one who maintained disquietingly good relations with the heretical English settlers of Aquidnett and Providence—the commissioners consent to Miantonimo's execution, provided that Uncas carry out the sentence in his own territory and "in a very faire maner . . . with due respect to his honour and greatnes" (507). This carefully worded stipulation on the part of the confederated colonies suggests that the analogy to Mary Stuart's fate may have occurred to other citizens of New England besides those who were acquainted with the colorful past of William Brewster. It is quite likely, too, that Bradford composed these pages of the history at some point not long after Charles I had suffered an equally "honorable" execution at the hands of the English Parliament. Brief though it was, New England's historical experience, as Bradford carefully renders it, was quickly proving to be a remarkable mirror of the larger world from which many of the original settlers had hoped to separate themselves.[31]

The subsequent intervention of the colonies into further Narragansett/Mohegan conflict over the next two years reflects the determination of the New England confederacy to adjudicate Indian differences as well as English ones, in the larger interests of domestic tranquillity. Colonial expansion, of course, could take place much more rapidly and securely without the threat of interruption by Indian wars. John Winthrop had explicitly acknowledged this link between peace and growth in his eagerness to bring the Pequot War to a swift conclusion. The 1643 confederation was one means to this end. Its provisions were intended to serve the long-term interests of the English, and though some of its language hinted at the intention of the colonies to regulate relations with the native people in an equitable way, none of the confederation members viewed it primarily as a forum for multiethnic cooperation. Nor did they view the deviant English communities of Pascataway or Rhode Island with much more favor than they did their Indian neighbors. Both of these smaller communities the confederation eventually hoped to absorb into one of their four constituent jurisdictions.[32]

Peace, however, was the confederation's immediate goal. Plymouth had found its outlying townships "marvelously unprovided of leade and powder" at the time that its magistrates first learned of a potential Narragansett threat.[33] Bradford does not comment on this surprising state of unreadiness in *Of Plimmoth Plantation,* but he makes clear in the pages of the history that it came as a great relief to have the impending war "stayed and prevented" by a comprehensive treaty of peace between the United Colonies and the Narragansett and Niantic peoples. Bradford transcribes this document, too, into *Of Plimmoth Plantation,* increasingly treating the book as a repository of primary sources during this period of rapid change (525). Despite the dictatorial English posture reflected in the treaty's terms, a broader conception of commonwealth is at least briefly visible in the English efforts to replace military conflict with diplomacy and to impose some central control over the sale of Indian land to English buyers. The evocative list of English and Indian signatories to the Narragansett and Niantic treaty of 1645 is carefully reproduced in Bradford's pages, the totemic marks of seven native sagamores following the names of the eight confederation commissioners for that year. Imperfect though it is, this understanding represents a brief interregnum between the rule of the old kingdoms of force and the outbreak of King Philip's War, thirty years later, when force will renew its grip on New England history.

In the closing pages of his book, Bradford subordinates the story of Plymouth's progressive diminishment in size and importance to this larger narrative of political evolution. His brief summary of the dispersal of Plymouth's church members, at the beginning of his chronicle for 1644, is far more prominent in the minds of modern scholars than it is in Bradford's narrative. Ancient mother Plymouth was physically "forsaken" by her children, Bradford concedes, as the population of the colony dispersed to outlying towns and more tempting agricultural prospects, but she remained central to "their affections." The original community may well be widowed, and "left only to trust in God," but such an exclusive reliance was scarcely a state of deprivation in the religious ethos that Bradford shared with most of his New England contemporaries (508–9).

Twice in the last years of his life, Bradford agreed to serve as president of the confederation commissioners at their annual meetings—once in 1648 and again in the fall of 1656, a few months before his death.[34] In a similar but far more dramatic fashion, Edward Winslow, too, accepted offers for "wider employment" in these momentous years, leaving Plymouth for London in 1646 to defend the colonies against the accusations of Samuel Gorton but remaining in the service of Oliver Cromwell's government for the rest of his life. Bradford appears to blame his old colleague, in the last sentence of his book, for this prolonged absence, but there are formal reasons for viewing Winslow's departure as consistent with the larger patterns of change that *Of Plimmoth Plantation* finally embraces. Winslow's willingness to enter this wider historical theater represents at once a reversal and a fulfillment of the course that William Brewster had taken a half century earlier, when he left the centers of power in Elizabethan London and retired to his birthplace, beginning the process of religious self-discovery and commitment that replaced the public career he had abandoned. In returning to that public sphere, Winslow symbolically carries with him—much as he carried *Good Newes from New-England* to the London press in 1623—the far more ambitious account of Plymouth's complete historical experience that William Bradford has so carefully prepared.

Conclusion

The High Preserver of Men

B RADFORD'S CHRONICLE FOR 1646, the last year that he covers in his book, is the shortest yearly account in *Of Plimmoth Plantation*—a fact that has encouraged many modern scholars to interpret his brevity as evidence of fatigue or despair. But there is no reduction in narrative scope or subtlety as Bradford brings his record to a close. The year of Edward Winslow's departure for England also witnesses the arrival of three ships, "in warrlike order," in Plymouth harbor, commanded by one Thomas Cromwell and commissioned by the earl of Warwick, a prominent figure in the forces of Parliament, to cruise for Spanish prizes in the West Indies. Warwick was one of the original signatories of the so-called Pierce Patent, from the Council for New England, under which Plymouth had been founded more than a quarter century earlier. He signed the 1630 patent that was reissued in William Bradford's name, after the original company of investors dissolved, and which Bradford in turn relinquished to the freemen of the corporation of New Plymouth ten years later. When Roger Williams went to England in 1643 to secure legal protection for Providence from the predatory designs of Massachusetts Bay, Warwick was a member of the parliamentary commission that gave him a sympathetic hearing. Samuel Gorton, too, found a receptive supporter in Warwick during his controversy with John Winthrop's government.

Nearly an exact contemporary of William Bradford, Warwick had been involved in New England's religious and political life since Robert Cushman and John Carver had first opened negotiations with the Virginia Company in 1617 and 1618, hoping to secure a patent under which the Leiden emigrants could safely establish a colony in North America. Warwick was one of Edwin Sandys's colleagues on that original royal body to which Robinson and Brewster had so cautiously appealed for the legal sanction and the financial resources that they needed to carry their enterprise through. The recurrence of his name in Bradford's closing chapter is more than an incidental detail. It marks the latest in a series of collisions between the community of settlers in Plymouth and the larger political entities whose patronage—or whose benevolent neglect—the colony had never ceased to require, even as it systematically resisted all forms of English interference in New England's affairs. Now, twenty-five years after Francis West and Robert Gorges had brought their ungoverned appetites for power and profit to Cape Cod Bay, another nautical emissary of English authority appears in Plymouth harbor.

Thomas Cromwell's company of eighty "lustie men" in 1646 have much in common with the self-destructive habits of Thomas Weston's ill-fated Wessagusset colonists from 1623—a bond that Bradford's formulaic phrase effectively highlights. Weston too had been fond of sending unruly bodies of lusty men to the woods of southern New England. Once ashore and thoroughly drunk, Cromwell's crew proved nearly impossible for Plymouth's authorities to control. They "did so distemper them selves with drinke," Bradford observes, that "they became like madd-men," and though they spent their wages freely in Plymouth, he suspects that they left behind more sin than money among the colony's citizens. After six weeks in Plymouth, Cromwell's ships departed for Boston, where Captain Cromwell was forced to strike one of his own mutinous sailors to the ground during their equally riotous visit there, inadvertently breaking his skull. Bradford called it a "sadd accident," and, indeed, a "counsell of warr" cleared Cromwell of any responsibility for this man's death, Bradford reports, though higher tribunals might not view his act in a similarly forgiving light. Three years later, Bradford writes, Cromwell himself died as a result of a fall from a horse, in which he was accidentally injured by the same rapier hilt with which he had struck his rebellious companion. "Other distempers" quickly brought him to a "feavor," Bradford notes, which proved fatal. "Some observed that ther might be somthing of the hand of God herein; that as the forenamed man dyed of the blow he gave him with the rapeir hilts, so his owne death was occationed by a like means" (527). Bradford keeps his distance from these speculations. The skeptical habits of a lifetime continue to resist the moralizing narratives that pervade the thinking of his contemporaries. One must not be bold with God's Providences.

Nonetheless, Captain Cromwell's momentous name offers a particularly convenient means for Bradford to suggest the disordered and violent world to which Edward Winslow had recently chosen to return—a militant England increasingly under the sway of Oliver Cromwell and his own Council of War, a nation still deeply divided by civil conflict and soon to embark on the first of several maritime wars with the Dutch in which Winslow will find himself embroiled as an official arms merchant to New England. In the space of a few paragraphs Bradford is able to evoke the full scope of Plymouth's long struggle to elude the old chronicles of European dominion and establish a religious community in some region that would not fall into the vortex of hostility that set Europe and England in "warrlike order" through the entire thirty-year period embraced by *Of Plimmoth Plantation.*

The volatile mixture of secular ambition, religious "arrogancie," and ungoverned appetite that repeatedly erupts, in different combinations, throughout Bradford's pages—in Thomas Weston, Thomas Morton, John Lyford, James Sherley, Christopher Gardiner, Arthur Peach, Thomas Granger, or Charles Chauncey—recurs once more, in Bradford's final chapter, through the agency of the earl of Warwick and his explosive privateer with the evocative name. There were, indeed, as Bradford recognizes, "great alterations in the State" that might plausibly keep Edward Winslow in England after 1646. But there were equally striking similarities between the political tempests of midcentury and the tempests of 1608 or 1620, in which the communal aspirations of the Leiden exiles had been formed. Winslow "fell into other employments," Bradford writes, when he entered the service of a triumphant Parliament, but he was also swept away by troubled seas, much as John Howland was during the *Mayflower*'s momentous voyage. No boat hook or topsail halyard was providentially at hand to rescue Edward Winslow. When he died of fever on board an English warship in the West Indies in 1655 and was buried at sea, Bradford may well have revisited these closing sentences as he recalled his old and valued friend. *Of Plimmoth Plantation*'s briefest chapter, then, is also among its most ambitious—a subtle reassertion of figurative command over Bradford's complex and unstable materials.

৯৯

THE WILL that William Bradford dictated on the day of his death makes no mention of the ambitious manuscript history that he was leaving in the custody of his heirs. Thomas Cushman, Thomas Southworth, and Nathaniel Morton recorded and witnessed Bradford's final wishes, though his wife Alice was surely present, along with at least some of Bradford's children. His illness must have progressed suddenly. Inveterate and accomplished penman that he was, Bradford had been planning to write out a will, with the help of Thomas Prence, a younger political colleague with whom he had shared many of the colony's public burdens, but some official business, perhaps, had kept Prence away until Bradford began to feel that death was unexpectedly close.

He called the attention of his three witnesses to "some smale bookes written by my owne hand," which he hoped, in their wisdom and discretion, they might be able to put to some use, "as you shall see meet." These certainly included the 1652

William Bradford his

Booke.

A⁰   1652

חָכְמָה וְ[אֵין] תְּבוּנָה וְאֵין עֵצָ[ה]
לְנֶגֶד יְהֹוָה

Ther [is] no wisdom, neither understanding,
nor [cou]nsell, against the Lord. pro: 21

dialogue or "Third Conference," between the colony's young and "Ancient" men, which has survived in the collections of the Massachusetts Historical Society, a neatly written volume not much larger than the shirt-pocket testaments that are sometimes distributed by evangelical organizations on university campuses today (fig. 11). Bradford singled out, in particular, the "sundry usefull verses" that he had been writing in recent years, contained "in a little booke with a blacke cover" that he did not want the supervisors of his estate to overlook. He may also have had in mind his Letter Books, official records of the colony's life that were, in some sense, public property. The fate of these documents, too, was evidently on his mind.[1]

Of Plimmoth Plantation, however, while not an imposing physical object on the order of John Foxe's volumes or Francesco Guicciardini's history, is in no sense a small book. Indeed, though surprisingly light for its size—a folio roughly eight by eleven inches—it was a sufficiently conspicuous presence on a bookshelf to invite an anonymous cataloguer, probably in the service of the bishop of London, to write "America" across its spine.[2] No New England reader would have been tempted to attach such a misleading classification to the book—certainly not Thomas Prince, whose New England Library, in the steeple room of Old South Church, housed *Of Plimmoth Plantation* through much of the eighteenth century. Anyone who had made even a cursory examination of the volume's contents would have recognized the inverse relation between geographical scope and narrative ambition that its title and its opening pages make plain. How could Bradford have neglected any direct reference on his deathbed to the intricate history that he had begun drafting, with such pains, nearly thirty years earlier and had only brought to a formal close in 1650?

The answer may lie in his pointed request to the three younger men at his bedside that they employ their wisdom and discretion in deciding how to make use of his remaining manuscripts. Bradford surely recalled, if only in general terms, John Robinson's comments on the utility of books in preserving the speech of the absent, in multiplying the avenues of instruction available to diligent readers, in blunting the passions that could easily flare up in the intimacy of oral exchange.[3] More recently, however, he had had occasion to remember that books were not immune to the destructive action of human resentment. In the earliest of his two surviving dialogues between the ancient settlers of Plymouth and their young successors, composed in 1648, Bradford had recalled a celebrated book-burning in the Nether-

FACING PAGE

Fig. 11. Title page of Bradford's manuscript book containing his "Third Dialogue" (1652). Courtesy of the Massachusetts Historical Society.

lands, in which Dutch authorities, acceding to English pressure, ordered a complete press run of one of Henry Barrow's and John Greenwood's Separatist tracts publicly destroyed in Middelburg.

Francis Johnson, at that time an English informer who had helped to seize the books, agreed to superintend their burning. As he did so, he idly picked two copies out of the fire—one for his own use and one for a friend—so that he could familiarize himself with the errors of his enemies. The repercussions of this casual act are dramatic. As Bradford's ancient spokesman observed, "Mark the sequel." At home in his study, Johnson began "superficially to read some things here and there" in the forbidden book, "as his fancy lead him." Before long the words "began to work upon his spirit," and he found himself poring over its pages:

> In the end he was so taken, and his conscience was troubled so, as he could have no rest in himself until he crossed the seas and came to London to confer with the authors, who were then in prison, and shortly after executed. After which conference he was so satisfied and confirmed in the truth, as he never returned to his place any more at Middleburg, but adjoined himself to their society at London, and was afterwards committed to prison, and then banished; and in conclusion coming to live at Amsterdam, he caused the same books, which he had been an instrument to burn, to be new printed and set out at his own charge.[4]

Such a fire as Johnson had presided over was clearly a surrogate for those in which the Marian martyrs had died, but burning a living body was futile, as well as barbaric, if the living words of the victim survived; and in the world of the printing press, burning words was extremely difficult to do. Even a single fugitive copy could rapidly grow into thousands of duplicates, which in the hands of thousands of readers would in time generate a library of successors to the original contaminated text. It is easy to see why metaphors based upon the model of infectious disease came to be applied so readily to the swift dissemination of ideas during the volatile decades of the Reformation.

Two years after Bradford had completed his first dialogue, a book-burning took place in Boston that may have reminded him of his anecdote about the conversion of Francis Johnson. William Pynchon, a prominent merchant and former magistrate of Massachusetts Bay, settled in the Connecticut valley, had arranged for the English publication of a book that he had written on the significance of Christ's mediatorial suffering, *The Meritorious Price of Our Redemption*. When copies of Pynchon's book reached Boston, in October 1650, the magistrates only had to glance at the title page to pronounce Pynchon's thoughts heretical and, with surprising speed, to direct that his work be burned by the common executioner in the

Boston marketplace. Pynchon himself was ordered to appear before the General Court the following spring in the hope that he would recant. When that meeting proved unsatisfactory, he was ordered to appear a second time, some months later. When Pynchon simply failed to attend this second hearing, the General Court made clear its determination to force the issue by arranging for a third appearance, but before the date arrived, Pynchon had left the colony to spend the rest of his life in England.[5]

Of Plimmoth Plantation was not a theological work, of course, but the treatment of Pynchon's unorthodox convictions made clear that Plymouth's increasingly powerful neighbor to the north would not tolerate the circulation of books that appeared, in the judgment of its leaders, to threaten the public well-being. Perhaps Bradford's implicit criticism of the Bay Colony's conduct in the Kennebec murders, in the trade and boundary disputes that had begun to shape their relations with Plymouth, or in the Pequot War would prompt a similar repressive response. William Pynchon had been able to protect his ideas by multiplying them in print. After returning to England, he revised and republished his controversial book, citing a number of English Puritan writers who were sympathetic to his position. *Of Plimmoth Plantation*, however, was still in manuscript, authored by a man who did not have the economic resources or the formal education that Pynchon possessed—important assets when persuading a printer to undertake a lengthy, secular history of a remote English colony, at a time when London was preoccupied with the drama of Oliver Cromwell's flirtation with the English crown. Keeping the existence of such a manuscript discreetly quiet, for the time being, may have seemed to Bradford and his heirs the best way to ensure its immediate survival. Roger Williams had written an elaborate account of his views on colonial land policy that simply disappeared, sometime after 1633, when it fell into the hands of the Massachusetts General Court.[6] It would not be surprising if William Bradford recalled this disquieting fact, too, as he lay dying, and counseled his three witnesses to use care in deciding how to manage this unique portion of his legacy.

About the importance of the legacy itself Bradford had no doubts. At some point in the opening months of 1651, he added to his manuscript a remarkable and evocative record of the original *Mayflower* passengers, grouped and numbered by household, in neat parallel columns on the page, followed by an account of "the increasings and decreasings of these persons" over the ensuing thirty years.[7] Although the preamble to New England's Articles of Confederation had obscured the issue of historical priority in the settlement of the region, Bradford's introductory inscription to these lists makes clear the unique status that this small body of emigrants holds. These are, Bradford declares, "The names of those which came over first, in the year *1620,* and were (by the blesing of God) the first beginers, and (in a sort) the foundation of all the plantations and colonies, in New-England" (531).

The claim is largely figurative, of course. Bradford recognizes that his companions on the first voyage were founders "in a sort" only. The metaphor of stepping stones, which the Leiden emigrants had initially employed to describe their imperfect vision of future possibility, is a more accurate reflection of the provisional expectations with which the small group of pioneers from John Robinson's English church had left Delftshaven in the late summer of 1620. The impact of Bradford's lists arises not from a retrospective appreciation for their documentary significance but from the narratives that they contain—the lives that they summarize and tally, as Bradford collates each household with the mortal interchange of deaths and births that constitutes the experience of each of these varied families through the first three decades in New England.

A painful process of separation, as well as the more hopeful one of union, lies behind each of Bradford's entries. The first names that he records in the list of original passengers, John and Katherine Carver, were childless. No wrenching decision had confronted them, like that faced by the Bradfords or the Brewsters, concerning which of their children might be old enough to bear the rigors of this initial phase of settlement and which would have to remain, for the time being, in Holland. Under the Carvers' charge, however, fell an assortment of younger adults and children—some emigrating as servants, but others traveling in a less clearly delineated relationship to the Carvers themselves that may have resembled the informal parental understanding that Bradford later established with Robert Cushman's son. In his tabulation of first beginners, Bradford recalls most of the names in John Carver's heterogeneous "family": "Desire Minter; and 2 man-servants, John Howland, Roger Wilder; William Latham, a boy; and a maid servant, and a child that was put to him called Jasper More" (531).

What accounts for the inexplicable deficiencies of memory highlighted in this simple entry? The Carvers' maidservant will marry in Plymouth and shortly die there, Bradford notes, when he sets down the destinies of each of these people, "taking them in order as they lye," in the second phase of his census. Her death, but not her identity, remains in Bradford's record. Jasper More's name is preserved, but only that he is "called" by it. Presumably his parents first called him this, but why are they not sailing to New England with him? Another group of children with the same surname, two brothers and a sister, were divided between the Brewster and Winslow households, but they appear to have been unrelated to Jasper. Of these four children, only one will survive the first winter in Plymouth. Jasper More, along with Roger Wilder, are the first in the Carver household to die, sometime in early 1621, "of the commone infection." Katherine Carver dies the summer after her husband succumbs to the unfamiliar heat of a New England April. Desire Minter, Bradford writes, whose parents were members of John Robinson's Leiden congregation, "returned to her freinds, and proved not very well, and dyed in England." William Latham lived twenty years in Plymouth—though how he spent them Bradford does not indicate—eventually emigrating once again to the Bahamas, where he died "for want of food" (534).

Of all the tiny federation of lives under John Carver's oversight in 1620, only John Howland thrived in New England, despite his near-fatal brush with the tempestuous North Atlantic on the *Mayflower*'s voyage. He married Elizabeth Tillie, whose own parents had died "a litle after they came ashore," Bradford wrote, and this vigorous couple "are both now living, and have 10. children, now all living, and their eldest daughter hath 4. children. And ther 2. daughter, 1. all living; and other of their children mariagable" (534). Bradford's prose can barely contain the exhilaration he feels at this stunning triumph of life over death. From the eight individuals listed under the Carvers' names at the beginning of his historical census, fifteen new lives have sprung. This childless couple proves to have presided, if only quite briefly, over one of the most prolific of the *Mayflower*'s households.

Initially, at least, Bradford is less than forthcoming about the reasons that prompt him to review these domestic histories. The great works of Providence "are to be observed," he dutifully notes, if only because such information "may be of some use to such as come after." But personal satisfaction alone is the immediate motive that he acknowledges in describing "such changs as hath passed over them and theirs" since the arrival in America. Not all of these changes share the wonderful and mysterious fertility of the Carvers' story. Christopher Martin, Robert Cushman's temperamental colleague during the planning stages of the *Mayflower*'s voyage, "dyed in the first infection," along with his wife and two servants. Thomas Tinker and his wife and son, all from the Leiden congregation, also died that winter, as did John Rigdale and his wife. These small families were completely extinguished within a few months of the ship's arrival. "John Crakston, and his sone, John Crakston," emigrated together on the *Mayflower* but left no third patronymic successor in Plymouth. The father died "in the first mortality," Bradford wrote, and his son a few years later: "having lost himselfe in the wodes, his feet became frosen, which put him into a feavor, of which he dyed" (536). The death rate among single male servants and hired men was also remarkably high.

But increasings far exceed decreasings, in Bradford's communal review. Rose Standish died in 1621, without children, but her formidable husband remarried and had four living sons at the time that Bradford made his lists. Oceanus Hopkins, son of Stephen and Elizabeth Hopkins, born at sea in 1620, grew up to become a sailor and died at Barbados, but the couple's daughter, Constanta, had twelve living children and their son Giles another four. Two of these names, at least, must have struck Bradford as uncanny in their ability to forecast the lives of those who bore them. Five of the Hopkins children were still alive in 1651, along with sixteen grandchildren. Francis Cooke—after William Brewster the second oldest passenger on the *Mayflower*—was likewise still alive as Bradford wrote "and hath seene his childrens children have children" (537). John Billington and his eldest son—the little boy whom the Nauset people had rescued from starvation in 1621—were both dead, but Francis Billington, the second child of this volatile family, was alive, married, and the father of eight children thirty years after his brother's memorable adventure among the Cape Cod tribes.

As Bradford summed up the results of his review, its significance had clearly come to exceed the merely personal dimension to which he had originally laid claim: "Of these 100. persons which came first over in this first ship together, the greater halfe dyed in the generall mortality; and most of them in 2. or three monthes time. And for those which survied, though some were ancient and past procreation, and others left the place and cuntrie, yet of those few remaining are sprunge up above 160. persons, in this 30. years, and are now living in this presente year, 1650. besids many of their children which are dead, and come not within this account" (539). Of the "old stock" of *Mayflower* emigrants themselves, Bradford added, nearly thirty were still alive as he completed his parallel lists—a triumphant fact that prompted the last words written in William Bradford's hand in the pages of his remarkable book: "Let the Lord have the praise, who is the High Preserver of men." The emigrants' small ship, well caulked and reinforced against the autumn storms, had indeed proved itself a kind of ark, delivering a remnant of John Robinson's church from the turmoil of European history long after their colleagues and relatives in Holland had dispersed and disappeared.

The figure of the ark, implicit in this double census that concludes *Of Plimmoth Plantation*, would scarcely have struck a seventeenth-century sectarian imagination as extravagant. It is particularly apt in view of the extraordinary communal history that evokes it. According to the inventory of personal property compiled by his executors, William Bradford owned two Bibles at his death. One was a practical, unadorned, 1596 English imprint on view today at the Pilgrim Hall Museum in Plymouth. No information exists about the second Bible that the inventory records, though it seems unlikely to have been simply a duplicate of its partner.[8] Either Bradford or Brewster may have also owned one of the larger, illustrated ver-

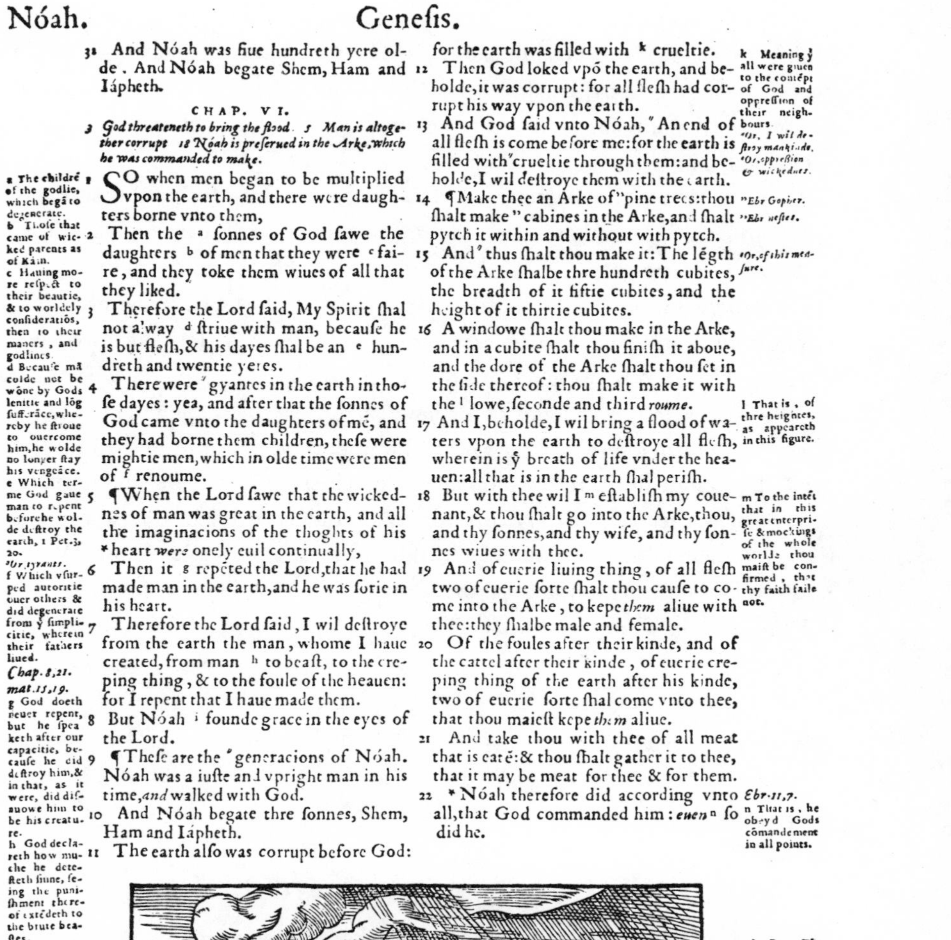

Nóah. Genesis.

31 And Nóah was fiue hundreth yere olde. And Nóah begate Shem, Ham and
Iápheth.

CHAP. VI.

3 God threateneth to bring the flood. 5 Man is altogether corrupt 18 Nóah is preserued in the Arke, which he was commanded to make.

1 SO when men began to be multiplied
vpon the earth, and there were daughters borne vnto them,
2 Then the [a] sonnes of God sawe the
daughters [b] of men that they were [c] faire, and they toke them wiues of all that
they liked.
3 Therefore the Lord said, My Spirit shal
not alway [d] striue with man, because he
is but flesh, & his dayes shal be an [e] hundreth and twentie yeres.
4 There were [*] gyantes in the earth in those dayes: yea, and after that the sonnes of
God came vnto the daughters of mē, and
they had borne them children, these were
mightie men, which in olde time were men
of [f] renoume.
5 ¶When the Lord sawe that the wickednes of man was great in the earth, and all
the imaginacions of the thoghts of his
* heart *were* onely euil continually,
6 Then it [g] repēted the Lord, that he had
made man in the earth, and he was sorie in
his heart.
7 Therefore the Lord said, I wil destroye
from the earth the man, whome I haue
created, from man [h] to beast, to the cre-
ping thing, & to the foule of the heauen:
for I repent that I haue made them.
8 But Nóah [i] founde grace in the eyes of
the Lord.
9 ¶These are the [*] generacions of Nóah.
Nóah was a iuste and vpright man in his
time, *and* walked with God.
10 And Nóah begate thre sonnes, Shem,
Ham and Iápheth.
11 The earth also was corrupt before God:
for the earth was filled with [k] crueltie.
12 Then God loked vpō the earth, and beholde, it was corrupt: for all flesh had corrupt his way vpon the earth.
13 And God said vnto Nóah, [*] An end of
all flesh is come before me: for the earth is
filled with [*] crueltie through them: and beholde, I wil destroye them with the earth.
14 ¶Make thee an Arke of [*] pine trees: thou
shalt make [*] cabines in the Arke, and shalt
pytch it within and without with pytch.
15 And [*] thus shalt thou make it: The lēgth
of the Arke shalbe thre hundreth cubites,
the breadth of it fiftie cubites, and the
height of it thirtie cubites.
16 A windowe shalt thou make in the Arke,
and in a cubite shalt thou finish it aboue,
and the dore of the Arke shalt thou set in
the side thereof: thou shalt make it with
the [l] lowe, seconde and third *roume*.
17 And I, beholde, I wil bring a flood of waters vpon the earth to destroye all flesh,
wherein is ŷ breath of life vnder the heauen: all that is in the earth shal perish.
18 But with thee wil I [m] establish my coue-
nant, & thou shalt go into the Arke, thou,
and thy sonnes, and thy wife, and thy sonnes wiues with thee.
19 And of euerie liuing thing, of all flesh
two of euerie sorte shalt thou cause to come into the Arke, to kepe *them* aliue with
thee: they shalbe male and female.
20 Of the foules after their kinde, and of
the cattel after their kinde, of euerie cre-
ping thing of the earth after his kinde,
two of euerie sorte shal come vnto thee,
that thou maiest kepe *them* aliue.
21 And take thou with thee of all meat
that is catē: & thou shalt gather it to thee,
that it may be meat for thee & for them.
22 * Nóah therefore did according vnto
all, that God commanded him: *euen* [n] so
did he.

a The childrē of the godlie, which begā to degenerate.
b Those that came of wicked parents as of Káin.
c Hauing more respect to their beautie, & to worldely consideratiōs, then to their maners, and godlines.
d Because mā colde not be wōne by Gods lenitie and lōg sufferāce, whereby he stroue to ouercome him, he wolde no longer stay his vengeāce.
e Which terme God gaue man to repent before he wolde destroy the earth, 1 Pet.3, 20.
*Or, tyrants.
f Which vsurped autoritie ouer others & did degenerate from ŷ simplicitie, wherein their fathers liued.
Chap. 8, 21. mat. 15, 19.
g God doeth neuer repent, but he speaketh after our capacitie, because he did destroy him, & in that, as it were, did disauowe him to be his creature.
h God declareth how muche he detesteth sinne, seing the punishment thereof extēdeth to the brute beastes.
i God was mercitul vnto him
*Or, histories.
k Meaning ŷ all were giuen to the contēpt of God and oppression of their neighbours.
*Or, I wil destroy mankinde.
*Or, oppreßion & wickednes.
*Ebr. Gopher.
*Ebr. nestes.
*Or, of this measure.
l That is, of thre heightes, as appeareth in this figure.
m To the intēt that in this great enterprise & mockings of the whole worlde thou maist be confirmed, that thy faith faile not.
Ebr. 11, 7.
n That is, he obeyd Gods cōmandement in all points.

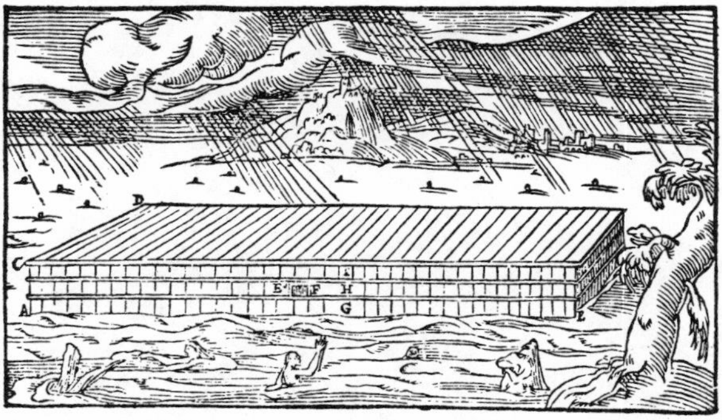

A. B. The length thre hūdreth cubites.
A. C. The breadth fifty.
D. E. The height thirty.
E. The windowe a cubite long.
F. The dore.
G. H. I. The thre heightes.

Fig. 12. From *The Bible and Holy Scriptures conteyned in The Olde and Newe Testament* (Geneva, 1560).

sions of the Geneva translation—certainly no more unusual a possession than Jean Bodin's *Six Bookes of a Commonweale* or John Foxe's ecclesiastical history. From his years in Leiden, at least, Bradford was almost surely familiar with the woodcuts that decorated many sixteenth-century editions of the Bible that the Marian exiles had lovingly prepared.

An illustration to the sixth chapter of Genesis, in the 1560 Geneva Bible, depicts Noah's ark in a fashion that is scrupulously faithful to the dimensions specified in the text: a great rectangular form, three hundred by fifty by thirty cubits, floating on the turbulent waters of the coming deluge (fig. 12). The Geneva engravers made no effort to represent a plausible seafaring craft. Instead they portrayed what appears to be a great book, much like the one that their fellow reformers had risked their lives to translate—a codex of inspired language, or perhaps an entire library, rather than a boat, a symbol of the profound importance of print to their religious revolt. The High Preserver of men chose to achieve his ends in remote biblical times through the medium of Noah's miraculous industry. Relying on the prudence of his heirs, and perhaps encouraged by this prophetically simple picture, William Bradford had some reason to hope that Providence might likewise prove to be the high preserver of books.

INTRODUCTION: THE OPERATIONS OF PRINT

1. The following paragraphs draw on Samuel Eliot Morison's account "History of a History," in the introduction to *Of Plymouth Plantation,* ed. Samuel Eliot Morison (1952; rpt., New York: Knopf, 1991), xxvii–xliii. See also Worthington C. Ford, "The Bradford Manuscripts," in *History of Plymouth Plantation 1620–1647,* ed. Worthington C. Ford, 2 vols. (Boston: Massachusetts Historical Society, 1912), 2:411–21.

2. *Bradford's History "Of Plimoth Plantation"* (Boston: Wright and Potter, State Printers, 1898), viii. I have elected to cite the Commonwealth Edition of the history for all quotations from Bradford's book, because it is the most widely available version that preserves the variations of contemporary spelling, which Bradford's manuscript shares with many printed books of his day. I have compared all quotations with Worthington C. Ford's 1912 edition, as well as with Morison's modernized text, and have corrected transcription errors in the Commonwealth Edition by comparing all cited passages to the 1896 facsimile of the manuscript: *History of the Plimoth Plantation . . . Now reproduced in facsimile from the Original Manuscript,* with an introduction by John A. Doyle (London: Ward and Downey; Boston: Houghton Mifflin, 1896). Throughout the book, page numbers in parentheses that identify passages from Bradford's history refer to the 1898 edition. Neither the 1896 facsimile nor the Commonwealth Edition observes Bradford's diacritical mark indicating how "Plimmoth" should be spelled. My own references to the title of his book, however, always do so: *Of Plimmoth Plantation.*

3. David Levin points to this relationship between Melville's novel and Bradford's book, among the many interpretive insights that he offers on *Of Plimmoth Plantation.* See "William Bradford: The Value of Puritan Historiography," originally written for Everett Emerson's collection *Major Writers of Early American Literature* (1972) but since reprinted in David Levin, *Forms of Uncertainty: Essays in Historical Criticism* (Charlottesville: Univ. Press of Virginia, 1992), 15–35.

4. On the relation between the policies of James I and the decision of Robinson's congregation to emigrate, see George F. Willison, *Saints and Strangers* (New York: Reynal and

Hitchcock, 1945), 11–58; and Bradford Smith, *Bradford of Plymouth* (Philadelphia: J. B. Lippincott, 1951), 40–63.

5. For a memorable account of the siege, see John Lothrop Motley, *The Rise of the Dutch Republic*, 3 vols. (New York: Harpers, 1856), 2:551–82.

6. Simon Schama, *The Embarrassment of Riches* (Berkeley: Univ. of California Press, 1988), 26–28, 178.

7. See the introduction to Morison's edition of the history, *Of Plymouth Plantation*, xxxix.

8. Schama describes this complex ambivalence most concisely in the chapter "Feasting, Fasting, and Timely Atonement," *The Embarrassment of Riches*, 130–220.

9. Smith, *Bradford of Plymouth*, 33.

10. Morison, *Of Plymouth Plantation*, xi.

11. John Foxe, *The First [Second] Volume of the Ecclesiasticall history contaynyng the Actes and Monumentes of thynges passed in every kynges tyme in this Realme, especially in the Church of England principally to be noted*, 2 vols. (London: John Day, 1570), 1:837.

12. Bradford Smith speculates on the purpose behind Bradford's borrowing this sum, with his house as security for the loan, in 1617, just as Brewster was beginning his printing business. See *Bradford of Plymouth*, 95.

13. Keith L. Sprunger, *Trumpets from the Tower: English Puritan Printing in the Netherlands, 1600–1640* (London: E. J. Brill, 1994), 133–44.

14. David Calderwood, *Perth Assembly* (Leiden: William Brewster, 1619).

15. For an illuminating discussion of the attempts to capture Brewster and to close down the Choir Alley press, see Daniel Plooij, *The Pilgrim Fathers from a Dutch Point of View* (1932; rpt., New York: AMS Press, 1969), 65–78.

16. See Annabel Patterson, *Censorship and Interpretation: The Conditions of Writing and Reading in Early Modern England* (Madison: Univ. of Wisconsin Press, 1984), 44–46, 105–7, for details on the notorious cases of Alexander Leighton and William Prynne in 1630 and 1633.

17. "To the Right Vertuous, Most Excellent and noble Princesse Quene Elizabeth, our Dreade Lady," in Foxe, *The Ecclesiasticall History*, 1:sig. 1r. Foxe could plausibly claim that his reference was to the Salome of Mark 15:40, but the disquieting note is impossible to dismiss.

18. Joseph Moxon, *Mechanick Exercises on the Whole Art of Printing*, ed. Herbert Davis and Harry Carter (1683–84; rpt., London: Oxford Univ. Press, 1958), 323.

19. See Moxon's description "Of the Press," ibid., 45–66; for his printer's dictionary, see 332–54.

20. James Deetz and Patricia Scott Deetz, *The Times of their Lives: Life, Love, and Death in Plymouth Colony* (New York: W. H. Freeman, 2000), 39. On seventeenth-century ships' tools, see Ford, *History of Plymouth Plantation 1620–1647*, 1:150 n. David Cressy notes that the screw "may have been part of a printing press," in *Coming Over: Migration and Communication between England and New England in the Seventeenth Century* (Cambridge: Cambridge Univ. Press, 1987), 168.

21. See Moxon's account of the spindle and its movements in *Mechanick Exercises*, 66–70.

22. Edward Winslow advised emigrants to New England to pack their meal so tightly in their casks that "you shall need an Ads or Hatchet to worke it out with." *A Relation or Journall of the beginning and proceedings of the English Plantation setled at Plimoth* (London, 1622), 63.

23. *Proceedings of the Massachusetts Historical Society, 1869–70* (1871): 396–464.

24. Harold Love, *Scribal Publication in Seventeenth-Century England* (Oxford: Clarendon Press, 1993), 35–46. See also Roger Chartier, *The Order of Books: Readers, Authors, and Libraries in Europe between the Fourteenth and Eighteenth Centuries* (Stanford, Calif.: Stanford Univ. Press, 1994).

25. Morison, *Of Plymouth Plantation*, 3–9. Morison follows Worthington C. Ford on Bradford's citation of authorities, though in doing so he perpetuates Ford's error on the source of the passage from William Perkins that Bradford quotes.

26. [William Whittingham], *A Brief Discourse of the Troubles begun at Frankfort in Germany anno domini 1554* (1575; rpt., London: Elliot Stock, 1908), 24–40. Patrick Collinson offers a persuasive challenge to Whittingham's authorship of this pamphlet. See "The Authorship of *A Brieff Discours off the Troubles Begonne at Franckford*," in *Godly People: Essays on English Protestantism and Puritanism* (London: Hambleton Press, 1983), 191–211.

27. The volumes by Peter Martyr and Jean Bodin may have passed from Brewster to Bradford at Brewster's death. See the estate inventories of the Brewster and Bradford libraries in *The Mayflower Reader: A Selection of Articles from* The Mayflower Descendant, ed. George Ernest Bowman (Baltimore: Genealogical Publishing Co., 1978), 139–45, 153–68. The most extensive bibliographic study of Brewster's books appeared in the *Proceedings of the Massachusetts Historical Society*, 2d ser., 5 (1889–90): 37–85. See also Lawrence D. Geller and Peter J. Gomes, *The Books of the Pilgrims* (New York: Garland, 1975).

28. Walter J. Ong, *The Presence of the Word: Some Prolegomena for Cultural and Religious History* (New Haven, Conn.: Yale Univ. Press, 1967), 236–41. On the controversial intent behind, and response to, the Rhemist Testament, see Evelyn B. Tribble, *Margins and Marginality: The Printed Page in Early Modern England* (Charlottesville: Univ. of Virginia Press, 1993), 43–50.

29. Keith Sprunger lists the titles printed by Brewster in appendix 2 of *Trumpets from the Tower*, 213–14.

30. Ong, *The Presence of the Word*, 250–51. See also "Latin Language Study as a Renaissance Puberty Rite," in Walter J. Ong, *Rhetoric, Romance, and Technology: Studies in the Interaction of Expression and Culture* (Ithaca, N.Y.: Cornell Univ. Press, 1971), 113–41.

31. Schama, *The Embarrassment of Riches*, 54.

32. For an account of the crisis and its roots in the negotiations that resulted in the truce of 1609, see Jonathan Israel, *The Dutch Republic: Its Rise, Greatness, and Fall 1477–1806* (Oxford: Clarendon Press, 1995), 421–77, as well as Israel's discussion of a contemporary plate on the Arminian Redoubt at Leiden, xix–xx. See, too, Pieter Geyl, *The Revolt of the Netherlands*, 2d ed. (London: Ernest Benn, 1958), 217–59; and Pieter Geyl, *The Netherlands in the Seventeenth Century*, pt. 1, 2d ed. (New York: Barnes and Noble, 1961), 38–63.

33. For Bradford's position on the question of the "National Church," see the opening of the first of his late dialogues, reprinted in *The Chronicles of the Pilgrim Fathers of the Colony of Plymouth*, ed. Alexander Young (Boston: Little Brown, 1841), 414–17. See, too, Edward Winslow's objections to the National Church, reprinted in Young, *Chronicles*, 390.

34. Patrick Collinson, *The Birthpangs of Protestant England* (New York: St. Martin's, 1988), 16–17. Jonathan Scott suggests that seventeenth-century English history is in large part an outgrowth of the internationalist consciousness of radical Protestants. See *England's*

Troubles: Seventeenth-Century English Political Instability in European Context (Cambridge: Cambridge Univ. Press, 2000).

35. On the existence and influence of the Dutch exile communities in the eastern English counties, near Norwich in particular, see Plooij, *The Pilgrim Fathers*, 12–14; and Willison, *Saints and Strangers*, 31–32. John Lothrop Motley estimates that by 1566, the year of iconoclastic mobs in Dutch towns and Protestant worship in the open fields of the Netherlands, there were thirty thousand Dutch exiles living in or near Norwich, a number that must have increased during Alva's subsequent persecutions. See *The Rise of the Dutch Republic,* 1:504. See also David W. Davies, *Dutch Influences on English Culture: 1558–1625* (Ithaca, N.Y.: Cornell Univ. Press for the Folger Shakespeare Library, 1964).

36. Keith L. Sprunger, *Dutch Puritanism: A History of English and Scottish Churches of the Netherlands in the Sixteenth and Seventeenth Centuries* (Leiden: E. J. Brill, 1982), 3–142.

37. See Willison, *Saints and Strangers*, 30–33, for a brief account of Browne's mixed career. On some implications of the Dutch presence in East Anglia, as well as the English emigrations to Holland, see Douglas Campbell, *The Puritan in Holland, England, and America: An Introduction to American History,* 2 vols. (New York: Harper and Brothers, 1892), esp. 2:243. Though dated, Campbell's work is a stimulating political and cultural history that went through four editions between 1892 and 1920, before James Truslow Adams simplistically dismissed its claims as "thoroughly unsound." See James Truslow Adams, *The Founding of New England* (Boston: Atlantic Monthly Press, 1921), 89 n.

38. On the special interest that a number of Renaissance linguists took in Hebrew, see Martin Elsky, *Authorizing Words: Speech, Writing, and Print in the English Renaissance* (Ithaca, N.Y.: Cornell Univ. Press, 1989), 132–46. For the scholarly case concerning Puritan "primitivism," see Theodore Dwight Bozeman, *To Live Ancient Lives: The Primitivist Dimension in Puritanism* (Chapel Hill: Univ. of North Carolina Press, 1988).

39. See Walter Ong's account of what he terms some of the "psychodynamics" of print, in *Interfaces of the Word: Studies in the Evolution of Consciousness and Culture* (Ithaca, N.Y.: Cornell Univ. Press, 1977), 230–71.

40. Wolfgang Iser, *The Act of Reading: A Theory of Aesthetic Response* (1976; rpt., Baltimore: Johns Hopkins Univ. Press, 1978), 107–18.

41. Peter Gay, *A Loss of Mastery: Puritan Historians in Colonial America* (Berkeley: Univ. of California Press, 1966), 42.

42. See Foxe's reply to "Alanus Copus" (Nicholas Harpsfield) for his insistence on the rigorous intellectual preparation necessary for one who would be "a controller in storye matters." *The Ecclesiasticall History,* 1:688.

ONE   ❧   WORDS AND WIND

1. Walter Benjamin, "The Storyteller," in *Illuminations,* ed. Hannah Arendt, trans. Harry Zohn (1968; rpt., New York: Schocken Books, 1969), 94.

2. Acts 27:20 in *The Geneva Bible: A Facsimile of the 1560 Edition* (Madison: Univ. of Wisconsin Press, 1969). All biblical quotations in this and subsequent chapters are from this reproduction of the Geneva translation.

3. Alan Howard, "Art and History in Bradford's *Of Plymouth Plantation," William and

Mary Quarterly 28 (April 1971): 245–46; Jesper Rosenmeier, "'With my owne eyes': William Bradford's *Of Plymouth Plantation*," in *The American Puritan Imagination: Essays in Revaluation*, ed. Sacvan Bercovitch (London: Cambridge Univ. Press, 1974), 97; Anthony J. Kemp, *The Estrangement of the Past* (New York: Oxford Univ. Press, 1993).

4. For a recent illustration of the critical prominence of this passage, see David Laurence, "William Bradford's American Sublime," *PMLA* 102 (1987): 55–65.

5. *History of the Plimoth Plantation . . . Now reproduced in facsimile from the Original Manuscript*, with an introduction by John A. Doyle (London: Ward and Downey; Boston: Houghton Mifflin, 1896).

6. William Wood, *New England's Prospect*, ed. Alden T. Vaughan (Amherst: Univ. of Massachusetts Press, 1977), 15.

7. See the facsimile of the original title page in *Mourt's Relation: A Journal of the Pilgrims at Plymouth*, ed. Dwight B. Heath (Bedford, Mass.: Applewood Books, 1963), xxvii.

8. See the facsimile of Smith's original title page in *The Complete Works of John Smith (1580–1631)*, 3 vols, ed. Philip L. Barbour (Chapel Hill: Univ. of North Carolina Press, 1986), 1:305.

9. Edward Winslow, *Good Newes from New-England: or A true Relation of things very remarkable at the Plantation of Plimoth in New-England* (London: William Bladen and John Bellamie, 1624).

10. See the facsimile of Higginson's title page in *A Library of American Puritan Writings: The Seventeenth Century*, vol. 9, *Histories and Narratives*, ed. Sacvan Bercovitch (New York: AMS Press, 1986).

11. Thomas Morton, *New English Canaan or New Canaan. Containing an abstract of New England, composed in three bookes. The first booke setting forth the originall of the natives, their manners and customes, together with the tractable nature and love towards the English. The seconde booke setting forth the naturall indowments of the country, and what staple commodities it yealdeth. The third booke setting forth, what people are planted there, their prosperity, what remarkable accidents have happened since the first planting of it, together with their tenents and practice of their church* (Amsterdam: J. F. Stam, 1637).

12. J. Paul Hunter, *Before Novels: The Cultural Contexts of Eighteenth-Century English Fiction* (New York: Norton, 1990), 167–224.

13. Leonard F. Dean, "Tudor Theories of History Writing," *University of Michigan Contributions in Modern Philology* 1 (April 1947): 3. See, too, Arthur Ferguson's account of "The tyranny of *res gestae*" in his *Clio Unbound: Perception of the Social and Cultural Past in Renaissance England* (Durham, N.C.: Duke Univ. Press, 1979), 5–27.

14. *The Twoo Bookes of Francis Bacon. Of the proficience and advancement of Learning, divine and humane* (London, 1605), 2:11v.

15. Stow's full title is *A Survey of London Contayning the originall, antiquity, increase, moderne estate and description of that citie* (London, 1598). Camden's English title is *Britain, or a Chorographicall Description of the most flourishing Kingdoms, England, Scotland, and Ireland*, trans. Philemon Holland (London, 1610). See also Barbara J. Shapiro, *A Culture of Fact: England, 1550–1720* (Ithaca, N.Y.: Cornell Univ. Press, 2000), 63–85.

16. Winthrop's most recent editors have not accepted Savage's title. See Richard S. Dunn, James Savage, and Laetitia Yeandle, eds., *The Journal of John Winthrop 1630–1649* (Cambridge:

Belknap Press, 1996), xxxviii–xxxix, 189, 551. Stephen Carl Arch makes the case for continuing to treat Winthrop's journals as a formal history. See *Authorizing the Past: The Rhetoric of History in Seventeenth-Century New England* (DeKalb: Northern Illinois Univ. Press, 1994), 20–23. John Smith's *The generall historie of Virginia, New-England, and the Summer Iles* (1625) is only an apparent exception to this ambivalence concerning the category of "history." Its title seems designed to indicate the heterogeneous nature of its contents—an anthology of accounts by various explorers and colonists in "general"—rather than Smith's particular generic ambitions.

17. On the development of the term in this period, see "The Varieties of History," in F. Smith Fussner, *The Historical Revolution: English Historical Writing and Thought 1580–1640* (New York: Columbia Univ. Press, 1962), 150–90; and D. R. Woolf, *The Idea of History in Early Stuart England* (Toronto: Univ. of Toronto Press, 1990), 3–76.

18. For a bibliographical assessment of the *Actes and Monuments,* see *John Foxe and the English Reformation,* ed. David Loades (Aldershot, Eng.: Scolar Press, 1997), 36–51.

19. John Foxe, "To the true Christian reader, what utilitie is to be taken by readyng of these Historyes," in *The First [Second] Volume of the Ecclesiasticall history contaynyng the Actes and Monumentes of thynges passed in every kynges tyme in this Realme, especially in the Church of England principally to be noted,* 2 vols. (London: John Day, 1570), 1:sig. 3r. See similar disclaimers from John Speed, John Stow, and Raphael Holinshed in Louis B. Wright, *Middle-Class Culture in Elizabethan England* (Chapel Hill: Univ. of North Carolina Press, 1935), 310–19.

20. Sir Walter Ralegh, *The History of the World,* ed. C. A. Patrides (London: Macmillan Press, 1971; originally published in 1614), 45. See, too, "Ralegh and the Dramatic Sense of Life," in Stephen J. Greenblatt, *Sir Walter Ralegh: The Renaissance Man and His Roles* (New Haven, Conn.: Yale Univ. Press, 1973), 22–56; and Woolf, *The Idea of History,* 45–55.

21. Christopher Hill, *Intellectual Origins of the English Revolution Revisited,* rev. ed. (Oxford: Clarendon Press, 1997; originally published in 1965), 189.

22. On the persistence of the medieval tradition of universal histories and chronicles into the sixteenth and seventeenth centuries, see C. A. Patrides, *The Phoenix and the Ladder: The Rise and Decline of the Christian View of History* (Berkeley: Univ. of California Press, 1964), 32–48.

23. See Walter Ong's account of Zwinger's book in *Interfaces of the Word: Studies in the Evolution of Consciousness and Culture* (Ithaca, N.Y.: Cornell Univ. Press, 1977), 171–77.

24. Patrides, *The Phoenix and the Ladder,* 36.

25. Bradford cites the "centurists" three times in the text of his third "Dialogue." *Proceedings of the Massachusetts Historical Society, 1869–70* (1871): 447, 449, 459.

26. Barbour, *The Complete Works of John Smith,* 1:310.

27. Ibid., 1:311–12.

28. George F. Willison, *Saints and Strangers* (New York: Reynal and Hitchcock, 1945), 106.

29. *A Relation or Journall of the beginning and proceedings of the English Plantation setled at Plimoth in New England* (London: John Bellamie, 1622), 65.

30. Leonard Dean, "Bodin's *Methodus* in England before 1625," *Studies in Philology* 39 (1942): 160–66. For an authoritative account of Bodin's significance as a historical theorist,

see Julian H. Franklin, *Jean Bodin and the Sixteenth-Century Revolution in the Methodology of Law and History* (New York: Columbia Univ. Press, 1963), 59–79, 137–54.

31. Bacon, *Of the proficience and advancement of Learning*, 2:151.

32. Cited in Franklin, *Jean Bodin and the Sixteenth-Century Revolution*, 150 n.

33. William Perkins, *A Faithfull and plaine exposition upon the 2 chapter of Zephaniah*, 5th ed. (London, 1609), 145.

34. On the influence of Perkins' book, see Barbara K. Lewalski, *Protestant Poetics and the Seventeenth-Century Religious Lyric* (Princeton, N.J.: Princeton Univ. Press, 1979), 218–26; and Eugene R. Kintgen, *Reading in Tudor England* (Pittsburgh: Univ. of Pittsburgh Press, 1996), 117–31. On contemporary efforts to inculcate techniques of "right reading," see Kevin J. Sharpe, *Reading Revolutions: The Politics of Reading in Early Modern England* (New Haven, Conn.: Yale Univ. Press, 2000), 38–62. Ian Green surveys efforts to shape the way readers approached the Bible throughout the seventeenth century. See *Print and Protestantism in Early Modern England* (Oxford: Oxford Univ. Press, 2000), 101–67.

35. William Perkins, *The Arte of Prophecying or A Treatise Concerning the sacred and onely true manner and methode of Preaching* (London, 1607), 32–33, 90–91.

36. Kintgen, *Reading in Tudor England*, 138–39.

37. George R. Potter and Evelyn Simpson, eds., *The Sermons of John Donne*, 10 vols. (Berkeley: Univ. of California Press, 1959), 4:266. A common reading culture does not necessarily mean that a common sermon style follows. John R. Knott stresses the sharp differences between Donne's pulpit performance and that of Richard Sibbes, a dissenting minister directly in William Perkins' tradition, six volumes of whose sermons were in William Brewster's library at Plymouth. See *The Sword of the Spirit: Puritan Responses to the Bible* (Chicago: Univ. of Chicago Press, 1980), 42–61.

38. Perkins, *The Arte of Prophecying*, 132–33.

39. Peter Martyr, "Letters," in *The Common Places of Peter Martyr*, trans. Anthonie Marten (London, 1583), 69.

40. Perkins, *The Arte of Prophecying*, 32.

41. Ibid., 31.

42. Perkins, *The Arte of Prophecying*, 31. For Tyndale's insistence on the "symple literall sense" of Scripture, see Kintgen, *Reading in Tudor England*, 126–27; and Evelyn B. Tribble, *Margins and Marginality: The Printed Page in Early Modern England* (Charlottesville: Univ. of Virginia Press, 1993), 14. John Robinson echoes this conviction that Scripture contains "but one proper, and immediate sense" in his chapter on biblical exegesis in *Observations Divine and Morall. For the Furthering of knowledg, and vertue* ([Leiden], 1625), 59.

43. Perkins, *The Arte of Prophecying*, 33. Perkins is describing the kind of systematic "re-writing" of a received text that Terence Cave has termed "generative reading." See "The Mimesis of Reading in the Renaissance," in *Mimesis: From Mirror to Method, Augustine to Descartes*, ed. John D. Lyons and Stephen G. Nichols Jr. (Hanover, N.H.: Univ. Press of New England, 1982), 149–65.

44. On the vitality (and controversy) surrounding contemporary marginalia, see Tribble, *Margins and Marginality;* and Christopher Hill, *The English Bible and the Seventeenth-Century Revolution* (1993; rpt., London: Penguin Books, 1994), 56–66. For Joyce's comic exploitation of these traditions of textual space, see *Finnegans Wake*, bk. 2, chap. 2.

45. Perkins, *The Arte of Prophecying*, 28–30. These instructions on keeping commonplace books were repeated in many sixteenth-century books. See Kintgen's discussion of Erasmus's advice on reading practices and commonplace collecting, *Reading in Tudor England*, 20–44. For an exhaustive and illuminating analysis of how one reader applied these methods throughout his life, see Sharpe's study of the reading practices of William Temple, in *Reading Revolutions*, 65–120, 180–205, 257–69.

46. For the fragment of the Letter Book that survives—the manuscript itself has been lost—see George Ernest Bowman, ed., *The Mayflower Reader: A Selection of Articles from* The Mayflower Descendant (1900–1906; rpt., Baltimore: Genealogical Publishing Co., 1978), 299–362.

47. In *Hypocrisie Unmasked* (1646), Edward Winslow reconstructs the farewell comments made by John Robinson at Delftshaven, to emphasize this acceptance of doctrinal change. See Alexander Young's reprint of Winslow's comments in *The Chronicles of the Pilgrim Fathers of the Colony of Plymouth* (Boston: Little Brown, 1841), 396–97.

48. Jeremy Taylor, *A Discourse of the Liberty of Prophesying* (London, 1647), 79.

49. Ibid., 80.

50. Glenn W. LaFantasie, ed., *The Correspondence of Roger Williams*, 2 vols. (Providence, R.I.: Brown Univ. Press; Hanover, N.H.: Univ. Press of New England, 1988), 1:379.

51. Neal Salisbury's repeated assertions of Plymouth's "militaristic bearing" toward neighboring Indians exemplify this scholarly distortion, though by comparison with Jonathan Goldberg's excoriation of "Bradford's genocidal text," Salisbury seems comparatively restrained. See Neal Salisbury, *Manitou and Providence: Indians, Europeans, and the Making of New England* (New York: Oxford Univ. Press, 1982), 124–29; and Jonathan Goldberg, *Sodometries: Renaissance Texts, Modern Sexualities* (Stanford, Calif.: Stanford Univ. Press, 1992), 223–46.

TWO   🐚   SUCH NEIGHBORS AND BRETHREN AS WE ARE

1. The Latin motto that Isselburg applies to his depiction of a military procession outside Nuremberg derives from the saying inscribed above the armory of the Venetian Republic. See Robert Burton, *The Anatomy of Melancholy*, ed. Thomas C. Faulkner, Nicolas K. Kiessling, and Rhonda L. Blair, 6 vols. (Oxford: Clarendon Press, 1986–2000), 2:188. The engraving itself is one of countless images that suggest the climate of impending conflict in central Europe, which intensified as the end of the truce between Spain and the Dutch Republic drew near. See Georg Hirth, comp., *Picture Book of the Graphic Arts 1500–1800*, 6 vols. (1882–90; rpt., New York: Benjamin Blom, 1972), 3:1041; and F. W. H. Hollstein, *German Engravings, Etchings, and Woodcuts 1400–1700*, vol. 15A, ed. Tilman Falk (Amsterdam: A. L. van Gendt, 1986), 143.

2. *A Relation or Journall of the beginning and proceedings of the English Plantation setled at Plimoth in New England* (London: John Bellamie, 1622), 40, 49–50.

3. Ibid., 51.

4. The colonists later resist Massasoit's demand for the severed head and hands of Squanto. See Edward Winslow, *Good Newes from New-England: or A true Relation of things very remarkable at the Plantation of Plimoth in New-England* (London: William Bladen and John Bellamie, 1624), 9.

5. *A Relation or Journall*, 45.

6. Lisa Jardine and Anthony Grafton, "'Studied for Action': How Gabriel Harvey read his Livy," *Past and Present* 129 (1990): 48.

7. Samuel Purchas, *Hakluytus Posthumus, or Purchas His Pilgrimes*, pt. 4 (London, 1625), 1828. Purchas was annotating a reprint of a report by the Council for New England entitled *A briefe Relation of the Discovery and Plantation of New England* (London, 1622).

8. Bradford certainly learned of the events of Dermer's visit from Squanto, who was one of the Indians captured by Thomas Hunt and who returned to New England with Dermer in 1620, but he also had access to a letter from Dermer, read before the Virginia Company in July 1621. See Frank Shuffleton, "Indian Devils and Pilgrim Fathers: Squanto, Hobomock, and the English Conception of Indian Religion," *New England Quarterly* 49 (1976): 108–16.

9. Robert Cushman, *A Sermon Preached at Plimmoth in New-England* (London: John Bellamie, 1622).

10. Winslow, *Good Newes from New-England*, 61.

11. Frances Yates, *The Art of Memory* (1966; rpt., London: Pimlico, 1992), 17–62. See also Karen Ordahl Kupperman, *Indians and English: Facing Off in Early America* (Ithaca, N.Y.: Cornell Univ. Press, 2000), 89–91.

12. *A Relation or Journall*, B2v.

13. Ibid.

14. Ibid., B3v. See for comparison Foxe's similar appeal for the melioration of offenses in "To the true Christian reader, what utilitie is to be taken by readyng of these Historyes," in *The First [Second] Volume of the Ecclesiasticall history contaynyng the Actes and Monumentes of thynges passed in every kynges tyme in this Realme, especially in the Church of England principally to be noted*, 2 vols. (London: John Day, 1570), 1:sig. 3v.

15. *A Relation or Journall*, B4r.

16. Ibid., 1, 4. The trope of the New World as a "howling wilderness" was widely employed for self-consciously rhetorical purposes throughout the seventeenth century. None of Bradford's contemporaries would have mistaken such language for an attempt at naturalistic description. See David Cressy, *Coming Over: Migration and Communication between England and New England in the Seventeenth Century* (Cambridge: Cambridge Univ. Press, 1987), 14.

17. *A Relation or Journall*, 2.

18. Ibid., 4–5.

19. Ibid., 6–8. James Axtell views Bradford's mishap with the snare as an instance of ethnohistorical humor, in *Beyond 1492: Encounters in Colonial America* (New York: Oxford Univ. Press, 1992), 186. But the incident also offers further indication of the English predisposition to admire Indian skills and to compare them favorably with European handicrafts.

20. *A Relation or Journall*, 11.

21. Compare Stephen Greenblatt's discussion of the experience of wonder as an element in European responses to the Indians, in *Marvelous Possessions: The Wonder of the New World* (Chicago: Univ. of Chicago Press, 1991), 16–25. See also Kupperman's emphasis on the complexity of the English response to native culture: *Indians and English*, 2–11.

22. *A Relation or Journall*, 19.

23. Ibid., 2.

24. See, for instance, the spare acknowledgment of sickness in *A Relation or Journall*, 25.

262 Notes to Pages 85–92

Bradford's more elaborate account of nursing practices in *Of Plimmoth Plantation* draws on a tradition of Christian historiography that dates at least from Eusebius. See William H. McNeill, *Plagues and Peoples* (1976; rpt., New York: Anchor/Doubleday, 1989), 135–36.

25. *A Relation or Journall*, 25, 14, 31.

26. Ibid., 29–30.

27. Ibid., 9, 13.

28. Nathaniel Morton is the first to print the names of the signers of the Compact, in *New England's Memoriall* (Cambridge, 1669), 15–16.

29. *A Relation or Journall*, 67. Compare Kupperman's account of the climate of anxiety in seventeenth-century England: *Indians and English*, 23–31.

30. The invidious passages in Cushman's portion of the *Relation* are often cited out of context and made to seem more representative than they are. See, e.g., James Axtell, *The Invasion Within: The Contest of Cultures in Colonial North America* (New York: Oxford Univ. Press, 1985), 137, 149. Irving's brilliant satire on seventeenth-century colonial apologetics is in Knickerbocker's *A History of New York*, collected in *Washington Irving: History, Tales, and Sketches* (New York: Library of America, 1983), 412–24.

31. *A Relation or Journall*, 69.

32. Cushman, "The Epistle Dedicatory," in *A Sermon Preached at Plimmoth in New-England*, A3v.

33. Anthony Pagden, *European Encounters with the New World* (New Haven, Conn.: Yale Univ. Press, 1993), 17–49.

34. Cushman, "The Epistle Dedicatory," A3r.

35. *A Relation or Journall*, 72. On the ideological dimensions of the radical Protestants' emphasis on industry and their correspondingly harsh attitude toward begging, see Christopher Hill, *Society and Puritanism in Pre-Revolutionary England* (New York: Schocken, 1964), 124–25, 273–85; and Margo Todd, *Christian Humanism and the Puritan Social Order* (Cambridge: Cambridge Univ. Press, 1987), 118–75.

36. One of the objections that English Presbyterians, as well as Anglicans, had to John Robinson's concept of church government involved his conviction that church "elders" or deacons (as well as pastors or ministers) had an obligation to preach, both in private gatherings and in the public church assembly. See John Robinson, *A Just and Necessarie Apologie of Certain Christians no lesse contumaciously then commonly called Brownists or Barrowists* (Leiden, 1625), 25–38, 50–53. Cushman was a deacon in the Leiden Church, but Robinson was prepared to allow ordinary members of the congregation to preach, informally, in public services as well, both as incitements to spiritual seriousness and as a means of identifying those whose analytical and speaking gifts might qualify them to be church officers in the future.

37. Cushman, *A Sermon Preached at Plimmoth in New-England*, 7. See, too, Mark L. Sargent's observations on the "pilgrim" trope, "Strangers on the Earth: William Bradford, the Epistle to the Hebrews and the Plymouth 'Pilgrims,'" *Fides et historia* 24 (1993): 18–41.

38. Cushman, *A Sermon Preached at Plimmoth in New-England*, 4, 5, 8, 16.

39. Ibid., 10.

40. Ibid., 13.

41. Ibid., 18.

42. See David S. Lovejoy, "Plain Englishmen at Plymouth," *New England Quarterly* 63 (1990): 232–48.

43. Winslow, *Good Newes from New-England*, A6, 52.

44. Ibid., 28. Winslow's disparaging view of the native shamans, in this scene, is consistent with the opinion he expresses near the end of his narrative, that Indian religion is largely devoted to the propitiation of the Devil. Alfred Cave seizes on this error in Winslow's understanding of Wampanoag culture and dismisses *Good Newes from New-England* as "garbled and distorted"—a blanket judgment that is at least as misinformed as Winslow's own assessments of native spirituality. See Alfred A. Cave, *The Pequot War* (Amherst: Univ. of Massachusetts Press, 1996), 21–22, 46.

45. Winslow, *Good Newes from New-England*, 28.

46. Ibid., 28–29.

47. Ibid., 31.

48. Ibid., 32. On the relation of revenge war to the Iroquois Confederacy, see Daniel K. Richter, *The Ordeal of the Longhouse: The Peoples of the Iroquois League in the Era of European Colonization* (Chapel Hill: Univ. of North Carolina Press, 1992), 30–49.

49. Winslow, *Good Newes from New-England*, 42.

50. Ibid., A6, 40–41. Indeed, Francis Jennings thinks Winslow's narrative is a calculated attempt to disguise Plymouth's unprovoked aggression against the Massachusetts people, but Jennings bases his judgment solely on George Willison's strained reading of Winslow's words, not on additional contemporary evidence. See Francis Jennings, *The Invasion of America: Indians, Colonialism, and the Cant of Conquest* (1975; rpt., New York: Norton, 1976), 186–87, 263–64. Compare Kupperman's more balanced—though still skeptical—treatment of Winslow's visit to Massasoit, in *Indians and English*, 180–83.

51. Winslow, *Good Newes from New-England*, 27.

52. Compare Hobomock's eulogy of Massasoit to Daniel Richter's account of the qualities called for, by Iroquois tradition, in one of that confederacy's leaders. See *The Ordeal of the Longhouse*, 40–41.

53. Winslow, *Good Newes from New-England*, 32–33.

54. James Merrell, *Into the American Woods: Negotiators on the Pennsylvania Frontier* (New York: Norton, 1999), 54–105.

55. Jean Bodin, *Six Bookes of a Commonweale*, trans. Richard Knolles (London, 1606), 11–12. See, too, Margo Todd's discussion of the role of common property as an ideal in Christian humanist social theory, in *Christian Humanism*, 130–33.

THREE ❧ ARTIFICIAL PERSONS

1. Worthington C. Ford, ed., *History of Plymouth Plantation 1620–1647*, 2 vols. (Boston: Massachusetts Historical Society, 1912), 1:79–80 n.

2. John Robinson, *Observations Divine and Morall. For the Furthering of knowledg, and vertue* ([Leiden], 1625), 225.

3. William Hubbard traces Lyford's movements after leaving Plymouth from Nantasket, to Cape Anne, and finally to Naumkeag, from which he departs for Virginia sometime before John Endecott's arrival in 1628. See Alexander Young, *Chronicles of the first planters of the colony of Massachusetts Bay, 1623–1636* (1846; rpt., New York: Da Capo Press, 1970), 20–27.

4. See Eugene R. Kintgen, *Reading in Tudor England* (Pittsburgh: Univ. of Pittsburgh Press, 1996), 18–57; Anthony Grafton and Lisa Jardine, *From Humanism to the Humanities:*

Education and the Liberal Arts in Fifteenth and Sixteenth-Century Europe (Cambridge: Harvard Univ. Press, 1986), 1–28; and Ann Moss, *Printed Commonplace-Books and the Structure of Renaissance Thought* (Oxford: Clarendon Press, 1996), 101–15.

5. Walter J. Ong, *Rhetoric, Romance, and Technology: Studies in the Interaction of Expression and Culture* (Ithaca, N.Y.: Cornell Univ. Press, 1971), 14–63. See also Louis B. Wright's survey of popular handbooks designed to foster copious speech or writing, in *Middle-Class Culture in Elizabethan England* (Chapel Hill: Univ. of North Carolina Press, 1935), 146–53.

6. Terence Cave, *The Cornucopian Text: Problems of Writing in the French Renaissance* (Oxford: Clarendon Press, 1979), 34.

7. Francis Bacon, *The Twoo Bookes of Francis Bacon. Of the proficience and advancement of Learning, divine and humane* (London, 1605), 1:17v–18r.

8. Cave, *The Cornucopian Text,* 147.

9. Thomas Hobbes, "To the Reader," unpaginated preface to *Eight Bookes of the Peloponnesian Warre,* trans. Thomas Hobbes (London, 1634). See, too, Peter Gay's observation that Bradford's credibility in the Lyford matter derives from his modesty: *A Loss of Mastery: Puritan Historians in Colonial America* (Berkeley: Univ. of California Press, 1966), 46–47.

10. In her discussion of problems of speech in Plymouth, Jane Kamensky terms Lyford an "ill-spoken" figure, who "made a mockery of Perkins's prophetic arts." These comments apply to Oldham's fits of uncontrollable anger, perhaps, but Lyford poses problems of fluency, not of ineptitude. *Governing the Tongue: The Politics of Speech in Early New England* (New York: Oxford Univ. Press, 1997), 59–60.

11. Erasmus makes this point in his influential textbook on the tactics for achieving abundant speech, *De duplici copia verborum ac rerum commentarii duo:* "The compressed style and the abundant style depend on the same basic principles . . . the craftsman in words who will be best at narrowing down his speech and compressing it will be the one who is skilled in expanding and enriching it with ornament of every kind." *Copia: Foundations of the Abundant Style,* trans. Betty I. Knott, vol. 24 of *Collected Works of Erasmus* (Toronto: Univ. of Toronto Press, 1978), 300.

12. David Levin's insistence on the importance of the letters to Bradford's sense of structure and of characterization has never been adequately explored. See "William Bradford: The Value of Puritan Historiography," in *Forms of Uncertainty: Essays in Historical Criticism* (Charlottesville: Univ. Press of Virginia, 1992), 25–27.

13. Claudio Guillen, "Notes toward the Study of the Renaissance Letter," in *Renaissance Genres: Essays on Theory, History, and Interpretation* ed. Barbara K. Lewalski, Harvard English Studies, 14 (Cambridge: Harvard Univ. Press, 1986), 100–101. The discussion of Bradford's exploitation of the narrative potential of letters, in the following pages, draws repeatedly on Guillen's provocative account of Renaissance epistolography.

14. Guillen cites Donne's lines from the verse epistle to Wotton to illustrate the dramatic emotional fiction of the letter: "Sir, more than kisses, letters mingle Soules; / For, thus friends absent speake." "Notes toward the Study of the Renaissance Letter," 80. See also Jonathan Goldberg's discussion of the letter as displaced speech in *Writing Matter: From the Hands of the English Renaissance* (Stanford, Calif.: Stanford Univ. Press, 1990), 249–57.

15. Elizabethan playwrights were particularly quick to exploit this dramatic vitality in letters. See Lisa Jardine, "Reading and the Technology of Textual Affect: Erasmus's Famil-

iar Letters and Shakespeare's *King Lear,*" in *The Practice and Representation of Reading in England,* ed. James Raven, Helen Small, and Naomi Tadmor (Cambridge: Cambridge Univ. Press, 1996), 77–101.

16. *Bradford's History "Of Plimoth Plantation"* (1898), 240. Bradford may choose to emphasize the correspondent's own "words" at this point in the history because the letter that he is about to transcribe, from James Sherley and his merchant colleagues, was actually written in the hand of Robert Cushman. See Bradford's Letter Book in *The Mayflower Reader: A Selection of Articles from* The Mayflower Descendant, ed. George Ernest Bowman (1900–1906; rpt., Baltimore: Geneological Publishing Co., 1978), 304–10.

17. See George Willison, *Saints and Strangers* (New York: Reynal and Hitchcock, 1945), 106–11; and Henry Martyn Dexter, *The England and Holland of the Pilgrims* (1906; rpt., Baltimore: Genealogical Publishing Co., 1978), 568–70, on the negotiations with the Virginia Company between 1617 and 1620.

18. On the role of the citation to Hebrews 11 in Bradford's understanding of Plymouth's circumstances, see Mark L. Sargent, "Strangers on the Earth: William Bradford, the Epistle to the Hebrews and the Plymouth 'Pilgrims,'" *Fides et historia* 24 (1993): 18–41.

19. See Samuel Eliot Morison, ed., *Of Plymouth Plantation* (1952; rpt., New York: Knopf, 1991), appendix 3, 360–66.

20. Thomas Prince wrote a note in Bradford's manuscript, indicating that since June 11, 1620, in the Old Style calendar was a Sunday, Cushman could not have been writing a letter on that date (66). But it seems more likely that Cushman's dating is accurate, that seventeenth-century Sabbath customs were not as unyielding as Prince imagined, and that Bradford has rearranged the order of the letters to emphasize the confusion of the emigration arrangements at this point in the history.

21. Bowman, *The Mayflower Reader,* 312.

22. Guillen, "Notes toward the Study of the Renaissance Letter," 99.

23. See Kevin Sharpe's introductory chapter on the origins of personal rule for a review of English political circumstances on the eve of the dissolution of Parliament in 1629, in *The Personal Rule of Charles I* (New Haven, Conn.: Yale Univ. Press, 1992), 3–62.

24. See Alfred Cave's chapter "Wampum, Pelts, and Power," in *The Pequot War* (Amherst: Univ. of Massachusetts Press, 1996), 49–68, for a treatment of the significance of wampum in the economy of southern New England.

25. See David Read's discussion of this pattern in "Silent Partners: Historical Representation in William Bradford's *Of Plymouth Plantation,*" *Early American Literature* 33 (1998): 291–314.

26. Edward Winslow invoked the spectacle of the Levellers in the reprint of *Hypocrisie Unmasked,* his 1646 attack on Samuel Gorton. See Edward Winslow, *The danger of tolerating levellers in a civil state, or An historicall narration of the dangerous pernicious practices and opinions wherewith Samuel Gorton and his levelling accomplices so much disturbed and molested the severall Plantations in New England* (London, 1649). See also Thomas Cartelli, "Transplanting Disorder: The Construction of Misrule in Morton's *New English Canaan* and Bradford's *Of Plymouth Plantation,*" *English Literary Renaissance* 27 (spring 1997): 258–80.

27. David Read compares Morton's intentions, as Bradford portrays them, to a parody of the Mayflower Compact, but the comparison to the anxieties of the Leiden church and

to the ideals of Robinson's farewell letter of August 1620 seems closer. See "Silent Partners," 298–305.

28. On the legal controversy surrounding Morton's weapons trade, see Charles Francis Adams' introduction to his edition of *New English Canaan* (1883; rpt., New York: Burt Franklin, 1967).

29. Lisa Jardine, *Worldly Goods: A New History of the Renaissance* (1996; rpt, New York: Norton, 1998), 3–90.

30. Cynthia J. Van Zandt attempts to defend these trading practices as a reflection of Allerton's cosmopolitan commercial education in the Netherlands. See "The Dutch Connection: Isaac Allerton and the Dynamics of English Cultural Anxiety in *The Gouden Eeuw*," in *Connecting Cultures: The Netherlands in Five Centuries of Transatlantic Exchange*, ed. Rosemarijn Hoefte and Johanna C. Kardux (Amsterdam: Vrije Univ. Press, 1994), 51–76.

31. Charles Francis Adams speculates about the nature of Allerton's defense, on the grounds of Morton's potential usefulness to Plymouth's interests. See *New English Canaan*, 36–37.

32. This focus on the colony's commercial affairs has prompted a number of critical objections to the "shapeless" nature of the second half of the history. The shape of the history is evident enough, but Bradford does not pretend that it makes for an appealing story. See, e.g., Robert Daly in "William Bradford's Vision of History," *American Literature* 44 (January 1973): 557; and Andrew Delbanco, *The Puritan Ordeal* (Cambridge: Harvard Univ. Press, 1989), 194.

33. Morison removes all three sections of Sherley's letter to the appendix of his edition of the history, making it impossible for readers to discern the textual wrestling match that Bradford stages in these pages. See *Of Plymouth Plantation*, 384–87.

34. Kevin Sharpe's account of the fiscal plight of the English government during the first five years of Charles' reign explains this level of official dependence on extorted revenue. See *The Personal Rule of Charles I*, 9–23.

35. Sherley's reference to golden keys is a garbled allusion to Acts 22:28. Bradford's comment on covetousness indirectly appeals to the pervasive suspicion of earthly riches in Proverbs.

36. Ashley would seem to invite the kind of praise for ethnological sensitivity that many modern critics reserve for Thomas Morton. Unlike Morton, though, he left no record of his assessment of Indian life. Michael Zuckerman is representative in his praise for Thomas Morton's adaptability, while passing over the intriguing (if shadowy) figure of Edward Ashley. See "Pilgrims in the Wilderness: Community, Modernity, and the Maypole at Merry Mount," *New England Quarterly* 50 (June 1977): 255–77.

37. See Thomas Dudley's comments on Gardiner's predicament in his March 1631 letter to the countess of Lincoln, reprinted by Young in *Chronicles of the first planters*, 333–34.

38. Richard S. Dunn, James Savage, and Laetitia Yeandle, eds., *The Journal of John Winthrop 1630–1649* (Cambridge: Belknap Press, 1996), 51–53, 90. See also Ford, *History of Plymouth Plantation, 1620–1647*, 2:140 n.

39. Sedgwick bases her character Sir Philip Gardiner on the Sir Christopher of Bradford's narrative. Her source is probably the edition of Mather's *Magnalia Christi Americana* that had been recently republished in 1820.

40. Foxe called Stephen Gardiner "a man hated of God and all good men . . . this vipers byrd." *The First [Second] Volume of the Ecclesiasticall history contaynyng the Actes and Monumentes of thynges passed in every kynges tyme in this Realme, especially in the Church of England principally to be noted,* 2 vols. (London: John Day, 1570), 2:1951.

41. Ibid., 2:1684. See, too, John R. Knott, *Discourses of Martyrdom in English Literature, 1593–1694* (Cambridge: Cambridge Univ. Press, 1993), 11–83, on the executions of Rogers and Hooper, as well as other victims of the Marian persecution.

FOUR   🐟   HERE IS THE MISERABLEST TIME

1. For a literary history of the medicinal metaphors that Bradford invokes, here and elsewhere in *Of Plimmoth Plantation,* see Stanley Fish's discussion, "The Aesthetic of the Good Physician," in *Self-Consuming Artifacts: The Experience of Seventeenth-Century Literature* (Berkeley: Univ. of California Press, 1972), 1–29; and Winfried Schleiner, *The Imagery of John Donne's Sermons* (Providence, R.I.: Brown Univ. Press, 1970), 68–80.

2. Alexander Young, ed., *Chronicles of the first planters of the Colony of Massachusetts Bay, 1623 to 1636* (1846; rpt., New York: Da Capo Press, 1970), 333–34. The Dudley letter is also reprinted in *Letters from New England: The Massachusetts Bay Colony, 1629–1638,* ed. Everett Emerson (Amherst: Univ. of Massachusetts Press, 1976), 67–83.

3. Christopher Hill, *Intellectual Origins of the English Revolution, Revisited,* rev. ed. (Oxford: Clarendon Press, 1997; originally published in 1965), 161–72.

4. Francis Bacon, *The Twoo Bookes of Francis Bacon. Of the proficience and advancement of Learning, divine and humane* (London, 1605), 2:10r, 17v–18r.

5. John Winthrop reports that some of Pierce's crew were drowned in this shipwreck. See Richard S. Dunn, James Savage, and Laetitia Yeandle, eds., *The Journal of John Winthrop 1630–1649* (Cambridge: Belknap Press, 1996), 89. According to William Hubbard, twelve people drowned in the *Lyon,* seven sailors and five passengers. See Hubbard's "General History of New England," *Collections of the Massachusetts Historical Society,* 2d ser., 5 (1815): 202.

6. On the plague outbreak of 1636, see Kevin Sharpe, *The Personal Rule of Charles I* (New Haven, Conn.: Yale Univ. Press, 1992), 622–24. Sherley's providentialist reaction to the epidemic is in fact quite conventional. See Alexandra Walsham, *Providence in Early Modern England* (Oxford: Oxford Univ. Press, 1999), 156–66.

7. Francis Bacon, *Advancement of Learning* (1605), 1:42r.

8. Ibid., 1:25r–v.

9. Ibid., 1:11r–2v.

10. Ibid., 1:9v.

11. Massachusetts authorities intervened in Salem's overtures to Williams in early April 1631. See Dunn, Savage, and Yeandle, *The Journal of John Winthrop,* 50. See also Glenn W. LaFantasie, ed., *The Correspondence of Roger Williams,* 2 vols. (Providence, R.I.: Brown Univ. Press; Hanover, N.H.: Univ. Press of New England, 1988), 1:12–29.

12. LaFantasie, *The Correspondence of Roger Williams,* 1:15. See John Winthrop's account of Williams' objectionable "treatice" on native sovereignty in Dunn, Savage, and Yeandle, *The Journal of John Winthrop,* 107–9.

13. Bradford's letter is printed among the Winthrop Papers in *Collections of the Massa-*

chusetts Historical Society, 4th ser., 6 (1863): 156–58. Winthrop's critical annotations on Brad-ford's view of Indian sovereignty were written on this letter and are reprinted with it.

14. For a summary of Williams' doctrinal scruples, see LaFantasie, *The Correspondence of Roger Williams,* 1:12–29.

15. Dunn, Savage, and Yeandle, *The Journal of John Winthrop 1630–1649,* 163.

16. The earliest usage the OED cites for *naturalist* is 1587; derogatory references come largely from works of theology printed before 1650. On the late-seventeenth-century trans-formation in New England providentialism that Bradford seems to anticipate, see Michael P. Winship, *Seers of God: Puritan Providentialism in the Restoration and Early Enlightenment* (Baltimore: Johns Hopkins Univ. Press, 1996). David D. Hall notes the prominence of the 1638 earthquake among contemporary collections of "wonders" in New England almanacs. See *Worlds of Wonder, Days of Judgment: Popular Religious Belief in Early New England* (Cam-bridge: Harvard Univ. Press, 1989), 82, 93.

17. *Collections of the Massachusetts Historical Society,* 4th ser., 6 (1863): 156. See Hall, *Worlds of Wonder, Days of Judgment,* 100–101, on the notoriety of the Hutchinson and Dyer births.

18. Nathaniel B. Shurtleff, ed., *Records of the Colony of New Plymouth: Court Orders* (1855; rpt., New York: AMS Press, 1968), 1:105. On Samuel Gorton, see Philip F. Gura, *A Glimpse of Sion's Glory: Puritan Radicalism in New England, 1620–1660* (Middletown, Conn.: Wes-leyan Univ. Press, 1984), 49–92, 276–303.

19. *Publications of the Colonial Society of Massachusetts* 22 (1920): 91–107.

20. Peach's service in the Pequot War casts some doubt on his relationship to Plymouth, since (according to Bradford) Plymouth's militia had not yet joined the Pequot campaign when word arrived that "the enimy was as good as vanquished" (424). Roger Williams reported that Peach claimed to be from Plymouth but that two of his accomplices were from Pascataway, or present-day Dover, New Hampshire. Peach could have grown familiar with servants living so far north of Plymouth, if he had been one of Plymouth's agents at their Kennebec trading post; or he may simply have lied to Williams about his origins. Massasoit described Peach to Williams as "Mr. Winslow's man" and identified Penowanyanquis as a Nipmuck, rather than a Narragansett. Jurisdictions and identities at this time could become quite confused, even in the reasonably confined territory of southern New England. See "The Murder of Penowanyanquis, August 1638," in Howard M. Chapin, *Documentary His-tory of Rhode Island* (Providence: Preston and Rounds, 1916), 81–89.

21. Shurtleff, *Records of the Colony of New Plymouth,* 1:93.

22. Ibid., 1:112–13. Winthrop reports Peach's penitential death. See Chapin, *Documentary History of Rhode Island,* 86.

23. Edward Winslow, *Hypocrisie Unmasked: By a true Relation of the Proceedings of the Governour and Company of the Massachusetts against Samuel Gorton, (and his Accomplices,) a notorious disturber of the Peace and quiet of the severall Governments wherein he lived* (London: John Bellamie, 1646).

24. Nathaniel Morton, *New England's Memoriall* (Cambridge, 1669), 146. Winslow begins his verses with an imperfect double anagram on Bradford's name that emphasizes the trait of judicial moderation: "I made Law for Bridl / For law I made Bridl." "See how God honoured hath this Worthy's Name," Winslow continued, "To make it spell his Virtue, and proclaime / His rare Endowments."

25. Shurtleff, *Records of the Colony of New Plymouth*, 1:127.

26. Francis Bacon, *The Essays*, ed. John Pitcher (London: Penguin Books, 1985; originally published in 1625), 223.

27. Bradford's "Ancient Men," in his 1648 "Dialogue," were especially determined to resist being labeled "Brownists" because of this "defection" on Browne's part. True Separatists "can no more justly be called Brownists, than the disciples might have been called Judasites." Alexander Young, ed., *Chronicles of the Pilgrim Fathers of the Colony of Plymouth* (Boston: Little Brown, 1841), 428.

28. John Robinson, *A Justification of Separation from the Church of England* ([Leiden], 1610).

29. Ibid., 3–4. Robinson is expressing the widespread conviction of his time that hypocrisy was the most pervasive sin in the late sixteenth and early seventeenth centuries. See William J. Bouwsma, *The Waning of the Renaissance 1550–1640* (New Haven, Conn.: Yale Univ. Press, 2000), 117–18.

30. Robinson, *A Justification of Separation*, 4.

31. Ibid., 6.

32. Ibid., 15.

33. Ibid., 48–49.

34. John Robinson, *Observations Divine and Morall. For the Furthering of knowledg, and vertue* ([Leiden], 1625), sig. Tt3r–v, for the table of contents at the conclusion of the text. The shift from "Cap" to "Chap" occurs after "Cap XXIIII Of Good Intentions," 141. This work is abbreviated ODM hereafter and cited parenthetically in the text.

35. Fish, *Self-Consuming Artifacts*, 150–54; Hill, *Intellectual Origins of the English Revolution*, 102–4.

36. See Gura, *A Glimpse of Sion's Glory*, 304–22, on Pynchon's ecclesiastical liberalism.

37. See also Margo Todd's account of Erasmus's principles on crime and punishment in *Christian Humanism and the Puritan Social Order* (Cambridge: Cambridge University Press, 1987), 38–39.

38. See, e.g., the punishments of Edward Michell and Edward Preston for "lude and sodomiticall practices," inflicted by the court in March 1642, seven months before Granger's trial: Shurtleff, *Plymouth Colony Records*, 2:35–36.

39. *The Common Places of Peter Martyr*, trans. Anthonie Marten (London, 1583), pt. 4, 248–55. The judicial practice of Leiden, during the years that Bradford lived there, reflects a similar ambivalence toward capital punishment. Between 1609 and 1619 only ten executions were carried out in the city, despite the dozens of capital crimes that came before its courts. Between May 23, 1614, and May 31, 1619, no executions were recorded—a remarkable record of judicial forbearance for the seventeenth century. See H. M. van den Heuvel, *De Criminele Vonnisboeken van Leiden 1533–1811* (Leiden, 1977–78), 92–143.

40. John R. Knott, *Discourses of Martyrdom in English Literature, 1563–1694* (Cambridge: Cambridge Univ. Press, 1993), 71–72.

41. Antonia Fraser, *Cromwell, The Lord Protector* (1973; rpt., New York: Grove Press, 2001), 691–93.

42. Dunn, Savage, and Yeandle, *The Journal of John Winthrop, 1630–1649*, 371–74.

43. Jonathan Goldberg suggests that Bradford dismisses Granger in "a merciless para-

graph," but by overlooking critical material in Morison's appendixes, Goldberg neglects the legal and punitive context that Bradford establishes. See *Sodometries: Renaissance Texts, Modern Sexualities* (Stanford, Calif.: Stanford Univ. Press, 1992), 225, 234–43.

44. This is the penalty that Anthony Bacon risked incurring when he was imprisoned for sodomy in Montauban in the summer of 1586. See Lisa Jardine and Alan Stewart, *Hostage to Fortune: The Troubled Life of Francis Bacon* (New York: Hill and Wang, 1999), 107–15.

45. Robinson, *A Justification of Separation*, 58–59.

46. David Cressy, *Travesties and Transgressions in Tudor and Stuart England: Tales of Discord and Dissension* (Oxford: Oxford Univ. Press, 2000), 259–65.

FIVE 🏵 CONTROLLER OF STORIES

1. Compare Nathaniel Morton, *New England's Memoriall* (Cambridge, 1669), 116–17, and the *Plymouth Church Records* in *Publications of the Colonial Society of Massachusetts: Collections* 22 (1920): 75 n.

2. Nathaniel Shurtleff, ed., *Records of the Colony of New Plymouth: Court Orders* (1855; rpt., New York: AMS Press, 1968), 2:73.

3. See George Willison's account of the "diaspora" of which Brewster's move was a part, in *Saints and Strangers* (New York: Reynal and Hitchcock, 1945), 312–43.

4. Bradford offers some scandalous disclosures from Guicciardini in the manuscript of his "Third Dialogue." *Proceedings of the Massachusetts Historical Society, 1869–70* (1871): 425. The page numbers that Bradford cites indicate that he owned the 1599 edition of Geffray Fenton's translation. For a review of the events that Guicciardini recounts in his book, see Lauro Martines's summary of Italian history between 1494 and 1530, in *Power and Imagination: City-States in Renaissance Italy* (1979; rpt., Baltimore: Johns Hopkins Univ. Press, 1988), 277–96. Kevin Sharpe records the prominence that Guicciardini's work held, as a storehouse of political knowledge, for at least one avid seventeenth-century English reader. See "The Mental World of Sir William Drake," in *Reading Revolutions: The Politics of Reading in Early Modern England* (New Haven, Conn.: Yale Univ. Press, 2000), 65–120.

5. Felix Gilbert, *Machiavelli and Guicciardini: Politics and History in Sixteenth-Century Florence* (Princeton, N.J.: Princeton Univ. Press, 1965), 123.

6. For the comparative ages of the *Mayflower* passengers, see Willison, *Saints and Strangers*, 437–43.

7. See Garrett Mattingly's account of Mary's execution and of Davison's fall from favor in part to placate the Scots, in *The Armada* (Boston: Houghton Mifflin, 1959), 1–21.

8. The origins and status of the Granger family in Scituate are unclear, but a large group of emigrants with that family name, including two named Thomas (perhaps father and son), arrived in Boston in 1637, listed as servants in various households. See Charles Edward Banks, *The Planters of the Commonwealth* (1930; rpt., Baltimore: Genealogical Publishing Co., 1967), 189.

9. Daniel Dyke, *The Mystery of Selfe-Deceiving, or A Discourse and Discoverie of the Deceitfulnesse of Man's Heart* (London, 1628), 6–10.

10. Ibid., 39.

11. Foxe collects the most impressive instances of divine retribution in a section titled "The severe punishment of God's mighty hand upon Priestes and Prelates." See John Foxe, *The First [Second] Volume of the Ecclesiasticall history contaynyng the Actes and Monumentes of thynges passed in every kynges tyme in this Realme, especially in the Church of England principally to be noted,* 2 vols. (London: John Day, 1570), 2:2298–302. This compilation belongs to a tradition of such collections; see Alexandra Walsham, *Providence in Early Modern England* (New York: Oxford Univ. Press, 1999), 65–115. Foxe takes note of the queen's loneliness and despair at her death in 2:2296–97. Winthrop's medical reports on Anne Hutchinson and Mary Dyer are in *The Journal of John Winthrop 1630–1649,* ed. Richard S. Dunn, James Savage, and Laetitia Yeandle (Cambridge: Belknap Press, 1996), 253–54, 264–66.

12. Thomas Granger, *A Familiar Exposition or Commentarie on Ecclesiastes* (London, 1621), sig. A4v, A7r, pp. 16–17.

13. Ibid., 141.

14. Ibid., 146.

15. Philip F. Gura, *A Glimpse of Sion's Glory: Puritan Radicalism in New England, 1620–1660* (Middletown, Conn.: Wesleyan Univ. Press, 1984), 263–67, 276–82.

16. See, e.g., the speech of Cardinal Giuliano Della Rovere, the future Pope Julius II, exhorting Charles VIII to continue with his invasion plans, in book 1, or the paired speeches on the design of the Florentine Republic by Soderini and Vespucci, early in book 2. Francesco Guicciardini, *The Historie of Guicciardin: Containing The Warres of Italie,* 3d ed., trans. Geffray Fenton (London, 1618), 32–33, 59–62. Sidney Alexander's modern abridgment offers a more accurate and accessible translation. See Francesco Guicciardini, *The History of Italy,* trans. Sidney Alexander (Princeton, N.J.: Princeton Univ. Press, 1969), 46–48, 76–83.

17. Alfred Cave is representative of many modern scholars who misread Bradford's efforts to distance himself from Winthrop's triumphal account of the Pequot War. See Alfred Cave, *The Pequot War* (Amherst: Univ. of Massachusetts Press, 1996), 152. For Wedgwood's summary of the outcome of the Thirty Years War, see C. V. Wedgwood, *The Thirty Years War* (1938; rpt., London: Folio Society, 1999), 463.

18. For the list of assistants in 1634, see Shurtleff, *Records of the Colony of New Plymouth,* 1:21.

19. Worthington C. Ford identifies the Plymouth trader whom Hocking killed. See *History of Plymouth Plantation 1620–1647,* ed. Worthington C. Ford, 2 vols. (Boston: Massachusetts Historical Society, 1912): 2:178 n.

20. The original text of the Commission was apparently in Latin. The translation may be Bradford's. See Ford, *History of Plymouth Plantation 1620–1647,* 2:183 n.

21. The dream was not, however, a very urgent one. See Kevin Sharpe, *The Personal Rule of Charles I* (New Haven, Conn.: Yale Univ. Press, 1992), 751–57, on the vacillating level of concern displayed by Charles' ministers concerning the question of asserting their control over New England.

22. See Ford's note on the deaths of Stone and Norton in *History of Plymouth Plantation 1620–1647,* 2:192.

23. Alfred Cave offers a detailed account of the developing trade competition in the Connecticut valley, as background to the Pequot conflict. See *The Pequot War,* 49–68.

24. Guicciardini's celebrated analysis of the perils of asking for or taking advice discloses the tangle of motives that diplomatic language characteristically disguises, in virtually all the political exchanges that the history records. See *The Historie of Guicciardin*, 45.

25. Winthrop reports that Bradford frankly accused Massachusetts Bay, in October 1636, of provoking war with the Pequot. See Dunn, Savage, and Yeandle, *The Journal of John Winthrop 1630–1649*, 192.

26. On the complex of motives shaping Massachusetts Bay policy in 1636 and 1637, see the two most balanced accounts of these events: Alden T. Vaughan, *New England Frontier: Puritans and Indians 1620–1675* (Boston: Little Brown, 1965), 122–54; and Cave, *The Pequot War*, 69–121. Vaughan has since modified his original, critical assessment of Pequot policy and behavior to conform more closely to Cave's emphasis on "English intransigence." Cave might better have stressed Massachusetts intransigence. The example of Plymouth's magistrates indicates that a homogeneous "English" position did not exist during this crisis, any more than a homogeneous "Indian" one did. See also Steven T. Katz, "The Pequot War Reconsidered," *New England Quarterly* (June 1991): 206–24.

27. This sacrificial wording is exemplified in the death sentence that Stephen Gardiner pronounces upon John Rogers; see Foxe, *The Ecclesiasticall History*, 2:1662. John Robinson's comments on sacrificial creatures are in *Observations Divine and Morall. For the Furthering of knowledg, and vertue* ([Leiden], 1625), 279.

28. David Levin's argument for the formal importance of the letters that Bradford transcribes in the history is especially pertinent to these pages. Without them it is impossible to grasp the scope of Bradford's critique of the Massachusetts Bay leadership. See *Forms of Uncertainty: Essays in Historical Criticism* (Charlottesville: Univ. Press of Virginia, 1992), 24–27.

29. Plymouth may have initiated the series of talks that led to the 1643 Articles by raising the issue of a defensive "league" against the Narragansett threat. See Shurtleff, *Records of the Colony of New Plymouth*, 2:47. Henry M. Ward summarizes the efforts that Massachusetts and Connecticut had made, immediately after the Pequot War, to arrive at some formal agreement for joint defense. See *The United Colonies of New England: 1643–1690* (New York: Vantage Press, 1961), 32–39; and Dunn, Savage, and Yeandle, *The Journal of John Winthrop 1630–1649*, 277–80, 292.

30. This conflict mediation arrangement is described in the Treaty of Hartford, signed on September 21, 1638. Alden Vaughan reprints the text in appendix 2 of his *New England Frontier*, 340–41. It is worth emphasizing that Plymouth played no role in this attempt by Massachusetts Bay and Connecticut to eradicate the Pequot's tribal existence and to contain Narragansett and Mohegan hostility. See Paul A. Robinson, "Lost Opportunities: Miantonomi and the English in Seventeenth-Century Narragansett Country," in *Northeastern Indian Lives, 1632–1816*, ed. Robert S. Gummet (Amherst: Univ. of Massachusetts Press, 1996), 13–28.

31. Charles was beheaded in January 1648/1649. Bradford indicates that he wrote the closing sentences of the history sometime after March 25, 1650, sixteen months later, making it likely that he composed his account of the Narragansett threat of 1643 at some point after news of the king's execution had reached New England.

32. Henry M. Ward notes that Massachusetts Bay insisted on excluding Pascataway

from the 1643 Articles, since the Boston government fully intended to absorb the Pascataway patents. Rhode Island was invited to participate in the United Colonies provided the Rhode Islanders would agree to join themselves to the jurisdiction of Plymouth. See *The United Colonies of New England*, 24–59.

33. Shurtleff, *Records of the Colony of New Plymouth*, 2:47.

34. Henry Ward lists the presidents of the meetings of the commissioners through 1689. See appendix C in *The United Colonies of New England*, 398–99.

CONCLUSION: THE HIGH PRESERVER OF MEN

1. See the text of Bradford's will, including the circumstances of its dictation, in *The Mayflower Reader: A Selection of Articles from* The Mayflower Descendant, ed. George Ernest Bowman (Baltimore: Genealogical Publishing Co., 1978), 139–40.

2. Bradford's book is in the George Fingold Library of the Commonwealth of Massachusetts, in the State House basement in Boston. I am grateful to Mary Bicknell, the special collections librarian, for allowing me to examine the manuscript volume closely.

3. John Robinson, *Observations Divine and Morall. For the Furthering of knowledg, and vertue* ([Leiden], 1625), 135–38.

4. Alexander Young, ed., *Chronicles of the Pilgrim Fathers of the Colony of Plymouth* (Boston: Little Brown, 1841), 425.

5. See Michael P. Winship, "Contesting Control of Orthodoxy among the Godly: William Pynchon Reexamined," *William and Mary Quarterly* (October 1997): 795–822.

6. Glenn W. LaFantasie, ed., *The Correspondence of Roger Williams*, 2 vols. (Providence, R.I.: Brown Univ. Press; Hanover, N.H.: Univ. Press of New England, 1988), 1:15–16.

7. George Bowman has shown that Bradford wrote these lists sometime between March 6 and April 3, 1651, just at the end of the year 1650 by the Old Style calendar. See *The Mayflower Reader*, 43–45.

8. It seems likely that at least one of Bradford's Bibles was a comparatively expensive edition. Thomas Cushman and John Dunham, who prepared the inventory of Bradford's estate, grouped his two Bibles together and assigned them a monetary value of one pound—twice the figure they had assigned to Guicciardini's *Historie of Guicciardin* and more than twice the value they affixed to Jean Bodin's *Six Bookes of a Commonweale*, both quite large and costly books. Two Bibles comparable to the 1596 Barker imprint would probably not have amounted to such a price.